SUSTAINING CIVIL SOCIETY

Strategies for Resource Mobilization

Edited by

Leslie M. Fox
and
S. Bruce Schearer

CIVICUS

CIVICUS
919 18th Street, NW, 3rd Floor
Washington, DC 20006 USA
Tel: (202) 331-8518
Fax: (202) 331-8774
Email: info@civicus.org

Publication design by ARTECH Graphics II, Inc.

Printed in the United States of America
ISBN   0-9644001-4-6

SUSTAINING CIVIL SOCIETY

Strategies for Resource Mobilization

Table of Contents

11 Building Indigenous Foundations That Support Civil Society **305**
S. Bruce Schearer

12 Tapping Social Investment Through the Market **327**
Malcolm Hayday

Institutional Reviewers of Chapters

1—A Strategic Guide to Resource Enhancement
CIVICUS: World Alliance for Citizen Participation

2—Earning Income Through Trade and Exchange
Philippines Rural Reconstruction Movement, Philippines

3—Foundation Funding: Venture Capital for Civil Society
European Foundation Center, Belgium

4—Individual Philanthropy
Child Relief and You (CRY), India

5—Building Grassroots Citizens' Organizations
Organization of Rural Associations for Progress, Zimbabwe

6—Public Resources From Government
West African Rural Foundation (WARF), Senegal
National Council for Overcoming Poverty (NCOP), Chile

7—Resources of Development Assistance Agencies
Young Men's Christian Association (YMCA), Lebanon

8—Engaging Corporations in Strengthening Civil Society
Hitachi Foundation, U.S.A.

9—Conversion of Debt: A Win-Win-Win Scenario?
Swiss Coalition of Development NGOs (SCDN)

10—Establishing and Operating Microcredit Programs
Centro de Fomento a Iniciativas Economicas (FIE), Bolivia

List of Acronyms

ADC	Abyssinian Development Corporation	FIE	Centro de Fomento a Iniciativas Económicas
APPC	Asia Pacific Philanthropy Consortium	FINCA	Foundation for International Community Assistance
BRAC	Bangladesh Rural Advancement Committee	FLO	foundation-like organization
CAF	Charities Aid Foundation		
CDFI	Community Development Finance Initiatives	FMDR	Fundacion Mexicana para el Desarrollo Rural
CEMEFI	Centro Mexicano para la Filantropía	FONAMA	Fondo Nacional Para el Medio Ambiente
C-GAP	Consultative Group to Assist the Poorest	FONGS	Federations des ONG Senegalaise
CLD	Center for Legislative Development	FPE	Foundation for the Philippine Environment
CRA	Community Reinvestment Act	GRO	grassroots organization
		Hivos	Humanist Institute for Cooperation with Developing Countries
CRY/India	Child Relief & You/India		
CSO	civil society organization	IAF	Inter-American Foundation
CSRO	civil society resource organization		
		IDAC	Instituto de Acao Cultura
EAPN	European Anti-Poverty Network	IDB	Inter-American Development Bank
EFC	European Foundation Centre	IDEPH	Institute for the Development of Philanthropy
EFJ	Environmental Foundation of Jamaica		
EU	European Union	IDR	Institute for Development Research
EZE	Evangelische Zentralstelle fur Entwicklungschilfe	IFAD	International Fund for Agricultural Development
FES	Fundación para la Educación Superior	IFI	international financial institution

IMF	International Monetary Fund	PBSP	Philippine Business for Social Progress
INAISE	International Association of Investors in the Social Economy	PRCF	Puerto Rico Community Foundation
INTRAC	International NGO Training and Research Organization	PRI	program-related investment
		PRIA	Society for Participatory Research in Asia
IRED	Development Innovations and Networks	PRRM	Philippines Rural Reconstruction Movement
IUCN	World Conservation Union		
IYF	International Youth Foundation	PWBLF	Prince of Wales Business Leaders Forum
K-REP	Kenya Rural Enterprise Program	RAFAD	Research and Applications of Alternative Financing for Development
MOU	memorandum of understanding	S/E-CSO	southern and eastern civil society organizations
NCNB	National Center for Nonprofit Boards	SEEP	Small Enterprise Education and Promotion Network
N-CSO	northern civil society organization		
NEFs	national environmental funds	SEWA	Self Employed Women's Association
NESsT	Nonprofit Enterprise and Self-sustainability Team	SPARC	Society for Promotion of Area Resources Center
NGO	nongovernmental organization	TNC	Transnational Corporation
NOVIB	Netherlands Organization for International Development Cooperation	UNDP	United Nations Development Programme
		USAID	United States Agency for International Development
NPI	New Partnership Initiative		
ODA	Official Development Assistance	VAT	value-added tax
OECD	Organisation for Economic Co-operation and Development	WARF	West Africa Rural Foundation
		WHO	World Health Organization
ORAP	Organization of Rural Associations for Progress	WWF	World Wildlife Fund

Preface

The world is changing rapidly, and so too are the dynamics and relations between the traditional "sectors" of society. In the new era, the "nonstate actors" from the market and civil society are playing increasingly important roles in cultural, economic, political, and social life. This new environment and set of relations present a variety of opportunities and possibilities for civil society organizations (CSOs), but they also present significant challenges and responsibility.

By their very nature and organizing principles, the other two sectors of society have ready-made sources of income: the state, through taxes and fees for public services, and the market through profits from the sale of goods and services. CSOs also possess the potential for solid support through the contribution of financial, in-kind, and voluntary support from their members, constituents, and communities. But these groups currently face significant obstacles in terms of both their own institutional capacity and the legal, policy, and regulatory framework, which does not always provide an environment that lets them generate sufficient resources from other sources. CSOs must therefore adopt comprehensive, long-term strategies to ensure the effectiveness and sustainability of their programs and organizations.

Since the inception of CIVICUS, a central part of the organization's work to promote civil society as a legitimate and effective partner alongside the state and market has been to bring attention to and help address the critical financial challenges facing our civil society colleagues around the world. The 500 representatives from more than 50 countries who came together at the first World Assembly of CIVICUS in January 1995 in Mexico City confirmed the organization's role as an international catalyst for development of civil society around the globe. The need to assess the resource needs of civil society and identify the potential sources of support and financing available to it has been the core mission of the International Task Force on Resource Enhancement established in 1995.

The Task Force's objective was to examine the many strategies and tools for resource generation for CSOs and gather them under one cover. Our intention was to publish a unique resource truly international in character, reflecting the richness of perspectives from the South, North, and East, from the grassroots as well as donor perspective. As a truly global network of CSOs, CIVICUS was well positioned to undertake this industrious task. We have been able to tap into the tremendous diversity of wisdom and experience of some of the greatest civil society thinkers and leaders and the most prominent institutions across the globe. Under the guidance of the International Task Force, we identified lead authors for each chapter and invited 14 prominent organizations with special expertise in resource mobilization from 10 countries and six continents to act as institutional reviewers for each. In this respect, the 16-month-long endeavor truly embodies the great plurality of opinion and approach that CIVICUS and its members represent and promote. Even with this review process, it should be noted that each chapter is the view of its author or authors, and does not necessarily reflect the views of CIVICUS; its directors, officers, and staff; or its funding organizations.

This immense enterprise required tremendous vision, courage, dedication, and knowledge. CIVICUS was fortunate to have S. Bruce Schearer, Executive Director of the Synergos Institute, as Chair of the International Task Force. Bruce's able and inspirational leadership was critical in seeing the book through from start to finish. CIVICUS has to pay special tribute to its lead consultant, Leslie Fox, for taking on the very daunting challenge of conceptualizing, coordinating, guiding, editing, re-editing, eventually rewriting portions, and completing this book while simultaneously ensuring the participation of Task Force members, authors, and case study contributors spread across the globe. Leslie's expertise, professionalism, and persistence were absolutely crucial to this enterprise.

Working closely with Leslie during the final months of the effort were Magdalena Wolinski and the team of Lee Davis, Katalin Zsamboki, and Nicole Etchart at a new international CSO—NESsT. Although their initial task was to identify and develop illustrative case material for each chapter, their contributions extended to a wider range of additional chores. CIVICUS also owes thanks to its Program Committee and its head, Rajesh Tandon, who provided us with the creative and intellectual stimulus to get this special project started.

CIVICUS is indebted to numerous others who have contributed in some way to the production of this book. We extend great thanks to the numerous authors, institutional reviewers, case study preparers, and other contributors credited individually throughout the book. Special appreciation also goes to our editor, Linda Starke, who helped ensure that this rich collection of information became more readable and coherent. And we owe a great deal to Chuck Frankel, who helped bring together the impressive individuals and institutions on the CIVICUS International Task Force.

Finally, we should also recognize the sustained and professional support of the core CIVICUS staff, without whom this book quite simply would not have been produced. Three individuals here were intimately involved in the project: Renée Hill and, later, Mary Gardner Abbott assisted the Task Force, and Jo Render shepherded the book to publication.

Miklós Marschall
Executive Director, CIVICUS

Foreword

In May 1995, the Board of Directors of CIVICUS met to review ways this relatively young global membership organization could play a useful role for civil society organizations (CSOs) across the world. Strategies for increasing the flow of sources available to groups was one of the first topics discussed. The Board decided to establish a working group to identify and promote strategies to enhance the resource base for civil society initiatives. The resulting 12-member International Task Force on Resource Enhancement held its first meeting in February 1996 in Washington, D.C., to decide how to contribute to this goal. Civil society leaders from Africa, Asia, Europe, Latin America, and North America reviewed the state of knowledge regarding resource development and concluded that no single source of information described all the principal avenues for acquiring resources. We decided to prepare a publication to fill this void.

How to Use This Book

Sustaining Civil Society addresses the practical realities that CSOs face in obtaining resources to support their work. It is concerned with fundraising as well as other forms of financing for CSOs. The book was designed to include and provide under one cover the principal strategies—both traditional and innovative—that CSOs have developed over the past four decades. In this regard, it provides a state-of-the-art in 11 areas of resource enhancement. At the same time, case studies provide concrete examples of how CSOs have used each strategy.

The book has an Overview and 13 chapters—introductory and concluding chapters and 11 substantive ones, each of which represents a specific resource enhancement pathway or strategy. Chapter 1 identifies four basic sources for resource enhancement and the key policy challenges to CSO financing. Each substantive chapter discusses the state-of-the-art that has evolved on a particular strategy and details two or more ways that CSOs have generated resources—financial and nonfinancial—for their organizations. And each chapter ends with a resource guide of organizations and reference documents related to the particular strategy.

Finally, Chapter 13 discusses what a successful overall resource strategy entails and the issues and policy implications of different strategies for CSOs, donors, the state, and private-sector stakeholders.

Sustaining Civil Society is not intended to be a detailed, step-by-step fundraising manual or handbook; such volumes already exist in significant numbers. Rather, its purpose is to provide concerned organizations with a "road map" of the full range of existing strategies that can guide their overall resource enhancement efforts, particularly by helping them determine which are most appropriate to their own situations and how strategies might be combined into an overall diversified approach to sustainable resource generation. Not every chapter will be relevant for all CSOs; in fact, some may not be at all applicable to local circumstances or experiences. Nor will all readers necessarily want to read the book in its entirety. Instead, you are encouraged to consider the broader principles and context of CSO resource generation introduced in the first and last chapters, read the Overview of the 11 strategies, and select additional chapters for further contemplation based on your own specific organizational situation or personal interest.

Who Should Read This Book

This book is intended for a wide audience:

- *Civil Society Organizations:* to provide CSOs throughout the world with an overview of the principal pathways for increasing financial and institutional resources, along with case illustrations and bibliographic information.

- *Civil Society Support Organizations:* to provide a comprehensive portrait of how the sector mobilizes its resources and how organizations that exist to support and promote civil society initiatives may best target groups.

- *Policymakers and Leaders:* to demonstrate to government and business-sector policymakers and leaders the scope and depth of the civil society sector, its modes of financing, and the ways it can enter into productive working partnerships with other sectors.

- *Researchers, Teachers, Trainers, and Students:* to provide an introduction to resource generation strategies and international case material to researchers and students of international development, civil society, and the nonprofit voluntary sector for practical use in the classroom or other nonformal adult education settings.

Moving into Action

The strategies described here are neither simple to implement nor immediate in their impact. They require a fundamental commitment by organizations to devote significant financial, managerial, and professional resources to building the internal capacity needed to garner adequate support. Only through such sustained, highly committed efforts are results likely to be achieved. But with such efforts, the possibilities and prospects for substantial growth in financial revenues are great.

In calling for this book, the members of the CIVICUS International Task Force on Resource Enhancement, who themselves are leaders in CSOs throughout the world, recognized the enormous burden most organizations face on a daily basis as they work to mobilize enough resources to meet their goals. The managers of most CSOs face constant pressure to conduct effective programs in response to huge and intense demands, and they typically have far too little time to devote to their established fundraising efforts, let alone to researching and developing entirely new strategies and methods. Under these circumstances, how can CSOs move effectively to action that will increase their resources?

The answer lies in leadership. Someone within the organization with the position and authority to do so needs to take the lead in order to break the lockhold of everyday demands and allocate time to begin a separate research, assessment, planning, and implementation process specifically targeted at resource enhancement. It is necessary to set aside sufficient time to structure and guide the research on what funding sources would be possible and appropriate, to conduct the institutional assessment of what strategies to pursue, to develop detailed operational plans, and to fund and oversee implementation of the plans. Once this process is started, a number of tools can be used to ensure its success, including this book and the numerous other works referenced at the end of each chapter. The members of the CIVICUS Task Force and the authors of each chapter constitute valuable resources who can be called on for advice. Civil society network and umbrella organizations in different parts of the world can arrange workshops for their members to share knowledge and information and help each other.

The CIVICUS Task Force hopes this book will help to stimulate and support that kind of commitment in CSOs of all kinds and in all locations—North South, East and West—in the years ahead. And we welcome learning about these efforts from you. We also hope that *Sustaining Civil Society* will serve as a basis for continued discussion and critical examination of the current status of financing for civil society around the world. Our hope is that it will encourage CSOs themselves, policymakers, and leaders to recognize the importance of the civil society initiative and the need to identify appropriate mechanisms to stimulate and support this critical work.

S. Bruce Shearer
Chair, International Task Force on Resource Enhancement
Executive Director, Synergos Institute

Overview
Themes in Resource Mobilization

It is the premise of this book that civil society organizations (CSOs) are playing increasingly important roles in the development process in all nations, particularly in developing countries and the newly democratic nations of Central and Eastern Europe and the former Soviet Union. These groups have at their disposal four general sources of revenues:

- earned income from fees and other self-generated income and investment earnings;

- contributions from domestic foundations, businesses, and individuals;

- domestic government subsidies and payments, including grants and contracts; and

- foreign aid (in southern and East European countries) from official development assistance (ODA) agencies and other external public and private donors.

The 11 resource generation strategies identified in *Sustaining Civil Society* to capture these revenue sources fit into three general categories: capturing existing wealth from public and private donors, generating new wealth through market-based approaches, and capitalizing on nonfinancial resources.

Capturing Existing Wealth from Public and Private Donors

Although CSOs around the world have traditionally approached resource generation from a position of dependency, the strategies identified in this book examine traditional relations in a new light. The strategies for leveraging resources from donor sources, both public and private, are reexamined in light of the decreasing pool of such resources, the increased competition for them, and the legacy of dependency these approaches have usually fostered. The key emerging trend is to redefine traditional relationships into longer-term, strategic joint ventures that invest in the institutional sustainability of civil society initiatives and promote a fundamental philosophy of transparency, local involvement, and mutual benefit.

This overview was prepared by Lee Davis of NESsT.

Chapter 3: Foundation Funding: Venture Capital for Civil Society

Chapter 3 describes traditional processes for identifying and garnering project-based and institutional grant support from private foundations as well as alternative ways that foundations can use their resources to promote a longer-term funding base for CSOs. It stresses the imperative for adequate access to information on foundation support, the need for clear and simple application processes, and the importance of transparency in foundation grantmaking. The chapter also identifies the benefits of increased public involvement in the decisionmaking and allocation of foundation resources to support civil society. Foundations need to foster longer-term, personal relations and partnerships with CSOs to shift this resource strategy from a short-term, project-based model into a long-term investment in CSO institutional development and sustainability.

The chapter identifies a variety of alternative mechanisms and strategies for foundations, including program-related investments, loans, loan guarantees, and other investment models to assist CSOs with immediate cash flow problems as well as to invest in the financial, human, and other resources they require to implement long-range organizational and programming plans. Finally, the chapter has fundamental implications for the autonomy and independence of CSOs around the world. It eludes to the foundation community as a critical component of civil society's overall sectoral infrastructure. Building endowed grant-making institutions that are locally based and controlled will allow communities and CSOs to be directly involved in identifying their own needs and funding priorities.

Chapter 4: Individual Philanthropy

Complementing the role of foundations is individual philanthropy, which Chapter 4 identifies in its purest form as "the disinterested giving of a person's own resources, as an expression of solidarity with fellow humans, even strangers." The strategy indicates the importance of local support for CSO initiatives, and challenges commonly held conceptions of the inability of local communities (and particularly the poor) in the developing world and emerging democracies to support their own civil society institutions financially.

The chapter illustrates how CSOs around the world have successfully generated sufficient support from within their communities, and the increased benefits of a broad base of support for the independence and autonomy of the CSOs as well as for the more general processes of fostering democracy, accountability, confidence, and stability in society. The authors point out that while many refer to this strategy as "alternative financing," CSO leaders must now recognize this as a fundamental element of their organizational sustainability. While it may be more difficult for a CSO to raise resources from 200 individuals, "having hundreds of supporters may lend stability to its income, dampening the impact of downturns in government, corporate, and institutional funding." It also increases groups' legitimacy with government and the private sector as partners in the making and implementation of public policy. However, the chapter realistically illustrates the difficulties of breaking from these "old financing habits" and the economic and cultural obstacles in shifting from a traditional model of donor dependence to one of broad-based, local community support.

Chapter 5: Building Grassroots Citizens' Organizations

Reinforcing this message is the strategy examined in Chapter 5. It focuses specifically on the fundamental contribution of grassroots organizations (GROs) and the strategies they use to sustain themselves as they promote members' shared interests and those of civil society more generally. The chapter reinforces the message that GROs and CSOs must look for resources first among their own members, within their own communities or neighborhoods. While these resources can consist of money, volunteer labor, or simply locally available materials from members, the central message is that CSOs and GROs "can be no stronger or more sustainable than the citizens who belong to them and the civil society that nurtures their growth and connects them to other groups and to the larger world."

Chapter 5 clearly indicates, however, that sustainability does not necessarily mean complete self-reliance. The authors recognize the valuable contributions of CSO intermediaries in providing support and services to GROs and their communities and in ensuring that GROs' voices are heard in public decisionmaking arenas outside the grassroots level. Beyond the valuable contribution that local diversity provides to GROs around the world, what is common to all these organizations is the fact that their members realize they can accomplish their individual social, cultural, and economic goals more effectively through joint action than alone. Whether the partnerships are with intermediary CSOs, local government, or donors, joint action multiplies effects and impacts. In the process, it builds the values of trust, tolerance, and cooperation—the "social capital"—that underlie all economic as well as social interaction.

Chapter 6: Public Resources From Government

The relative health of relations between civil society institutions and those of the state is of critical importance to the sustainability of civil society. The government not only often represents the single largest potential source of funds for CSOs, but through its political and legislative capacity it defines the policy and regulatory environment in which CSOs operate.

The downsizing of central governments and the move toward decentralization has led governments toward contracting the services of both for-profit and nonprofit organizations. More and more government ministries in developing countries are awarding contracts to private entities through competitive bidding, replacing the practice of directly executing programs in such diverse areas as housing, public works, environmental protection, education, and others. This is opening an important new source of funding for both civil society and the private sector. As Chapter 6 points out, however, there may be fundamental differences in values and approach between CSOs and their governments. And although the state may be a considerable source of support for CSOs in their efforts to serve the public good, ensuring a minimum degree of societal welfare remains the overall responsibility of government.

Leveraging resources from the government in the form of grants, contracts, or loans may well provide increased local control and effective use of resources. Furthermore, channeling government resources through CSOs may also increase access to critical public decisionmaking and policymaking processes. Alternatively, however, grant and contracting relationships may be dictated solely by government will and politics, and may also be interpreted more as "a danger to [CSOs'] independence rather than a solution to their sustainability." Civil society dependence on governments, particularly in developing countries with relatively weak democratic traditions, can be risky. Co-optation, manipulation, and political instrumentation are constant dangers. Political shifts can also signify sudden losses of revenue and institutional sustainability, and can divorce CSOs from their constituencies and missions.

The effective use of this strategy must be based on a mutually beneficial relationship between CSOs and government, consisting of a more strategic and entrepreneurial approach. The relationship must include room for significant negotiation and mutual decisionmaking and be based on a commonly defined mission that capitalizes on the strengths of the stakeholders and defines an enabling regulatory environment for CSO initiatives.

Chapter 7: Resources of Development Assistance Agencies

The portion of official development assistance allocated to CSOs from governments as well as the assistance channeled through northern civil societies to locally based CSOs has increased significantly over the past three decades. This strategy examines how the traditional relations between northern official agencies and nongovernmental organizations (NGOs) can be transformed into a long-term, strategic approach that recognizes CSOs as legitimate public actors in the formulation and implementation of sustainable development policies.

As the authors point out, CSOs need to be viewed less as "instruments" of northern donor development policies and more as "partners" in helping to shape and formulate these policies. Since a significant percentage of the current resources of CSOs in the developing South and transitioning East comes from ODA, there is a real danger of not only dependency but also the loss of organizational autonomy and decision-making power among local CSOs. The cases and critical analysis presented in this chapter indicate a variety of alternative models that are emerging to redefine the nature of official development assistance to CSOs and the relations between CSOs, NGOs, and donors. CSOs and policymakers alike must recognize the role that civil society should play in influencing donor policy and restructuring the system of technical cooperation at the country and global levels.

Chapter 8: Engaging Corporations in Strengthening Civil Society

Out of either uncertainty, ideology, or inexperience, CSOs have traditionally underestimated or overlooked the opportunities and value of engaging the private, for-profit sector in leveraging additional resources in support of their work. As the process of decentralization and privatization grips countries around the world, however, and as corporate profits rise, pressure from governments and citizens for broader corporate social responsibility and community engagement has increased.

The greatest challenge for CSOs around the world now is to define a relationship with private-sector institutions that is a strategic, win-win approach that appeals to the corporate agenda of financial gain and the "bottom line." As the author illustrates, many CSOs have found this to be difficult and uncharted territory, fearing that engaging companies might overwhelm or undermine CSO efforts and that corporate agendas would reign supreme to the detriment of communities in question.

The first task in approaching this strategy is overcoming the stereotypes and distrust that often serve as an insurmountable obstacle to constructive engagement of the private sector. CSOs must approach businesses in a discriminating and critical way to prevent co-optation or abuse. But they must also come forth with a creative and entrepreneurial strategy that shifts the emphasis for business from altruism and charity to strategic alliance and mutually beneficial ventures. The challenge is to try to extend these alliances so that business decisions and actions integrate community interests. At the same time, CSOs must press governments to provide an enabling fiscal and regulatory environment that encourages private-sector contributions to CSOs through tax deductions and other community investment incentives.

Generating New Wealth Through Market-Based Approaches

The private sector has become an increasingly important source of support for community programs and CSOs throughout the world. With the departure of many foreign donors from Latin America and from Central and Eastern Europe, for example, CSOs are looking to the private sector for support and alternative models of resource generation.

The growing importance of the market and of business activity offers numerous revenue-generation opportunities for CSOs. These include fees for services and the production and sale of goods and services to public and private "clients" or "customers," business ventures, debt swaps, the management of investment portfolios, and other creative financial transactions. These approaches vary from the simple sale of T-shirts to incredibly complex financial transactions.

CSOs that provide credit to microenterprises and the informal sector have become proficient at generating income from their lending operations to sustain some or all of their administrative costs. In some cases, these CSO intermediaries reach a volume of credit that enables them to become formal financial institutions; others become partners with banks by drawing on lines of credit to relend to microentrepreneurs. Grassroots and community organizations have also successfully achieved financial independence through production and access to local and international markets.

While tapping the private sector should not be considered a panacea to the problem of CSO resource dependency on other funding sources, it does represent a new and potentially rich arena of opportunity. The creation of "new wealth" for CSOs can strategically offset—not replace—the resources garnered from public and private donors, and simultaneously contribute to the overall autonomy and independence of CSO initiatives. Several strategies in this book examine creative options for using private-sector tools in CSO resource generation.

Chapter 2: Earning Income Through Trade and Exchange

Chapter 2 discusses the most obvious and direct application of market approaches in CSO resource mobilization. The strategy questions the commonly held notions and stereotypes about the divisions between the "for-profit" and "nonprofit" sector. CSOs around the world have increasingly recognized the unique opportunities for combining efforts to provide job training and lasting employment and economic opportunities for their constituents with revenue generation for the organization itself. These cost recovery, mission-related, and non-mission-related approaches to revenue generation are not without significant obstacles, however, both internal and external.

Although earned income approaches can provide CSOs with a potentially sustainable source of unrestricted income, free of the conditions and time constraints of donor funds, they can be tremendously risky, often fail, and can result in significant loss to CSOs. Nevertheless, if they are implemented successfully, earned income strategies can contribute not only to the financial and programmatic objectives of CSOs, but to the process of democratizing and redefining the current marketplace mentality to include the value of social as well as economic capital.

The earned income strategy goes hand-in-hand with the strategy identified in Chapter 8 of engaging the private sector. In addition to attracting philanthropic support from the private sector, there are numerous opportunities for engaging businesses in joint, mutually lucrative, revenue-generating ventures. These strategies therefore also promote a variety of methods for redefining the traditional set of relations between the private sector and civil society.

Chapter 9: Conversion of Debt: A Win-Win-Win Scenario?

The debt conversion approach examined in Chapter 9 is a way to mobilize resources for CSOs that has recently gained attention around the world. As with any new strategy, CSOs and policymakers should examine it critically, lest the few documented cases of success and the current flurry of interest create unattainable expectations. Indeed, the debt conversion approach represents a unique and mutually beneficial strategy for creditor, debtor, investor, CSO, and community. The contribution of debt conversion to overall debt reduction is minimal, but its potential as an alternative way to leverage local resources for environmental and development initiatives is significant.

Debt conversions are incredibly complex financial transactions, further complicated by political dimensions, legal and tax regulations, and significant uncertainty and risk. There is no clear-cut sequence of steps, and the authors state clearly that this revenue generation approach is not recommended—or even possible—for small, inexperienced CSOs. Typically, only larger CSOs with a well-established financial division should consider this as a viable resource mobilization option. In its most ideal form, however, debt conversion represents a unique instrument for cooperation between CSO intermediaries, private-sector financial institutions, and government. It holds great promise as a method for converting debt into local currency to fund local projects or to set up special funds to benefit domestic CSO initiatives.

Chapter 10: Establishing and Operating Microcredit Programs

As a resource enhancement strategy for CSOs, microcredit programs are similar to earned income in that they engage the market and involve the trade and exchange of goods and services. In this case, credit is the service offered, for which the clients pay by way of interest. Numerous cases from around the world indicate that lending to the poor can make excellent business sense. Just as in debt conversions, microcredit strategies entail often complex financial transactions and management practices. And as with earned income strategies, becoming a financial institution for microcredit operations means transforming the "nonprofit essence" of a CSO into a profitmaking entity that is still dedicated to a mission of service and common good.

As with most market-based strategies for resource mobilization, this is a difficult transition for many CSOs—particularly for the inexperienced. No matter how socially driven CSO-initiated microcredit programs are, they must be established and operated as if they are commercial enterprises. Even though the CSO will necessarily be not-for-profit, its guiding principles must be cost recovery, capitalization, and full pricing—in other words, efficiency-oriented quality financial services to ensure full self-sustainability and to build an equity base. In the long term, it is hoped that this business-mindedness will translate into increased sustainability and broader outreach, thereby fulfilling the CSO's mission better in addition to generating income.

Despite the growing public support for and attention to microcredit approaches, there are both pros and cons to this approach. Many microcredit programs are heavily subsidized by donors, and the question remains as to whether CSOs are the most appropriate or effective model for microcredit financing. Furthermore, increased efforts must be made by CSOs and others to ensure that CSO-based microcredit programs are further integrated into the formal financial sector. In this respect, microcredit represents another opportunity for partnership between CSOs, the private sector, and government.

Chapter 11: Building Indigenous Foundations That Support Civil Society

In Chapter 11's assessment, civil society resource organizations (CSROs) are a resource mobilization strategy that applies to a small number of CSOs but that benefits many. As a method for building local grantmaking institutions that provide funds to other CSOs, the CSRO strategy illustrates the potential for both capitalizing on and transforming existing donor funding sources as well as generating new, local streams of resources in support of CSO initiatives. CSROs represent a mixed model in this respect, since they receive funds from a variety of sources, including official aid agencies, northern NGOs, local and national governments, debt swaps, or their own earned income strategies. CSROs are therefore a useful CSO model both in their effectiveness in attracting diversified funding sources and in their role as intermediaries for passing on smaller grants to local CSOs.

As with developing any sizable organizational endowment, the principal limitation of the CSRO approach is the difficulty inherent in establishing a fund large enough to generate a meaningful and sustainable stream of income. In addition to committed and effective leadership and a clear, compelling vision, successful CSROs require the capacity and experience to tap into potential financing and to manage and develop this grantmaking and intermediary support role. When successful, however, CSROs are a valuable model of intersectoral cooperation and partnership. Successful CSROs are sophisticated institutions with a wide range of contacts and working relationships, among them ties to donors, government agencies, the business sector, and northern CSOs. As the author points out, as indigenous intermediaries rooted in their own communities, CSROs can play a uniquely valuable role in mobilizing civil society participation in national development and policymaking.

Chapter 12: Tapping Social Investment Through the Market

In keeping with other market-based resource mobilization strategies for CSOs, the author suggests in Chapter 12 that "development is an asset-based process." The chapter makes clear that "long-term, broad-scale community development relies on core economic principles familiar to any private-sector business. The values may be different, but the tools are the same." In this vein, tapping into private-sector social investment resources to support CSOs is one additional method of creating both economic and social wealth.

Related to the strategies on earned income and market engagement, this approach appeals to social investors who see their involvement as potentially lucrative. "Productive borrowing" through social investment—whereby an investor receives a return from lending funds that exceeds the costs of borrowing them—is a definite financial incentive. For CSOs, it may also provide a bridge during financially difficult times of restricted cash flow and a longer-term solution by providing investment funds for organizational development, equipment, building or refurbishing of facilities, staffing, or other needs to launch or expand activities.

The social investment approach relies heavily on an environment in which governments recognize the contribution of CSOs to promoting social cohesion and in which savings and banking legislation does not inhibit the development of a financial infrastructure to support them. This strategy also requires a certain level of CSO organizational capacity and a familiarity with for-profit business-disciplined investment practices. As some CSOs have become larger and more like social businesses, they require investment to help them increase their long-term financial capacity so as not to have to rely on any single source of funding. Most social investment institutions are currently very small, and many remain undercapitalized to allow for activities on a larger scale. Furthermore, one considerable challenge of these new funding sources is their ability to build links with the formal financial sector and integrate their activities into the financial mainstream.

Although still on a relatively small scale, successful social investment represents one alternative method—similar to the program-related investment strategies of private foundations identified in Chapter 3—for obtaining capital needed for longer-term organizational sustainability. Philosophically, social investment strategies also encourage a shift from the traditional donor-donee relationship to one based more on principles of business partnership, joint venture, and investment. Locally based and capitalized social investment funds, village banks, cooperative loan funds, revolving credit associations, and so on can also position communities and CSOs to better anticipate and respond to critical financial needs and provide a sense of local participation and ownership.

The Bottom Line of Market-Based Approaches

As these strategies all illustrate, global trends in marketization and capitalization are having dramatic effects on CSOs around the world. Even in the "nonbusiness" strategies described earlier, business language, principles, and approaches are creeping into the culture of CSOs and civil society more generally. As Chapter 4 notes, in attracting individual philanthropic funds, CSOs—including grassroots citizens' organizations—are finding that they must behave as commercial entities in an environment increasingly competitive for resources and attention. Learning from business marketing and sales, CSOs are targeting and positioning themselves to "sell" their services to potential donors and the public alike, treating them as respected customers, clients, or business partners.

CSOs too quick to disregard a market-based approach to resource enhancement will eliminate a great many opportunities to promote their social change and development objectives. As pointed out in Chapter 2, the commonly held stereotypes about the divisions between the "for-profit" and "nonprofit" sectors is a barrier to identifying alternative sources of income for CSOs. Although resource generation strategies using private-sector instruments allow CSOs to tap into potentially "new" sources of wealth, there are indeed both positive and negative issues in greater private-sector engagement. A market-based approach to CSO revenue enhancement may make good business sense, but it runs the risk of potentially capitalizing on (or appearing to capitalize on) poor constituents, so its ethical and moral utility are often questioned.

The "bottom line" of business efficiency may therefore be in direct conflict with the social or economic needs of society. This raises the familiar question of whether socially motivated programs can become self-supporting and independent from outside subsidy, considering that they address the needs of the poor. It also raises the issue of microcredit programs or other fee-for-service activities of CSOs charging an exorbitant rate of interest in pursuit of establishing a self-supporting structure or attempting to finance their own structures themselves.

In other strategies, too, CSOs may find private-sector language and approaches "too cold" and "too businesslike." Strategies prescribed for "cultivating donors" may smack of opportunism or manipulation to some, and can raise fears of losing sight of a CSO's original mission. CSOs clearly face significant difficulties in balancing the profit motive with their social goals.

Finally, it is important to point out that this increased attention to market-based resource mobilization strategies does not prescribe—nor should it imply—a decreased level of responsibility or support to CSOs from the public sector. Instead, it raises a crucial question: what is the proper balance of social services between the nonprofit and public sectors, particularly at the local level? The answer is not whether there is a role for public-sector institutions, but what that role should be. As is evident in debates echoing from the United States to Sweden, the issue is hardly unique to countries in the South and East.

Capitalizing on Nonfinancial Resources

CSOs everywhere typically underestimate the true value of their assets by overlooking one of the most crucial elements and strengths of civil society—the ability of organizations and communities to leverage support in the form of volunteered time, labor, goods, equipment, experience, and other in-kind gifts. Common to nearly all 11 strategies in this book is the critical role that such nonfinancial resources play in ensuring the long-term sustainability of CSOs.

In the discussion in Chapter 4, pledging time, sweat, or counsel to CSOs is cited as a pure expression of individual philanthropy. While the chapter focuses on leveraging monetary donations from individuals, much of the discussion applies equally to gifts of goods and volunteered work.

The grassroots citizens' organizations discussed in Chapter 5 look specifically at the range of financial and nonfinancial resources that can be mobilized from their communities or members. The latter represent one of the most valuable and ready-made supports for these institutions, in the form of volunteer labor, locally available materials, and exchanged services or goods. Even more important, however, are the human resources and capacities these organizations possess. Their effectiveness in developing leadership, multiplying the value of local community and citizen resources, and promoting a civic and participatory environment among their constituents represents a critical and oftentimes undervalued asset.

In the discussion of garnering resources from government, the authors of Chapter 6 rightly point out that opportunities for in-kind gifts and subsidies to CSOs from government in the form of equipment, seconded staff, or other training or technical assistance are increasing as governments privatize economic enterprises and scale back in the direct delivery of social services. The divestiture of production units or selling off of state-owned industries has allowed many CSOs to "inherit" facilities and property that may have otherwise represented a drain on state resources in maintenance and upkeep alone. Although these nonfinancial donations may have clear benefits to both sets of stakeholders and assist in breaking down barriers between them, CSOs need also to weigh carefully the symbolic and practical costs they may entail. Groups need to have a clear and precise idea of the terms under which government is providing the "subsidy" so as not to be pulled away from the CSO's intended mission.

Similar trends in relations between CSOs and private-sector institutions are under way. Companies are shifting emphasis in their engagement of resources and activities; they increasingly use in-kind giving and volunteerism to support civil society initiatives. As the author of Chapter 8 points out, corporate funds are under extraordinary pressure, and the financing available for strategic social investment will always be severely limited since expenditures unrelated to core business operations are always the first to be eliminated. It is often easier for companies to contribute their products and services than to allocate scarce funds for financial contributions. CSOs stand to gain more value through in-kind giving and volunteerism than companies can provide from grant funds.

Nonfinancial resources represent the single greatest opportunity to engage companies in community problem-solving from both an expertise and a cost-effectiveness standpoint. Furthermore, in building stronger, long-term partnerships between CSOs and the private sector, nonfinancial resources can play a central role. As Chapter 8 notes: "There are few strong relationships anywhere in the world that are based solely on money. Therefore it is important to build partnerships involving people, exchanges, and assets far more valuable than mere money."

In Chapter 10 on microcredit, nonfinancial resources clearly play an important role. Redefining the financial requirements of "collateral" could have tremendous implications for the ability of CSOs and the poor around the world to gain access to mainstream financial institutions. Encouraging financial institutions and governments to adapt lending laws to accept what CSOs and communities value and have to offer as a guarantee—something that would be difficult for the borrower to replace if it were seized—would provide mainstream validation to many nonfinancial resources that CSOs and GROs possess. What such groups usually have to offer as "assets" is time, professional expertise and experience, and a vision of development.

As noted in Chapter 7 on development assistance, official donors have provided significant nonfinancial resources to CSOs. This has included capacity-building assistance, opportunities to participate in development fora from the local to international levels, and, perhaps most important, a commitment to promoting an enabling environment that has facilitated CSO participation in national, regional, and international sustainable development policymaking and implementation efforts.

Finally, it is imperative for CSOs to recognize the high stock of "public capital" they possess as well as the critical need to preserve and promote it. Throughout this book the authors discuss the financial, physical, human, and social capital that CSOs require to become fully sustainable and effective actors in society. The importance and value of this public capital is perhaps best summarized in Chapter 7:

> Over the last four decades, building some form of "capital" has been one of the principal strategies of policymakers, although the focus has moved from physical to human and then social capital. In general, building capital has meant raising the quality of stock or resources in one of these areas. CSOs are often held to a higher moral standard in the conduct of their operations than are players in the state or market. The idea that civil society in general and CSOs in particular should have a highly normative dimension centered on notions of integrity, credibility, and legitimacy is a just and accurate one.
>
> In most cases, CSOs have a high stock of public capital—at least in terms of their members or clients—just because they are neither governmental nor market-based. This public capital is the greatest resource that CSOs have at their disposal, and one that should be maintained and even increased. The reaction to a CSO's request for assistance is likely to depend on its perceived legitimacy, including the grounding in local society, and the integrity of its dealings with the larger social and political environment.

Chapter 1
A Strategic Guide to Resource Enhancement

S. Bruce Schearer, Miguel Darcy de Oliveira, and Rajesh Tandon

Increasing demands are being placed on civil society everywhere. The democratization and government decentralization taking place in most parts of the world have created the opportunity and indeed the necessity for citizens to become more engaged than ever before in the political, social, and cultural lives of their nations and of the world as a whole. Civil society in every region today is providing a broad and powerful means for mobilizing such citizen participation.

Concepts of what makes up civil society vary. Although there is no single authoritative definition, in its first book, *Citizens: Strengthening Global Civil Society* (1994), CIVICUS explained civil society as:

> men and women, groups and individuals, getting together to do things by themselves in order to change the societies they live in. In the last two decades, people of all classes, creeds, and ethnic backgrounds have organized themselves to defend democracy and human rights, to fight for more equitable development and a safer environment, or, more simply, just to help those in need or improve the quality of daily life in their neighborhoods and communities.

Figure 1 provides a working anatomy of the civil society sector in terms of the types of organizations it encompasses. The aim of this book is to be as inclusive as possible, with particular emphasis on development-oriented civil society organizations (CSOs).

Over the past several decades, the functions of civil society have expanded in the areas of citizen participation and the delivery of social, economic, cultural, educational, and scientific services. In both cases, the need for additional human and institutional resources to perform these public interest functions has also increased. In order to build up the needed capacities within civil society so that it can scale up its efforts, much larger, more sustainable flows of financing are needed.

This book is concerned with how these additional institutional capacities can be acquired and how expanded flows of financial resources can be obtained. It presents

13

FIGURE 1: An Anatomy of Civil Society

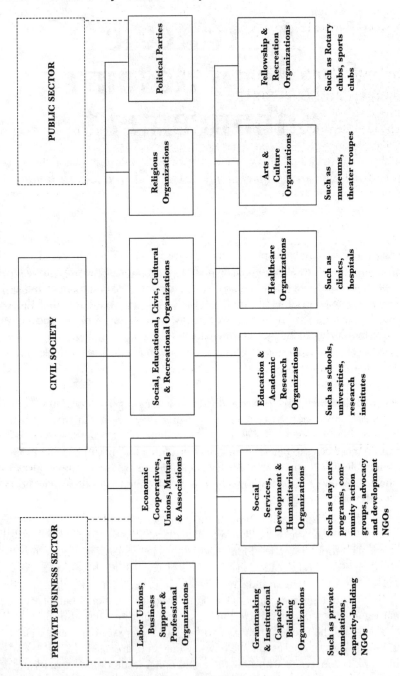

Source: S. Bruce Schearer and John Tomlinson, "The Emerging Nature of Civil Society in Latin America and the Caribbean: An Overview." The Synergos Institute, New York, 1997.

a systematic, comprehensive approach to resource enhancement for the civil society sector. *Sustaining Civil Society* examines the principal sources of financing available to CSOs and describes how these sources can be developed and used.

The Importance of Mission, Organizational Capacity, and Leveraging

The point of departure of this book is that in most circumstances resources are available if civil society organizations pursue a mission and perform functions that are valuable to society, and if they undertake well-designed efforts to obtain the resources needed to perform these functions.

Whether a CSO's goal is to influence government policies through advocacy, organize local communities to act in their own interests, deliver social or economic services, or advance in other ways the concerns of citizens, a deeply held mission is vital to their mobilization as well as their use of resources. A mission lies at the motivational heart of all civil society organizations.

An organization's mission ultimately flows from those who created the group and those who will benefit from it; taken together, these form its "constituency." In order for a CSO to establish institutional capacities and attract human resources to conduct its programs, its constituency must develop the mission, both conceptually and in terms of human caring and commitments. The mission provides the leading focus for mobilizing human, institutional, and financial resources. Resource mobilization must flow from and be congruent with the mission of the organization—not the other way around.

It is no secret that well-organized, effectively operated CSOs generally have a greater impact—and raise more financial resources—than disorganized, poorly managed ones. They not only possess greater organizational capacity, they also typically have stronger reputations and are associated with a larger number of talented volunteers and supporters. Although the greater access to funding for their work undeniably helps such groups be more effective and have greater impact, few would deny that superior organizational capacities and successful execution of their programs are the starting point. The finances come as a result.

The lesson is profound: without a vital, relevant mission and strong organizational capacity, financial resources are not likely to be forthcoming no matter how worthy a group's intentions. And, even more important, financial resources alone do not generate the extent of program results or the impact that could be achieved if an organization's management, planning, and ability to evaluate its role and work are as well developed as they can be.

Once a strong mission and effective program and institution are in place, the most important action that CSOs can take to enhance their financial base is to strengthen and deepen the professionalization of their resource development capacities. This is true within every type of organization as well as for the sector as a whole. Currently, the proportion of institutional capacity devoted to fundraising compared with program development and implementation within organizations is far too small in most groups. To secure an adequate stream of income and to take advantage of and develop the potential for expanding income levels, CSOs need to give higher priority to resource development in their budgeting and staffing.

Another critical ingredient for raising financial resources and using them for maximum impact is collaboration and partnership with other groups. In an era of scarce resources and expanding needs, no one organization—or, for that matter, sector—is likely to have the capacity to solve major social problems or bring about institutional change on its own. For this reason, a third vital component of resource enhancement is the organizational capacity to develop and operate effectively in close working partnerships with other civil society groups, with government bodies, and with the private sector. This lets CSOs leverage their individual resources and have much more powerful results.

How CSOs Can Increase Their Resources

In order to develop effective resource enhancement strategies that are appropriate to their particular institutional assets and roles, civil society organizations need to first analyze their own situations. All such groups raise revenue to cover the costs of their activities from four basic sources:

- earned income, including fees, other self-generated income, and investment earnings;
- contributions from domestic foundations, businesses, and individuals;
- domestic government subsidies and payments, including grants and contracts; and
- foreign aid (in southern and eastern countries) from official development assistance agencies as well as from private external groups such as churches, nonprofit organizations, and global corporations.

The balance among these four basic sources varies greatly from organization to organization. Some groups rely almost exclusively on one source, such as government funding or foundation grants. Others have streams of income from a diversity of sources. Often CSOs have never thoroughly analyzed how they might expand the sources they rely on.

Within these four basic sources, it is possible to identify 11 separate yet complementary pathways to resource enhancement for civil society organizations. Each of the chapters in this book provides an overview of a different resource enhancement strategy, emphasizing the most effective practices, as well as the strengths and limitations of each strategy. The final chapter examines how the different pathways of resource mobilization can be put together by CSOs to achieve adequate and sustainable flows of funds and other resources to undertake their missions successfully.

The book begins in Chapter 2 with revenues from various types of earned income, which in many, perhaps even most countries is the largest source of revenues for the civil society sector (excluding religious organizations). Chapter 10 on microcredit programs also essentially deals with an earned income pathway. Near the end of the book, this subject is revisited in a new guise in Chapter 12, "Tapping Social Investment Through the Market," which deals with a rapidly emerging area that blends earned income with contributions, called "social investments."

Chapters 3, 4, 5, and 8—on foundation funding, individual philanthropy, grassroots citizens' organizations, and working with corporations—all deal with strategies that entail giving resources in the form of contributions to CSOs. Government revenue sources are discussed in Chapter 6. This is often the second largest—and sometimes the largest—source of revenues for the civil society sector. Typically, it is far larger than revenues from contributions. Governments are also a source of revenues through conversions of debt, covered in Chapter 9.

Foreign aid, which often figures in debt conversion, is discussed as a major pathway in Chapter 7. And finally, Chapter 11 on indigenous foundations that support civil society offers a mixed pathway that combines all the others.

It is evident from this picture of overall sources of financing that many CSOs can benefit by stepping back from their day-to-day demands and fundraising activities to take a strategic view of resource enhancement possibilities. In addition to chapters on the major revenue sources, *Sustaining Civil Society* also contains information on innovative sources of financing, such as debt swaps, forming foundation-like organizations or microcredit intermediaries, or using new market-based mechanisms.

The fundamental approach is to tap as many of the pathways as professionally as possible. This will result in multiple sustainable streams of income, which will not only enhance the overall resource base of the organization, but also make it more secure and sustainable by virtue of the diversification of sources.

Some Basic Policy Challenges to the Financing of Civil Society

The overall political and regulatory climate in which civil society organizations seek to mobilize and use resources is often not as supportive as the demands being placed on the sector require. In many cases, it is hostile to such efforts by CSOs, thus undermining their contributions to national development. This section looks at some policy changes that various national and global actors could make to improve the climate and thereby strengthen financing for civil society.

The Need for Greater Stability of Funding

All the four basic sources of income for civil society groups are variable, by definition. Earned income levels and user fees tend to fluctuate in association with economic cycles. Revenues from government vary according to political changes, as does income from foreign aid. Contributions from foundations and corporations are geared to those institutions' interests and objectives, which typically undergo frequent revision and refinement. Contributions from individuals are one of the most stable sources, but they, too, depend on cycles in the overall economy, as well as on changes in public interest.

CSOs can respond to the challenge for greater financial stability in three ways:

- they can diversify their income sources to minimize dependence on any single source;

- they can build working cash reserves and establish lines of credit and other mechanisms to provide financial cushioning when changes occur outside their control; and

- they can build endowments, capital funds, and other forms of permanent assets that give them a "safety net," as well as collateral for borrowing when necessary—where such assets are invested to produce net income, this income can be held for emergencies and fluctuations in financial resources.

Policymakers need to remove obstacles to the multiple routes for resource mobilization described in this book. Also, training and other programs of professional capacity building for resource development are urgently needed if civil society is to raise more resources. Multilateral and bilateral donor agencies and national governments need to supply a portion of the financing for such training.

Private banks in many countries increasingly see CSOs as potential clients for lines of credit and working capital funds. Governments and private donors should support these financial services for not-for-profit groups in all countries as a matter of common practice.

Policymakers and donors can also support the financial stability of CSOs by adopting policies and funding practices to establish endowments and permanent capital funds. Those types of funds may not be appropriate to all groups, but they would make an enormous contribution to the stability and independence of many of them. They can be built up slowly over time through the entrepreneurial efforts and savings of CSOs, but the national policy and legal framework to permit such action must be in place.

The Need to Regularize Government–Civil Society Relations

As long as civil society and government question and threaten each other's legitimacy, civil society cannot meet its goals, and governments expose themselves to increasing levels of citizen criticism and protest. The starting point is to regularize the roles of government and civil society in each country. This requires both sectors to accept the notion that state, market, and civil society share responsibility for meeting national needs, and that each has a legitimate and complementary function.

In regularizing state–civil society relations, countries around the world have chosen different approaches and established different sets of policies and mechanisms in accordance with their national cultures and histories. There is clearly no "right answer," but there are many models of what can be done.

Governments and the bilateral and multilateral agencies that support them urgently need to use a comparative legal and governance perspective to develop a new clarifying and enabling body of law and regulation that provides civil society in each country with a clear-cut way to participate in national policy and priority setting and in national development efforts.

At the most fundamental political level, national governments in consultation with civil society must decide how much they wish to share responsibilities—and the state's revenues—with CSOs in different sectors of national life. At this operational level of collaboration, the challenge is to identify and construct a blend of mechanisms that can be used by government departments and CSOs to work together in various programmatic fields, such as education or health. To support this collaboration, a variety of forms of government funding need to be developed, among them transparent, merit-based contracting and grant procedures. A rich menu of experience and "best practice" examples for this exists around the world.

The Need for Improved Legal and Regulatory Environments

The third major challenge to enhanced financing of civil society is to establish a supportive environment of law, regulation, and policy among governments and international agencies to enable the sector to raise revenues from the four basic sources mentioned earlier. Present laws and policies create major obstacles to each of these, and they work against the interests of both civil society and the public interest as a whole.

For example, many governments constrain nonprofit organizations from earning income even when that income is used to support their own programs. In many countries, legal obstacles and unfavorable policies make it difficult for nonprofit organizations to be direct recipients of foreign aid. Tax laws discourage philanthropic contributions in some countries. The ability of nonprofit groups to accumulate capital funds or property is also restricted in many countries. In many places, adverse regulations and arbitrary practices impede the provision of government funds to nonprofit groups.

What is needed is a supportive set of basic principles and laws along with transparent, favorable, regulated policies within nations to permit CSOs to be as effective as possible in raising the resources they need to finance their activities. Since earned income and government funding are such important sources, an enabling legal and policy environment in these two areas is especially critical.

The Need to Release and Mobilize Untapped Potential

The fourth major challenge goes beyond financing to human, institutional, and technological resources. Private, for-profit corporations are increasingly concerned about the increase in major social problems. And CSOs need the knowledge, skills, technology, and institutional know-how that private corporations are potentially willing to contribute. But civil society groups are not yet making effective use of these resources. Businesses and global corporations possess enormous management and technological capacities that could benefit nonprofit groups. The subject of corporate citizenship and social responsibility needs to be much more widely discussed and put into action through pragmatic new multisectoral partnerships, as discussed in Chapter 13.

Similarly, citizens everywhere are looking for ways they can contribute to making society better. But much more effort is needed by CSOs to design practical mechanisms for tapping this resource. The potential contributions of time and skills by citizens need to be captured through a wide variety of volunteering mechanisms. Civil society today is responding to these challenges with increasing vigor at the global and national levels, but much more is needed and can be done.

One of the most important steps policymakers and official donor agencies can take to support this—as well as the other policy challenges outlined above—is to provide program financing for widespread education to inform the public at large about the contributions and relevance of civil society to national well-being. It is only through such broad public understanding and support that long-term resource mobilization from society as a whole can be generated. This challenge is one that international donor agencies are especially well placed to help local civil society groups meet.

Chapter 2

Earning Income Through Trade and Exchange

Horacio R. Morales, Jr.

Civil society is often referred to as the "nonprofit" sector. Its main objective is to fulfill a public purpose or charitable mission that in most cases has had nothing to do with business, profit-making, or the market. In contrast, the main purpose of business firms is to generate profits through trade and exchange in the marketplace. Yet these commonly held notions and stereotypes about the divisions between the "for-profit" and "nonprofit" sectors represent a barrier to identifying alternative sources of income for civil society initiatives. They need to be reevaluated and reconstructed.

In light of reductions in and constraints on traditional sources of funds from public and private donors, civil society organizations (CSOs) around the world are increasingly turning to the market to earn income and mobilize local resources. This trend has developed out of concern over long-term sustainability and self-reliance. Furthermore, CSOs have recognized the potential impact of market involvement on their efforts to provide economic opportunities and lasting employment at the local level. Job training and employment programs, for example, as well as trade and marketing efforts to promote the products of local farmers, fishers, and other small producers can benefit from direct market engagements. Other benefits of CSO interaction with the market include the injection of principles of social and environmental responsibility into the business community.

The recognition of these benefits has paved the way for CSOs to become involved with the trade and exchange of goods and services, an approach previously associated only with the selfish motives of for-profit firms and running counter to CSO priorities of community welfare and environmental protection. Groups are using this strategy not just out of profit motives and the financial bottom line, however. They have stamped these endeavors with their own unique characteristic of social objectives.

This chapter was prepared with the assistance of Lee Davis of NESsT.

Paying Your Own Way, Carrying the Message

This chapter addresses several "earned-income" strategies for CSOs in developing and transition countries. It is important to note, however, that these are not intended as isolated resource enhancement strategies. Oftentimes earned income is quite wrongly considered a replacement for official development assistance (ODA) or for funding from northern nongovernmental organizations (NGOs) and foundations. Instead, earned income is one of several ways that CSOs can diversify their funding base and generate a portion of their income from "untied" or "unrestricted" sources.

Three approaches to earning income are discussed in this chapter:

• cost recovery,

• mission-related, and

• non-mission-related.

The chapter excludes an examination of earned income within microcredit programs, debt swaps and conversions, and endowments even if they are part of a strategy to engage the market, as these are covered in other chapters.

Many CSOs have used cost-recovery approaches or fee-for-service schemes for years, and indeed this is the most widely used and evenly distributed geographically of the three strategies for earning income. It involves charging direct beneficiaries either the partial or full cost of providing a good or service. Family planning organizations charge clients for condoms, pills, and other birth control methods. Primary health care units charge patients for immunizations and other services. Medical CSOs charge patients for basic curative treatments. Many CSOs bill governments or private clients for consultancy services in such areas as capacity-building and training, research, and policy analysis and formation. Other CSOs charge fees for civic education and election monitoring, agricultural extension services, marketing, and management of government or donor programs and projects. The rise of ecotourism has prompted some CSOs to charge fees and recover costs when sponsoring tours.

Mission-related earned income refers to revenues generated through activities and enterprises that fall within the mission or mandate of the CSO. In this sense, cost recovery approaches are part of mission-related income. What distinguishes the latter is the fact that there is no direct link between services rendered to beneficiaries and revenues generated. This is typically a less extensive source of revenue for CSOs, largely because it requires a set of skills that differ from the specific services normally provided by the CSO. For instance, a CSO providing medical services to a depressed tribal community may decide to sell tribal products to increase beneficiaries' income. The CSO may not immediately have the equipment, personnel, or skill to do the job effectively. In many cases, mission-related income includes adding a good or service for sale, sometimes produced or provided by its beneficiaries, in order to finance the main services provided.

Non-mission-related income is generated from business and enterprise activities that may have no relation to the original mission or program objectives of the CSO (although the term may be a misnomer for CSOs that accept the promotion of social enterprises and corporate social responsibility as a part of their mission). They are pursued to generate financial resources or investment capital for the CSO and may not be rationalized within the framework of the CSO's mission. It usually entails not only additional equipment, personnel, or skills but also investment capital, which is usually difficult to obtain for any group other than large, well-established CSOs.

There are fewer but increasing numbers of attempts among CSOs to undertake non-mission-related income initiatives. Falling into this category are businesses such as restaurants, hotels, shops, and speculative ventures such as investments in real estate, stocks, treasury bills, and so on. These ventures involve far greater investment and risk than cost-recovery and mission-related approaches to earned income. When they succeed, non-mission-related ventures can produce a significant source of funding for CSOs. But when they fail, they can do significant financial damage and have an altogether demoralizing effect on an organization. In fact, if available statistics regarding the success rates of for-profit small business start-ups around the world are any indication, entering the business market is a highly risky and oftentimes unsuccessful venture.

Despite this, some CSOs have modified their revenue generation strategies to include earned income through direct market activities. The Philippine Rural Reconstruction Movement (PRRM), for example, has a resource mobilization strategy for 1996–2000 that states:

> The institution shall pursue a comprehensive resource-building strategy that would ensure its financial sustainability and that of its programs and allied institutions. This shall be pursued through a combination of building the institution's endowment fund; pursuing the translation of its local, national and global advocacy into concrete support for programs and projects; multilateral and bilateral partnership [with] donor agencies supportive of sustainable development; and business/enterprise development.

Benefits and Limitations

Earned-income strategies can serve several important purposes for CSOs. Those that successfully adopt such an approach typically do so to offset reductions in donor support or to become more financially self-sustainable and less dependent on external assistance. Financial sustainability—whether from cost recovery, mission-related, or non-mission-related income—leads to greater CSO autonomy. Earned income can provide funds that CSOs can allocate without any conditions or constraints; it helps groups overcome the pitfalls of becoming a donor-driven organization or a mere implementer of donors' predetermined programs. CSOs will be free to design and implement programs that are more responsive to the needs of their members or beneficiaries. They will also be free from the reporting and accounting requirements of donors.

"Financial sustainability" or "financial autonomy" can mean something different for every CSO. As mentioned earlier, an earned-income approach to resource generation is not a panacea for all troubled organizations, nor is it intended to replace completely income from public and private donors. In fact, a core question for CSOs to answer before considering an earned-income approach is, What do we hope to achieve with an earned-income strategy? The answer to this question alone can help determine the nature and scale of earned-income strategies most suitable for a given CSO.

FUNREDES, DOMINICAN REPUBLIC

The Fundacion Redes y Desarrollo (FUNREDES), the Networks and Development Foundation, was established as an international nonprofit NGO in 1993 in Santo Domingo. It was set up to facilitate and accelerate the spread of and access to information and communication technologies throughout Latin America by supporting the development of national networks and providing access and training for potential users from a variety of fields, including NGOs, universities, and scientific communities.

FUNREDES received seed support from Union Latina and ACAL to begin its activities in 1993. The full-time staff of four is helped by a group of FUNREDES consultants and national correspondents throughout the region who have expertise in documentation, computer science, satellites, multimedia, and telecommunications. The largest single source of FUNREDES' income (70 percent) is from fees for services, product sales, and consulting. The organization receives none of its resources from governments or from its membership (apart from in-kind donations). More than 50 percent of FUNREDES' earned income is from consulting and contract activities.

A number of for-profit competitors provide similar Internet services to the private sector in the Dominican Republic, but to date FUNREDES has not had any direct problems with competition. In attracting partners, FUNREDES argues that its knowledge and skills in the Internet field and in Web site design are superior to those of many private-sector service providers, and that TELESINERGIA will be competing as an equal player in the market. In the process of negotiating agreements to launch its enterprise activities through TELESINERGIA, the Foundation also managed to arrange deals for funding some of its nonprofit networks with local telecom operators.

Information obtained from Daniel Pimienta, Executive Director, FUNREDES. This case study is based on Lee Davis, "New Directions in NGO Self-Financing."

Is the objective to generate all or just a portion of income? The level an organization aims for can have significant effects on the CSO itself. Some, albeit few, CSOs succeed in generating 100 percent of their income. If this were so easy, however, more would be doing it. Most CSOs instead attempt simply either to cover the costs of a given program or activity or to generate only a portion of annual income from earned-income activities—typically enough to cover administrative or operational expenses or staff salaries, leaving funds from external donors or local philanthropic gifts to cover project-related costs.

Earning even symbolic amounts or up to 20–40 percent of a CSO's annual income can provide significant freedom for an organization. It can serve as leverage for CSOs in the South by allowing them to act from an independent position while lobbying on ODA and private development assistance from the North. As CSOs in the South establish their capacity to mobilize resources from the market, they will be able to exercise more independence and initiative in their negotiations with northern CSO partners and ODA donors. With enough earned income to cover the general operations of their work, CSOs can choose whether and what funds to accept without the immediate concern of financial ruin. They can start to exercise real power in terms of defining the course of their own work and the terms of development assistance generally.

Earned-income strategies can also provide the opportunity for CSOs to become critical players in democratizing the market by promoting corporate social responsibility and serving as a model of how to use market tools for public benefit. CSOs can therefore help to slowly loosen the grip of big corporations that dominate and manipulate local and international markets. Groups can also become significant actors in shaping the needs and meeting the demands of the public at large through earned-income ventures. They can therefore pave the way for more socially responsible, environmentally friendly investment, production, consumption, and exchange among individual consumers.

Within the three strategies for earning income, cost-recovery strategies can have a number of positive effects on organizational and programmatic performance. Some CSOs have found that they help decrease expenditures through better systems and operations. Likewise, CSOs that charge clients for goods provided or services rendered, whether through cost recovery or mission-related activities, are likely to be more accountable to their clients. Clients who pay tend to demand higher-quality goods or services and tend to have a greater voice in the design or implementation of the good or service. The CSO may, in turn, find itself more efficient and effective in reaching its beneficiaries.

Typically, cost-recovery methods tend to be more successful when the service or good being provided leads to income-generating opportunities for the CSO's constituency. Credit programs of CSOs or CSO marketing services for members' or beneficiaries' products or services are therefore more often and easily accepted and successful. These types of cost recovery are generally more likely to recover a bigger percentage of their costs than those of CSOs engaged in educational or outreach services (such as AIDS education).

A major problem with cost-recovery approaches is that in many developing countries, the reality of poverty makes charging fees for services, especially from the poor, practically and morally unjustifiable. Thus many CSOs in these areas have refused or are simply unable to use this approach. This dilemma has been resolved by some groups through some form of "cross-subsidization"—subsidizing the poor with fees collected from better-off clients.

While mission-related and non-mission-related resource generation activities avoid this pitfall, they raise other issues of concern. Such ventures run the danger of distracting CSOs and their members from their primary mission, if not subverting their lofty values altogether. At the same time, CSOs often do not have the skills or expertise required to make a business activity successful. A business venture requires specific skills in accounting, marketing, financial management, personnel management, and quality control. The cost of gaining such skills often exceeds the expected revenues from the business activity, since most CSOs do not want to impose big profit margins and the enterprises they choose often tend to be small-scale, with minimal earnings.

Another major drawback in these cases, particularly for non-mission-related income projects, are the legal complications that come with earning income. In most countries, CSOs are classified as nonprofit organizations, and are not subject to income tax. Once they start earning income beyond cost recovery, their nonprofit status is put into question. One way to resolve this is to spin off mission- and non-mission-related income activities into an institutionally distinct subsidiary or a separate entity. This can protect the integrity of the CSO and its services and programs. Another advantage of this is that it will force the separate business entity to keep a distinct set of accounts. This protects the use or misuse of other sources of income, and the problem of funds from grants subsidizing the enterprise or business activities.

Future Trends

As external resources continue to decline or shift priorities, CSOs will have to resort to earned-income strategies of one kind or another. As they gain more experience in cost-recovery methods, mission-related provision of goods or services, and business ventures, and as the principles of social entrepreneurship or corporate social responsibility are adopted, the number of these projects should rise. Many lessons are sure to be learned from both successful and failed endeavors. To date, however, there have been no comprehensive attempts to document and draw lessons from the earned-income approaches of CSOs around the world. There is a relative dearth of knowledge on this topic and little understanding of the best approaches for nurturing or replicating earned-income initiatives.

As more and more CSOs generate a portion of their own income, civil society's nonprofit character will continue to evolve. Critics of earned-income approaches argue that this could undermine the value-oriented and voluntary nature of CSOs. The reverse claim could also be true, however: CSOs who overlook the opportunity to use private-sector tools to their benefit could face significant consequences in light of dwindling external resources. Earning income through trade and exchange could therefore be seen as a strategic move to preserve the very integrity of CSOs. The current dependency paradigm, in which CSOs remain purely "nonprofit" in character and continue to compete for a smaller pie of external resources, needs to be reassessed. Earning income from trade and exchange is one way to accomplish this.

Key Issues

As CSOs mobilize resources through engagement with the market in varying ways, this strategy should be seen as complementary rather than competitive with more effective efforts at CSO advocacy for increasing ODA and local public expenditure for just and sustainable development. In this respect, it is important for CSOs to become more effective advocates and have an impact in terms of increasing the allocation of funds to CSOs in ODA and government budgets, as well as investing in development education to upgrade fundraising campaigns for the northern public or to increase public support for ODA. Merely replacing a strategy of engagement with the state with one of engagement with the market would lose sight of the bigger battle on the structural dimensions of poverty, inequity, and environmental decline at the national and global levels.

A number of key issues influence the effectiveness or viability of earned-income approaches. As noted earlier, this is not an easy strategy to undertake, since it not only entails a significant reevaluation of traditional fundraising methods, it questions the fundamental division between the for-profit and nonprofit sectors. The concept of an enterprising approach to NGO finance is a two-part problem, requiring both a philosophical and a practical paradigm shift.

On the philosophical level, CSOs must question their dependence on public and private giving for both its limitations and its consequences. Many CSOs are accustomed to depending on the "easy money" of outright grants. They sometimes have little motivation to look elsewhere for income. The earned-income approach requires a fundamental shift of attitude about resource options, with adoption of a more entrepreneurial approach in lieu of charity and welfare. But this philosophical shift also needs to take place among donors, who need to reevaluate the traditional project-based funding approach and replace it with a model that facilitates a longer-term investment in individual CSO development.

On a practical level, a number of very real obstacles exist for CSOs trying to earn income. The barriers are internal and organizational (management skills and experience, planning and capacity) as well as external, created by the policy and regulatory environment that governs CSO economic activity (that is, legal and tax issues, issues of public perception, and relations with private businesses, the state, and donors).

Recovering the Costs of Goods or Services

At the local, national, regional, and global levels, a range of different broad-based membership organizations, intermediary and primary development NGOs, specialized CSOs, and grassroots groups have used various forms of cost-recovery approaches or fee-for-service schemes. The services and goods provided span the whole range of CSO involvement. They can thus be categorized thematically or functionally.

There are at least four major categories of goods and services:

- basic social goods and services, including health, education, relief and rehabilitation, housing, water, and energy;
- goods and services that deal with livelihood and economic development;
- goods and services related to environmental and natural resource management; and
- goods and services that promote organizational development, empowerment, and responsive governance.

Some of the more common products or services are:

- education, training, and capacity building;
- publications and multimedia development communication;
- community organization and technical services extension;
- research, policy analysis, and formulation; and
- planning, monitoring, and evaluation.

SAMUHIK ABHIYAN, NEPAL

SAMUHIK ABHIYAN is a nonprofit social development organization established in 1992 in Kathmandu, Nepal, by a group of professional trainers committed to the empowerment of local people through organizational and human resource development, savings and credit promotion, planning and management, and other training and awareness-raising activities.

In an effort to move away from the tendency of NGOs in Nepal to depend entirely on external grants for programs, SAMUHIK ABHIYAN attempts to use local innovative mechanisms to generate resources for its activities. Those under its Institutional Development Support and Advocacy Programs are entirely financed with internal resources. The group's resourcing strategy includes sales of professional services, training packages, souvenirs, and publications, along with membership contributions. Local social development organizations that request training or technical support are required to mobilize local resources to meet part of the cost. The organization's journal and booklets are also sold for a minimal price to lessen the need for external resources to maintain publication.

Information obtained from Bhuwan Acharya, Chief Executive, SAMUHIK ABHIYAN.

In recent years, management services related to various aspects of organizational development have also become common, such as human resource management, financial management, and computer-based information/communication systems development. One typical service offered has been the organization and documentation of seminars and conferences.

Clients for these goods and services include members of CSOs and the public at large (usually specific sectors or segments); peoples' organizations, NGOs, and other CSOs, including donor NGOs; academic institutions and churches; government bodies and intergovernmental organizations; and even business corporations.

Key Best Practices

For some CSOs that are set up to provide specific goods and services, cost-recovery approaches are built into their financial strategy from the very start. And in a few cases (such as management consulting CSOs or groups built to provide a specific service to members, defined clients, or a specific segment of the market), cost-recovery schemes are the main source of income.

The question of both the market demand for a given product or service and the ability of constituents or other clients to pay for the product or service is a critical one in determining the most effective method for implementing cost-recovery approaches. A strong knowledge of both the market and potential clients is necessary for appropriate planning and pricing schemes. The social and economic realities within given countries can dictate or significantly influence the likelihood of success.

In Central and Eastern Europe in recent years, for example, most environmental training activities have been donor-driven, and existing programs have been too expensive or the participants have been reluctant to pay the full costs of training delivery. A number of members of the Environmental Management Training Center Network, an NGO established in 1994 with funds from U.S. and Hungarian donors, have attempted to collect fees for their training services in order to recover at least a part of their costs. In the Czech Republic, the Center for Environmental Analyses has attempted three times to charge fees at its workshops, with mixed success: "When the conference had participants from industry, we have had 100 percent success with the fee. When the conference had participants from NGOs, almost all participants asked for some sort of financial help or couldn't attend. When the conference had participants from city and regional offices, 50 percent paid the full amount and 50 percent asked for some sort of financial assistance."

Many other lessons about cost recovery can be found in the cooperative movements around the world. Cooperatives, especially at the local level, are set up to provide specific services for members, often at a lower cost than prevailing market rates. As long as they at least break even, they remain sustainable providers that improve the income or quality of life of the households of their members.

Success stories of small-scale projects are plentiful at the village level, but big-scale projects are harder to find. Examples of successful multipurpose cooperatives at the primary level providing services for their farmer members include KASAMA and the Dugong Multipurpose Cooperative in Cotabato, Mindanao. These cooperatives retail credit obtained from the government's Land Bank of the Philippines. They also manage the use of various farm implements (hand tractor and thresher) and postharvest facilities (a drier and a mini-rice mill) for members. They charge service fees that are below the prevailing market prices and interest rates, and way below the high rates offered by informal moneylenders in the area. The incomes of the farmers who are members have increased 25–50 percent after they used these services.

Any CSO that implements a cost-recovery approach will have to examine the potential for actually recovering the cost of providing the service or good. CSOs have to analyze their membership, client, or public market in terms of people's capacity to pay for the service or good. It is a workable strategy to consult clients or include them in determining what cost should be recovered and the price they should pay or are able to pay.

Some clients, especially the unemployed, are likely to be unwilling or unable to pay for certain goods and services. In this case, CSOs should look at other sources of income such as donor grants or government subsidies to support the service or good. Those that provide "public services" should have a right to share "public" funds generated from national or local tax revenues for these purposes. (See Chapter 6.) In many countries, however, access to these "indirect" cost recovery resources is not available, which unfortunately often coincides with facing the realities of poverty in developing countries. This makes it more difficult for them to justify cost-recovery approaches.

One solution is cross-subsidizing the delivery of services. PROSALUD, for example, is a Bolivian health care NGO that serves about 300,000 lower- and middle-class people. Since 1985, PROSALUD has used a cross-subsidization strategy whereby prof-

CZECH CLEANER PRODUCTION CENTER

The Czech Cleaner Production Center (CCPC) has used an innovative cost-recovery approach for its training courses. CCPC offers a 10-month cleaner production course for governments and businesses in the country to develop strategies for optimizing energy and material flows and reducing their impacts on the environment. A part of the course and the main evaluation criteria for participants is carrying out a cleaner production project in a participating company. Participants form teams that then implement projects. They receive course certificates only if their recommendation yields results (that is, is implemented by the company).

All results undergo a detailed evaluation by a special committee in order to determine whether the achieved results (in terms of monetary savings) are real. Each company whose personnel enrolls in the course signs a contract with CCPC committing itself to paying half of the fees for the senior expert who supervises each team as well as a share (up to 10 percent) of the annual savings realized as a result of the project. This amount can actually turn out to be quite substantial, since some of the recommendations lead to as much as US$100,000 in annual savings—resulting in US$10,000 for CCPC.

Information obtained from Environmental Management Training Center Network, Regional Environmental Center for CEE.

itable services such as selling contraceptives, condoms, and pharmaceuticals subsidize unprofitable services, while profitable health centers subsidize unprofitable centers.

Each health center applies its own fee schedule. Most, however, do not test the income of clients but apply a fee that is higher than the public health system's but lower than the private fee would be. The policy is to charge enough to survive. Sometimes they offer free services as well, but the share of clientele receiving this usually does not exceed 3–10 percent. Some of the centers providing services for richer patients charge higher fees. At present the system covers 80 percent of the operating costs of the health centers; some of the health centers produce 100–110 percent of their operating costs, while others cover approximately 40 percent. The average level of self-sustainability has been increasing through the years.

In addition to cross-subsidizing services for the poor with fees collected from wealthier constituents or clients in their own countries, CSOs have also begun to identify methods of recovering costs from donors and foreign visitors. Close relations between CSOs and agencies in the North and South have created a new category of tourist—those who seek a more realistic view of society than presented by government and corporate tours. These human exchanges can take a lot of time and energy away from the CSO's main mission. But groups are investigating ways to make the effort pay for itself.

Similarly, a growing number of CSOs are capitalizing on the natural beauty of their surroundings to recover costs through tourist dollars. Environmental CSOs that manage parks and protected areas have increased efforts to charge fees for entrance

ECOLOGICAL DEVELOPMENT TOURISM PROGRAM, PHILIPPINES

In recent years, the Philippine Rural Reconstruction Movement—the oldest and largest primary development NGO in the Philippines—together with its partner community organizations has charged foreign visitors to see its various areas of operation. This approach arose from PRRM's own internal assessment, which showed that significant staff time and resources were spent hosting visitors every year. A number of PRRM's NGO partners in the North, particularly the Kanagawa People to People Aid Movement in Japan, were continually asking PRRM to handle groups of 5–20 "development tourists" from trade unions, cooperatives, citizens' groups, and local governments as a means of promoting support for specific aspects of PRRM's core program (largely funded by the Dutch overseas aid agency, NOVIB).

PRRM offers tour packages for specific areas that already are tourist destinations (such as a Natural Museum Tour in Ifugao, home of the famous rice terraces) and, on request, adds relevant areas of PRRM operations across upland, lowland, and coastal communities. For the time being, PRRM's ecodevelopment tourism program is able to partially or fully recover the costs of both the institution and its partner community organizations in hosting the tourists. Charging based on the visitors' capacity to pay is a difficult issue. Clear guidelines need to be made in this respect, as it can be a source of misunderstanding.

PRRM and its partners have plans to spin this program off into a separate enterprise. To make this transition, they have realized the importance of market segmentation and research to determine if indeed a large enough market exists and can be tapped.

Case study prepared by Philippine Rural Reconstruction Movement.

and for ecotours. The Philippine Eagle Foundation in southern Philippines, for example, charges tourists entrance fees for its eagle park in Davao City; the National Trust of St. Lucia, which manages the Pigeon Island National Landmark Park, also charges entrance fees for tourists and other visitors in addition to renting space in the park as a wedding venue and open-air concert area. The money generated goes toward maintenance and conservation expenses in the park.

Thousands of CSOs involved in education and research sell publications or charge fees for seminars. Since 1978, the IBON Databank, a Philippine research institute, has been able to generate local resources from the sale of their research studies, books, diaries, and calendars. A bimonthly *Facts and Figures* research digest has helped other CSOs and the public at large to better understand major policy issues and socioeconomic problems. The revenues generated have helped reduce IBON's dependence on external grants. The Regional Environmental Center in Szentendre, Hungary, also attempts to cross-subsidize through its publication sales. Its research and policy reports and other directories and publications on environmental issues are offered for free to CSOs and for a fee to governments, businesses, and western constituents.

Major Conclusions for Practitioners

Before embarking on a cost-recovery strategy, CSOs should first consider whether the good or service is (or was) provided by government or other for-profit sector institutions. If it is not provided by others, can it be considered a public good or service that should be provided by government through public funds? If so, then the CSO should lobby for government subsidies or interventions. If it succeeds in getting public funds, this will help the CSO in providing better goods or services and perhaps reach a larger market.

CSOs should consider a number of other key questions before undertaking any new cost-recovery project. What value would be added by the CSO providing the service? Is there a strong demand for the service? What is the capacity or willingness of the clients to pay for the service?

Other issues that arise from CSO involvement in delivering goods or services that otherwise would have been public have to do with the consistency of cost-recovery approaches with community empowerment or self-governance strategies and with CSO advocacy for responsive governance. Groups that are advocating community empowerment in relation to the delivery of basic social services (such as preschool education or primary health care) should take care that cost-recovery approaches do not detract from community capacity-building efforts, which aim to increase communities' ability to deliver services themselves.

Service NGOs especially need to ensure that cost-recovery approaches are pursued side-by-side with capacity-building and phaseout schemes, so that recovering costs from direct service delivery can at best be a transition strategy. The objective of setting up community-based systems for the delivery of basic social services that are subsidized by the government should be part of CSO advocacy for empowerment and responsive governments. Therefore, CSOs need to adjust the magnitude of cost-recovery approaches at the community level to suit local conditions.

If the CSO determines that charging fees for goods or services delivered is a reasonable option, then in collaboration with the clients it should establish a realistic fee structure. This is critical particularly in developing countries, where many of the CSO clients are underprivileged. The CSO should also see how the clients may help deliver the service or take it over altogether after a period of time.

Mission-Related Earned-Income Strategy

This strategy differs from a cost-recovery approach in that the activities involved are not directly linked to the goods or services mandated by the CSO mission. It includes many initiatives that nonprofit organizations providing relief, welfare, safety net, or education services undertake to mobilize resources from the general public in order to finance their programs, outside of direct solicitations and fundraising campaigns.

This is a less extensively used approach to earning income. It is used mainly by bigger and more established CSOs. For example, the Bangladesh Rural Advancement Committee (BRAC), the largest NGO in Bangladesh, maintains a multimillion-dollar annual operating budget and has numerous commercial operations that generate resources for its programs. As of 1994, up to 31 percent of BRAC's income of US$70.1

million was generated from mission-related activities. That figure was expected to reach 38 percent by 1996.

BRAC's mission-related resource-generating activities and enterprises include 14 Training and Resource Centers, handicrafts production and marketing at home and abroad, provision of services by a computer center and BRAC Printers, a group of profitable retail shops and export business for local craftspeople, a cold storage facility built to help very small tenant farmers store potatoes beyond harvest time, and several garment factories. Similarly, the Population and Community Development Association in Thailand operates a number of for-profit enterprises, including a fruit orchard, as well as numerous non-mission-related businesses through its for-profit subsidiary Population Development Corporation.

Several large northern NGOs, such as the International Federation of Red Cross and Red Crescent Societies (Red Cross), are also involved in mission-related, earned-income activities. The Red Cross has successfully pursued mission-related earned-income strategies in various countries based on a threefold revenue-generating strategy: make a profit, meet a valid social need, and strengthen the movement or organization.

Beyond the efforts of these larger NGOs, which are either international in character or very highly connected or subsidized by external donor funds, the challenges of starting up and running this type of earned-income strategy among smaller CSOs remains largely undocumented—and oftentimes extremely difficult. Numerous small community CSOs around the world have also attempted, often with mixed success, to use mission-related earned-income strategies. Several areas of CSO activity have typically lent themselves to extensions into mission-related, earned-income initiatives. Organizations within the fields of economic opportunity, job training, and employment generation have been particularly active. Many groups have extended their program activities into a profitable earned-income venture that simultaneously furthers their mission.

In Hungary, for instance, the Gondviseles Alapitvany (or Caretaking Foundation), founded in Budapest in 1992, serves the needs of mentally handicapped youth (18–30 years old) and their families through small, group-based care and the provision of employment opportunities. It has evolved into an organization with a full-time staff of 25 and an annual operating budget of approximately US$65,500. Nearly one third of the foundation's income in 1996 was generated through its own income-generating activities, including a child care equipment rental shop and the production and sale of children's toys.

Handicapped employees work to assemble and package children's toys and "logic sets." The work itself has a fundamental teaching value to mentally handicapped youth, intended to improve logical, three-dimensional, and numeric recognition through enjoyable, playful, colorful, creative, and productive work. Meanwhile, the employees earn their own living expenses, receive medical insurance coverage, and even contribute to their state retirement pension. According to foundation staff, the difference between its income-generating activities and those of other NGOs is that Gondviseles' handicapped employees do not just make the toys to sustain the NGO, they make them to sustain themselves. The income generation activities are an integral part of the foundation's programmatic mission.

THE JAIROS JIRI ASSOCIATION, ZIMBABWE

The Jairos Jiri Association, probably the largest of its kind in Africa, serves more than 10,000 disabled people annually in Zimbabwe. It has a wide range of programs, including schools and psychotherapy treatment centers for children, a scholarship program to assist secondary and post-secondary students, a training center and farm for agricultural education, and outreach and follow-up integration programs; altogether, there are 16 centers all over the country.

One of the Association's main activities is the provision of specialized education plus vocational training for the disabled. It operates five craftshops, two furniture factories, and a farm that produces food for nearby residents and graduated trainees. These craftshops provide a great opportunity for disabled people to obtain skills and to produce high-quality goods including furniture, artificial limbs, wood, metal and leather crafts, and china.

In addition to serving as training centers and as a way to publicize the Association, the craftshops generate a considerable amount of revenue for the association. Jairos Jiri began to generate earned income in 1959 to support its programs. The goods produced by the disabled clients are sold in goodwill stores to the general public, including tourists. The association covers 43 percent of its expenses from the revenues of these shops. They started their operation with donor funds (about US$200,000) and have been producing profit since establishment.

One important lesson for Jairos Jiri is that the stores could not be managed as part of the charitable programs. According to the Executive Director, they should have been operated as a separate business activity from the beginning, adopting business principles and strategies.

Information obtained from C.B. Zharare, National Executive Director, Jairos Jiri Association.

Similarly, CSOs working in the field of trade and promotion of economic opportunities for local craftspeople have also ventured heavily and oftentimes successfully into the earned-income arena to generate income as well as provide dependable employment for local artisans and entrepreneurs.

One important advantage of mission-related income is that the project is a natural extension of the CSO's current work, capitalizing on an existing activity, skill, or capacity. This alone tends to reduce the risks involved in enterprising activities by CSOs, since it requires less of an investment of time and resources to get going immediately. The organization may also be simply more comfortable with such an activity due to its familiarity. But as with cost-recovery strategies, it is not always easy, particularly for CSOs working with poor or marginalized constituents, to identify activities related to their mission that are lucrative. Some organizations, however, have been able to capitalize on lucrative staff skills by offering computer and Internet services to for-profit companies in order to generate resources for expanding such services to nonprofit, educational, and research constituencies.

ASSOCIATION NAJDEH, LEBANON

Association Najdeh is a Lebanese nongovernmental organization funded by private donors that is run by women for women. Its aim is to transform marginalized Palestinian women into productive members of society through education, health care, and income-generating projects. Real economic independence for Palestinian women (and men) is Najdeh's main goal. Within Lebanon, the political and civil rights of Palestinian refugees are restricted. The jobs available to them are limited, but they need to earn income to survive.

Najdeh started 17 years ago to generate income and, equally as important, to revive a skill that was part of Palestinian women's cultural heritage: embroidery. Najdeh's embroidery project, called Al Badia, is the commercial arm of the NGO. In 1977, Al Badia established its first embroidery workshop. The project currently maintains 10 workshops in Palestinian camps all over Lebanon, employing 350 women. In 1995, the project generated US$250,000 in sales. Embroidery workshops also serve as social units: embroiderers and their families often partake in Najdeh's social services, join a technical training program, or take literacy and family health courses.

More than half of Najdeh's sales come from two stores in Beirut. Most of their export sales come from international solidarity groups, alternative trading organizations, and committed individuals. The income from the sales goes to the embroiders and to cover the program's organizational costs.

Information obtained from Nina Smith, Executive Director, The Crafts Center.

Earning Income Through Activities Unrelated to Mission

Historically, CSO initiatives in non-mission-related earned-income strategies were the precursors of the philosophy of corporate social responsibility. (See Chapter 8.) The earliest practitioners of this were institutional owners of pension funds in industrial countries—the trade unions. They were the first to start defining a set of criteria for socially responsible investments mainly related to their mission of upholding workers' individual and collective rights and welfare. So CSOs that go into non-mission-related business and adhere to principles of corporate social responsibility may in fact be furthering their mission by serving as a model.

For a number of reasons, this is the least used of the three approaches to earning income. Non-mission-related income strategies are usually used by CSOs that have the advantage of an asset base that can be transformed into investments. PRRM in the Philippines, for example, just started to venture into this area after it successfully negotiated in January 1996 the sale of property it acquired through a donation of a U.S. company in exchange for leasing it back to them for three decades. This was possible because of a historical circumstance in the early 1970s that led to the end of parity rights in landownership afforded Americans in the Philippines. It was not possible before, as PRRM did not have what could become investment capital.

The non-mission-related earned-income strategy is therefore particularly difficult for small CSOs to conduct on a scale allowing them to manage the risk and make a sizable enough investment with existing resources, both human and financial. A great deal of preparation, planning, and market research are necessary in order to identify the viability of a given venture.

Key Best Practices

Because a non-mission-related earned-income strategy typically represents a venture into a foreign arena of enterprise activity, the risks are far higher than with other activities for earning income. And so is the investment of resources—both human and financial. Access to start-up resources, whether venture capital, loans, or needed equipment, is also a significant obstacle.

CSOs have developed a number of unique approaches to non-mission-related earned-income ventures. It is common for less well endowed groups to start ventures with donated or in-kind gifts of funds or equipment. Some organizations have capitalized on the interests and skills of staff and members to undertake viable business ventures. In some cases, groups have tapped the initial skills of their founders in the field of design, marketing, computers, or the visual arts.

Other successful CSOs have ventured far deeper into business activities that have no relation to the original mission or program objectives of the organization. Some have set up distinct enterprises or invested in the market to generate income that is then plowed back into core or regular programs. As noted earlier, an increasing number of CSOs have entered into business enterprises such as restaurants, hotels, shops, and speculative ventures such as real estate, stocks, treasury bills, and so on. The management of a viable and profitable business portfolio requires an able, experienced, business-savvy leadership to ensure that the decisions made both result in profitability and do not jeopardize the nature and social mission of the CSO itself.

Another practice that has emerged in recent years has been the use of business enterprises by intermediary CSOs to build a capital or endowment fund to support their organizational activities while providing an on-going source of funds for other local social initiatives. This can also create a corpus of funds to serve as a "foundation-like organization" to support the initiatives of other CSOs in the country through grantmaking. (See Chapter 11.) This approach is a unique and effective means of using market-based instruments to generate capital through an intermediary CSO while shielding smaller, local community organizations from the risks and uncertainties of venturing into the market and allowing them to focus on their mission-related activities.

Major Conclusions for Practitioners

Non-mission-related income is probably the most controversial among the three strategies covered in this chapter. Being dominated by big corporate interests, there are real pitfalls that a CSO has to face when dealing with a highly competitive market. Foremost is the danger of degeneration into a pure profit endeavor, and some CSOs have—

CHILD RELIEF AND YOU, INDIA

Child Relief & You (CRY) is an independent, nongovernmental public trust established in India in 1979. It began as a small initiative of Rippan Kapur, an employee of Air India who gathered six friends to respond to the unjust living conditions of Indian children. The group Kapur brought together were experienced in a variety of fields—artists, copywriters, photographers, graphic designers, accountants, and advertising and marketing experts. They began by producing and selling greeting cards to raise resources for children's programs. Kapur hoped to illustrate that collective effort among individuals could make a difference without the assistance of government support, and that anyone's contribution and talents could be translated into support for impoverished children.

Initially, CRY was able to rely on the donated products and services of artists, paper merchants, professional advertisers, and publicists to print and market its cards. The sales served two purposes: to raise resources for programs supporting children, and to increase public awareness of issues facing impoverished children. CRY has grown from a single office in Mumbai (formerly Bombay) to a major national mainstream NGO with approximately 200 staff and offices in five cities across the country and an affiliate in the United States. Over the last 16 years, CRY has disbursed more than US$3.5 million, supporting some 650,000 children through 188 child development projects around the country. CRY operates as a foundation-like organization, directing the resources it generates to voluntary organizations throughout India dedicated to helping underprivileged children. CRY believes that, released from the burden of fundraising, these grassroots NGOs are then free to concentrate on their child and community development work.

In 1996, the paper product sales generated 49 percent of CRY's annual income—its largest single source. CRY's early greeting card sales have now grown into a multimillion-dollar paper products business. CRY products are stocked and sold by a network of independent retailers throughout India. The group receives no support from the Indian government, which gives it greater freedom to set its own policies and direction. The organization does receive some indirect benefits in the form of tax exemptions, however. CRY receives a sales tax exemption and duty waivers on imported paper, and a tax exemption on donations.

Information obtained from Nomita Abreu, CRY-USA. This case study is based on Lee Davis, "New Directions in NGO Self-Financing."

rightly or wrongly—justified following this path. For this reason, a separate entity is often needed to implement this strategy, with the CSO as beneficiary. Even then, the CSO cannot wash its hands of the responsibility of ensuring a level of corporate social responsibility. Many CSOs have been criticized by constituents, by the public, or by private, for-profit competitors for venturing into non-mission-related activities.

FUNDACIÓN SOCIAL, COLOMBIA

Fundación Social, a Colombian foundation founded by a Jesuit priest in 1911, is committed to the elimination of the structural causes of poverty and the transformation of Colombian society. It was established to provide a sustainable source of funding for social development projects without relying on the government or any other source. Originally, Fundación Social was funded solely by the Caja Social de Ahorros, a savings fund generated by the workers who benefited from the fund's resources. The fund's profits were invested and the income used to fund community self-help initiatives. Today, Fundación Social's revenue base continues to come from private companies that are owned by the foundation.

Unlike many successful businesses, the Fundación Social is not a business that has its own philanthropic foundation; it is a foundation that has its own group of businesses. The board of directors and executive staff of these companies are the same as those of the foundation. With assets of more than US$2 billion, Fundación Social has 14 for-profit companies and numerous social programs serving some 3 million clients throughout Colombia.

The foundation's companies span the industries of finance, construction, health, recreation, and communication. They are highly competitive and growing, particularly those in the financial sector, laying to rest the myth that financial services geared to low-income populations cannot yield profits. The largest and most profitable is the original Caja Social de Ahorros, with thousands of small deposits from low-income individuals and families whose profits are then invested and used for social development.

After reinvesting a portion of annual profits to conserve patrimony, compensate for inflation, and keep its enterprises on the cutting edge, Fundación Social is left with approximately $4 million of its $35 million annual profits to support social programs, which are integrated local development programs in some of

---

At least initially, CSOs are better off not undertaking productive activities unless they are related to the purpose and on-going programs of the organization. Furthermore, the product and service should have a ready market and be related to a tangible asset of the organization, such as the staff's skills or knowledge.

CSOs may not have the resources to offer competitive salaries to attract qualified professionals. Furthermore, regulatory issues, including legal and tax complications that come with earning income, may also hinder CSO enterprises. Even creating a distinct subsidiary may introduce added management and accountability issues that CSOs must be prepared to address. In short, there are a great number of internal organizational issues and external regulatory and other obstacles and issues that may hinder or beleaguer CSO enterprise efforts (Davis, 1997).

The internal issues to consider include:

- *Conflict of Culture*: To many CSO leaders, "profit" is an offensive word associated with only the worst of corporate intentions. Accepting private-sector, market-

Colombia's most challenging areas. They tend to focus on the poorest sectors of society and generally use long-term, holistic, replicable strategies.

Fundación Social's success rests on a series of strengths that have important implications for replication:

- a relatively secure source of working capital for social projects leveraged from an expanding market;
- a mechanism for supplying financial services to low-income people regularly denied access to credit and savings opportunities;
- competition from market forces, which makes the organization efficient and carries over into the social programs to stimulate a focus on sustainability criteria;
- a large clientele of low-income individuals and families, which effectively disperses risk; and
- by operating in the market, a foothold from which to influence the market on behalf of poor people.

At the same time, there are several constraints to this approach: capital is only available once the enterprise establishes a certain level of profitability, and the 14 companies operate at different levels of profitability; as with any business, there is always risk of failure; it may be difficult to assemble a management team that combines business acumen and social commitment; and a precarious balance must be maintained between the financial health of the enterprise and the social investment.

Through this unique self-financing strategy, Fundación Social has broken the traditional approach that centered on projects in favor of a long-term, results-oriented, program-support strategy.

This case study is adapted from Steven Pierce, "Grassroots Development and the Issue of Scale: A Colombian Case," Grassroots Development, *Vol. 19, No. 2, 1995.*

oriented approaches to generating CSO resources may seem unethical to some CSO leaders, if not the veritable antithesis of CSO values.

- *Business Management Skills and Experience*: Although many people working in CSOs are skilled in particular vocational or social service areas, most lack the business and financial management skills needed to manage earned-income strategies effectively.

- *Planning/Allocating Human and Financial Resources*: Assessing the CSO's internal resource capacity—both financial and human—to undertake enterprise activities is a critical concern. CSOs often overestimate their capacity in this regard.

- *Appropriate Management Structure*: Determining the most effective structure for management and accountability of earned-income strategies is critical. CSOs must decide whether to manage the activity within the existing organizational structure, manage it through a separate department or team, or establish a completely separate subsidiary or other legal entity to manage the venture.

Several external issues also merit attention:

- *Access to Capital*: Access to the necessary financial capital to launch or expand earned-income initiatives is a significant obstacle to CSOs. Because of their non-profit or voluntary legal status, they are often denied access to traditional small-business loan funds from private banks or other lending agencies. Often the only available alternatives are to use internally generated funds; donor funds; donations from staff, members, boards, or friends; or in-kind donations.

- *Public Perception*: CSOs need be concerned about public scrutiny of earned-income efforts. Poorly marketed or misunderstood intentions can bring unwanted negative public perception either of tax evasion or of "cashing in" on poor constituents.

- *Legal Status*: Many governments allow CSOs to engage in some form of economic or commercial activity. However, legal treatment of earned-income activities varies in both form and clarity from country to country.

- *Tax Treatment*: There is wide variation from country to country regarding the tax treatment of earned-income activities of CSOs, as well as on the levels of monitoring and enforcement of these regulations.

- *Competition with Business Sector*: In some countries, private small businesses have objected to CSOs entering local markets while enjoying "unfair" competitive advantages in the form of tax exemptions and so on.

- *Relations with Donors*: Earned-income approaches have ramifications for defining new relationships between donors and recipients as well as between northern and southern CSOs.

The Red Cross has developed a comprehensive set of guidelines for evaluating the potential of a nonprofit organization to venture into the world of commercial competition, for selecting and evaluating a business concept, and for preparing a business plan. Its publication *Generating Revenue* is a useful tool for CSOs assessing their readiness to undertake earned-income strategies of any kind.

Even keeping numerous practical obstacles and useful guidelines in mind, a strategy to mobilize resources by earning income through one of the strategies described in this chapter is a difficult method to replicate. No equation or formula is available, and it is impossible to determine in advance an optimal level or type of earned-income strategy appropriate for all organizations.

As noted earlier, the earned-income approach is not appropriate for all CSOs, and for those that do implement it, it is far from a solution for all fiscal difficulties. It often requires a considerable dedication of human and financial resources, which is sometimes simply beyond the capacity of CSOs. As with any resource-generation technique, CSOs must weigh the costs and benefits in light of their own circumstances.

RESOURCE GUIDE

Reference Documents

BRAC, *BRAC at 20: 1972–1992* (Dhaka: BRAC Printers, September 1995).

Crimmins, James C., and Mary Keil, *Enterprise in the Nonprofit Sector* (New York: Partners for Livable Places and Rockefeller Brothers Fund, 1983).

Davis, Lee, "New Directions in NGO Self-Financing," Social Change and Development Occasional Papers 1997 (Washington, D.C.: The Johns Hopkins University, Nitze School of Advanced International Studies, 1997).

Gafud, R. et al. "Social Investment Fund Proposal and Feasibility Study" (Quezon City: 1996).

Grassroots Development, A Journal of the Inter-American Foundation, Vol. 19, No. 2, 1995.

"The Greening of Global Investment," Economist Publications Ltd., January 1991.

Holloway, Richard, "Income Generation," in Noorton, Michael, ed., *The Worldwide Fundraiser's Handbook: A Guide to Funding for Southern NGOs and Voluntary Organisations* (London: International Fund Raising Group and Directory of Social Change, 1996), pp. 107–122.

International Federation of Red Cross and Red Crescent Societies. *Generating Revenue* (Geneva: 1994).

Lovell, Catherine H., *Breaking the Cycle of Poverty: The BRAC Strategy* (West Hartford, Conn.: Kumarian Press, 1992).

Morato, Eduardo A., *Social Entrepreneurship and Enterprise Development: Text and Cases.* (Makati, Metro Manila: Asian Institute of Management, 1994).

Neighborhood Development Collaborative, "Entrepreneurship in the Non-Profit Sector: 1982" (Flint, Mich.: Charles Stewart Mott Foundation, May 1982).

NOVIB Coordinating Office (NCO)-Philippines, "Investing in People: The Path to Self-Help and Interdependence" (Manila: 1996).

Philippine Rural Reconstruction Movement, *SEED Workshop Documentation*, 1996.

Randel, Judith, and Tony German, eds. *The Reality of Aid 1996: An Independent Review of International Aid* (London: Earthscan Publications, 1996).

Rangan, V.K., "The Aravind Eye Hospital, Madurai, India: In the Service for Sight" (President and Fellows of Harvard College, Harvard Business School, 1994).

Serrano, Isagani R., *Civil Society in the Asia Pacific Region* (Washington, D.C.: CIVICUS, 1994).

Sherman, Jeremy, and David Bonbright, *Changemakers: Non-Profits: The New Resourcefulness* (Calcutta, India: Ashoka Foundation, 1996).

Skloot, Edward, *The Nonprofit Entrepreneur: Creating Ventures to Earn Income* (New York: The Foundation Center, 1988).

Vincent, Fernand, ed., *Alternative Financing of Third World Development NGOs*, Vol. 1–2 (Geneva: Development Innovations and Networks, 1995).

Vincent, Fernand, and Piers Campbell, *Towards Greater Financial Autonomy: A Manual on Financing Strategies for Development NGOs and Community Organizations* (Geneva: Development Innovations and Networks, 1989).

Concerned Resource Organizations

Prof. Victor Tan, Associate Dean
Asian Institute of Management
Center for Development
Management
Joseph R. McMicking Campus
123 Paseo de Roxas, MCPO Box 2095
1260 Makati
Metro Manila
Philippines
Tel: (63-2) 892-4011
Fax: (63-2) 817-9240 or 894-1407

Fazel Hasan Abed, Executive Director
Bangladesh Rural Advancement
Committee
66 Mohakhali C.A.
Dhaka 1212
Bangladesh
Tel: (880-2) 863633 or 601604 or
600161
Fax: (880-2) 883542 or 883614

Prof. Eduardo A. Morato
FREED/ODI
106 Kaimito Ville
Valle Verde I
Pasig
Metro Manila
Philippines
Tel: (63-2) 892-4011

Darcy Jameson, Program Manager
Institute for Development
   Research
Sustainable Development Services
44 Farnsworth Street
Boston, MA 02210-1211
Tel: (1-617) 422-0422
Fax: (1-617) 482-0617
E-mail: idr@jsi.com

Betty Scheper, Head, South East Asia
   Bureau
Max Van Den Berg, Secretary General
Netherlands Organization for
International Development
Cooperation
Mauritskade 9, PO Box 30919
2500 GX The Hague
The Netherlands
Tel: (31-70) 342-1621
Fax: (31-70) 361-4461
E-mail: admin@novib.nl

Nonprofit Enterprise and Self-
sustainability Team (NESsT)
Lee Davis, Nicole Etchart,
and Katalin Zsamboki, Co-Directors
3104 Grindon Avenue
Baltimore, MD 21214
Tel/Fax: (1-410) 426-3671
E-mail: nesst@igc.apc.org

Horacio R. Morales, Jr., President
Philippine Rural Reconstruction Movement
Kayumanggi Press Building
940 Quezon Avenue
Quezon City
Philippines
Tel: (63-2) 928-1715 or 927-0079 or 410-5233
Fax: (63-2) 928-7919

Fernand Vincent
Research and Applications of Alternative Financing for Development
1, Rue de Varembe, P.O. Box 117
CH-1211 Geneva 20
Switzerland
Tel: (41-22) 733-5073
Fax: (41-22) 734-7083

Dr. S. Bruce Schearer, Executive Director
The Synergos Institute
100 East 85th Street
New York, NY 10028
Tel: (1-212) 517-4900
Fax: (1-212) 517-4815
E-mail: bschearer@synergos.org

Chapter 3

Foundation Funding: Venture Capital for Civil Society

Elan Garonzik

Providing and Using Information on Foundations

The documents and professionals that encourage, facilitate, and provide information on the work of foundations and corporate funders are known as the philanthropic information infrastructure. Although this chapter talks a great deal about documents and texts, people are actually the most important part of the infrastructure: librarians assisting grantseekers in a funding information center, editors carefully reviewing funding information before it goes to print, directors of centers and of foundation associations who freely give their advice and guidance to other organizations, board members and staff of foundations, and corporate funders who provide not only funding but also their wise experience.

Fundamentally, the infrastructure in this sector has two mutually dependent and supportive elements. Both are needed, and both should be provided at the same time in order to assist the work of foundations, corporate funders, and their grantseeking partners. The two elements are:

- a public record objective—across a broad spectrum, foundations and corporate funders support educational, cultural, social, recreational, and scientific programs. This objective documents and provides a public record of this work. Foundation directories are the clearest examples of public record tools, but also included are funding bibliographies, on-line information, and the many publications issued by funders themselves.

- public information service objective—funding information is important to funders seeking project partners, associations in search of resources, and governmental bodies and other organizations that work with the foundation and corporate funding community. This objective aims to ensure that this information is available and accessible close to those who need it, with some open-access, professionally run library services.

Over the past seven years, Europe has made great strides in developing the right information infrastructure, largely through the work of the European Foundation Centre (EFC) and its partners across Europe. The EFC's special information project in this area is called the Orpheus Programme, which provides a public record and a public information service on foundations and corporate funders active in Europe.

Before continuing, it is important to define some of the terms used in this chapter. Defining foundations for a global audience presents a challenge, due to the many different legal and tax environments that exist and to subtle differences in language and culture. For example, the Foundation Center in the United States begins its definition with "nongovernmental, nonprofit organization," yet there are many important governmentally linked foundations in Europe, notably the German political foundations. The EFC's *Typology of Foundations in Europe* defines foundations as:

> separately constituted nonprofit bodies with their own established and reliable source of income (usually, but not exclusively) from an endowment or capital. These bodies have their own governing board. They distribute their financial resources for educational, cultural, religious, social or other public benefit purposes, either by supporting associations, charities, educational institutions or individuals, or by operating their own programmes.

In both Europe and the United States, by far the largest group of foundations is strictly active at a very local level, supporting community or regional programs. A far smaller share of foundations is active at a national level, and an even smaller group is active at international and intercontinental levels. For example, of the 38,807 foundations reported in the Foundation Center's *Foundation Giving, 1996 Edition*, only 3–4 percent have program interests outside the United States.

Corporate funding may be done through a separately constituted corporate foundation or directly by the business concern. It can include financial support as well as gifts-in-kind, such as equipment or supplies. Corporate citizenship refers to a broader action by a business in support of its community, through employee volunteerism, the loan of executive staff, financial contributions, and other means. It is rare for a business to undertake citizenship programs in locations where they do not have operations or plants. (See also Chapter 8.)

Private or independent funding refers to the financial support provided by foundations and corporate funders. This is in contrast to public funding, whereby a government agency provides support to a nonprofit organization, either through a direct grant or through a contract for services to be delivered.

The Infrastructure's Importance

A philanthropic information infrastructure is important in order to accomplish the following:

- expand philanthropy—when information on philanthropy is available, potential donors have a way to learn of the work of existing foundations and corporate funders; they will have models to adapt for their own philanthropic work, and can be encouraged to take their place at the table.

- promote philanthropy—with reliable information on the many contributions of organized philanthropy, funders can effectively advocate for an improved legal and fiscal environment for their work.

- facilitate philanthropy—good information can help independent funders locate possible funding partners, should they wish to form a funding consortia for a specific project.

- assist grantseekers—with the right documentation and professional guidance, grantseeking associations will have a better understanding of the independent funding community, and how to research and approach funders that may be interested in their projects.

- aid public authorities—with the retreat of the welfare state and new information on the effectiveness of nonprofit organizations in jobs creation and service delivery, public authorities increasingly seek to gain from the experience of independent funders.

- help scholars, researchers, and the media—reliable, accessible information assists those researching the foundation, corporate funding, and association communities, as well as those writing about them.

- support the nonprofit sector and society as a whole—independent funding is just one part of the larger nonprofit sector, yet it is a crucial part; independent funding is the "venture capital" for the sector, supporting innovating projects that may have long-term implications for society.

Benefits and Limitations

The benefits of building a philanthropic information infrastructure are clear from the importance of this information to a wide variety of actors in the nonprofit sector. The chief limitation is that national and regional funding information centers must focus primarily on their own foundation community. For international and intercontinental information, they depend on the existence of professional centers in other regions of the world, and on having good working relationships with these offices. The Foundation Center, for example, often advises U.S. grantseeking associations needing information on Europe to contact the EFC. Similarly, the EFC refers Europeans with questions on Asia to the Asia Pacific Philanthropy Consortium.

At a 1994 EFC Orpheus Programme workshop for librarians of participating centers, Margaret Haines, chief librarian at the King's Fund, told participants one truth of the library world: No one can do it all. You must collaborate and form partnerships. This is particularly true in the field of funding information. The Foundation Center maintains five offices and works with 207 cooperating library collections across the United States. The European Foundation Centre works with 33 network centers across Europe, and it seeks to increase this number.

The dictum "you cannot do it all" needs to be emphasized in a multinational setting. Europe is composed of at least 35 countries, and there is also the vibrant, quickly developing "European-level" nonprofit sector. At national and regional levels across

ASIA PACIFIC PHILANTHROPY CONSORTIUM

The Asia Pacific Philanthropy Consortium is an informal network of grant-making philanthropic institutions and organizations that support the growth and development of Asian grantmaking philanthropies. It is governed by a six-person Executive Committee with members from Australia, Japan, South Korea, the Philippines, Thailand, and the United States. The Consortium has received funding from more than a dozen private and corporate foundations in Australia, Japan, Korea, and the United States.

The Consortium's objectives are to increase the flow and effectiveness of philanthropic giving within and to the Asia Pacific region, to increase public awareness and promote the role of philanthropy in addressing critical social needs, to help strengthen philanthropic institutions in the region, and to facilitate efforts by Asian Pacific philanthropies to identify and collaborate on issues of mutual concern.

Three of the Consortium's current major activities are related to building the philanthropic infrastructure. First, a comparative research project on the legal and regulatory frameworks affecting philanthropic organizations and the nonprofit sector in 10 East and Southeast Asian countries is establishing a baseline of legal information and will facilitate ongoing efforts at legal reform and policy improvement. Country reports are being prepared by legal specialists using a common analytic framework.

Second, the Consortium is creating electronically linked databases and information centers on the nonprofit sector in Australia, Hong Kong (China), South Korea, Japan, the Philippines, and Thailand. Each center will contain directories and other information about the country's nonprofit sector, bibliographies, and a list of bibliographic materials available at each center. These are scheduled to become operational in fall 1997, and the databases will be accessible through the World Wide Web.

Third, the Consortium is encouraging networking among regional philanthropies. In September 1995 it helped the U.S.-based Council on Foundations organize and fund a conference in Hong Kong on Corporate Citizenship in Asia. Representatives of 95 Asian, American, and European corporate foundations and giving programs met to share experience and best practices in several program areas.

Case study prepared by Barnett Baron, Asia Pacific Philanthropy Consortium.

Europe, each nonprofit sector is distinct. Each has its own values, traditions, and needs. And the staff of a grassroots organization doing funding research will probably not speak fluent English. They should expect—and receive—assistance in their mother tongue.

Although the Foundation Center's cooperating library collections exist largely for information dissemination, in Europe the Orpheus network centers serve the dual purposes of information dissemination and information collection. Working in their national languages, these centers have created funding databases, published directories, and advocated for the independent funding community within their nation or region. Thus in Europe two levels of activity are occurring simultaneously:

- at the European level, the EFC focuses on cross-border, "European-level" funding information, and has published directories and bibliographies that it shares throughout the network; and
- at national and regional levels, network centers such as the Portuguese Foundation Centre, the Hungarian Foundation Centre, and the Centre for the Third Sector in Slovakia focus on funding information with regards to their own country or region.

This limitation can also be a benefit. Through this partnership, everyone gains. The network centers have information on funders active in their nation, as well as European-level funding information. The EFC can turn to the network with specific questions, and it knows that its information tools are available to a wide audience. When the EFC receives an information request from a grantseeker in a specific country, it can refer the association back to the relevant network partner.

The EFC network is not perfect. It exists as an ideal, but the reality is different. Certain centers are stronger than others. In some large countries, such as the United Kingdom or Poland, the centers are found in the capital, and other cities and smaller towns are not as well served. Other countries—Ireland and Italy, for example—do not yet have centers. To address these issues, the EFC has developed two special projects that are largely about network facilitation and network center strengthening. The Orpheus Civil Society Project focuses on centers in Central and Eastern Europe, while the EFC Philanthropy Network Project is strengthening the information base of centers throughout Europe.

Future Trends: Computerized Data and More Information Centers

The Internet is the fastest growing communications medium ever. At last count, more than 40 million people in 168 countries had Internet access. The World Wide Web provides 80 million pages of information, and this is doubling every four to five months.

This new information technology holds out a great promise for the philanthropic community, for it is an effective bridge-builder across national and cultural boundaries. The Internet allows for efficient, cost-effective exchange of accurate, up-to-date information from one country to the next—with almost immediate access. It also enables organizations to reach out and publicize their activities at a European, indeed at a global level. And the Internet and the Web can prepare today's youth—already growing up as computer enthusiasts—to be the leaders of the philanthropic community of tomorrow.

Funders and the organizations that serve them are quickly exploiting the World Wide Web to their benefit. The advantages of a Web site are clear:

- It can put a funder's information within a logical context, particularly with the Web presences of the EFC, certain Orpheus network centers, the Foundation Center, and the Council on Foundations.
- The information is accessible 24 hours a day, 365 days a year, from anywhere in the world.

A DECENTRALIZED NETWORK OF RESOURCE CENTERS

Launched in 1994, the EFC Orpheus Civil Society Project develops and sustains indigenous information and support centers serving foundations and associations in Central and Eastern Europe. As of April 1997, 24 resource centers in 15 countries participated in this decentralized network.

The monumental restructuring efforts in Central and Eastern Europe have continued to focus attention on the need to nurture civil society in newly emerging democracies. Critical to the underpinning of civil society is the development of capable and viable foundations and citizens' associations. From the early 1990s, information and support centers were being created to serve national foundations and associations. There is considerable evidence suggesting that investing in these resource centers is an effective strategy to accelerate the sector's development.

Charities Aid Foundation-Russia (CAF-Russia) elected to join the Civil Society Project in 1994. CAF-Russia itself is helping develop an information and support network throughout Russia. So the challenges it faces have much in common with those of the whole network of resource centers in the region. Being a relatively strong organization, CAF-Russia is playing a leading role in working toward the goals of the Orpheus Civil Society Project. To date, these include preparing long-term strategic plans, extending services from capital cities to the provinces, organizing management training, developing legislative and fiscal consultancy services, building advocacy skills, conducting research, and creating a documentation base. Most recently, CAF-Russia held a successful marketing seminar for the resource centers in the network, preparing the ground for each center to develop its own marketing strategy.

- It is cheaper and quicker to publish up-to-date information electronically. Funders note it is far cheaper to give prospective grantees their Internet address than an annual report, and, given the shelf life of annual reports, the Internet presence may be more current.

- A funder's grantees, prospective funding partners, potential grantseekers, and the public are kept informed of the funder's activities.

Philanthropic Web sites already provide a considerable source of rich information, yet they present three problems for users. The information being added has been developed as if by a publishing house without editorial stewardship. And information is used as if it were a library without reference assistance. Concerning information synthesis, the Web provides information one computer screen at a time, and this is most likely inappropriate for newcomers to the funding field. Both the Foundation Center and the EFC have developed projects to address these issues.

CAF-Russia is also beginning to work closely with the GURT resource center in Kiev, Ukraine, and with NGO Centrs in Riga, Latvia. Planned assistance includes:

- mutual study visits to examine in detail the workings of the centers and the services offered,

- internships for the executive director and legal consultant of GURT at CAF-Russia,

- extending Russian language nonprofit information exchange service to Ukraine and Latvia,

- internships for Ukrainian trainers in the training programs of CAF-Russia,

- sharing CAF-Russia's experience with national and local governments in the context of building an enabling legislative and fiscal environment for the nonprofit sector,

- a seminar on ethics in Ukraine, and

- sharing of trainers to deliver a seminar for small NGOs in Latvia.

In addition to these skill-building achievements, the most significant aspect of Orpheus Civil Society Project activities is the development of mutual trust and co-operation between peoples divided by history and the recent divisive practices of the communist period. The centers report a sense of moral obligation to assist and seek assistance from one another, without the constraints of a centralized institution. They believe that this, in itself, is a most fertile soil for future growth of individual organizations, the network, and the foundation and association sector as a whole.

Case study prepared by Olga Alexeeva, Deputy Director at CAF-Russia, and by Eric Kemp, EFC Orpheus Civil Society Project Coordinator.

The second key trend in infrastructure is the growing number of information centers around the world. Lester Salamon notes that there has been a marked increase in the nonprofit sector globally in recent years. To serve this, there has also been a marked growth in funding information and support centers. The EFC was established in 1989, and the early 1990s witnessed the establishment of similar centers and associations throughout Central and Eastern Europe, as well as in Asia, Africa, and Latin America. Given this proliferation of centers, there are practically no accompanying agreements between them with regards to the exchange of information. The exceptions are the EFC Orpheus Programme, which focuses on Europe; the good working relationship between the EFC and the Foundation Center in New York; and certain signed cooperative agreements between the EFC and centers in Asia and Latin America. (There was a previous international agreement between existing centers, in the late 1980s.)

The Council on Foundations is planning an International Meeting of Associations Serving Grantmakers, to be hosted by the Mexican Centre for Philanthropy (CE-MEFI, for Centro Mexicano para la Filantropía), February 8–11, 1998. It is being

DEVELOPING PHILANTHROPIC SERVICES IN MEXICO

The Centro Mexicano para la Filantropía (CEMEFI) is a nonprofit civil association founded in December 1988. Its mission is to promote a culture of social responsibility and to strengthen the organizations of civil society. With headquarters in Mexico City, CEMEFI is active throughout the country.

As a membership-based organization, CEMEFI's stakeholders include 182 charitable and voluntary organizations as well as foundations, corporations, and individuals. It is funded by foundations, affiliates, and other contributors. Over the coming years, CEMEFI expects to generate important income from diverse products and services that are being developed.

In the pursuit of its objectives, CEMEFI offers major programs on Government Relations and Public Policy, Communications, Research, Corporate Philanthropy, Development, and Professional Development.

CEMEFI's research program is building a base of knowledge about the sector and the environment in which it works. For example, CEMEFI cooperates with the Johns Hopkins Non-Profit Sector Comparative Study, and it actively promotes the development of the sector's research capacity. The goal of the Government Relations program is to improve the political and regulatory environment for charitable and voluntary organizations across Mexico.

organized by a Planning Committee with representatives of associations from North America, Latin America, Europe, Africa, and Asia. Though the meeting is looking primarily at the membership associations of funders, some of these, such as the EFC and CEMEFI, are also information providers. Planned outputs of this meeting include a directory of the association of grantmakers and a directory of support organizations. The meeting's agenda includes a special session to address the needs of the various funding information centers worldwide, and to begin to discuss guidelines for information exchanges among them.

Ownership and Resource Needs

Developing a philanthropic information infrastructure that can serve both private funders and grantseeking associations will require ownership as well as resources—professional and financial. Ownership refers to the development of an information center that reflects the values, traditions, and needs of a specific nonprofit sector in a country or region. It cannot be done externally. Models exist, but they usually must be highly adapted to fit the specific needs of a country or region.

For example, the EFC benefited from advice from the Foundation Center on its database structure, but the ultimate European database varies greatly from the U.S. model. Similarly, grantseeking customs differ from one country to the next. U.S. funders expect

Regarding services, the Centro de Información Filantrópica (CIF), the first of its kind in Mexico, is an information center that offers services on documentation of philanthropy and the third sector. The bibliographic data bank includes the CIF collection and, in the near future, will be available on CEMEFI's Web page. The CIF is in initial phases of design, and in the future it will link up with similar philanthropic information centers.

CEMEFI also convenes meetings and releases regular information products. Notable publications and services include:

- *Directory of Philanthropic Institutions*—this data base, available in print and on diskette, registers detailed information on 3,865 organizations throughout the country, two thirds of which were created in the last 30 years;

- a newsletter published every two months, covering information about philanthropic initiatives in Mexico and abroad, with interviews, information about membership, and stories on important meetings and upcoming workshops;

- the magazine FILANTROPIA, published quarterly and developed by an Editorial Board made up of individuals from different member organizations; and

- professional consultation concerning legal and fiscal issues, fund development, and institutional development.

Case study prepared by Vivian Blair, Director, Institutional Development, CEMEFI.

a project proposal of about 10 pages, while those in the United Kingdom wish more succinct proposals of 5 pages. One U.S. fundraising manual suggests holding private dinners, with the host asking guests to contribute to a specific cause. Polish colleagues have noted that this custom would be practically unacceptable in that country.

It is the EFC's experience that ownership begins with a meeting of a country's leading nonprofit organizations to determine their needs and whether these needs include a support center that focuses on funding information, among other topics. If there is no need—or perhaps no consensus on various competing needs—perhaps the time is not right to begin developing the philanthropic information infrastructure. Outside observers can be invited to these meetings, but they should be there to offer advice and perhaps technical assistance, not to make decisions or do work.

Concerning professional and financial resources, any new funding information center will need a program plan and an accompanying project proposal to raise support and move the plan into action. Funding will most likely consist of a consortium of domestic funders and possibly international funders that are interested in the development of the philanthropic information infrastructure. This has been the case for the EFC, CEMEFI, and the Asia Pacific Philanthropy Consortium, as well as additional centers and associations of foundations that provide funding information services.

From one country to the next, costs will vary greatly, largely due to differences in the charges of professional staff and in expenses related to rent, utilities, equipment, and overhead.

BOX 1

STEPS TO BUILDING A FUNDING INFORMATION CENTER

First, establish consensus. Talk to key nonprofit sector leaders in your country or region. You may want to call a meeting, or attach this subject to a nonprofit sector conference or forum being held in your country. Ask a number of crucial questions: Is this information service needed? Can you begin to obtain local funding information? If you start in a capital city, how will other regions and cities be served? Can you get commitments from partners to assist in this endeavor? Can there be a consensus on ownership of your funding information center?

Second, develop a plan in writing. You or a team of people should be able to develop a program plan on how you are going to begin and develop your center. This plan should be easy to adapt into a project proposal, as outlined in this chapter. Of the range of information needs, which are most critical? Where should you begin—with a directory? with library services? Which organizations may fund your project, including both indigenous and foreign funders? Who will sit on your steering committee or board to provide leadership and oversight of the project?

Third, learn from other models. You will no doubt benefit from visiting an established funding information center. If you cannot do this, get their publications or visit their World Wide Web sites, for these will indicate their level and areas of service. (See Resource Guide at the end of this chapter.)

Fourth, secure certain start-up resources. Can you or one of your partners donate a small office space, some books, and maybe a computer? Is there a volunteer who

---

Building and Strengthening the Philanthropic Information Infrastructure

This section describes some of the tools to be developed in order to meet the broad objective of building and strengthening the philanthropic information infrastructure. To create a public record, for example, a classification system can be set up to track types of foundations as well as their subjects, population, and geographic interests. And a database can be established to store foundation information and make it available through print and on-line means.

Tools to meet the objective of providing a public information service include a bibliography on literature concerning the foundation and corporate funding community, and professionally run open-access library services that provide both private funders and grantseeking associations with information services.

As an aid to those just starting out, Box 1 describes the steps needed to begin developing a national funding information center.

could help you? Could your project possibly rely on a more established organization during your start-up years? For a small nonprofit, even stamps are important; could a partner organization donate these? You can obtain annual reports from foundations and corporate funders, most of which are free.

Fifth, begin credible services, no matter how minimal. *The European Foundation Centre began open-access library services one day a week, and gradually built on this. Starting to provide some services establishes your credibility and assists in your fundraising efforts. You should release a newsletter or bulletin to spread information on your project.*

Sixth, ensure your steps can be built upon. *The EFC's first directories and bibliographies were simply word-processed documents. Later this information was transferred to a computer database. Similarly, the* Australian Directory of Foundations, *now in its 8th edition, is based on word processing.*

Seventh, continue building partnerships. *Develop a broad mailing list, and ask to be put on the lists of other organizations. Share information openly with partner organizations, so that they begin to naturally turn to you for your expertise. Attend nonprofit sector meetings locally or internationally, even as an observer. Seek and accept visitors, domestic and foreign, to ensure that your organization and its services are known. Begin with personal contacts, and know that these can be followed up with faxes and e-mail.*

Finally, ask for help. *You would be surprised at how many people and organizations are willing to help, but just have not been asked.*

Classification Systems

Classification systems allow us to make sense of our many different worlds. When they work well, they allow us to compare and understand readily national or international nonprofit work. When they do not work, they hide meaning and distort facts. We are asked to compare apples and oranges.

In 1983, the National Center for Charitable Statistics, a project of Independent Sector, began work on a U.S. classification system for the nonprofit sector. Up to that point, many major foundations and nonprofit agencies had their own systems. They could not talk to one another. They defined as basic a field as education differently, so it was practically impossible to compare the Foundation Center's statistics on educational funding to those from the Conference Board or those presented in *Giving USA*.

Four years later, the project's steering committee realized they could not agree on anything. They finally decided to hand over to Russy Sumariwalla of United Way the development of the spine or framework for the new U.S. system, and agreed to work with what he suggested. This brought about the National Taxonomy of Exempt

Entities, which is now used by the Foundation Center, *Giving USA*, and scores of foundations and other organization across the country.

For philanthropic information services, classification can be broken down into five areas:

- foundation type—the source of financial resources, control of the governing board, and approach to the distribution of resources;

- subject interests of funding program—the specific fields of interest of the foundation or corporate funder, such as culture, education, environment, health, or social welfare;

- population group interests of funding program—specific population groups that the funder seeks to assist, such as the elderly, disabled, women, or youth;

- geographic interests—the regions or countries where the foundation has program interests; and

- type of support provided—the specific purposes of grant monies that may be awarded, such as general support, program development, research, or scholarships.

Four classic types of foundations are found in the United States: independent, corporate, operating, and community foundations. The Foundation Center reports on the growth and funding interests of these four types in its annual publication, *Foundation Giving*. To a large extent, these types are determined by American tax laws—one country, one legal and fiscal system. By comparison, the foundation landscape in Europe is richly varied, in part due to the many languages and cultures in Europe and the different legal and fiscal environments from one nation to the next. Thus whereas the British typically refer primarily to trusts, the Dutch will refer to a *stichting*, the French to a *fondation*, the Germans to a *Stiftung*, the Spanish to a *fundación*, and the Swedish a *stifstelse*.

Along with the many different names for foundations, there are many different foundation types in Europe. Endowed foundations exist, as do community, operating, and corporate foundations. Certain foundations in Europe benefit from the proceeds of lotteries or gambling. Some foundations may be considered to be collector/distributor foundations, gathering funds from various sources, including the general public, to serve their operational or grantmaking programs. Indeed, certain foundations in Europe are hybrids, combining several elements noted above: for example, the King Baudouin (Belgium) is largely an operating foundation, with an endowment, benefiting from lottery proceeds and raising funds from the general public on a continuing basis, and with a grants program.

To provide an order within this diverse landscape, the EFC developed the *Typology of Foundations in Europe*, a collaborative effort by the EFC, its members, and the Orpheus network centers. The typology presents 18 of the most common foundation types in Europe, grouped initially into four generic categories: independent foundations, corporate foundations, governmentally linked foundations, and fundraising foundations. The EFC used the typology for the first time in its directory *EFC Profiles*. Although the main goal of the document is to provide foundations and corporate funders with an overview of the different types of foundations found in Europe, it is also of key relevance to grantseekers. For example, it is helpful to know that the Wellcome

Trust in the United Kingdom is not a corporate foundation but an independent trustee-controlled foundation. Similarly, the Volkswagen Foundation is not a corporate foundation, though its name might imply that.

In another important classification area, the subject interests of foundations and corporate citizenship programs, the EFC looks to the considerable experience of the Johns Hopkins Comparative Study and its International Classification of Non-Profit Organizations. Other countries and regions with classification needs should study this system seriously.

Databases and Directories on Funding

To edit and publish foundation directories, it is a distinct advantage to be a "database junkie." There are now close to 40,000 private and community foundations in the United States, and the EFC estimates that there are some 80,000 to 100,000 foundations in Europe. Directories on foundations and corporate funders, most of which are produced from a database, provide information on these funders within a logical framework. In the funding information field, everyone seems to be working on a funding database. Across Europe, there are 15 national- or regional-level funding directories that are produced from a database, and also the EFC's European-level directories. The Asia Pacific Philanthropy Consortium is working on a funding database. There are also database-produced funding directories from Australia, Canada, and Japan, and work has begun on one in Latin America.

Usually, an organization will need two complementary staff elements—editorial and technical—working closely together to deliver databased information effectively. The EFC's database on foundations and corporate funders presents a host of information according to six general areas.

- *Contact information:* funder name; street address; telephone, fax, and e-mail numbers; name of the primary person to contact.

- *History and background:* a description of the history and philosophy of the funding organization. For corporate funders, this describes the corporate link. Includes establishment date, any former name of the foundation, or corporate funder.

- *Program interests:* details on the funding organization's major interests and activities, and the geographic focus of these interests. Subject indexes, such as arts, health, or science, are linked to program interests.

- *Financial information:* the year of record for the data provided; total assets or capital endowment; gifts received for the accounting year; total expenditures; total grants expenditures; total program expenditures (for operating foundations). For comparative purposes, the EFC provides information both in national currency and in ECU.

- *Application procedures:* restrictions on the giving program, such as no grants to individuals; any specific application forms and deadlines; any requirement for an initial, brief letter of inquiry; details of funder publications on how to get further information.

PUBLISHING A FUNDING DIRECTORY

The Australian Association of Philanthropy was established in 1975 as a national body to represent the shared interests of trusts and foundations in Australia, as well as to represent philanthropy to government and the community. The association now has 85 members, including family trusts, philanthropic individuals, private trusts and foundations, trustee companies, and corporations. The name was recently changed to Philanthropy Australia.

Although the association exists to serve its member trusts and foundations, it also provides information to those seeking funding. This is achieved primarily through publishing the *Australian Directory of Philanthropy*, the only reference tool of its kind in the country.

A major change over the years has been the increased willingness of trusts, foundations, and corporations to be included in the *Directory*. It has proved to be of great benefit not only to those seeking funds but also to those who—sometimes against their better judgment—allow information on their programs to be included. For them, the *Directory* has resulted in an increased diversity of grant applications, a depth of projects, and much better "tailoring" of project applications to appropriate sources of funding.

The *Directory* has proved to be a major revenue source for the association,

- *Board members and key staff:* names and positions of individuals who provide management and governance oversight; list of any honorary/advisory committee; key staff, with their areas of responsibility.

Directory editors must be scrupulous in their work, and toward this end there are three areas to be aware of. First, information gathering. The EFC believes that the very best sources of information about foundations and corporate funders are those that they release themselves. Funder publications can be annual reports, newsletters, grants lists, press releases, or information on the World Wide Web. The EFC would advise against sending a blank questionnaire to a funder in the hope that they will complete it satisfactorily. Rather, you should obtain this information and prepare a draft database entry.

Second, information verification. Once you have completed a draft database entry on a funder, mail or fax it to them for their review. This enables a funder to update financial or program information, and to ensure its portrayal in a directory will be accurate. Most funders will appreciate the work done in compiling a draft database entry, and they will provide corrections as needed. The EFC has a 98-percent response rate on verification.

Third, information maintenance. Establish and keep up to date a log on every funder to be included in a database and directory. The log will help you know at a glance what you have completed and where each point of information stands. Log entry points include: Has source information been gathered? Has it been keyed, reviewed, proofread, and corrected? Has it been mailed to the funder for verification? Have final

whose budget comes approximately one third from membership fees and two thirds from publication sales and services to grantseekers. When the association published the eighth and most recent edition, in August 1996, it resolved to update the *Directory* annually. The 1996/1997 edition had 300 entries, and the next will have at least 400.

To gather information for the *Directory* database, the association relies on grantseekers who contact it for information, sometimes asking why a particular trust or foundation they know is not listed. It also leans heavily on friends who act as the association's "eyes and ears." These individuals scan newspapers, see an interview about a new foundation, hear an interesting radio broadcast, or pick up some information of philanthropic interest over dinner. The association then contacts the foundations to verify any details, and asks if it can include them in the *Directory*. Because Australia does not have a regulatory legal framework to check details such as these, this hands-on approach is the only useful form of research.

A major difference between Philanthropy Australia and similar associations elsewhere is that Australia is too small for there to be a separate organization for grantseekers. Based partly on the popularity of the *Directory* with grantseekers, the association is looking at ways to accommodate their needs, and it is considering the possibility of establishing a separate business entity that will cater to grantseekers.

Case study prepared by Elizabeth Cham, Philanthropy Australia.

corrections been keyed and proofread? Has the responsible editor signed off on each entry? Watch out for last-minute changes.

Bibliographic Information

There is wonderful work being done in the funding publishing area in Europe. The Fondation de France published *Repères A Travers le Monde des Fondations*—a review of the world of foundations. Charities Aid Foundation (UK) released its useful *Dimensions of the Voluntary Sector*. The Portuguese and Hungarian foundation centers publish their foundation directories bilingually, in their national language and in English. There are two foundation directories in Germany—one on funders with scientific interests and one covering all 7,000 German foundations. The Dutch publish a superb reference tool. After a new foundation law was enacted in Spain, the text was quickly available in English. Excellent publications are emanating from European participation in the Johns Hopkins Comparative Study.

The European Foundation Centre plays a key role by serving as a convener, bringing independent funders together so that they can share information and experience. Bibliographies are in fact information conveners. They cull together information on publications from a wide variety of sources, and then make it available to a wider audience. They also serve two highly practical purposes. Bibliographies alert funders as well as network centers to new, important tools they may need for their work. They also allow network centers to provide, from afar, information on demand.

In 1994, the EFC published the *Select Bibliography on Foundations and Corporate Funders in Europe*. This is updated with a quarterly bibliographic newsletter, the *efc bookshelf*, and a second edition of the *Select Bibliography* is planned. Entries fall into seven broad subject areas:

- foundation directories;

- corporate citizenship literature;

- international, intercontinental, and European institution funding information;

- national issues for the foundation and association community;

- international and intercontinental issues;

- nonprofit management titles related to funding; and

- the legal and fiscal environment for funding.

The *efc bookshelf* also notes funder annual reports recently received by the EFC. The *Select Bibliography* includes a listing of the publication types of EFC members, such as annual reports, newsletters, information brochures, or application guidelines. Librarians and documentalists in the Orpheus network of funding information centers note that these listings are highly valuable, for they alert the public to important documents that funders release themselves.

Occasionally it is important to highlight bibliographic data. When *Voluntas*, the international journal of the voluntary sector, released an issue that focused exclusively on the foundation community, the EFC documentalist wrote a lengthy abstract to bring the volume to readers' attention.

Bibliographic efforts are a two-way street. Earlier the importance of partnerships was noted, and this is certainly true in a multinational setting. The EFC asks each network center to provide us with copies of their important publications, and a bibliographic entry in English. In turn, each center receives relevant information on volumes published across the continent. Also, the EFC uses the *efc bookshelf* as an ordering form for the libraries in the Orpheus network centers. Each center notifies the EFC of what volumes they need, we order them in bulk, and then pass the discount on to each center.

Open-Access Library Services

The EFC library holds orientation sessions for a group of grantseekers on the last Tuesday of every month. The documentalist reviews the EFC and the EFC Orpheus Programme and explains how to use the resources in the EFC library to research foundations and corporate funders. After each session, usually 10–15 grantseekers can be found in the library studying information in directories and guides. The Foundation Center's New York library is similarly filled with researchers every week day, and ICN, the Czech funding information center, reported 2,324 library visitors in 1996.

Open-access library services serve two primary audiences—independent funders and grantseekers. Of course, the libraries also serve the broader audience of scholars, researchers, the media, government bodies, and all others interested in the work of foundations and corporate funders.

For Foundations and Corporate Funders

Open-access library services to independent funders are at once both practical and political. At the practical level, foundation and corporate funders often "camp out" at such libraries for extended periods of time. New foundations want to explore what other funders are doing in specific fields of activity, so that they may use their resources to address potential funding gaps. Existing foundations may be looking for funding partners or hoping to learn from the experiences of their colleagues.

Yet the political and structural services of these libraries may be even more important. Loren Renz, Vice President for Research at the Foundation Center, has noted that when public authorities begin asking questions about independent funders, open-access library services are the first line of defense. Through these libraries, funder information is not just summarized in a directory and not just available by writing to a foundation. It is immediately and publicly available, acting as a shield to deflect criticism of foundation secretiveness.

To understand the need for this, it is useful to look at U.S. foundation history. In the early 1950s, during the McCarthy era, some U.S. policymakers were convinced that the broad grantmaking latitude afforded foundations had permitted them to engage in "un-American activities" (code words at the time for the promotion of Communism). Serious new legislative and regulatory restrictions on foundations were headed off, but it was clear that the lack of even the most basic information about U.S. foundations and their activities presented a danger to the field itself. In the words of Russell Leffingwell, a Carnegie Corporation board member at the time, "Foundations should have glass pockets."

Sara Engelhardt, President of the Foundation Center, notes that the center was established in 1956 precisely to work for the transparency of foundation pockets. Indeed, its initial name was the Foundation Library Center, and its initial programs consisted of a New York library, which collected annual reports, and the periodic publication of the *Foundation Directory*.

The European Foundation Centre is doing its part to work for the transparency of foundation pockets in Europe. In 1994, the European Parliament resolution on "Foundations and Europe" could have been damaging to the independent funding community and its work in support of civil society within the European Union, indeed across the whole continent. The transparency provided by the EFC Orpheus Programme, combined with effective lobbying by EFC members, deflected this threat.

For Grantseeking Associations

Work with grantseekers comprises most of the day-to-day work in open-access libraries. Their services are a major element of a funding information infrastructure because they provide professional guidance to a great deal of disparate information, and they help grantseekers to synthesize this information according to their needs.

Funding directory listings are, by their very nature, summaries. They can help researchers identify foundations that may be included on their "prospect" list. But rarely do they contain all the detailed information that lets a grantseeker know whether this foundation should remain on their list.

THE FOUNDATION CENTER OF
THE UNITED STATES

The Foundation Center, incorporated by a small group of U.S. foundations in 1956, is the prototype information resource for organized philanthropy. Its mission is to promote public understanding of the foundation field. It accomplishes this by collecting, organizing, analyzing, and disseminating financial, programmatic, and grants information on private foundations and, to the extent possible, on corporate, community, and other institutional grantmakers in the United States.

The center's mandate explicitly precludes a public relations role in favor of serving as an "information agency." Its initial primary advocacy role was to encourage foundations to publish annual reports as a way to shed public light on their activities. Failing that, the center could resort to the annual information reports required by the Internal Revenue Service (IRS) as a means of documenting foundation spending and other vital information. Ultimately, the center plays the dual role of a shield against public criticism of foundations and a clearinghouse of information from public sources and from foundations themselves. In this latter role, it has become the premier resource for fundraisers interested in attracting foundation grants.

Originally the center was a library of whatever information could be assembled from other sources. Over time, it began recording its own data, taken primarily from foundation reports to the IRS, and publishing them in the *Foundation Directory*. The center now maintains a database of information on some 43,000 grantmaking

One specific document of great assistance to U.S. grantseekers is the 990PF, the tax returns of private foundations. By law, these are public documents. Through an agreement between the Foundation Center and the U.S. Internal Revenue Service, these documents are microfilmed. The New York and Washington offices of the Center hold complete collections of these documents, updated on a continuing basis. Field offices in Atlanta, Cleveland, and San Francisco hold collections for their regions of the United States, as do certain cooperating library collections.

The 990PFs are detailed and rich documents. In addition to providing the financial details for a foundation for a year, they include lists of board members, top executive staff, program statements, and a complete list of grants paid during the year. After researchers have reviewed a foundation's summary listing in a directory, they often turn to the 990PF to see if this foundation is really appropriate for their funding needs.

In countries without similar documents, a funding information center should be an avid collector of the publications of foundations and corporate funders such as annual reports, newsletters, grants lists, conference proceedings, information brochures, and other documents. They are often the best information about a funder, because funders state explicitly what they fund and what they cannot fund due to policy. As not all funders release public documents, it is also helpful to collect newspaper articles. The Foundation Center, in addition to its 990PF collection, holds all these types of documents.

entities, with the grants of some 1,000 of the largest of these coded according to its own Grants Classification System, based on the National Taxonomy of Exempt Entities. The center publishes some 50 different directories from this database, as well as *FC Search: The Foundation Center's Database on CD-ROM.*

In 1994, to strengthen the philanthropic information infrastructure further, the Foundation Center created a World Wide Web site on the Internet with the dual goal of delivering valuable new services and reaching new audiences. This has significantly extended its audiences outside the United States. In addition to information about the center's own resources, the site features a weekly digest of the print media's coverage of philanthropy, highlights and excerpts of its latest research studies, a variety of educational resources for grantseekers, and a comprehensive annotated directory of Internet sites related to philanthropy. The directory of foundations on the Internet contains well over 150 hyperlinks to U.S. grantmaking foundations. The site now includes an "electronic reference desk," staffed by an online librarian, to provide answers via e-mail. An online publications catalog and order form permits those without access to the library network to buy center publications related to their particular interests.

The Foundation Center serves as a model for groups committed to the transparency of foundations in other countries. While many of its information-gathering procedures make use of resources unique to the United States, its publishing, education, and research programs have been observed and emulated by groups from all parts of the world.

Case study prepared by Sara L. Engelhardt, President of the Foundation Center.

One way to collect annual reports is to attach to your own annual report a small card that requests a funder's annual report in return. This lets the foundation respond quickly. It is a highly effective way of keeping a library collection up to date. To be thorough, a library should hold the publications of funders located in that country as well as those outside that have program interests in the region.

To be of broader assistance to funders as well as grantseekers, a funding information library should also contain:

- guides on program planning and proposal writing—documents that explain how to think through and develop a project, and how to approach funders for support. There are many excellent English-language texts, but the best one will probably be in a native language. Some fundraising texts also provide solid advice on alternatives to foundation support.

- manuals on nonprofit management—these cover topics such as strategic planning, administration and accounting, and working with volunteers. On the topic of board development, there are the fine publications of the National Center for Nonprofit Boards, located in Washington.

- texts on the legal and fiscal environment for funding—these can help funders that may be considering work in your region to understand what is required by public authorities, and how to work within those requirements.

SUCCESSFUL FUNDRAISING FROM FOUNDATIONS

The European Anti-Poverty Network (EAPN), based in Brussels, is an independent network of nongovernmental organizations (NGOs) fighting poverty and social exclusion in the European Union. It brings voluntary antipoverty NGOs together into national networks, to allow representative delegates to form a Europewide umbrella organization. Twenty-three European specialist networks also belong to EAPN.

At an EAPN seminar in Budapest, Hungary, NGOs from East and West had the chance to share their experiences. Participants identified the need for clear information on NGO funding. Accordingly, EAPN began planning a second seminar, to expand on East-West exchange in the area of social exclusion. The seminar would focus on "Working with Children and Young People in the Local Community." EAPN also began plans to publish a funding guide.

Toward these purposes, EAPN developed a project proposal that included two items:

- cofunding for a seminar in Romania, with strong participation of NGOs from Eastern Europe, and

- a funding guide to inform NGOs on potential funding sources, both private and public, for their work—in particular where transnational work and exchange is involved.

As a first step in researching additional funding, EAPN visited EFC headquarters in Brussels. EAPN staff explored its options by consulting the *International Guide to Funders Interested in Central and Eastern Europe* and the detailed information available in the EFC Library. As a result, they drew up a shortlist of potential

- documents on the nonprofit sector in that country as well as elsewhere—these enable funders to have information on the values, traditions, and needs of the nonprofit sector, and to identify the major umbrella organizations that serve it. They enable grantseekers to locate colleague organizations in their given field of interest, facilitating the sharing of experience and partnership formation. They can also allow a comparison of nonprofit sectors in other countries. On this last point, there are helpful publications available from the Johns Hopkins International Comparative Non-profit Study, particularly *The Emerging Sector*.

Major Conclusions for Practitioners

Given the number of tasks to be confronted, one major conclusion for practitioners would be to establish priorities. Is there a current directory on foundations and corporate funders in the nation or region? If not, this would be a logical place to begin, for, as noted, most private funders are active locally, and international funders would want to know if they could leverage their funding against local sources of support. If

foundations that might support the seminar and the funding guide. An initial letter of inquiry was sent to this group, explaining why funding was being sought and asking whether it would be useful to make a formal application. Initial responses were negative.

EAPN then attended a meeting on the Council of Europe's project on Human Dignity and Social Exclusion. A brief staff presentation on EAPN explained activities with NGOs in Eastern Europe, including the planned seminar. The Charles Stewart Mott Foundation heard the presentation and indicated that the seminar and funding guide might support its work in reinforcing the role of NGOs in Eastern Europe, as well as work in the area of the fight against exclusion. On the basis of these discussions, EAPN made a proposal to the Mott Foundation for cofunding for the seminar (specifically, for NGO participation from Eastern Europe) and for the funding guide. This proposal was successful.

At the same time, EAPN was also developing a working relationship with the Soros Foundation. Contact in this case was through the Spanish member of the EAPN Task Force, who was working with partners in Romania. The partners were able to obtain agreement from the Soros Foundation in Romania to partially fund the seminar—for interpretation and part of the materials costs on the spot.

This presented a possible dilemma. What would be the views of the two foundations regarding cofinancing? Would they be concerned about being associated with a project already supported by another foundation? Discussions with the EFC indicated that this should not be the case, and, at least in this instance, it was seen as positive to have two foundations involved in one project. Therefore, EAPN discussed this issue openly with both the Mott and Soros Foundations, and cofinancing was agreed.

Case study prepared by Pauline Geoghegan, Development Officer, EAPN.

there are extremely limited sources of local support, is there a directory of international funders that have stated interests in the country or region? Notably, the first EFC funding directory was its *International Guide to Funders Interested in Central and Eastern Europe*, published in 1993.

If such fundamental tools exist, is there an open-access library or small resource center where these tools can be used in context? Can this library begin collecting the support documents, such as funder publications and nonprofit management guides? Are there partnerships that can be formed in the country? Could one organization publish a funding directory, and another tend to the responsibilities of an open-access library?

Once priorities have been established, practitioners should consider asking existing funding information centers for technical assistance and guidance. As noted, the Foundation Center provided considerable assistance to the development of the EFC's funding information services, and the EFC in turn has helped centers across Europe. Centers in Central and Eastern Europe are currently developing a "twinning" program, whereby more experienced centers are aiding those just getting started. At the very least, any representative of an information center who is travelling internationally should schedule a visit to any funding information center in that area.

Researching and Approaching Foundations and Corporate Funders

This section reviews how grantseekers should use the information in a library or center to research and approach private funders effectively. In the experience of the EFC Library, many grantseekers simply want "the list." They hope they can get the perfect list of funders for their project from the library, and rush off to a meeting. Unfortunately, this simply does not work. Nor do circular appeals or mass mailings to funders. Each foundation and corporate funder is distinct. Each has its own personality and character with regards to its program interests. Accordingly, detailed research is necessary. Indeed, it will be the work of the grantseeking organization—the board of trustees, top management, and staff responsible for funding—to develop a list specific to that organization and its priorities.

An estimated 90 percent of funding requests are declined immediately. Many are declined because they fall outside a funder's stated interest areas or because they are inadequately prepared and do not reflect an organization's strengths and its ability to carry out a proposal's objectives.

Getting support from a foundation or corporate citizenship program can be as difficult as getting a job, and involves many of the same steps. Before applying, know your funder well. You want to ensure that your organizational expertise falls within the funder's stated program interests. And you will want to put your project in writing. This involves writing a project proposal that is as clear and professional as a written job application. Many excellent grantseeking guides can help you understand and structure this process. (See the Resource Guide at the end of the chapter.)

Successful Funding Begins Within Each Organization

Successful funding from foundations and corporate citizenship programs should be based on the development of a deliberate organizational strategy and a linked project proposal (see Box 2).

Developing an organizational strategy usually involves intensive work on the part of an organization's management and board of trustees or directors. It also may involve work with other organizations in the same field that share similar goals. In developing a strategy, the following questions should be answered clearly and directly:

- What is the unique purpose of the organization?
- What audience does it serve?
- Does this audience receive similar services from any other organization?
- What important need or needs does the organization aim to fill?
- Does the board of trustees fully support the initiatives to begin to respond to these needs?

Box 2

KEY ELEMENTS OF A PROJECT PROPOSAL

Introduction—Aim	*Summarizes clearly the aim of the project and the organization's abilities and qualifications to accomplish this aim.*
Needs Statement	*Reviews the need for the project and may detail a specific problem that the proposed project will answer and resolve.*
Objectives and Goals	*The aim should be broken down into measurable objectives, and the objectives into measurable goals. Goals are more detail-oriented. They are the specific projects or tasks that will be undertaken to achieve the aim and resolve the need or problem.*
Evaluation	*Explains how the success of achieving your stated goals will be measured. Often, this involves an advisory committee that guides and reviews the project regularly.*
Budget Summary	*Notes the total project cost and other sources of funding, if any.*
Future Funding Plans	*Describes the financial resources needed to continue the project once the support requested has ended, and how the organization will obtain these resources.*
Detailed Budget	*A realistic, accurate budget that details project expenses. Standard budgetary items are: personnel; travel/meeting costs; equipment; office running costs such as rent, telephone, and postage; publications; and computerization. Itemize all costs more than US$100.*
Appended Information	*Include in an appendix meaningful information that helps support the proposal. This may be detailed work plans, the latest annual report, and any documents that support the organization's credibility.*

Developing a "Prospect" List

Blanket or scatter-approach funding, whereby requests are sent to a wide group of foundations and corporate funders, is ineffective and can damage an organization's credibility. Funding directories are not the end of the funding research process; they are the beginning. Accordingly, they should not be used to develop a mailing list for requests for funding. Such attempts will waste an organization's time and, in addition, can seriously harm your future funding efforts.

Research on funders' stated program interests is essential. Once an organizational strategy and linked project proposal have been developed, this research process can begin. The goal is to find those few funders that have interests in line with the orga-

THE ASSOCIATION OF CHARITABLE FOUNDATIONS (UK)

The Association of Charitable Foundations (UK) is the resource body for grantmaking trusts and foundations in the United Kingdom. Membership has grown from 60 groups in 1989 to more than 250 in 1997. The members range from the world's largest philanthropic foundation (the Wellcome Trust, which funds medical research), through generalist and specialist national foundations, to small and local bodies.

Membership is open to independent (that is, nongovernmental) grantmaking trusts and foundations. Full members must have an assured income from endowment or another source, have a well-established regular public appeal, or be a company that has made a long-term commitment of funds. Other grantmaking bodies can join as associate members, and affiliation is also allowed for corporate bodies that act as administrator or trustee for several grantmakers. Operational charities (including operational foundations) cannot join unless they also make grants; fundraising and grantseeking are not allowed at association meetings.

The association's funds come mainly from members' subscriptions, which are charged on a graded scale. Initial grants from founder members will terminate at the end of the first 10 years, in 1999, leaving the association fully funded by subscriptions and income from events and publications.

The association's work includes:

nizational and project objectives. One overarching principle guides research for funding: if you do not qualify, do not apply.

Funder research is a two-step process. The first step aims to develop an initial "prospect" list of 10–15 funders who have general interests in the subject area of your organization or project. The second step involves further research and refines this list to the three or four funders you may approach.

Information in funding directories can help grantseekers develop a prospect list. Most directories are indexed to major fields of interest, such as culture, education, the environment, health, and science. As grantseekers are researching foundations and corporate funders, they should bear in mind the following:

- Does the funder support the specific subject area for which funds are being sought? For example, anyone seeking funds for a program involving university education should immediately cross off the prospect list those funders only interested in the education of young children.

- Does the funder indicate an interest in the country or geographic region? Just because a funder has program interests in Europe does not mean that it is active in every European country.

- Is the funder an operational foundation? Operational foundations prefer to carry out their own programs and usually do not accept funding applications. They can, however, offer valuable expertise in their stated program interests.

- a program of good-practice seminars aimed at improving techniques in grant assessment, evaluation, and related topics;

- research, discussions, and publications on grantmaking policy, particularly on such matters as the relationship between trusts/foundations, corporate givers, and government grant programs;

- publications such as handbooks on "Good Grant-Making," "Fairness in Funding," and "Guidelines for Funders of Voluntary Organisations";

- a bimonthly magazine, *Trust & Foundation News*;

- 20 interest (or affinity) groups of foundations on specialist grantmaking themes, such as the arts, environment, housing, and international giving;

- a regional forum of grantmakers; and

- support groups for trust personnel with different roles and attributes (such as assistant or deputy directors, black trustees and staff, and treasurers or finance directors).

Information for NGOs seeking grants in the United Kingdom is provided not by the association but by independent directory publishers such as the Charities Aid Foundation and the Directory of Social Change. Coordination and support for U.K. nongovernmental groups is provided by bodies such as the National Council for Voluntary Organisations.

Case study prepared by Nigel Siederer, Director, Association of Charitable Foundations.

- Does the funder make grants for the type of support being requested? For example, anyone seeking funding for a conference should not approach a funder that explicitly states it does not support conferences and seminars.

- Does the funder only support major infrastructure projects that may involve a number of organizations, including government partners? For example, it is inappropriate to request support to equip a single school laboratory from a funder that is only interested in the development of the administration of a country's education system.

- Does the funder make grants for the amount of money being requested? It is inappropriate to request 20,000 ECU from a funder that never made a grant above 5,000 ECU. Also, funders may not wish to support the full cost of a project; they may expect the organization to find additional sources to share the full cost.

- Does the funder accept full project proposals, or does it prefer an initial, brief letter of inquiry?

Further Research Refines the Prospect List

The very best sources of information about foundations and corporate funders are those that they release themselves. Funder publications can be annual reports, newsletters, grants lists, press releases, application guidelines, and other documents. In

CREATING AN ARTS LOAN FUND

Program-related investing is often perceived exclusively as a tool of the large endowed private foundations, used principally to increase the supply of capital for large-scale housing and economic development projects. At the Dade Community Foundation in Miami, however, program-related investing has followed a different path.

As the Dade Community Foundation's assets have grown from US$5 million in 1984 to US$48 million, grantmaking has increased proportionately. Annual discretionary grantmaking is currently around US$250,000, with the arts receiving roughly 10 percent. Not surprisingly, the need for funding by local arts groups is far greater. In fact, annual requests to the foundation total US$50,000 to US$100,000. Most come from ethnically diverse arts and cultural organizations operating at the grassroots level. Though relatively small, many of these organizations are well established, highly professional, and dynamic. Together, they play an important role in bringing together Miami's many ethnic and racial groups.

One way the foundation supplements discretionary grantmaking and increases the flow of dollars to local nonprofit agencies is through special purpose funds. In 1989, the Miracle Fund, devoted exclusively to arts and culture, was created through a US$50,000 gift from the principals of the Miracle Center, a new specialty mall. Although it was set up as a permanent endowment, the fund's limited size would have generated only US$2,500 annually, adding little to the existing arts grant budget.

Based on a study of community needs, the foundation decided to create a revolving loan fund that would complement discretionary arts-and-culture grantmaking. Short-term financing was identified as a critical need of small and emerging groups that depend in part on funding from public sources, such as the local arts council. Yet long delays between the commitment of grant funds and their release can cause groups to falter, cancel performances, or forgo important marketing efforts.

The foundation's feasibility study indicated that a pool of loan funds, to be disbursed in amounts no greater than US$5,000 for on average three to nine months, would meet the typical needs of small arts groups. Specifically, the loans would:

recent years, certain international funders have begun publishing their annual reports in a second or third language, or at least including translations of significant text. After initial research, if a funder remains on the prospect list, copies of its annual report and application guidelines should be requested.

Funder publications will give you a comprehensive overview of a funder's priorities and the areas that it will and will not fund. In reviewing an annual report, look for the information that will help determine whether the funder should remain on the prospect list. Pay careful attention to stated program interests, restrictions, geographic limitations, and other qualifications.

Grants lists, contained in many annual reports, can also provide valuable information. Usually these lists include the name and address of the organization funded, the

- serve as bridge funds between the close of one season and income from subscription sales for the next season;
- guarantee a short-term loan;
- advance funds for running a benefit;
- pay a marketing, development, or public relations consultant;
- finance the preparation of a grant application; or
- provide the advance needed to start a state or federally funded program.

The revolving loan fund concept was approved by the board, which set an annual interest rate of 2 percent and required a fund balance of US$25,000 as a loss reserve. In terms of guidelines for the program, three policies have distinguished loan processing from discretionary grantmaking: the loan approval process takes no longer than one to two weeks; applicants are assessed for their payback potential; and the foundation president is authorized to approve loans directly, to ensure a speedy response. As of 1997, the foundation had made 30 loans totalling US$123,000, and all but two of these have been repaid in full.

Most of the decisionmaking related in the Miracle Fund is similar to that involved in grantmaking. What is distinct is the need to focus on the payback potential of the applicant. Three small theater groups received loans at times of extreme cash flow problems. In those cases, the risk level the foundation was prepared to assume was highly related to the importance of the applicant institution to the community, the match between its mission and the foundation's focus on using the arts for intercultural bridge building, and the applicant's prior financial history.

The fund has clearly improved the stability of small grassroots arts and cultural groups. The foundation administers it as part of its grantmaking program, with backup from its financial office. The loan negotiation itself provides an opportunity for arts groups to evaluate their current financial position in a way that grants never accomplish. Most important, the use of the Miracle Fund has turned a small endowment into an annual source of US$25,000 of working capital for the arts.

Case study prepared by JoAnne Chester Bander, former Vice-President, Programs and Projects, Dade Community Foundation.

amount of the award, and a brief descriptive text on the purpose of the grant. Unlike program area statements, which describe what a funder aims to do, grants lists show what they actually did. Grants lists reveal the types of organizations a funder tends to support and the average size of the grants.

Another useful means to extend funding research is to be well informed about colleague organizations that work in a similar field. Most established associations publish an annual report, usually listing their funders for a year of record. Accordingly, an effective grantseeker needs not only the annual reports of funders, but also the annual reports of colleague organizations. Before concluding funding research, it would be advisable to obtain these annual reports and see if any additional names should be added to the prospect list. This is a key point that many associations overlook.

Finally, as noted earlier, the World Wide Web is an excellent way to broaden and deepen research. The Web sites of the Foundation Center and the EFC provide lists of funders active in the United States and Europe, respectively, with automatic links to the Web pages of funders listed. There is also a host of additional information on the Web for grantseekers, most of it in English.

Program-Related Investments

One special type of foundation support is not actually a grant but rather a loan—often an interest-free loan. Program-related investments (PRIs) are loans, loan guarantees, and other investments made by foundations for charitable purposes. The range of PRI "tools" available to funders also includes asset purchases and linked deposits. PRIs represent a small percent of annual philanthropic dollars. But grantseekers who have an established relationship with a funder should consider their effectiveness in certain program areas, particularly community development and job creation.

At certain points in a nonprofit's development, loans would actually be preferable, for three reasons. First, if a nonprofit has a large grant from a government body, there is often a serious delay from the receipt of the grant letter to the receipt of the funds. A loan can help bridge this period and ensure that a project begins on time. Second, sometimes a nonprofit has an irregular cash-flow pattern, for structural reasons. A membership organization, for example, may not receive regular dues payments, particularly when a member's dues need to be board-approved. A loan fund can help smooth out monthly finances. Third, certain large, long-term projects, particularly in community development, can have complex financial arrangements, with a number of funders involved from the government, business, and nonprofit sectors. A loan fund can provide much-needed capital to bridge funding from grant to grant, to support an organization's or project's financial credibility when seeking new funds, and to assist in short-term periods with heavy expenditures.

In 1995 the Foundation Center completed a national survey of PRI funders and recipients, a project supported by the Ford Foundation. Funders' principal motivations for making PRIs were to maximize the impact of their program interests and to provide an alternative form of financing where grantmaking is inappropriate or insufficient. Nonprofits most often seek to borrow through PRIs due to need for capital, either short-term or long-term.

The Center reports that since this funding became available, 74 funders have disbursed or guaranteed PRIs totalling $719 million. Per funder, the median PRI amount disbursed was $1.7 million, and the median number was three. Three fifths of PRI funders hold assets of $50 million or over, and they accounted for 87 percent of all PRI activity. Most funders receive requests for PRIs exclusively from nonprofits, but financial intermediaries—credit unions, venture capital and loan funds, development banks—are favored by several of the largest PRI providers.

Community development, housing projects, job creation, micro-enterprises, and health projects represent the largest program areas of PRIs. Nevertheless, funders also use PRIs to support the arts and media, human services, education, and the environment. Nearly two fifths of PRI dollars are for projects that serve the economically disadvantaged. The majority of PRIs are for cash flow and bridge financing, and for the purchase and construction of facilities.

Funding Usually Commences at the Top Level

Successful funding usually commences at a top-management to top-management level, from director to director or board member to board member. Usually, foundations and corporate funders do not simply support the words and texts of written project proposals; they fund the people who can execute these proposals effectively.

Most funding directories and nearly all funder annual reports include the names of the board of trustees of the funding organization, the chief executive officer, and often the program officer responsible for specific areas of interest. Before an initial letter of inquiry is sent, the organization's own board and top management should be consulted about these names. Do they know any of these individuals personally? Have they met them at conferences or international meetings? It is always more effective to have a board member or top manager send a personal letter to an individual at a foundation. Following this initial top-level contact, if a funder is interested in a proposal, further contact may continue at the staff level.

Funding Involves Long-Term Relationships

On approaching a funder, the grantseeker should be willing to undertake the responsibilities of a long-term relationship. This involves communication in the form of effective and timely reporting as required by the funding organization—few funders are willing to make an award in exchange for a half-page report a year later. It also involves keeping the funder informed of any significant changes in the written project proposal.

Over time, such communication may evolve into mutually beneficial professional relationships, with both the funding organization and the grantee working to achieve specific aims in an area of shared interest.

RESOURCE GUIDE

Reference Documents

A Women's Fundraising Handbook (Menlo Park, Calif.: The Global Fund for Women, 1995), 16 pp.

This publication shares some thoughts about raising money and giving it away. It explores how the Global Fund for Women developed, and the lessons it learned when implementing its program. The volume also includes lists of ideas and organizations that are possible sources of financial and other resources.

Carlson, Mim, *Winning Grants Step by Step: Support Centers of America's Complete Workbook for Planning, Developing and Writing Successful Proposals* (San Francisco, Calif.: Jossey Bass, 1995), 115 pp.

Structured in nine individual steps to lead an applicant through the grant-proposal writing process so that the workbook exercises and grant proposal are completed together. Sections also provide a bibliography, extra work sheets, and additional tips on writing letters of intent and conducting research on grantmakers.

Clarke, S., *The Complete Fundraising Handbook* (London: Radius Works, 1993), 256 pp.

A guide to raising money for charity, covering the range of funds available and the different fundraising techniques. Includes case studies and examples of good practice and covers the major sources of funds from government and company donations in the United Kingdom.

European Foundation Centre, *European Foundation Centre Profiles* (Brussels: 1995), 159 pp.

A comprehensive directory aimed at providing foundations, corporate funders, government bodies, and grantseekers with a public record of the funding interests of EFC members, both in Europe and intercontinentally. Offers detailed profiles of 112 foundations and corporate funders active in Europe or intercontinentally. The profiles contain contact information, funder's origin and purpose, a review of financial information and major activities, and a list of trustees and executives. Profiles also review a funder's geographic interests, any restrictions on the funding programs, application procedures, publications, and EFC membership category.

Geever, Jane C., and Patricia McNeill, *The Foundation Center's Guide to Proposal Writing* (New York: The Foundation Center, 1993), 191 pp.

A comprehensive guide to proposal writing. The book includes each step of the process, from preproposal planning to writing, as well as the essential follow-up. Incorporates interviews with 18 foundation and corporate citizen programs.

Getting Started: A Funding Guide For Non Governmental Organisations in Central and Eastern Europe Seeking Funds and Partners (Brussels: The European Anti-Poverty Network, 1996), 105 pp.

Offers advice to NGOs in Central and Eastern Europe involved in the field of poverty and social exclusion. Advice on fundseeking from their own county, the European Union, and western foundations. Also includes foundation addresses.

Le Guide Complet de la Collecte de fonds au Québec (Montreal: Les Éditions de L'AQSEP, 1996).

A practical guide to raising money for charity, covering different fundraising techniques such as the creation of fundraising events or telemarketing. Includes list of foundations and corporate funders in Quebec.

Guide to Funding for International and Foreign Programs (New York: The Foundation Center, 1996), 356 pp.

Contains portraits of more than 700 U.S. grantmakers active at an international level, including address, financial data, priorities, application procedures, and names of key officials. An additional insight into foundation funding priorities is provided by the descriptions of recently awarded grants. This edition has a range of indexes including the type of support, subject field, and geographic field, which allows funders to be easily located.

Ingram, Richard, *Ten Basic Responsibilities of Nonprofit Boards* (Washington, D.C.: National Center for Nonprofit Boards, 1994), 22 pp.

Profiles fundamental responsibilities of boards, focusing primarily on the board viewed as a single entity.

International Foundation Directory 1996 (London: Europa Publications, 1996), seventh edition, 817 pp.

Contains details on more than 1,450 institutions in some 104 countries worldwide. Entries are arranged alphabetically by country. Each entry contains address, phone and fax numbers, function, primary aims and activities, finances, publications, and key executives and trustees. Includes an alphabetical index of entries by name and an index by activity to identify foundations working in particular fields.

Kiritz, Norton J., *Program Planning and Proposal Writing* (Los Angeles, Calif.: The Grantmanship Center, 1980), 48 pp.

Designed to assist both applicants for grants and grantmakers. As a proposal format, it will help in preparing a clear application, which states the aims of the organization and the purpose of the funding. It is especially useful where there are no specific guidelines provided for proposals, and its proposal format has been adopted by both government agencies and foundations. The paper is a part of the Grantsmanship Center reprint series and maintains its relevance.

Norton, Michael, *Writing Better Fund-Raising Applications* (London: Radius Works, 1992), 80 pp.

A practical guide to costing projects, improving communication skills, assessing applications, and creating worksheets.

Renz, Loren, Shaista Qureshi, and Crystal Mandler, *Foundation Giving 1996. Yearbook and Figures on Private, Corporate and Community Foundations* (New York: The Foundation Center, 1996), 131 pp.

Provides a comprehensive overview of the latest grantmaking trends and reviews changes in growth and distribution patterns. Includes various statistics on giving trends illustrated in 116 tables and graphs. New features include a geographic analysis of corporate and community foundations.

Salamon, L.M., and H.K. Anheier, *The Emerging Sector: The Nonprofit Sector in Comparative Perspective: An Overview* (Baltimore, Md.: Institute for Policy Studies, The John Hopkins University, 1994), 140 pp.

Recent changes in social and economic conditions and in public attitudes toward government are focusing new attention on private nonprofits throughout the world. This report, based on research findings developed by The John Hopkins Comparative Sector Project, summarizes findings with regard to the scope, structure, and financing of these institutions across a broad range of countries and identifies a set of issues these findings raise for the future of the sector.

Selected Bibliography on Foundations and Corporate Funders in Europe (Brussels: European Foundation Centre, 1994), 69 pp.

An annotated bibliography including 263 entries of regional, national, and European-level funding directories; legal, fiscal, and management titles; and the publications of members of the EFC. Updated each quarter by the *efc bookshelf.*

Seltzer, Michael, *Securing Your Organization's Future* (New York: The Foundation Center, 1987), 514 pp.

A guide to fundraising strategies. Section 1 focuses on the founding and running of an organization. Section 2 provides an overview of the range of revenue sources available to nonprofits and information for securing the support of the various sources presented. Section 3 documents appropriate fundraising strategies.

Typology of Foundations in Europe (Brussels: European Foundation Centre, 1995), 13 pp.

The typology provides foundation and corporate funders with a comprehensive overview of the different types of foundations in Europe. It is also of key relevance to grantseekers, scholars, researchers, the media, and governmental bodies that work with Europe's foundation community. The publication is the result of a collaborative effort of the EFC, its members, and the Orpheus Networking Centres. In establishing this typology, three criteria were reviewed: the source of the foundation's financial resources, the control of decisionmaking, and the approach to the distribution of financial resources. The typology presents 18 foundation types in Europe, grouped under four generic categories: Independent Foundations, Corporate Foundations, Governmentally Linked Foundations, and Fundraising Foundations.

von Rotterdam, Ingrid, *Building Foundation Partnerships: The Basics of Foundation Fundraising and Proposal Writing* (Toronto: Canadian Centre for Philanthropy, 1994), 88 pp.

Provides an overview and current trends in the Canadian foundation community. Also reviews the most efficient fundraising strategies, from research to proposal development.

Concerned Resource Organizations

Asia Pacific Philanthropy Consortium
Information Center (APPC-IC)
c/o Institute for East and West Studies
Yonsei University
134 Shinchon-dong
Seodaemoon-Gu
Seoul 120-749
South Korea
Tel: (822) 361-3506
Fax: (822) 393-9027
Web site: http://www.iews.yonsei.ac.kr/appcic

Association of Charitable Foundations (UK)
4 Bloomsbury Square
London WC1A 2RL
United Kingdom
Tel: (44-171) 404-1338
Fax: (44-171) 831-3881

Charities Aid Foundation—Russia
10 Yakovoapostolsky Perulok
103064 Moscow
Russia
Tel: (7-095) 928-0557
Fax: (7-095) 298-5694

Council on Foundations
1828 L St., N.W.
Washington, DC 20036
Tel: (1-202) 466-6512
Fax: (1-202) 785-3926
Web site: http://www.cof.org

Dade Community Foundation
200 South Biscayne Blvd.
Suite 2780
Miami, FL 33131
Tel: (1-305) 371-2711

European Anti-Poverty Network
Rue Belliard 205, bte 13
B-1040 Brussels
Belgium
Tel: (32-2) 230-4455
Fax: (32-2) 230-9733

European Foundation Centre
51 rue de la Concorde
B-1050 Brussels
Belgium
Tel: (32-2) 512-8938
Fax: (32-2) 512-3265
Web site: http://www.efc.be

EFC Civil Society Project
Regional Office
Jaracza 3/39
00-378 Warsaw
Poland
Tel and fax: (48-22) 625-2979

The Foundation Center
79 Fifth Avenue
New York, NY 10003
Tel: (1-212) 620-4230
Fax: (1-212) 691-1828
Web site: http://www.fdncenter.org

Fourth Iberoamerican Third Sector Meeting (in 1998)
c/o Federation of Argentine Foundations
Avenida Santa Fe 2161, Planta Baja
Buenos Aires 1123
Argentina
Tel: (54-1) 825-8429
Fax: (54-1) 826-7943

Group of Institutes, Foundations and Enterprises
Alameda Ribeirão Preto 130
Conjunto 12
01331-000 São Paulo
Brazil
Tel: (55-11) 287-8719
Fax: (55-11) 287-2349

The Hong Kong-America Center
6/F, Tin Ka Ping Building
The Chinese University of Hong Kong
Shatin, N.T
Hong Kong
Tel: (852) 2609-8748
Fax: (852) 2603-5797
E-mail: hk-amcenter@cuhk.edu.hk
Web site: http://www.cuhk.edu.hk/hkac

Institute for the Development of Philanthropy (IDEPH)
c/o Puerto Rico Community
Foundation
Royal Bank Center, Suite 1417
Hato Rey, Puerto Rico 00917
Tel: (1-787) 754-2623
Fax: (1-787) 751-3297

Mexican Centre for Philanthropy (CEMEFI)
Mazatlan No. 96
Colinia Condesa
06140 Mexico City DF
Mexico
Tel: (52-5) 256-3739
Fax: (52-5) 256-3190

National Center for Nonprofit Boards
2000 L St., N.W.
Washington, DC 20036
Tel: (1-202) 452-6262
Fax: (1-202) 452-6299
Web site: http://www.ncnb.org

Philanthropy Australia
Level 3
111 Collins Street
Melbourne 3000, Victoria
Australia
Tel: (61-3) 9650-9255
Fax: (61-3) 9654-8298

Chapter 4
Individual Philanthropy

Daniel Q. Kelley and Susana García-Robles

Creating a Culture of Philanthropy

Unless a civil society organization (CSO) has an endowment, financial self-sufficiency and peace of mind come from diversifying sources of income. What better way to diversify than to promote individual philanthropy and receive donations from many individuals? People want to be part of something important. They want to give their resources to turn dreams into reality. Civil society can help them.

In the past, a mass of cash from governments and international donors tended to dam up the traditional wellsprings of people helping people. As those institutions have cut back on their support for civil society, however, CSOs around the world have tapped into the reservoir of goodwill of their fellow citizens.

"Philanthropy" is not a term preferred by CSOs everywhere. Its etymology—love of other people—has in some places degenerated into a denotation of paternalism—*asistencialismo*, as they say in parts of Latin America. But some word must be used to describe this individual form of support for CSOs, and philanthropy is used here for that purpose. In its purest form, individual philanthropy means the disinterested giving of a person's own resources, as an expression of solidarity with fellow humans, even strangers. True philanthropists expect nothing in return for their gifts.

This ideal, of course, has nuances. Humans cannot act without some motive, be it as lofty as the hope of happiness in a life to come. A challenge for the CSO, then, is to discover what will motivate each potential donor to turn a good intention into a gift. Small tokens of appreciation from a CSO are always in order, because it is as human to be grateful as it is to give. Fostering individual philanthropy, however, is different from selling goods and services, and it is better for civil society than are lotteries and games of chance, when the emphasis is on "my luck" rather than "our work."

"Strangers" were just mentioned in this notion of philanthropy, to contrast with the worldwide phenomenon of one wealthy individual or family always giving to only one organization, which they often control. This is not bad, but society benefits even more if everyone is open to donating to causes that make a compelling case for support based more on results than on who founded them, works in them, or directs them. To pledge personal time, sweat, money, or goods to strangers is the purest expression of solidarity with fellow citizens. (Although this chapter talks mainly about money, much of the discussion applies equally to gifts of goods and volunteered work.)

The Space of Individual Philanthropy

While individual philanthropy is praiseworthy, a CSO should not neglect other sources of funding. As a matter of fact, although each has a unique core, there are no bright lines separating individual, business, foundation, and government support. How do you classify it when a couple's gift to a CSO comes from the checkbook of their company—business or individual? When Germans decide to dedicate a part of their taxes to a certain religious group, is that individual or government support? It does not matter.

The point of this chapter is not to classify, but to make the case that asking individuals for support is worthwhile, and must be done thoughtfully. Part of what this chapter says about donor relations applies to businesses, foundations, and governments, because, after all, individuals are found there, too—one of the reasons why individual philanthropy is fundamental to the growth of civil society.

If individual philanthropy intersects with other modes of philanthropy, what makes it special?

- It deals with large numbers of potential and actual donors. The techniques of identifying them and asking them for resources are special.

- It engages several (or many) active solicitors. They do not have to be experts, much less professional fund developers, but it helps if they are supported by a trained staff.

- It has a long-term commitment, not only to this abstract strategy, but also to certain individuals. People typically start with a small donation—if any—and CSOs have to help them increase their contributions over time.

- Its proposals are simple, unlike those demanded by governments, foundations, and sometimes businesses. (Although this does not mean that appeals to individuals require little thought.)

- It feels a special need to join with other CSOs in creating a culture of philanthropy, increasing the notion and understanding of disinterested giving, which will benefit all of civil society.

The burden of creating a culture of philanthropy lies disproportionately on CSOs, which have to be transparent and accountable to the people they claim to serve. People do not deposit their money into black holes. What is more, CSOs need to be professional regarding the other side of the coin of philanthropy, their fund development (a term preferable to fundraising, which is taking on a mechanical, impersonal connotation). The techniques of fund development—the techniques of promoting individual philanthropy—do have a lot in common with business marketing and sales. A CSO should make the effort to "sell" its service intelligently to potential donors, but fund development does not begin with sales. It ends there.[1]

Strategic Questions

The first and most basic question for any CSO is, What do we want to accomplish? In other words, what is our mission? The CSO must know what it wants to accomplish in the long run. Furthermore, each and every person involved in fund development must be convinced of the organization's mission and be able to enunciate it in a succinct, compelling way.

Further strategic questions lead to the three strategies in individual philanthropy described in this chapter. Marketing strategies, for example, arise out of answers to three questions: Who loves our mission? Who should love it? Who do we want to love it? The term "marketing" may seem formidable, but it comes from common sense. The executives of a CSO, who are often passionately committed to their mission, tend to imagine that nearly everyone would share their feelings if they only heard about it. This leads to disappointments. Just as a for-profit business has to market its product or services, the CSO has to market its mission, or, better yet, its results. Of course, the CSO has to satisfy several markets—its clients, its staff, its Board—but when discussing philanthropy, the market of interest is potential donors.

In deciding on a role, it is important to remember that the CSO is not a beggar. Assuming that it offers something worthwhile to society, it should carry itself with confidence. Second—and important for anyone leery of the workload in what has been said thus far—the CSO should be a team. A common obstacle to realizing the enormous opportunities of individual philanthropy is that founders or executive directors think that they have to or can do it all alone.

Answering the question of who a CSO is points to the need to train all staff—paid and unpaid—in how to treat past and future donors with respect, which is what all businesses that succeed in open markets do. This is the essence of the second strategy. Those who do fund development should avail themselves of ongoing education in this field. Consultants' advice can be invaluable, but they do not raise money—the CSO does. They deserve a fair day's wages for a fair day's work. The largest professional association of fund developers in the world considers it unethical to work on commission.

CSOs with a legal personality have one or more formal bodies that are responsible to society for the actions of the organization. They should consider helping some or all of these persons learn how to be leaders in obtaining individual donations. CSOs that are informally organized may want to consider setting up a similar development committee, which is the third strategy discussed in this chapter.

Aside from these strategic questions, there are minor ones—When do we ask? Where do we ask?—from which flow a variety of tactical options that will be covered in the discussion of marketing.

A final piece of advice is the importance of experimentation, to see what works for each CSO. There is no philanthropic recipe that works for everyone.

Importance and Scale of Individual Philanthropy

We may know how many shrimp are caught in the world each year, but we do not have the foggiest idea how many philanthropic dollars people give to people. The scanty data that do exist cover mainly industrial nations, and any comparisons be-tween countries are extremely difficult to make.

Nevertheless, some rough estimates can be pulled together. (See Chapter 1.) According to one painstaking study, individual donations account for 6 percent of civil society's income in seven countries.[2] It surprises many people that 47 percent of civil society's income derives from fees and revenues, 43 percent from government, and only 10 percent from private sources, including companies, foundations, and individuals. Of this 10 percent, the lion's share—60 percent—comes from individuals. European CSOs receive from 2 percent (in Germany) to 7 percent (in the United Kingdom) of their total income from individuals. In the United States, the figure is 14 percent, while in Japan it is less than 1 percent. Considering their recent socialist past, Hungarian citizens are amazingly forthcoming: their direct contributions finance 5 percent of civil society there.

It is important to note that these figures exclude contributions to houses of worship and religious groups and congregations. While the study considers them to be a part of civil society, they are such a big part that the authors could not begin to gather sufficient data on them for most countries. True, in some countries, such as France, mainly religious purposes count for next to nothing. But elsewhere they change the picture.

In the United States, 80 percent of private giving comes from individuals, and most of it goes to religious organizations; money used for worship and doctrinal instruction was not counted in the 14 percent just cited, but money used to build a hospital or run a school was. Counting all of it, the portion of individual income donated to civil society in the United States rises from 0.57 percent to 1.19 percent. For Germany, it rises from a relatively small 0.18 percent to a relatively high 1.12 percent.

In other parts of the world, there are indications that individual giving is tied to religious institutions. Islam encourages the formation of endowed social service centers, *waqf*, a practice first used centuries ago to build hostels for pilgrims. It preaches tithing: the *zakat* is 2.5 percent of a person's income. If it were all complied, this would make certain countries' statistics look twice as good as those for the United States and Germany, where "tithe" means 10 percent to the Christian majorities, and is a custom more honored in the breach than in the practice. In Lebanon, 50 percent of the funding of Islamic CSOs—usually social welfare organizations—seems to come from *zakat*, and more comes from occasional donations. Some 3,000 Egyptian mosques that are affiliated with *zakat* committees raised $5 million in 1989. It seems that many individuals practice such philanthropy throughout the Islamic world, but how many and how much money is involved are unknowns.[3] We do know, however, that all the world's major religions, and most of its philosophies, encourage philanthropy.

Although we will make the case for individual philanthropy on philosophical grounds, as a financial phenomenon it is relatively small. Nevertheless, in some countries the absolute numbers are large: $116 billion from individuals in the United States in 1995, for example.[4]

And aggregate data do not tell the whole story. Donations from individuals are a vital source of income for many CSOs. They are also quite important for different sectors of civil society in different countries—for education and the arts in the United States, health and the arts in Western Europe, and recreation in Hungary, for example. On the other hand, to the extent that civil society receives fees from clients and support from governments, individual donations are small, probably because they are not perceived as needed. Such is the case with health care in the United States and Germany, and with education in the United Kingdom and France.[5]

In the United States, there is interesting information about income groups. For the whole population, including non-givers, the more wealthy people are, the more they give—slightly—as a proportion of their income. This is not surprising. But among those who contribute to CSOs, the poor donate more than others. Once Americans give, in other words, the poor donate proportionately more than the Rockefellers: 4.3 percent versus 3.4 percent of gross income.[6] Is this true the world over? Is compassion stimulated by hardship, or do varying economies and societies, differing tax rates and deductions, blur the picture?

There does seem to be a relation between giving and tax deductions, but it has to do with systems as well as with percentages. Where lower deductions are offered—or where the mechanism is complicated, as in the United Kingdom, or where it is ambiguous, as in Italy—individual philanthropy is hindered. There is also a hint that where the tax burden is high, individual contributions to civil society are low.

CSOs everywhere use a wide variety of asking methods, but there are regional preferences. In the United States and Canada, the church collection plate is the most successful vehicle. Outside of religious giving, personal solicitation looms large. In the United Kingdom, people give to collections and at events. The national lottery is a huge fundraiser, although as noted earlier, gambling is on the edges of true philanthropy. The French respond much better than others to direct mail and advertisements, they are gracious when there is a knock on the door or a can held out at a street corner, but they are adverse to the Anglo style of personal interviews, where a level of contribution is hinted at.[7]

Japanese giving has traditionally been directed toward family members or, in the case of the wealthy, to a limited number of charitable and educational works that they call their own. So individual giving to civil society is not widespread, and does not amount to much. But it seems to be on the upswing: in spite of an almost total absence of tax incentives, Japan Foster Plan had 55,000 sponsors who gave $33 million in 1993.[8] Direct mail now works in Japan.

On another front, "although exact numbers are not available, corporate donations dominate over individual giving in Croatia, Estonia, and Poland, while individual donors' contributions have the highest position in Bulgaria and Slovenia. In Hungary, the number of private donors more than doubled, and the size of average donations more than quadrupled between 1988 and 1990."[9]

Latin America has a long history of philanthropy by the wealthy. It is a big region, with many countries, so generalizations must be taken with a grain of salt. That said, anecdotal evidence suggests that as a middle class emerges, individual contributions have become first possible and then important, in spite of governments' suspicion of civil society and lack of tax incentives for it. As in other parts of the world, it is difficult to distinguish among donations from individuals, families, companies, and foundations, because matriarchs and patriarchs have tended to rule all.

Mexico has 35 years of experience in systematic fund development. Annual and capital campaigns are common. There are professional fund development consultants who supplement the in-house talent of universities, hospitals, and museums. All over the region, affinity credit cards and automatic payments are the order of the day. Argentina and Brazil, probably because they are so big, stand out as practitioners of sophisticated media and collection techniques. Rio de Janeiro offers data from 140 of its thousands of CSOs: about 6 percent of income is derived from private sources—corporations, foundations, and individuals. The figure omits transfers from the Catholic Church, some of which presumably originates from individuals.[10] In any case, if individuals accounted for half of the 6 percent—an upper-end hypothesis—then they would represent 3 percent of all income, close to the figure in France.

Benefits and Limitations of Strategy

Suppose that it would take a CSO more time and effort to raise its annual operating budget from 200 individuals than from grants from one government, two foundations, and three companies, combined. Would any CSO bother with the individuals? It might, for political and long-term economic reasons. Having hundreds of supporters may lend stability to its income, dampening the impact of downturns in government, corporate, and institutional funding. The strategy may also increase autonomy, diffusing the power that a few major grantmakers can wield over the values, mission, and operations of the CSO.

Of course, these benefits come from having a broad base of support of any and all types, not just individual philanthropy. Peculiar to this strategy, however, are its simple proposals. Compared with institutional grant requests, the documents required are not elaborate, and negotiations are brief. The appeal to an individual must be thoughtful, certainly; simple is not the same as easy. Yet the resultant contributions are easy to administer, with few if any of the strings that institutions attach to their money.

Individual contributions enrich not just the recipient organization, but civil society in general, which has been described as voluntary association for the common good, and private voluntary initiatives for the public good. When you give your resources, you are giving a part of yourself to others, you are associating. Who builds civil society more: a project manager currently employed by an NGO but who could be hired by a construction company tomorrow, or a child whose pennies helped pay the manager's salary today? This consideration alone will not convince a service-providing CSO to turn from institutional to individual funds, but it has already motivated grantmaking institutions to encourage local individuals to donate time and money to those CSOs.

This strategy fosters democracy, grounding certain CSOs firmly in their community, making them accountable to a wide constituency that has voted for them, so to speak, with its donations. In particular, it recognizes the fact that the poor are capable of mobilizing resources for the organizations they themselves create to deal with their problems. Broad support gives confidence to governmental, corporate, and institutional donors that the CSO works in the public interest. Governments often demand this if the CSO wants fiscal and legal privileges.

While the philanthropic impulse is universal, it expresses itself in a variety of ways, and sometimes is even stifled by systemic forces. In different countries at different times there have been a relatively few very wealthy families, hardly any middle class, and many poor people. Some rich families may have run their own charitable organizations. One or more religious institutions may have raised money from those with means, distributing it to religious networks of social services, resulting in a further centralization of service delivery and a distancing of the philanthropist from the ultimate beneficiary. The rise of strong central governments has often meant centralization of social services and cultural activities, sometimes a usurpation of religious networks, and a dampening of the type of giving discussed here.

Citizens in such societies tend to expect either a religious group or the state to solve everyone's problems. Official and private aid from abroad has sometimes contributed to this attitude. Self-help groups still exist, and generosity is certainly abundant for family and fellow villagers. But philanthropy adds a new element: it is the disinterested giving of resources even to strangers. Promoting it involves bucking entrenched mentalities.

Where there is no culture of giving, there is no culture of asking. The CSO may feel intimidated by the prospect, at a loss as to how to approach individuals. It may be daunted by the long-term commitment involved. It may think it is degrading to have to "market" itself. The one technique of individual fund development that it practices—events like dinners and concerts—may be wearing thin on donors. These are certainly drawbacks, but confidence and training can overcome them. In conducting more than 100 training workshops since 1992, the International Federation of Red Cross and Red Crescent Societies (the Red Cross) has distilled some strategies to help transfer fundraising experiences between cultures. (See Box 1.)

Developing countries and transition economies present special challenges. Direct mail—any mail—and phones have not worked well. Despite universal traditions of philanthropy, some places have a limited number of wealthy donors, and they may feel inundated by requests. Even in North America and Western Europe, 20 percent or less of total contributions to civil society come from private giving. The highest figure we know of—the share of CSO income in the United States, including from religious worship, that comes from individuals—is only 20 percent. It is not a panacea, particularly in developing countries and Eastern Europe.

Current Trends

Given the explosion in the number of CSOs everywhere, particularly in the developing world, over the last 25 years, competition for financing is increasing. This is heightened by the cutbacks in some government and international development assistance funds, along with sudden shifts of institutional funds from issue to issue and from one region to another. No wonder more and more CSOs are trying to diversify their sources of income. There are reasons to believe that individual philanthropy will increase, especially in the South and East. The question is how big a role it will play.

Certain winds are blowing in its direction. Governments are decentralizing some functions, privatizing others, deregulating commerce and industry, and cutting off subsidies; businesses conglomerates are breaking up into their parts, and the parts in turn have several profit centers that say they listen more and more to workers on the shop floor. In some countries of Latin America and Asia, this seems to have caused the macroeconomic indicators and many people's incomes to go up. Seeing this

Box 1

Transferring Fundraising Experience

- *Before doing training, assess program viability, funding needs, and skills gaps. This sounds terribly basic, but often we put on a training program because we happen to have it ready, not because it connects with real needs.*

- *Plan follow-up before you plan the training. . . . The follow-up is the hard part, but it is critical to implementing new ideas generated at the workshop. Training is expensive. Protect your investment by outlining in advance certain action steps that will ensure that the training is put to work. Agree on these steps in writing with participants before the workshop closes.*

- *Show what others are doing. It helps to see real examples: "Here's what someone else is doing to raise money. How could you make something like this work for you?" One way to do this is by video—expensive to produce, but it can be an effective training tool.*

- *Examine principles behind what works elsewhere. After watching a video that documents a successful commercial activity in Zimbabwe, for example, the trainer might lead participants in a discussion of the reasons for success of that program. . . .*

- *Acknowledge local realities and tap local resources. In Tajikistan, a branch of the Red Crescent Society borrowed an example they learned from Finnish Red Cross trainers and organized a door-to-door campaign. Rural people with no cash donated goats and vegetables, which were then converted to cash. This first-time effort provided encouragement to volunteers and a good base for future campaigns.*

- *Use specialists/consultants. In Nairobi, a BBC correspondent and an advertising agency added professional perspective to a regional seminar on information and fundraising. In Gambia, the Gambia Women's Finance Association shared small business expertise in a regional workshop with West African Red Cross Societies. In South America, a fundraising professional is now assisting our regional delegation to provide tailored, ongoing guidance to five Red Cross Societies.*

- *Make your training as participatory as possible. Involve participants in planning the training and as true "doers" in workshop sessions and even as facilitators. We find it useful to invite participants to identify obstacles at the outset of training, then look for practical ways of dealing with those blocks. Also, ask participants to generate fundraising ideas, to practice presenting requests to corporations, and to do a feasibility. . . analysis of a fundraising project or commercial activity.*

Source: Michael Hayes, Senior Officer, Resource Development, Red Cross, Geneva.

growth, and breathing the airs of subsidiarity—the principle that those who are closest to a problem or activity should take on maximum responsibility for managing it—more and more people think that it is a good thing for local individuals to give money to local CSOs to improve the quality of local life.

The average CSO in the South and East will agree, but old financing habits are hard to break. Throughout history, much of civil society has expected to be funded by a powerful institution: first by large religious organizations, then by governments, then by international entities. Now CSOs are turning with great expectation, and sometimes a hint of self-righteousness, to a supposedly monolithic business sector. To negotiate with well-to-do individuals would represent even more of a change of heart for the many CSOs that started life as agents of change against authoritarian or incompetent regimes identified with traditional moneyed interests. The collapse of communism sharpened their thinking about the roles of government, private enterprise, and citizens in creating wealth and using it wisely, but these CSOs are not about to go out of their way to praise and promote individual philanthropy. To sum up, the average CSO will not take the initiative, but rather will respond to a culture of giving and to the leadership of those who aim to create or revive it.

An important trend in North America and Western Europe is that donors are becoming more discriminating: they are tending to earmark their gifts, rather than make them unrestricted, which means that the successful CSOs are those that work the hardest at marketing themselves. It also helps to keep administrative costs low, as donors increasingly examine the ratio of overhead to total expenditures. CSOs starting to do individual fund development might be well advised to address this issue from the beginning.

Other evidence that donors are more discriminating includes that federated appeals, while still important in several countries, are slightly less popular in the United States. A heated debate has erupted there also about the mushrooming number of "donor-directed" funds administered by community foundations, a seeming self-contradiction. This type of discriminating philanthropy correlates positively with levels of education and negatively with age.

Some data indicate that the age of donors is becoming more important than their nationality in determining what they give to. Indeed, in the United States, there is less giving for strictly local causes, which may reflect how often the youngest two generations change their place of residence. Young donors are not only more discriminating about how a CSO uses their gift, they tend to give to different CSOs than their parents. Given the considerable wealth young people are in line to inherit, CSOs will continue to facilitate planned giving, and they will learn how to best approach the increasingly diverse population that holds all this wealth.

Women, for example, control an increasing amount of wealth. They outlive their partners in wealth-generation in unprecedented numbers, and they deposit paychecks in their personal accounts like never before. In the United States, their donation patterns so far are not very different from those of men, so fund developers have to pay attention not to the mission of the CSO, but to the women themselves, and who asks them for funds and how they prefer to be asked.

Key Issues

Economy

Naturally, a healthy economy helps all types of philanthropy. A CSO may not be able to do much about the economy, but it may want to protect itself from drops in corporate contributions during troughs in the business cycle by always asking individuals for money, too. A bad economy may not be the time to adopt this strategy, but it is also not the time to abandon it. People have hearts, and sometimes savings. If cash is a problem, the CSO can ask for contributions of goods and services. It may also wish to be an advocate for a wide distribution of the benefits of a growing economy, which would broaden and stabilize its donor base.

Globalization

As economies and societies intertwine, strategies and techniques of fund development learned through trial and error in any part of the globe should find increasingly receptive audiences in other areas. But aside from this crossnational exchange of information, it is debatable whether globalization results in a crossnational giving of money by individuals. Certainly donors are increasingly aware of problems in other countries, so they may want to give a donation. Problems that used to seem local are now seen as international—environmental ones are the most obvious—and this should motivate foreign donors even more. A recent bilateral tax incentive for donations between Mexico and the United States may yet prove useful, despite attempts to sabotage it.

On the negative side, however, Western Europe, which as a leader in international giving by institutions seems like fertile ground for crossnational giving by individuals, talks little about it and does less. There is a growing feeling that, whenever possible, local people should solve local problems. Many northern and western CSOs that used to run relief or development programs abroad have changed their focus, trying instead to strengthen CSOs they think can more effectively meet the challenges within their own societies. The wealthier CSOs provide training in management skills and fund development, help start formal and informal networks of CSOs, convene conferences, and so on. Unfortunately, they are finding that their own donors are not interested in this capacity building or institutional strengthening, which can seem like a layer of bureaucracy. Donors would rather give to CSOs that solve people's problems directly. But they have no tax incentive to give to a foreign CSO, nor do they know which ones they can trust.

Credibility

A well-managed CSO, responsive and accountable to its donors, has a better chance of success. Beyond this, every CSO should be concerned about every other CSO's integrity, because a culture of giving depends on the public image of all of civil society. History already makes the sector suspect in many eyes.

Where one person or family has dominated each CSO, shams and corruption have not been unknown, and the whole sector's accountability to the public has not been clear. Where civil society has surged in defiance of oppressive and incompetent regimes, it has made political enemies. In Latin America, Africa, and Asia, the sector is perceived as being leftist, and not every potential donor likes that. Where states think they are doing a favor to citizens by letting them associate among themselves, CSOs have to behave cautiously, not giving out information that can be used against individuals unfairly, albeit legally. What starts as an understandable defense mechanism ends up as a lack of transparency, an important issue with donors. And there is plain old greed, graft, and grubbiness, as witnessed by recent scandals at certain CSOs in the United States and Western Europe. These angered their donors, and frightened everybody else's.

Even though citizens' associations opposed them, totalitarian and authoritarian regimes have perverted the notions of voluntary association and widespread volunteering by the public. In newly independent states and in several Central and East European countries, people were pressured into "helping the community." After the adrenaline of revolution against these regimes wore off, the sour taste of a lifetime of "volunteer, or else. . ." has remained. Some people just want to be left alone. To them, civil society is a meddler.

In the face of these obstacles, a civil society that wants to promote individual philanthropy has to promote itself—its legitimacy and accomplishments. CSOs have to work together, for example by organizing media campaigns extolling the importance of their sector, as a precondition to broadening their base of donors and volunteers. There is strength and credibility in numbers. Some large international foundations are spreading the theory and best practices of civil society, including the promotion of local individual philanthropy. In Mexico, they have joined with individuals, businesses, CSOs, and other institutions to form CEMEFI (see Chapter 3), which has carried out an important campaign of public education about the benefits of giving and volunteering. Fundación Esquel in Ecuador has done the same, and Argentina's Foro del Sector Social is about to. And CIVICUS is trying to raise the public consciousness worldwide.

Ethical standards and guidelines have become important in countries and cultures with a history of private giving. They are equally important—maybe even more so—in countries with little experience and history of personal philanthropy. Donors want to be treated fairly and need to know that funds will be solicited and used properly. The National Society of Fund Raising Executives, the largest U.S. association of fund developers, encourages the dissemination of a concise and incisive Donor Bill of Rights.

Enabling Environment

It is important to have technique, but more important to operate in a society with attitudes, policies, laws, regulations, and enforcement that promote giving and make civil society worthy of it. Tax treatment matters. U.S. civil society was greatly stimulated by changes to the tax laws in the 1930s that provided deductions for individuals making donations to a broad range of CSOs, as well as exempting CSOs from the payment of taxes. There is currently a debate about whether to continue these incentives or eliminate them, which would lower tax rates and thus leave more money in people's pockets, which in turn should increase their donations. This theory may prove true, but not according to large coalitions of CSOs that vehemently oppose it.

Whichever path may be better in the long run, incentives can certainly induce nongivers to give. This was taken to extremes in Peru in the 1980s, when in-kind donations to certain CSOs were a money-making proposition. Perhaps more typical is the current United States, where studies show that a tax deduction—in the context of 30–50 percent marginal tax rates—may not convince many nongivers to give, but it significantly increases the total amount of dollars contributed. Taxes on accumulated wealth and on inheritance also have great impacts on philanthropy.

But favorable tax treatment is pointless where there is widespread tax evasion. Civil society is not an alternative to the state. It needs the right amount of government—enough, at least, to collect taxes. No doubt the state intrudes too much in many parts of the world, for example by making it difficult to start and operate CSOs. But civil society can choke on unbridled freedom, as is the case in much of Eastern Europe. The lack of regulation and supervision has thrown civil society to the dogs of corruption. No wonder it has trouble there raising money from the public.

Culture

No CSO needs to be told that some or all of these observations on individual philanthropy are at odds with their culture. They already know it. Words of warning are for foreign donors and consultants. In some places, a personal gift has a deep meaning, perhaps demanding a reciprocity that a CSO cannot or should not fulfill. In many places, planned giving through wills and bequests carries such a notion of mortality and intrusion on family prerogatives that it is off-limits. Information about individual donors may be lacking, or its knowledge may be offensive: in some places, the only research on prospects is done by the secret police. Jealousies and rivalries can preclude donations to certain groups. Soliciting a friend may not seem like sharing a way to be useful, but using a friendship selfishly. Asking for help may appear degrading to asker and asked. Foreigners should bear all such cultural considerations in mind, and natives may want to consider experimenting with new appeals as the prevailing culture changes.

Marketing: Reaching Out to Donors

As noted earlier, a CSO does well to have a marketing mentality. When it comes to fund development, it can be considered a not-for-profit business and its donors are customers. To discover a market, or make one, the CSO has to make time for research and analysis. A classic way of approaching any market involves three basic premises: a business has to satisfy certain wants of its customers, customers who share a common characteristic tend to have similar wants, and it is more efficient to approach a homogenous group than the same number of disparate individuals.

First, segment the market.[11] Try to find patterns in current donations. Ask donors what they like about the organization, its mission, its activities, and its results. If some patterns within current donations can be identified, you will have discovered certain segments of the population that are prime candidates for fund development efforts. Ask others—friends, colleagues, wealthy people—what they would like to see in an organization like this one, and again look for patterns. What do similar CSOs do to attract donors?

Second, target one or more groups. Armed with some insights into current and potential donors, choose what groups or individuals you will make the effort to solicit. Although only so many things can be done at the same time, some CSOs may decide to approach a dozen different segments of the market at once.

Third, position your CSO. Decide how it will make sure it appeals—in word and in deed—to the interests of its target group or groups. How will it stand out from

HELPAGE INDIA

HelpAge India is the only secular voluntary organization working at the national level in India for the welfare of elderly individuals. Projects supported by the group include old age homes, rehabilitation programs, day care centers, and medical outreach programs. Funding for these projects has been possible only through the generosity of the public.

Direct mail is one of the fundraising techniques used by HelpAge India. The organization is constantly looking out for and acquiring addresses of potential donors through such means as newspaper advertisements. Relevant data are computerized and updated regularly. Potential donors are kept on the mailing list for up to five years.

Since direct mail involves only written communication, a good appeal letter is critically important. The appeal letter is sent first to a small segment of the target audience to test both its effectiveness and the mailing list being used. If the response rate is over 2 percent, a large-scale mailing follows.

A first-time donor is a "hot prospect" who must be nurtured. He or she is sent newsletters, annual reports, birthday greetings, brochures, project lists, and personal letters. The aim is to develop a close relationship with each donor and keep the person as informed about HelpAge India as possible.

The budget for direct mail is strictly monitored; HelpAge India has been able to keep the cost/benefit ratio at 1 to 5—that is, for every dollar spent on a mailing, five dollars is generated in donations. Each direct mail campaign is coded so that the response rate can be measured and analyzed. Donors are then assigned a priority according to their income, frequency of giving, and size of each donation; a donor profile is compiled based on these varying factors, and subsequent mailings are targeted so as to increase the donation revenue per mailing.

Direct mail now provides 15 percent of HelpAge India's funding. The donor base has increased from approximately 3,000 donors in 1990, when direct mail started, to more than 50,000 donors in 1997. The organizers attribute much of this success to careful planning, constant testing and evaluation of the mailing lists, and increased public awareness of the organization's objectives.

Case study prepared by A.W. Limaye, Director General, HelpAge India.

other CSOs in its field? Look at it from the donor's point of view: why should they give to you and not to another CSO that seems to be doing the same thing?

Fourth, pick when and where you will ask.

Key Best Practices

While fund development is often called an art, having scientific tools doubtless gives any organization a leg up on its competition. A CSO that represents a foreign dance ensemble, for instance, would clearly waste time and money approaching someone who has a track record of contributing only to local, not international or even national causes. Many CSOs would do well to spend time and money updating their data on current and potential donors, which begins with maintaining simple mailing lists. (See also Chapter 3.)

Mailing lists are essential not only for sending information to donors, but for keeping track of them in order to sooner or later ask for ever larger contributions. CSOs buy lists from other organizations and they create their own in numerous creative ways. For example, participants at an event may be eligible for a door prize if they fill out a card with their contact data; the organizing CSO keeps the cards at the end of the evening. Some CSOs produce fancy magazines and send them out—at or below cost—mainly because they know that avid readers will take the initiative to report any change of address.

The CSO has to position itself right in front of some donors. This is not a question of changing a mission to suit donors, but of thinking about what motivates likely supporters and then showing them how the CSO is already doing what they want. Of course, a CSO that is not attracting any support should re-examine its mission. Maybe it needs to create a niche for itself by adding a new program or by pouring existing resources into an existing activity to the point where it is deservedly famous in the field.

In any case, when it comes to asking for money, a CSO may find it worthwhile to shine a special light on what it does, or present different aspects of its work to different potential donors. The trend, as mentioned, is for donors to be more and more discriminating, preferring to give to a specific program, activity, beneficiary, or building rather than to "general purposes."

One way to help people feel a part of the CSO, and therefore more likely to contribute, is to invite them to sponsor some part of the program. The best known and most successful sponsorships involve the care of children, but museums, hospitals, and universities have learned to emphasize different departments to different target groups. Donors pledge a regular contribution and are moved to fulfill their promise when they receive periodic news and photographs about how their little girl has made it to high school, or their village now has clean water, or their inner-city neighborhood has an arts festival this year.

Once it settles on a strategy, the CSO can intelligently respond to the tactical question, When do we ask? Here are some standard answers.

- *All the Time:* This wears out donors and CSOs, all year long, as they lurch from crisis to crisis. It is not a good answer, according to experienced CSOs. It is wise to focus everyone's attention and energy for a limited time on a definite goal.

- *Annual Campaigns:* Every year, for a month or longer, the CSO concentrates on raising all the funds necessary to cover annual operating expenses, usually through a large number of small donations obtained at workplaces, at events, through the mails, on the phones, and perhaps using mass media publicity.

- *Capital Campaigns:* Occasionally, the CSO solicits donations for something new, typically for a building, but perhaps to start a new program or fund an endowment. A capital campaign may last years, never supplanting the annual campaigns on which the organization relies for steady income. The CSO invites

EDUCATIONAL COOPERATION SOCIETY, NIGERIA

In an effort to support leadership development by providing a more well rounded educational experience to young Nigerians, the Educational Cooperation Society (ECS) planned a campaign to raise US$1.4 million. The money would be used for permanent building facilities for the Irawo University Center, a private activities center and residence for students of the University of Ibadan.

The ECS positioned the campaign as a project of "distinction and excellence" in order to appeal to the high-status potential donors they would be targeting. To reach these wealthy individuals, fundraising committees called Patron Boards were established in Ibadan and Lagos. The Ibadan Boad was headed by an investor who also served as director of many local and international companies. The Lagos Board was a more diverse group of cosmopolitan Nigerians with some cultural or ethnic identity with Ibadan, including a widely respected retired Chief Justice as Chairman. Because of their prestige, both Boards were very successful in obtaining funding that would otherwise have been hard to get.

The ECS projected the "upscale" image of the project in several ways. The Board Members, highly respected in both social and corporate environments, gave the project instant name recognition. The world-class academic and physical level of the future Center was emphasized. A personal one-on-one appeal was used; correspondence was limited to letters from Board Members. This was very important, as a highly publicized campaign would have jarred with the serious academic nature and upscale image of the project. High-quality promotional materials were used, including a distinctive color brochure. Finally, donors were recognized with plaques that were hung in a room of the new building. The larger the donation, the larger and more prominent the room in which the plaque appeared.

Construction work was programmed in phases, with the common and dining room areas completed first, which allowed fundraising events in the facility before it was finished. Proud of the progress already made, Board Members toured potential donors around the building and encouraged them to help or to give more generously if they had already contributed. The project was completed in 1992.

Case study prepared by Timothy Keenley, Independent Consultant, Global Work-Ethic Fund.

wealthy people to exercise leadership for the broader public by making major gifts. Personal interviews are necessary.

- *On a Moment's Notice:* Some CSOs—for example, those doing relief work—are poised to launch mini-campaigns as soon as disaster strikes. They can use mass media, the mails, and the telephone effectively if they have already decided to adopt this strategy and have planned accordingly.

Copious information exists on the techniques of annual and capital campaigns, which are standard operating procedure for many CSOs all over the world, especially in North America, including Mexico, and Western Europe.

AL-AMAL CENTER FOR CANCER CARE, JORDAN

The Al-Amal Center for Cancer Care provides comprehensive cancer care to the people of Jordan and the surrounding region, including early detection, treatment, and rehabilitation of cancer patients, public awareness and education, and research.

The General Union of Voluntary Societies, under the guidance of its president, Dr. Abdullah El-Khatib, formed a National Task Force for the Establishment of Al-Amal Center in 1984. Following the death of his daughter, Dalia, from leukemia at the age of 13, Dr. El-Khatib recognized the urgent need for a cancer center to provide effective cancer treatment then available only in industrial countries and at high cost.

Dr. El-Khatib and the Task Force developed a capital campaign to raise the estimated US$30 million needed for the center. With the help of media and word of mouth, Jordanians became aware of the Center's goal. Many wealthy individuals began to donate generously, and other contributions flooded into the General Union of Voluntary Societies, which also contributed a great deal. About 25,000 students joined a nationwide "Knock on the Door" fundraising campaign. Construction began in 1989, after some US$2 million had been collected.

The second tactical question is, Where do we ask?

- *In Person:* The larger the desired gift, the more personal should be the contact with the potential donor. In some areas of the world, however, even small donations are received in person. Such is the case where the mails are unreliable. People make a one-time or a periodic pledge, and the CSO sends out carefully screened and supervised volunteers to collect and also to give something in return, for they are trained to keep donors informed about what is new and interesting at the CSO.

- *At the Workplace:* CSOs can convince employers not only to handle the administrative chores of a collection, often by a payroll deduction, but even to solicit employees. For many companies, it is a point of pride to have "100 percent participation." But for some workers, it must be said, this is irritating. Workplace appeals can take place almost anywhere. In a federated appeal, some CSOs choose to rely on an intermediary organization to solicit funds from certain donors, and to divide up the proceeds according to a mutually agreed formula, which can reflect various parameters: the size of a given CSO, the number of direct beneficiaries it has, the amount of money it raises on its own, and so on. Donors appreciate not being solicited by great numbers of organizations. They feel confident about giving to a large, trusted intermediary. For the CSOs, this arrangement provides an inexpensive way to raise funds. In Canada, it is the most cost-effective method of all.[12]

An Al-Amal Center Support Week held in 1992 under the patronage of His Majesty King Hussein and Her Majesty Queen Noor was one of the largest Jordanian charity fundraising efforts ever. It included another "Knock on the Door" campaign, as well as a charity march of thousands of people from Al-Hussein Sports City to Al-Amal Center. The week ended with a 16-hour live telethon, in which Jordanians donated more than US$10 million, the largest amount in the nation's history. In 1993, United Way International named Dr. El-Khatib "Volunteer Fundraiser of the Year."

Almost 26,000 donors contributed to the Al-Amal Center, 6,500 of whom did so in the memory of a loved one lost to cancer. Today, the center includes a 120-bed inpatient hospital complete with an Intensive Care Unit, Children's Section, Women's Center, and Bone Marrow Transplantation Unit. Outpatient chemotherapy, diagnostic radiology, and various other advanced testing are also available.

Obviously important to the success of the capital campaign was the commitment to the cause and the excellent preparation and planning by all involved. A clearly defined goal gave potential donors something to aim for, and the fact that so many people had friends and loved ones with cancer helped create a special sense of national sympathy and unity.

Case study prepared by Dina Ra'ad and Sady Shakaa, Al-Amal Cancer Center.

- *At Events:* The value of a charity ball, a concert, or a walkathon lies not so much in the money raised but in the publicity generated and the institutional capacity built—that is, by volunteers and talents rising to the surface in the press of events. This is why they still take place even where they are the least cost-effective approach available, which is the case in Canada in general and for many CSOs in the North and West. For their publicity value, special events typically launch and close campaigns.

- *Through Direct Mail:* This term refers to mailing appeals to carefully targeted potential donors. Building up a profitable mailing list takes time, money, and brains. In the United States, Canada, and the United Kingdom, where direct mail is widespread and scientific, a well-managed effort may take two or three years to pay off—but then it does so handsomely. Obviously, where the mail is unreliable or people cannot be located, this technique is inappropriate.

- *On the Phone:* Telephone calls seem to be most effective in helping existing donors increase their gifts, reclaiming donors who no longer respond to direct mail, and providing some personal contact with small donors. It is an art form that in some countries is regulated by governments, particularly regarding "cold calls"—those to individuals who have never supported the CSO before. The phones and mails are becoming reliable for use in campaigns in the South and East. Their use may be saturated in the North and West.

GOLDEN BRANCH FOUNDATION, HUNGARY

Aranyag Alapitvany—The Golden Branch Foundation—was established in 1995 by a private film company and by prominent Hungarian individuals, including a member of Parliament, a high-ranking official in the Ministry of Welfare, a university professor, and a television producer. Its mission is to support and improve the children's health care system in Hungary by raising money through a highly publicized media campaign.

In May 1995, the most popular artists entertained Hungarian families for six hours during a telethon broadcast on national television, the first ever in the country's history. Viewers were able to call in their pledges using 15 telephone and 3 fax lines. They could also bid on many valuable items that had been donated for the campaign. Some US$300,000 collected during the telethon was distributed among 21 children's hospitals throughout Hungary. During the campaign, The Golden Branch Foundation also received in-kind donations of hospital equipment valued at more than US$170,000.

In 1996, the Foundation introduced new ideas in its fundraising campaign. People could send contributions by check, but since personal checks are not used in Hungary, special checks were made available in every post office. The Foundation received more than 12,000 checks and raised approximately US$100,000. Another new initiative connected the main televised campaign to local fundraising campaigns organized in five other cities to benefit children's hospitals in the respective communities.

The success of The Golden Branch Foundation is surprising in a country where a large part of the population has become impoverished during the past five years. It may be due in part to the lack of competition from other NGOs in public fundraising, but it can also be attributed to the strong support and influence of the media.

Case study translated by Kati Zsamboki of NESsT from Web site—http://www.elender.hu/aranyag/index.html

- *In the Media:* Newspapers, magazines, radio, television, and the Internet are used to solicit contributions, to announce campaigns, and to publicize the virtues of a CSO or of civil society in general. Traditional mass media normally make sense for large, established organizations or for those that can capitalize on a newsworthy occurrence and can afford to hire media experts. Newspapers and magazines have the most impact when an emergency is in the public eye. People will have already decided to give; they only need to be told how. Free, "public service" time on radio and television is a boon to civil society. Large CSOs throughout the world also find it cost-effective to pay for advertisements, documentaries, entertainment specials, and telethons. The World Wide Web on the Internet is effective for disseminating information, especially of a long-term nature. Grant-making CSOs have been inundated with requests for information via the Web, however, and the same thing could happen to any unprepared CSO. It is not yet a proven way to solicit resources, but the smart CSO will monitor developments in this medium.

Major Conclusions for Practitioners

- CSOs should take the time to find the needs of certain donors and fill them.
- A CSO needs to dedicate resources to research and take the time to think and plan, not choosing tactics until it settles on a strategy.
- Special thought should be given to targeting the following groups of proven good donors:
  - volunteers and adults who were volunteers when they were young;
  - people aged 55–65 (before 55, they are too busy making money to think about giving it away, while after 65, they are too insecure to give it, or too tired to think about it);
  - religious people; and
  - current and former voters and members of civic associations.
- To obtain major gifts, someone in the CSO needs to win the confidence of the prospective donor.

The Donor as a Respected Customer

There is but one essential in donor relations: respect. As noted earlier, there is always a motive behind a donation. Philanthropy is a transaction. The CSO wants, to put it bluntly, money or goods or services. What do donors want? As Dorothea Leighton put it, every individual needs to feel that he or she is "a worthwhile member of a worthwhile group."[13] Because you respect your "prospects," you offer them the opportunity to join you in making a difference in the world. Let us dissect this phrase.

First, the opportunity. The main reason that people do not donate to civil society is that no one asks them. In North America and Western Europe, individuals are twice as likely to give and volunteer if they are asked to do so. Societies whose tradition of generosity is different from this philanthropy, or where it has been interrupted, may want to take note of this basic observation.

The second point concerns "joining" the CSO. People give to people, meaning two things. First, donors mean to give not to the CSO itself but to the ultimate beneficiaries of its activities: the poor little girl, or the proud new voters, or those whose humanity has been enriched by the chamber music ensemble. Although the importance of "positioning the CSO" has been discussed, successful CSOs do not put themselves in front

SOLIDARIOS, LATIN AMERICA AND THE CARIBBEAN

Solidarios, the Council of American Development Foundations, is a Latin American and Caribbean umbrella organization of 26 National Development Foundations (NDFs). The NDFs are based in various countries throughout the region and provide financial and technical assistance to low-income microentreprenuers in urban areas and to farmers in rural areas.

Since the organization's inception in the 1960s, a key characteristic has been the participation of business executives, professionals, and civic leaders in the organizational structure and decisionmaking process. This has been fundamental to the nature of the NDFs, since their institutional mission is not only to improve the quality of life and promote the empowerment of low-income groups, but also to involve private-sector individuals in the social, economic, and democratic development of society.

All members of an NDF have the right to vote in the general assemblies and to be elected to the Board of Directors, since democratic participation is essential to the success of each NDF. Individual members agree to pay an annual fee as follows: regular member, US$100; sponsor, US$165; and patron, US$225. Memberships for organizations in these same categories are US$250, US$560, and US$870. Each member is then listed by category in the Annual Report. They receive a plaque indicating their membership, which they can display in their office or home. Also, lapel pins are given to members and can be worn at special events, meetings, and elsewhere.

The NDFs hold membership campaigns fairly regularly in order to recruit people who will bring new ideas to the organization. Typically, Board Members are responsible for recruiting new members by contacting friends, customers, suppliers, and so on by mail or by telephone, although help from the members at large is always appreciated.

A typical NDF may have 300 members and may collect approximately US$150,000 in membership fees each year, which is often enough to cover administrative costs. Although the income generated by membership fees is certainly welcome, it should always be remembered that the most important purpose of membership is to allow the exercise of social responsibility by all members of the community.

of donors. Center stage belongs to the people they are serving. Publicity materials center on what these people accomplish, not on how the CSO has some nice programs. The tone should be positive, even when discussing disasters and poverty: "We are improving the situation; join us." The CSO certainly does not talk about its own leaky roof and mortgage payments. Donors have enough problems of their own.

Second, people do not throw their money away, but they may choose to entrust it to somebody. The CSO can only win their trust by operating effectively and efficiently, something it is worth sending out frequent reminders about. Large donations come from people that someone in the CSO—an executive, a board member, even a paid consultant—has befriended over the years. Fund developers sometimes talk of "cultivating donors," and some CSOs recoil at a phrase that smacks of opportunism, manipulation, and coldness. But for fund developers who are successful over many years, this is just a term of art. They work for causes that they believe in, they like people, they share their accomplishments and dreams with them. And people respond.

If they respond positively, you thank them immediately. If they say no, you still thank them, and you send requests and thank-yous for as long as you can afford the rejection, especially when your studies indicate there should be a match between you and them. For those who do contribute, express your gratitude in the most personal way possible, all things considered. In the United States, it is said that if you thank a donor seven times this year, they will give more next year. There are certain formulas of gratitude used to acknowledge the hierarchy of gifts—from form letters to newsletters to personal P.S.'s on letters to plaques to names of buildings—but generous donors do not like being treated like Pavlov's dogs.

Fund development is a transaction in which two parties help each other. Compared with satisfying businesses, foundations, and governments, satisfying individuals is easy. Organizations want justifications and documentations, while individuals are content with a brochure and some photos—and increasingly, for sophisticated donors, some assurance of cost-effectiveness. But the main point holds true: individuals, more than other types of supporters, are looking for something for the heart.

Key Best Practices

Wise CSO leaders never want to lose a donor, so they lavish attention on beneficiaries, present and past. These participants, patients, theatergoers, students, alumni, and so on may be able to return a favor in the future. In any case, people who are grateful are civil society's products. They are what donors want to hear about, so the CSO should keep in touch with them.

As a most basic sign of respect for donors, CSOs should try to make it easy for them to make contributions. The remainder of this section discusses some of the many instruments available for this.

Collections, whether in public places or door-to-door, are most successful where the CSO already enjoys credibility with the public. It is in the best interest of the organization to screen and supervise those doing the collecting. The more badges, pamphlets, and paraphernalia the solicitors carry, the more credible they seem.

Automatic payment systems are successful everywhere, and are most necessary where monthly reminders to donors do not arrive in the mails, where sending money through the Post Office is not feasible, or where people are plugged into banks, are technical and organized, or just like the convenience. If the CSO can have people accept a monthly

AIGLON COLLEGE, SWITZERLAND

Aiglon College, a British international boarding school in Chesihres-Villars, Switzerland, is attended each year by approximately 300 students between the ages of 9 and 18. Many of the 3,000 alumni continue their education in some of the world's finest universities.

Alumni have an important role in the life of every independent school. Aiglon clearly benefits from the monetary contributions made by alumni. Although its primary source of income is school fees, personal solicitations from parents and alumni since 1994 have raised more than SFr 4.2 million (about US$2.9 million). Since the inception of the Alumni Annual Fund program in 1996, more than SFr 100,000 (US$70,000) has been contributed by approximately 100 alumni.

When previous attempts to solicit funds from American alumni were unsuccessful, the college hired a Campaign Director with U.S. independent school experience to manage its capital campaign for facilities and endowment, as well as to begin the Alumni Annual Fund. A Campaign Coordinator was hired to assist with database management and communications, and the former Headmaster and his wife joined the endeavor part-time to focus on enhancing the life-long relationship between alumni and the school.

Individual alumni have had a very important role in the planning and imple-

charge against their credit card or bank account, they have a long-term donor. (The financial institution requires a certain number of participants for such a program to work.)

Affinity credit cards bear the name of a CSO that has made a deal with the financial institution that issues it: the CSO promises to have a lot of people apply to participate in the card, and the issuer promises to give a specified percentage of all charges to the CSO. This has been wildly successful for the CSOs that first introduced it. After two or three years, however, as lots of other organizations join in, it can become just one more little source of income. But even in the competitive atmosphere of Brazil, Abrinq (a large foundation) covers 50 percent of its operating costs from affinity credit cards by being focused, professional, and aggressive in its marketing of them.

Payroll deductions are most often a tool of the federated appeals mentioned earlier. Although declining in popularity in the United States, they are still important there and in Canada, and are taking hold elsewhere. The Charta 77 Foundation in the Czech Republic is happy to have recently discovered this tool.[14] The ups and downs of payroll deductions and federated appeals may be part of an evolution of philanthropy that shows itself to be at different stages in different countries.

The most sensitive issue in fund development worldwide is bequests to CSOs and other provisions by the dying to support favorite causes. In most cultures, the topic

mentation of the Alumni Association and the Alumni Annual Fund. The association President secured the commitment of the Board of Governors, and enlisted a volunteer Alumni Association Executive Committee, including the Alumni Annual Fund Chairman. These two volunteers drove the policy and implementation decisions, including fundraising goals. Their commitment to Aiglon College and to the purposes of the Alumni Annual Fund as well as their own example were the essential ingredients in motivating other alumni to volunteer and to make personal gifts to Aiglon College.

They discovered that non-American alumni were less knowledgeable and therefore less confident about asking their peers to contribute. It was important to offer them a script they could use for telephone calls and personal meetings; each possible objection from a prospective alumni donor was identified, and responses were prepared for the volunteer.

The results and benefits of creating an Alumni Association and beginning an Alumni Annual Fund have been significant. Now more than 40 percent of the Board of Governors at Aiglon are alumni, and alumni are more actively involved in identifying prospective students from their communities. A new source of income has been created with enormous opportunity for growth, making Aiglon College less dependent on fees and therefore more financially stable.

Case study prepared by Mary K. Carrasco, Aiglon College Campaign Director.

cannot be mentioned. In Anglo-Saxon countries, however, it has become a major topic in fund development, and planned giving is becoming big business. In those countries, the personal and tax implications of retiring from work and life have become quite convoluted, and they are not taboo. People facing those realities welcome advice from someone they trust about how they can provide for themselves, their family members, and the causes they have come to support. CSOs explain planned gifts to them.

Donors can, for instance, bequeath an asset to the CSO and still receive a fixed income based on it; when they die, the asset goes to the CSO. Naturally, financial and legal arrangements and instruments vary from country to country, and CSOs hire experts to advise them and prospective donors. Groups interested in this approach should also be prepared to deal with the various types of bequests that may be received, including property, shares, and even livestock.

Effective fund development in the North and West helps small new donors become major donors over time. In a modification of the classic Giving Pyramid, the Golden Pyramid has many steps of equal height, each of which represents a donor. The base is a huge square step containing a mass of solid gold, representing one donor's extremely large contribution, which inspires others to give—albeit lesser amounts.

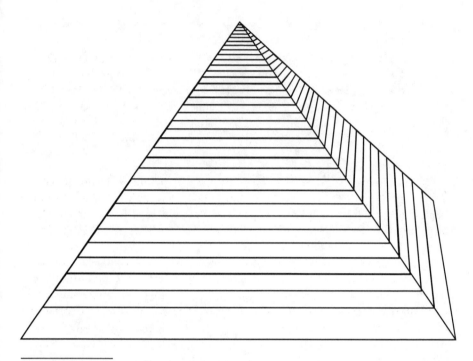

© The Global Work-Ethic Fund, Washington, 1996.

Toward the top, the many small steps of relatively little value represent the many small, first-time gifts of money and volunteer work contributed by the general public. Annual campaigns and emergency appeals are typically the times when new donors are found. Knowing that it costs six times more to recruit than to retain a donor and that 75 percent of tomorrow's big donors are today's little donors (based on experience in the United States), organizations allocate proportional money, time, and effort in making them feel appreciated. People like to receive a membership, which gives them special privileges or discounts, for example, or front-row seats at the events of a performing arts group. And just being listed as a member makes them feel special. CSOs, for their part, like the way memberships create a lasting bond with donors.

People who donate their time feel a special bond when the CSO treats them well—they feel like appreciated, albeit unpaid, employees. When they are not taken for granted, volunteers become prime candidates to add cash to their already valuable contribution.

Capital campaigns are usually the time when the CSO makes a concerted effort to help many donors make a big move down the steps. They must be escorted: a personal relationship with them is critical. On the way down the pyramid, it becomes clear that a lot of the golden steps are really made of stocks and bonds and real estate. The huge blocks of gold at the base are planned gifts that involve wills and bequests.

Twenty years ago, in mature CSOs with well-functioning individual philanthropy programs, 20 percent of individual donors accounted for 80 percent of the total funds. Now, a ratio of 10/90 is common, and a 5/95 split has occurred in the billion-dollar campaigns of some universities. Still, the top of the pyramid, consisting of

BRITISH ORTHOPAEDIC ASSOCIATION

The British Orthopaedic Association (BOA) was founded in 1917 and represents approximately 2,000 orthopedic surgeons throughout Great Britain. In response to reductions in government funding earmarked for medical specialties, its members created a subsidiary fundraising arm—the Wishbone Appeal, later renamed the Wishbone Trust—to raise money for innovative research in the specialty of orthopedics.

Grateful patients are an obvious constituency for any medical cause looking for a supporter base. Since U.K. data confidentiality law prohibits giving patient names and addresses to organizations, the BOA asked orthopedic surgeons for help; they wrote to their own patients and invited them to take part in the first "Great Hip Walk" in 1989 to raise money for the Wishbone Trust.

In 1991, a second walk raised US$2.2 million and an initial database of approximately 8,000 people was compiled. One striking fact was that 20 percent of the participants were 75 to 99 years old; 75 percent were over normal retirement age. With these statistics in mind, it was natural to suggest the use of planned giving as a fund development strategy. The form of planned giving that was chosen was simple bequest pledges, whereby donors pledge a share of their estate to the Wishbone Trust.

A fundraising professional hired by the BOA determined that March was the month when many people wrote their wills. In January, mailings were sent out specifically on the subject of bequests for the Wishbone Trust. Of the 8,000 individuals contacted, more than 100 pledged a share of their estate in their wills. Though the number may not seem large, research has shown that the average share of an estate donated to a voluntary organization is more than US$43,200. Hence these 100 pledges could eventually bring more than US$4.3 million. An unexpected bonus was that cash donations totalling US$6,400 came in with the pledges, easily covering the cost of the initial mailing.

Planned giving is clearly not for organizations looking for a quick way to generate revenue. The average time between a bequest made to the Wishbone Trust and its receipt is 4.2 years, with cash bequests averaging US$3,520 and estates worth on average US$43,200.

Since older individuals often have a different concept of money, it is better to ask them for a percentage of their estate rather than for a specific amount—"5 percent" seems like less than "$500" even if the two amounts are exactly the same. It was also found that donors "gave with their heart and not with their head," so complex explanations of the tax advantages they would receive through planned giving were unnecessary.

newer and smaller givers, is needed for the money it represents, for the larger future gifts it promises, and as a proud and encouraging sign to major donors that the CSO is popular and successful.

Major Conclusions for Practitioners

Many of the above best practices come from the experience of large CSOs in industrial countries. Nevertheless, some conclusions can be drawn that are more universal.

- Offer people an opportunity to do something worthwhile.
- To find out what donors are looking for, put yourself in their shoes. Listen to them, and spend time with them.
- Tell them about your beneficiaries.
- Appeal to the heart as well as the head.
- Thanks come from the heart, and have an eye to the future.
- Thank donors seven times a year.
- Soliciting major gifts from individuals is most cost-effective, but small gifts have their place: major donors like to see that they are not alone, and minor donors can become major.
- Be aware of the variety of vehicles available to help donors be more generous.
- In appropriate cultures, help them provide for their passing.

The Role of the Board and Development Committee

The more people inside a CSO, the more friends it has outside. This can translate into more money. So a Development Committee is important.

The executive director or director cannot do it all. That person has other key responsibilities, and in addition, may not be very good at fund development. Donors, for their part, respond most generously to the right person asking for the right gift. The director cannot know every potential donor well enough to know what the right gift is, and cannot possibly be the right person for every potential donor, although civil society does boast of many charismatic founders who come close.

In addition, a good number of donors hesitate to give if the request comes from someone whose salary more or less depends on the answer. Staff and consultants just provide support services to the prestigious volunteers who do the asking. They can provide moral support during visits to potential donors, but they try to stay in the background.

Any director needs six good volunteers. At least, that's the case in the United States. Successful campaigns, no matter how big or small the CSO or how many tens of thousands of donors they reach, need only some 50 key supporters, and these can be discovered by just a half-dozen committed solicitors. The directors, however, need to find, train, manage, and constantly encourage these people.

Where to find the soliciting six? These volunteers are not like those who stuff envelopes. Some may already be members of the Board of Directors (the shorthand used here for the formal governing body of CSOs that have legal personality).

Shouldn't those who are legally responsible for the operations of a CSO feel responsible for its financial health?

This assumes that they are on the Board to help. In some countries, this is not always the case; government officials may be there to inspect if not to control the CSO. No matter what the country, many CSOs do not seem to appoint "real" people to Boards, just their names. This can be useful in raising money, but other CSOs find it more helpful to align themselves with the classic paradigm of the effective, functional Board: one third wisdom, one third work, and one third wealth. Some are there for their advice, some for their energy, and some mainly for their donations.

All Board members are asked to help in some way with the financial campaigns, according to their time, talents, and interests. Even those who do not respond with work or wisdom are asked to make a cash contribution as a good example to prospective donors. Board members who eventually ask other people for resources are filled with confidence and authority if they have previously emptied their own pockets.

Donors will follow a leader. Rightly or wrongly, they will give time to people with whom they feel comfortable, or whose very presence in their home or office flatters them. Thus it is important to have solicitors who are well known and admired in the social circles of the prospects. More rightly than wrongly, donors will entrust money to people whom they admire.

Of course, this sketch of a CSO is of the ideal. Reality is not so rosy, and civil society organizations have always been characterized by a tension in leadership. There is the charismatic founder and/or director—charismatic, but often chaotic. For the sake of continuing the mission, there is the Board—permanent, but often plodding. The golden mean for a CSO is not the valley formed where weakness digs in against weakness. When there is good will, strength builds on strength, and a peak rises up; there is effective association for the common good—civil society.

Key Best Practices

Boards of Directors are delicate beasts; they have authority over the Director, but they usually do not know as much and they can never do as much. In terms of the Board's role in asking for resources from individuals, a few important lessons have been learned. A steady turnover of members is not a bad thing. People get tired and stale. It is common to have staggered term limits for all members—say, three years—with perhaps one possible renewal term voted on by the rest of the Board. This makes for a gracious way of saying good-bye to members. An informal, less demanding Advisory Board can be a holding station for ex-members whose contributions should be retained, as well as for promising new members whose commitment needs to be examined.

It is helpful to make sure that incoming members of the Board know what is expected of them regarding meetings, financial contributions, fund development, and so on. Sometimes they even sign an acknowledgment of having been informed of these matters.

It is common practice to form a Development Committee—the name varies—to supervise a fund development campaign, whether annual or capital. Being a committee of the Board, this consists of some members and perhaps some outsiders. Everyone is on the lookout for others who will help with not only their money but

MEXICAN RURAL DEVELOPMENT FOUNDATION

In Mexico City in 1963, some members of the Union de Empresarios Catolicos (Catholic Union of Businessmen) set out to find solutions to some of the nation's many social problems. They formed the Central de Servicios Populares, Asociacion Civil (SERPAC) in 1965 to provide technical assistance, offer training, and promote educational, cultural, and social activities for the rural population.

By 1969 SERPAC wanted to expand its program in order to have a wider impact. The members organized the Fundacion Mexicana para el Desarrollo Rural (FMDR), or Mexican Rural Development Foundation, as an institution of private individuals to carry out programs on a national scale. The basic motivations behind the genesis of the FMDR were an understanding of poor rural living conditions, the drive of Christian solidarity, and the business identity of its members.

Three types of people are sought as Board Members: those with economic resources, those who possess social prestige, and those who have time for the cause. They are asked to contribute approximately US$50 each month to FMDR—or more if they are able. The presence of highly regarded businessmen and women on the Board of Directors gives FMDR legitimacy when facing donors and state

their time. The staff of the CSO should be concerned about training committee members—or having them trained by experts—about the techniques of fund development, including how to ask someone for money. As common sense dictates, studies show that the money raised increases proportionally with the number of people who ask for it. Leadership is crucial to the success of the campaign.

Some CSOs charge a free-floating entity, one with no legal responsibility, with the task of fund development. It sometimes is lethargic, because people best respond when they know they are responsible. The arrangement only works if the group has ardent adherents of the mission who do not mind being left out of policymaking. Educating and motivating them may be a constant concern of the CSO's executives.

During a fund development campaign, the committee holds regular meetings. A intensive capital campaign of 6–12 months may demand biweekly or weekly gatherings in which progress is examined and goals are set for each solicitor, or each captain of each team of solicitors, until the next meeting. The goal is to constantly expand and refine a list of possible donors, each of whom has at least one piece of data written next to their name: Who will ask them for the contribution? And often, How much will they be asked for?

Major Conclusions for Practitioners

- Passionate and knowledgeable leadership on the Board of Directors will raise money for the CSO.
- The executive director of the CSO should want Board members to feel responsible for fund development, and should help them to feel this way.
- The right person should ask the right person for the right gift. To obtain

authorities; they have also played an influential role in opening up the Mexican political system to the social problems present throughout the country.

FMDR Board Members are critical to the success of the organization and are expected to meet the following obligations:

- study the philosophy and methodology of FMDR,
- visit at least one of FMDR's farmer groups each year,
- attend monthly Board meetings,
- attend FMDR's national events,
- participate as a delegated Board member and/or in a work Committee,
- recruit new donors,
- disseminate the work of FMDR in the community and in their social circles,
- financially support FMDR,
- contribute ideas for improving the FMDR Movement, and
- take five friends on a field visit every year.

Case study prepared by Magdalena A. Wolinski, Consultant, CIVICUS.

large donations, influential people should be on the Board and its Development Committee.

- The more who ask, the more you get.
- The Board should tell prospective members what is expected of them, and then demand it.

Notes

1. Peter F. Drucker, *Managing the Non-profit Organization* (New York: Harper Business, 1992), p. 99.

2. Salamon, L.M., and H.K. Anheier, *The Emerging Sector: The Nonprofit Sector in Comparative Perspective: An Overview* (Baltimore, Md.: Institute for Policy Studies, The John Hopkins University, 1994).

3. Discussion of Islam largely based on Amani Kandil, "The Status of the Third Sector in the Arab Region," in Miguel Darcy de Oliveira and Rajesh Tandon, coords., *Citizens: Strengthening Global Civil Society* (Washington, D.C.: Civicus, 1994), p. 117.

4. Ann E. Kaplan, ed., *Giving USA* (AAFRC Trust for Philanthropy, 1996).

5. Salamon and Anheir, op. cit. note 2, chap. 4.

6. Data are for 1995, according to a Gallup Organization poll for Independent Sector, cited in *Chronicle of Philanthropy*, 17 October 1996. Donations for specific income ranges vary from year to year. In 1993, for example, the top income group of donors gave more than the lowest income group. But generally, for those who make donations, the lower the income, the greater the percentage given away.

7. Charities Aid Foundation, *International Giving and Volunteering* (London: 1994).

8. Numbers for Asia from Yuko Iida Frost, "Managing Strategic Changes of American NGOs in Asia," paper for 1995 Annual ARNOVA Conference, November 1995.

9. Ewa Les, "The Voluntary Sector in Post-Communist East Central Europe: From Small Circles of Freedom to Civil Society," in de Oliveira and Tandon, op. cit. note 3, p. 220.

10. Salamon and Anheir, op. cit. note 2, p. 91.

11. Cf. Drucker, op. cit. note 1, pp. 73–94.

12. Interview with Patrick Johnston of the Canadian Centre for Philanthropy, May 1997.

13. Cited in Harold Seymour, *Designs for Fund-Raising* (Rockville, Md.: The Taft Group, 1988).

14. Aftab Hladíková, "Fundraising in an Emerging Country," paper delivered at the International Conference on Fund Raising of the National Society of Fund Raising Executives, Dallas, Texas, March 1997.

RESOURCE GUIDE
Documents

This list covers a few of the books used in writing this chapter. There are thousands of books on fund development and civil society written for audiences in the North and West. The Foundation Center is a good place to begin learning about them.

Charities Aid Foundation, *International Giving and Volunteering* (London: 1994).

Doyle, Liam, ed., *Funding Europe's Solidarity: Resourcing Foundations, Associations, Voluntary Organizations and NGOS in the Member States of the European Union* (Brussels: Association for Innovative Cooperation in Europe, 1996).

International Federation of Red Cross and Red Crescent Societies, *Resource Development Handbook* (Geneva: 1994).

Kelley, Daniel Q., *Dinheiro para Sua Causa*, Textnovo Editora. (An expanded version of the Spanish-language original, adapted and translated for Brazil.)

National Society of Fund Raising Executives Institute, "Glossary of Fund-Raising Terms," 1986.

Seymour, Harold J., *Designs for Fund-Raising* (Rockville, Md.: The Taft Group, 1988).

Sherman, Jeremy, and David Bonbright, *Non-Profits: The New Resourcefulness, Changermakers*, Special Issue 1996 (Calcutta, India: Ashoka Foundation, 1996).

Wilson-Grau, R./SAT, "Alternative Sources of Income for Novib Partners," Novib, Amsterdam, 1994.

Periodicals

Chronicle of Philanthropy
PO Box 1989
Marion, OH 43305
Tel: (1-800) 347-6969
E-mail:
subscriptions@philanthropy.com
Web site: http://www.philanthropy.com
  Excellent biweekly newspaper, mainly but not exclusively on the United States.

International Philanthropy, a publication of the World Fundraising Council
24 Concord St.
Fairfield, CT 06430
Tel: (1-203) 319-1011
Fax: (1-203) 319-1012
E-mail: jfrost@cda.com
  Outstanding newsletter with news and commented lists of resources, including Internet.

Tercer Sector
Serrano 2297
1425 Buenos Aires
Argentina
Tel: (54-1) 832-1762 or 832-7996 or 832-7985
E-mail: sector3@satlink.com
Web site: http: //www.intr.net/com-intar/sector3
  Mostly Argentina, and mostly on CSO programs; a little on fund development.

Case Study Contacts

Richard M. McDonald
Headmaster
Aiglon College
1885 Chesihres-Villars
Switzerland
Tel: (41-24) 495-2721
Fax: (41-24) 495-2811
E-mail:RMMCDONALD@
    compuserve.com

William B. Cargill
President
**Aiglon College Alumni
Association**
67 Westway Road
Southport, CT 06490
Tel: (1-203) 845-6206
Fax: (1-203) 849-8463
E-mail: bcargill@actmedia-hq.com

Dina Ra'ad
Director, Public and International
Relations
Al-Amal Cancer Center
P.O. Box 1269 Al-Jubeiha
Amman 11941
Jordan
Tel: (962-6) 849387
Fax: (962-6) 835868

Aranyag Alapitvany
Taltos u. 4
1123 Budapest
Hungary
Tel: (36-1) 175-9968
Fax: (36-1) 175-2444
Web site: http://www.elender.hu/
    aranyag/index.html

Russell Vallance
Fund-Raising Consultant
former Director of The Wishbone
Trust of the **British Orthopaedic
Association**
6A Bridge Square

Farnham, Surrey GU97QR
United Kingdom
Tel: (44-1252) 737-346

for **Educational Cooperation
Society:**
Timothy Keenley
Global Work-Ethic Fund
1521 16th Street, NW
Washington, DC 20036
Tel: (1-202) 232-1600
Fax: (1-202) 232-1533

**Fundacion Mexicana para el
Desarrollo Rural**
La Quemada 40
Colonia Navarte
C.P. 03020 Mexico City
Mexico
Tel: (52-5) 530-0442
Fax: (52-5) 519-2054

A.W. Limaye
Director General
HelpAge India
C-14, Qutab Institutional Area
New Delhi 110016
India
Tel: (91-11) 696 6641
Fax: (91-11) 685 2916

Enrique A. Fernández
Secretary General
Solidarios, Council of American
Development Foundations
Calle 6 #10 Paraíso
P.O. Box 620
Santo Domingo
Dominican Republic
Tel: (1-809) 549-5111
Fax: (1-809) 544-0550
E-mail: solidarios@codetel.net.do

Promoters of CSOs and Local Philanthropy

Esquel Group Foundation
1003 K St. N.W., Ste. 800
Washington, DC 20001
Tel: (1-202) 347-1796
Fax: (1-202) 347-1797
U.S. member of a network of CSOs in several Latin American countries; promotes civil society, including fund development for CSOs.

Foundation Center
79 Fifth Avenue
New York, NY 10003
Tel: (1-212) 620-4320
Fax: (1-212) 691-1828
Web site: http://www.fdncenter.org
Important resource center on all aspects of civil society, especially fund development.

Global Work-Ethic Fund
1521 16th St. N.W.
Washington DC 20036
Tel: (1-202) 232-1600
Fax: (1-202) 232-1533
E-mail: info@globalfund.org
Web site: http://globalfund.org
Advisory service on fund development from local and U.S.-based sources.

International Center for Not-for-Profit Law
1511 K St., N.W. Ste.723
Washington, DC 20005
Tel: (1-202) 624-0766
Fax: (1-202) 624-0767
E-mail: dcicnl@aol.com
Web site: http://www.icnl.org

International Fund Raising Group
352 Kennington Rd.
London, SE11 4LD
United Kingdom
Well known for training seminars on fund development in Europe and Latin America.

National Center for Nonprofit Boards
2000 L St., N.W., Ste. 411
Washington, DC 20036
Tel: (1-202) 452-6262
Fax: (1-202) 452-6299
E-mail: ncnb@ncnb.org
Gopher://ncnb.org:7002
Worldwide training of staff and Boards of CSOs.

National Charities Information Bureau
Web site: http://www.give.org
The National Charities Information Bureau's mission is to promote informed giving and charitable integrity, to enable more contributors to make sound giving decisions, and to do all we can to encourage giving to charities that need and merit support.

National Society of Fund Raising Executives/NSFRE
1101 King St., Ste. 700
Alexandria VA 22314
Tel: (1-703) 519-8469
Fax: (1-703) 684-0540
E-mail: resctr@nsfre.org
Web site: http://www.nsfre.org
The world's largest professional association of fund developers; chapters in Canada and Mexico, as well as the United States.

NonProfit Forum
http: //ourworld.compuserve.com/
    homepages/nonprofit
    Libraries containing resources
    on topics including trusteeship,
    leadership, management, planning,
    evaluation, marketing, legislative
    issues, and a heavy emphasis on
    philanthropy, fundraising, and
    planned giving; membership is
    US$15/month or US$150/year.

UK Fundraising
Web site: http://www.fundraising.co.uk
    A wealth of information and links
    for U.K. and international fund
    development.

University of Washington Development Office
Web site: http://weber.u.washington.
        edu/~dev/others.html
    Links to alumni associations and
    university fund development offices,
    so you can see what others are up to.

Chapter 5

Building Grassroots Citizens' Organizations

Fernand Vincent and William LeClere

The Building Blocks of Development

By the early 1990s, sustainable development had begun to emerge as the new development paradigm guiding the actions of development policymakers and practitioners. "Ordinary" people moved from being the objects of development—-passive entities to whom development happened—-to its principal subjects: empowered actors with political as well as social and economic rights who participate in defining their problems, setting priorities for their solution, and, when appropriate, acting to resolve them.

The wave of democratic transitions that swept through the developing South and transitioning East starting in the late 1980s helped people consider themselves "citizens," in many cases for the first time. But their ability to exercise their newly acquired citizenship effectively—including the pursuit of improvements in their own welfare and that of their families and communities as well as the larger society—has been constrained by, among other things, their lack of experience and relative weakness compared with other political actors participating in public life.

This chapter looks at grassroots organizations (GROs) and how they sustain themselves in their role of promoting shared member interests—including, at times, larger societal goals—through collective action at the most local level of association. Grassroots citizens' organizations are defined here as the primary or base unit of civil society—that is, the smallest unit of organized, voluntary, autonomous, and nonprofit social interaction that participates in defining, defending, and promoting the public good at the local level and beyond.

The use of "public" here is deliberate and has a twofold meaning. First, as noted throughout this book, public does not equal government; civil society, including GROs, has a right to participate in all matters pertaining to the public good, whether that involves defining and setting priorities for public problems, making public policy, or delivering public services. Second, public is meant in both the larger societal context as well as in smaller, nonstate (or civil society) publics, which would include the members of a specific community or neighborhood or, in this case, the members of a GRO. The principal criteria for whether an action is "public" is if it touches a self-defined community, based on either shared residential location or a common interest. Viewed in this light, all civil society organizations (CSOs) have some public character. As discussed in greater detail later, this chapter is concerned with CSOs that engage in public actions at both the societal and grassroots levels, and in all those public spaces in between.

GROs have been variously called peoples' organizations, community-based organizations, and self-governing associations. What they have in common is that they are formed voluntarily by individuals coming together to promote shared interests, solve common problems, or articulate collective aspirations. They are citizens' organizations in that they have an essential political function, in addition to economic and social ones, that they undertake on behalf of local people throughout the world. They do not engage in "partisan" politics per se, but in order to improve the welfare of their members or the larger community, they must confront powerful interests in both the state and market and use collective power to overcome these interests.

Challenging imbalances in power relationships is a political act. It is civil society's role in defending and advancing societal interests and promoting civic values and good governance practice that distinguishes sustainable development from previous development paradigms that failed. None of these fundamental civil society functions will be achieved, however, unless they start with and fully involve citizens' organizations at the grassroots level. GROs are the building blocks of social and economic development and the place where ordinary people are able to practice the art of associating together in common purpose in a participatory way without fear of sanction or reprisal. It is among these base units of democracy and development that the greatest likelihood for financial sustainability and autonomy exists.

The chapter takes the perspective of a grassroots group—looking for resources first within its community or neighborhood base, and then outward to the larger world, which often conditions its ability to operate and achieve its stated goals. Because GROs have been voluntarily formed to address a locally identified problem often resolved through the provision of a good or service, their ability to charge fees and earn income from them is greater than might be the case of other nonlocally based providers (such as government or national development groups).

Resource mobilization for GROs is to a large extent tied to the nature of the goods or services they provide to their members and the larger community. Although there are a wide range of cultural associations and social clubs at the local level, the discussion here is concerned with grassroots groups that undertake any of the following:

- delivery of social and safety net services (includes parent-teacher associations, village pharmacies, mothers' clubs, potable water system committees, neighborhood watch groups, community flood management committees, and village health management groups);
- management of natural resources and environmental protection (includes water user, irrigation, and grazing associations; community forestry committees; and buffer-zone management committees);

- promotion of economic growth through job creation and income generation (includes producer groups and cooperatives, credit unions, savings and credit clubs, women's income generating groups, and artisanal and peasant associations); or
- maintenance of the social peace and conflict management/resolution.

In addition to addressing these basic social and economic problems, GROs have increasingly begun to engage local powerholders in government and business sectors as well as traditional authorities over issues of concern to their members. In a very real sense, then, GROs are multipurpose rather than specialized or single-purpose organizations, in line with the problems that confront people at the local level.

On behalf of community-level producers, GROs not only provide a range of services to increase production, they try to ensure that rural and urban producers obtain the maximum return on their investment, including their labor. And on behalf of consumers at the local level, GROs ensure that goods and services, particularly essential public services, are available and that their quality meets acceptable levels of safety—whether the group provides the good or service or it comes from outside providers. Thus GROs require resources for a combination of productive, social, and political purposes contributing to the goal of empowered citizens and communities at the grassroots.

The chapter also looks at CSO intermediaries that provide GROs and their communities with a range of services, including that of representation so that their voice is heard in public decisionmaking arenas beyond the grassroots level. In short, it aims to connect grassroots groups with social, economic, and political processes and institutions at levels of policymaking that they cannot directly touch or influence themselves.

Strategy Importance and Scale

Most grassroots community-based organizations have traditionally affiliated around such characteristics as clan, caste, ethnicity, linguistic group, age, gender, or religion. For the most part, these affiliations were dictated at birth, so membership could not necessarily be considered "voluntary," which is a fundamental characteristic of civil society, including citizens' organizations. Most such grassroots associations were formed to address a specific social, cultural, or economic need, often dealing with survival issues within a given community. With the wave of democratic changes beginning at the end of the 1980s, however, not only was there a major proliferation of voluntary associational life at all levels, but the very nature of these organizations began to change as well.

The first type of changes centered on the membership of grassroots groups as well their functions and relationship to the wider community. The internal governance structure of traditional associations has often reflected the norms and values of their larger society. This has often meant an unelected leadership, largely if not solely male-dominated, centralized, and hierarchical. Women's associations (discussed in greater detail later) are a principal exception to this pattern. In most cases, where traditional authorities—such as a chief and his counselors, religious leaders, or the heads of important cultural societies—have been the principal decisionmakers at the grassroots level, they have often exercised leadership in local associations by either de facto or de jure means.

CITIZENS' REVIEW PANEL, CZECH REPUBLIC

Plzeň is an industrial Czech city of 200,000 inhabitants that is currently dealing with major increases in its urban traffic. Local environmental NGOs concerned about proposed responses to this problem asked the Center for Community Work (CCW) for assistance. CCW is an association of Czech NGO-based community organizers who undertake projects to build representative municipal coalitions of NGOs that then organize public participation pilot projects.

In 1996, a public hearing on this topic was attended by more than 300 citizens affected by the proposed expansion of the roads in Plzeň. During a subsequent Accountability Forum held for members of the Executive Municipal Council, some 100 local citizens and the city's coalition of NGOs asked City Hall to test the effectiveness of a Citizens' Review Panel in addressing traffic problems. In this way, the traffic problem became a political issue in the city and made the municipality clearly accountable for a proper solution.

As a result, the Executive Municipal Council established in 1997 a pilot Citizens' Review Panel and provided it with an independent mandate and resources for

What has been most noticeable among recently established grassroots associations is a growing emphasis on internal democratic practice and increased participation of members in the selection of leaders and in group decisionmaking. While consensus still remains an important element in group dynamics in many cultures, there has been a qualitative change in relationships among members leading to greater equality and value of the individual voice in the group setting, as well as increased accountability of leaders to members and transparency in decisionmaking and resource use. This increases the quality of associational life not only at the grassroots level, but also in local communities and ultimately the larger society.

The second notable change concerns relationships between grassroots citizens' organizations and their external environment. Traditional groups, whether they are about using a natural resource or providing mutual aid, have often meant the difference between subsistence living and improved levels of social and economic well-being for the members. They have not, however, been well integrated into the formal market economy or linked to larger political processes, both of which are critical determinants of socioeconomic welfare at the local community or neighborhood level. The same can be said for relationships with other civil society actors beyond the local level. What distinguishes today's citizens' organizations from traditional associations, therefore, is a recognition that they can no longer rely solely on themselves or their communities to achieve group social and economic objectives.

GROs, and the CSO intermediaries that work with and represent them, have been created first and foremost to address the concrete problems of their members in social, economic, and environmental areas. Today's associations, in addition to providing individual members with a means for tackling social or economic problems collectively, also address the fundamental problem that has essentially marginalized people in much of the South and East for decades—their lack of political power to ensure that their

basic operation. Consisting of four NGO representatives and four representatives of the public administration, the panel is an ad hoc working group of the Municipal Assembly; it was given the mandate to solicit and analyze suggestions of local citizens and to design optimal solutions to the traffic problem. Public hearings, interactive public exhibitions, and surveys are used to determine citizens' concerns and suggestions for solutions. The resources allocated by the Municipality—approximately US$3,000—cover expenses associated with public relations activities of the panel as well as 25 percent of the salary of each NGO representative.

The project has enjoyed great success and has considerably improved the position of the city's coalition of NGOs in the eyes of the Municipal Council. Local media attention has also helped participating NGOs to increase their visibility in the city. With this success, City Hall has expressed interest in developing the concept of Citizens' Review Panels, recognizing that empowering citizens to contribute to decisionmaking results in sound ideas and myriad alternative solutions to a city's problems.

Case study prepared by Jiri Dusik, Regional Environmental Center for CEE.

interests and problems are heard and acted on by those with the power to do so. Thus the true value and importance of building GROs is that the principal resource being built is citizen empowerment, from which all other resources flow.

The diversity of GROs is only limited by the interests and ingenuity of the people who create them. Associations of fisherfolk, artisans, and peasants stretch from Eritrea to Peru to the Philippines; groups concerned about livestock grazing, water use, and forest conservation are emerging in such diverse locales as Lesotho, Tajikistan, and Nepal; and primary-level producer groups, local trade unions, cooperatives, and credit unions are reemerging as independent, democratically run organizations after decades of subservience to one-party states in countries as diverse as Bangladesh, Bolivia, Latvia, and Zambia. What is common to all these organizations is the fact that their members realize that they can accomplish their individual social and economic goals more effectively together than alone. In the process, they can build values of trust, tolerance, and cooperation—or what Robert Putnam has so aptly called social capital, which underlies all economic as well as social interaction.

Generating resources from activities that raise incomes or create jobs appears at first glance to be more likely goals than activities that aim at delivering social or safety net services to those unable to pay for them. True, microenterprise, agricultural production, transformation and marketing activities, and some areas of conservation and natural resource management are able to generate a stable flow of financial resources to sustain the operations of grassroots associations. But new GROs that provide education, health, and safety net services to their members or clients are increasingly demonstrating the willingness of local people to support organizations that address local problems and are rooted in their communities.

In general, countries and regions that endured or still live under the rule of totalitarianism are more likely to experience difficulty in building autonomous and sustainable grassroots organizations. Somewhat less difficulty will be experienced in countries that experienced years and even decades of authoritarian one-party or military rule but where at least some measure of space existed for nonstate organizations. Thus, in general, the newly independent states of the former Soviet Union and Central and Eastern European countries will see a slower emergence of GROs than most Latin American, many African, and a significant number of Asian countries. Not only did 50–70 years of communist rule virtually extinguish all voluntary and autonomous associations, but the values of volunteerism, philanthropy, and social capital that underlie civil society were prevented from developing. Again, although there may be many formal and national-level civil society actors in evidence in all these countries, it is the nature—the quality as well as quantity—of associational life at the grassroots level that ultimately will determine the successfulness of this strategy in a given locale.

Benefits and Limitations

This strategy has long been a favorite of development practitioners who have promoted popular participation and empowerment at the grassroots level. Its lineage can be traced back to the early 1960s in Latin America, Africa, and Asia with the emphasis on peasant power and "conscientization," and more recently in the teachings of liberation theology and "peoples' power." The inability to promote and support this strategy successfully over the last 30 years has been due to the less than free and open political systems that marked most eastern and southern countries. Because such basic rights as freedom of association and speech were absent in many countries, the fundamental conditions or "enabling environment" for the formation and growth of healthy and vibrant civil societies were equally absent.

While the situation has obviously improved in the 1990s, the gains are still tenuous overall, and civil society is constrained in its actions by the unfriendliness of the larger political environment. Thus the strategy's principal limitation is one that has been with it for decades. What is unique about the chances for success today, however, is that GRO resource enhancement and sustainability are inextricably linked to the larger phenomenon of peoples' movements seen from the local to the global level and challenging the status quo of social and economic inequality and environmental degradation. While the struggle that this represents will be a long one, civil society will be in the forefront. And as its successes mount, so will its fortunes, literal as well as figurative.

This larger framework of constraints and opportunities is found in a number of ways at the practical level. Basically, this strategy is premised on the growth and empowerment of both citizens and civil society. Politically enfranchised, rights-bearing, and responsibility-laden men and women and a public realm of intermediary voluntary and autonomous associations and networks of civic engagement are not born or created; they evolve over time. Not only is this a long-term endeavor, it is one that takes a considerable measure of capacity building and institutional development. GROs, in short, can be no stronger or more sustainable than the citizens who belong to them and the civil society that nurtures their growth and connects them to other groups and to the larger world.

A measure of reality must also be brought to the discussion of sustainability, for both grassroots organizations and intermediary CSOs. GROs and their manifestation beyond the local level in the form of intermediary CSOs are the most likely members of civil society to achieve institutional sustainability. It is unrealistic, however, to think that they can do so solely from resources that exist at the local level, or that 100 percent of their costs can be completely covered at all times without significant inputs from outside actors. Because many GROs and CSOs will be delivering public goods and services that may have been previously provided by government, it is not unreasonable to think that government, whether central or local, should provide some degree of support to them. While GROs and CSOs undertaking more productive services are more likely than those providing social and safety net services to achieve a high degree of sustainability, there should be few illusions that this will happen quickly or fully.

The aim of this strategy is to identify and determine a level of resource sustainability that ensures a minimum degree of organizational autonomy. GROs and CSOs should be able to cover core institutional costs from revenues other than those from governments, donors, or business. Or these external sources should account for no more than a certain percentage of overall resources. As pointed out elsewhere in this book, CSOs in the North generate close to 50 percent of their overall resources from their own efforts and slightly less than this from public resources made available by government.

For citizens' organizations operating at the grassroots level, a more appropriate figure might be that at least two thirds of their total resource base could come from local sources and be self-generated. The nature of the relationship of intermediary CSOs to their grassroots counterparts as well as the functions they carry out at the grassroots will largely determine the extent to which these groups can achieve resource sustainability themselves, as discussed later.

Future Trends

Despite the many setbacks to and reversals of democratic transitions in southern and eastern countries over the past decade, it is clear that the future belongs to citizens, their organizations, and peoples' movements on a global scale. This may not be empirically verifiable in the short term, but the march of civilization can certainly be seen as one that places individuals' rights and obligations at the heart of any political system and certainly as the basis for making societal decisions. Citizens' organizations provide their members with a permanent means to participate in local matters and, when necessary, are the principal channel for extending their voice beyond the local level.

Donors, who increasingly finance attempts to strengthen civil society as a component of larger democracy promotion and sustainable development programs, are slowly realizing that their initial focus on support to more formal, national-level civil society actors does not necessarily lead to either strong democracies or sustainable and equitable economic growth. This "quick fix" donor strategy of support to institutions and processes at the macro-political level has little relevance to the vast majority of citizens and citizens' organizations at society's base.

While promoting democracy as an end in itself is obviously desirable, unless this is integrated into the daily lives of people in local communities it will lose its luster and the promise of ensuring true and lasting individual, community, and societal change. Thus donors are beginning to allocate their resources to promote the more inclusive strategy of sustainable development that ties democracy and good governance objec-

ORANGI PILOT PROJECT, PAKISTAN

In 1980, a community organization was established in Orangi, a squatter settlement in Pakistan with a population of approximately 1 million. The organizers spent the first six months of the Orangi Pilot Project (OPP) meeting with the squatter settlers to find out about their problems and to gain their trust. The main problem discussed was the lack of a sewage system, which residents blamed for health problems as well as damage to their homes from waterlogging. The solution, they decided, was to build a self-maintained, self-managed, self-financed, low-cost sewage system.

Four main obstacles initially impeded progress on construction of the sewage system. First, the settlers believed that it was the duty of the government to build sewage lines for them, free of charge. Second, sanitary latrines and underground sewage lines built by government or commercial agencies were beyond the means of low-income families. Third, the settlers did not have the technical skills required to construct the underground sewage lines themselves. Finally, the construction of underground sewage lines also required the ability to organize for collective action.

To overcome these obstacles, OPP set up a small office with a team of social organizers and technicians. Nightly meetings were held to discuss the benefits of the project and motivate the settlers to join together for the common good rather than wait for government assistance. The technicians surveyed the roads, prepared estimates, and mapped out each step of the project. They found the homeowners competent and willing to assume the responsibility of construction and

tives to improvements in the social and economic welfare of all a country's people. GROs are the logical focus of such programs as they are the principal means to achieving sustainable development at the local level.

The final trend that will ensure the continued importance of this strategy for the foreseeable future is the increasing focus on local government as the most effective "locus" of sustainable development. Decentralization has been a strategy for promoting economic growth and improved social welfare since the earliest days of the first development decade. It has never lived up to its promise, however, for the same reason that development in its many iterations has failed to deliver—that is, the lack of freedom for citizens to participate in constructing their own futures. Because most central governments today are no longer as able or in many cases willing to intervene in the social and economic life of their countries, there is pressure on local governments to take on these many and diverse "public" responsibilities.

Increasingly, local governments are being democratically elected and thus more open to considering new ways of relating to local citizens and their organizations. This allows increased participation of GROs in defining their problems, formulating solutions to them, and, where appropriate, implementing activities that follow from the solutions prescribed. The ability to participate as a legitimate partner alongside local government in making public decisions increases the likelihood that pub-

maintenance of latrines in each home, the underground sewage lines, and the collection drains. The main drains and treatment plants, however, would remain the responsibility of a central authority.

The technicians also spent several months studying how to make construction affordable for poor homeowners. By simplifying the design of the system and using standard parts, the costs were reduced to less than one fourth the contractors' rates. OPP also trained some of the homeowners as masons, loaned them tools, and provided guidance and supervision, thus eliminating kickbacks and profiteering. The homeowners elected representatives who collected money, bought the necessary materials, and hired laborers.

Several months were required to organize a group of families to begin construction, but once a section of the settlement was complete, it served as an excellent incentive for other homeowners. More than 70,000 flush latrines have been constructed and sewage lines have been laid in approximately 5,000 of the settlement's roads, for a total investment of approximately 60 million Rupees.

What was important to the success of this project was that the scope of the work was clearly identified, the roles of each homeowner and other individuals were defined, and the community was made a partner in the development of the sewage lines rather than a passive recipient dependent on government. The Orangi Pilot Project has been so successful that it is now being replicated in other areas, and UNICEF has accepted the model for its Urban Basic Service Program.

Case study based on Anwar Rashid, "Self-Financed, Self-Managed, Self-Maintained, Low-Cost Development Sanitation."

lic resources controlled by that government will be allocated to GROs for implementation. Even where a legal devolution of authority or resources to local government has not taken place, because of the weakness of many central governments there has been a de facto decentralization of at least the authority to act, even if the resources have been lacking. This is precisely why GROs have gained a greater voice in these same countries—because they can mobilize local resources from their members and communities.

Issues

One of the principal issues raised by this strategy is the role of intermediary CSOs. These groups exist, in principle, only insofar as they serve the needs of the local level, which include generating or finding needed resources. The pattern to date, however, has placed traditional development nongovernmental organizations (NGOs)—the most prominent type of intermediary CSO—at the center of most development strategies, particularly those supported by donors. As noted earlier, NGOs are normally institutionally separate from the communities and GROs with which they work. Without doubt, NGOs have been a primary force within civil society promoting the new paradigm of a politically empowered citizenry and citizens' organizations. But the fact that many of them deliver services to local communities that could perhaps be delivered by GROs calls into question their long-term role at the grassroots level.

Many development practitioners and policymakers alike see NGO intermediaries as catalysts in the promotion and strengthening of GROs, and increasingly in helping to regroup them into higher-level unions and federations. Where NGOs do deliver services—whether health care, conservation management, or credit administration—some see this as a temporary measure until GROs or federations of grassroots groups are capable of assuming these responsibilities themselves. Just as the operational role of international NGOs in southern and eastern development is generally agreed to be at the end of its useful life, the role of their local counterparts in grassroots development is being rethought. Serving as a catalyst for and providing support to GROs and federations is now being increasingly discussed as the longer-term role for NGOs. Whether this is what develops for NGOs remains to be seen. It will have a major impact on resource enhancement at the grassroots level.

On a more practical level, the issue of "nonprofit" must be considered for GROs that engage in activities that generate some form of revenue or financial resource. For a GRO to be labelled nonprofit does not mean that it should not try to cover its expenses any more than it means that it is not professional in how it conducts its affairs. Whether a GRO charges a fee for medicines provided to a community, or takes a percentage of the credit or loan provided to its members, the resulting income is treated as revenue. When a grassroots group has a surplus of revenue over expenditures in the delivery of a given good or service, the balance is a net surplus that is then reinvested in the organization. As discussed in greater detail later, GROs should and must cover a component of their costs from the goods and services they provide to their members. This is essential to any strategy that attempts to promote autonomy as well as sustainability. It is ultimately what distinguishes successful and effective GROs from those that are not.

Mobilizing Resources at the Grassroots

To achieve a significant degree of autonomy and sustainability in their operations, GROs must first establish a strong resource base from among their members and the surrounding community. This is consistent with their essentially local focus and their emphasis on either solving member problems or advancing their particular interests. It also recognizes that financial sustainability and organizational autonomy are intimately tied to political empowerment, of both citizens and their organizations. GROs operate in a limited area—one or more villages in a rural area, for instance, or several neighborhoods within a city. Thus their potential sources of income as well as the individuals with power to influence their activities are most likely well known to them and can be approached one-on-one.

Mapping and Analyzing Resources

The first step in any resource mobilization strategy is to identify and inventory the range of financial and nonfinancial resources that are potentially available from either GRO members or their communities. Normally the financial side of the equation is fairly straightforward. But nonfinancial resources can benefit from an organized exercise that maps and analyzes what is immediately available from the surrounding environment.

A number of innovative self-assessment inventory instruments and methodologies have been developed for use by grassroots organizations. (See Box 1 for one example.) In general, the inventory will assess—depending on the type of good or service being provided—existing natural resources, such as water, land, or energy supplies; human resources, including skills and expertise; and capital assets such as livestock, farming or fishing equipment, and even trees that have been planted for either domestic use or to generate income.

It is extremely important for the GRO to review existing and available technologies currently in use. This can include traditional practices and technologies, whether related to agriculture or medicine, as well as those that have been introduced and are considered "modern" and innovative. The point is to ensure that traditional practices and technologies in such areas as pest control and management, grain storage, savings mobilization and credit administration, traditional medicines, family planning, conflict resolution, and group decisionmaking are included in the mix of resources considered by GROs in the formulation of strategies to deliver goods or services. The resource mapping exercise not only provides GROs with necessary information about their ability to meet needs from available means, it shows that financial resources may not be as important as previously thought.

Membership Strategies

As noted earlier, a distinguishing feature of grassroots organizations is the fact that they are formed, owned, and operated by their members. Moreover, they are voluntarily formed, although in many cases an external catalyst may have provided the initial spark to mobilize and bring people together. And increasingly, GROs are democratically structured to govern their affairs, including making collective decisions and choosing their leaders. The combination of these factors points clearly to the fact that the members are the most important resource of the organization and the likeliest source of financial as well as nonfinancial contributions.

Membership fees provide the first possibility for obtaining cash or financial resources. The decision on how much to levy on each member is one that must be jointly arrived at through the GRO's normal governance process, which it is anticipated will be a democratic one. Even if obligatory membership dues are required, as happens in some groups in the Sahel and South Asia, these should have been clearly agreed on in the original charter or constitution and in the bylaws of the GRO. In addition to an entry or annual membership fee, the GRO can assess members an agreed-upon amount for special purposes, such as the establishment of a local development fund, the one-time purchase of a piece of equipment, or the establishment of a guarantee fund so that local banks will be more likely to lend them money for their productive activities.

The issue of savings must also be considered. One of the principal resources that GROs can mobilize from their members and the surrounding communities is their savings. Credit programs have been found to be most successful when a person's receipt of credit is tied to a contribution of savings. The traditional assumption has

Box 1

THE REFERENCE BOOK OF THE VILLAGE

MYRADA, a large, integrated development program begun 30 years ago in India, has published a model for an inventory of nonfinancial resources available at the village level. The following are some of the elements found there.

People: number of families and houses; number of men and women; literacy rate; employment and unemployment rates

Skills: farmers, carpenters, blacksmiths, weavers, potters, craftsmen, mechanics, salesmen, small businessmen

Education: number of schools; distance from village; number of girls and boys in school; number who have left school; examples of non-formal education

Health: number of hospitals, pharmacies, dispensaries, doctors, nurses; distance from village; equipment

Drinking Water: number and location of open wells, tube wells, ponds, rivers, irrigation tanks, lakes

Communication: accessibility to bus and other means of transportation; types of roads in the area

Housing: types of houses in the area; distance at which timber, cement, and iron are available

Lighting: available energy resources for lighting; distance to nearest electrical supply station

Agriculture: total area of cultivatable, cultivated, fertilized, irrigated, and non-irrigated land; loans available for agricultural purposes; cost and availability of fertilizer and pesticides; amount of produce per hectare

---

been that poor people do not save, but empirical evidence over the past two decades has demonstrated that in a range of productive activities they are able not only to save but to repay loans. In some cases in the Sahel, for instance, savings and credit unions have too much liquidity that could be turned into productive investments. So before GROs look beyond their membership or their communities for funds, they should first look within themselves for savings that can be used to finance some level of their activities or to leverage additional resources from the outside.

In general, GROs have between 10 and 100 members, with the average size depending on the nature of the good or service being provided and the size of the surrounding community. Beyond 100, size becomes as much a resource constraint as a strength, because it becomes more difficult for the organization to manage its affairs with the level of member participation that is viewed as indispensable to effectiveness and even survival.

Equipment:	*wood, iron, conventional or improved sowing equipment, grinders, carts, water-pumps, tractors, vans*
Rainfall:	*in millimeters per year, and amount per month during the last 10 years*
Animal Husbandry:	*number of farm animals for food and for work; nearest veterinary clinic; total production of milk, chicken, and beef; distance to markets where produce can be sold*
Irrigation:	*land irrigated through well water, through borings, through canals or tanks; depth at which water available; list of people who have irrigation systems; amount of irrigated land in hectares*
Nature of Earth:	*type, texture, and composition*
Forests:	*distance of village from the nearest forest; what forest products are used for*
Cooperatives:	*names of cooperatives; capital, location, and distance from the village; list of members of the management committee of cooperatives*
Credit Cooperatives:	*types of approved loans; amount of total loans given; amount of nonrepayment*
Marketing:	*number of marketing centers; number of wholesalers and retailers*
Prices:	*amount paid to peasants for different products; prices of different consumer products at the nearest market*
Salaries:	*amount paid to workers in agriculture, carpenters, blacksmiths, construction workers, forest workers, farmers, and others*
Bank:	*names of banks and distance from village; types of loans; interest rates; number of savings accounts in banks and amount of deposits*

While the membership of a GRO may coincide with a given residential area, this is by no means automatic because many goods and services provided by GROs are based on addressing the interests or concerns of a well-defined group who come together voluntarily. Even where the problem identified may concern the entire residential unit, separate groups may be formed because, for instance, women want to ensure that they are treated fairly (in savings and credit clubs, for example), or because everyone in the community does not want to be involved in the delivery of a service (perhaps a parent-teachers association or community water supply committee). In these cases, because membership is voluntary, it is also self-limiting.

Given the size of most GROs, the amount of funds that can be collected from members will cover only a small share of the total costs of delivering any goods or services. As modest as member contributions—financial and nonfinancial alike—may

CREDIT UNIONS IN LESOTHO

In an attempt to increase local investment in agriculture in Lesotho, the National University of Lesotho Extension Program—a partnership between the National University of Lesotho and the Canadian-based St. Francis Xavier University, the Canadian International Development Agency, and Misereor (a Catholic development organization based in Germany)—suggested that credit unions be formed. Village leaders organized community meetings at which the Extension Service explained how a credit union works. After this orientation, the community members were responsible for deciding whether they wanted a credit union; if so, they had to take the initiative to invite the Extension Service back to provide training. The commitment of time, effort, and resources on the part of the community firmly rooted the project at the local level.

Once the decision to form a credit union is made, village members form study groups and commit a year of study to become thoroughly knowledgeable about the concepts and operations. Then several members are selected to participate in an intensive course on bookkeeping and financial management. They were required to pass qualifying exams in order for the credit union to be formally established and officially registered with the Ministry of Agriculture and Cooperatives. Each credit union is managed and administered entirely by its members, who are responsible for all decisionmaking. The members also elect a nine-member Board of Directors, an Auditing Committee, a Credit Committee, and an Education Committee. Once the credit unions are established, it is the government's responsibility to conduct an annual financial audit.

The World Council of Credit Unions and the Canadian-based Caisse Populaire provided training materials and assistance in establishing an umbrella organi-

be, however, they form the core of the overall strategy of promoting autonomy and sustainability, and focus the organization on the need to look internally before going outside its borders for resources.

Generating Resources by Providing Goods and Services

Earned income from the goods or services provided by the GRO offers one of the most promising areas for resource enhancement. Chapter 2 details the earned income strategies used by all kinds of civil society organizations. The emphasis here is on how grassroots groups can generate income from the goods and services they have decided to provide to their members and the surrounding community (identified as mission-related earned income in Chapter 2). Although some GROs have developed projects and income-generating activities that have nothing to do with their primary missions, this is a risky endeavor and one that is normally undertaken by intermediary CSOs, if at all.

Productive or Economic Activities

Several services and activities that GROs undertake are by their very nature intended to generate income or in-kind resources. One of the best known and most frequently pro-

zation, the Lesotho Cooperative Credit Union League (LCCUL). At one point, when the government announced its intention to take over the credit unions and use them as a base for a national bank, the cooperation of the communities with LCCUL proved a formidable force in fighting this government initiative.

The movement eventually led to the formation of more than 70 credit unions throughout the region. Membership has increased steadily over the years; given the extended families of the average member, the credit unions reach more than 250,000 direct beneficiaries. Their program has diversified to include a number of income-generating activities such as communal gardens and crafts cooperatives, and some unions have even constructed their own facilities, which can be rented out to earn income. Due to its success, Lesotho has been selected as the site for the African Cooperative Savings & Credit Association training center for southern and eastern Africa.

Establishing a credit union gives members an opportunity to save regularly, borrow in times of need, learn how to manage their own finances, and develop habits of thrift and honesty. They use the skills they acquire and their access to capital to start their own small enterprises. Approximately 30 percent of credit union members hold leadership positions throughout the village in development committees, churches, and political parties. In addition, at least 45 percent of the credit union members have learned how to read and write. And since many of the men are absent from the village for long periods working in South Africa, women have played a prominent role within the credit unions, which helped give them visibility as capable and responsible leaders.

Case study based on Dr. Dele Braimoh and Dr. A.M. Sets'abi, "Improving the Material Conditions of Rural Communities in Lesotho through Credit Unions."

vided services is securing funds in order to extend credit to members for a range of on-farm and off-farm income-generating and microenterprise activities. The GRO acts as a credit administrator of a joint fund on behalf of individual member-borrowers. The group normally manages the individual loans that have been approved by its governing board, ensures collection of repayments, and perhaps provides some simple advisory and accounting services to borrowers. In return, it may either charge a fixed administrative fee or take a percentage of the total borrowed to cover some share of its costs. (See Chapter 10 for information on intermediary CSOs establishing and operating credit programs.)

The groups that provide this service range from traditional revolving credit associations and savings clubs, such as the *esusu* and *tontine* found throughout Africa, to more formalized grassroots units of larger savings and credit schemes such as the Grameen Bank in Bangladesh, to the primary units of countrywide savings and credit unions. Again, the concern here is with the GRO—the smallest unit of voluntary, nonprofit, and autonomous association that provides a good or service to its member-owners. This is where the issue of nonprofit needs to be considered.

In addition to credit programs, the other principal "productive" GRO type is the one that provides a common good or service to its members. This includes primary cooper-

JARDIM SHANGRI-LA, BRAZIL

The shantytown of Jardim Shangri-la is a haphazard cluster of small shacks made of scrap lumber and cardboard, with no running water or sewage, perched alongside a putrid, garbage-strewn river. Taking advantage of the headway generated by a local branch of the Citizens' Campaign Against Hunger and Poverty and For Life (the Acao da Cidadania Contra a Fome, Miseria e Pela Vida) from a nearby shantytown, 16 families in Jardim Shangri-la banded together to tackle long-standing community problems. For years they had waited for government help; now they realized that with limited outside help and their own sweat and ingenuity, they could take effective action. They established the Cooperativa Habitacional Jardim Shangri-la to upgrade their housing and generate much-needed income.

Cooperative members began by holding bingos and raffles and pooling their money to buy land for a brick-making factory. Next, they received a $7,000 grant from the Fundo Inter-Religioso, a small-projects fund operated by an ecumenical coalition of church groups and NGOs, to purchase a simple motor-run press to produce cement bricks and concrete slabs. Eight local residents were hired to work at the factory, which would cover their salaries from the profits of brick sales.

atives or precooperatives, peasant or artisanal associations, a range of producer groups (such as those on food and cash crops, or cattle and sheep), and a number of natural resource user associations (such as those on irrigation or forest management). These organizations may provide a necessary production input or good, transform a primary product into a usable form, or market a product to or on behalf of its members. They may also ensure that a valuable service is undertaken, such as managing an irrigation system, providing extension education, or advising on markets. Increasingly these groups are undertaking new services—or returning to traditional ones—made possible by the advent of democracy, such as the resolution of conflicts that arise among members, or lobbying local powerholders for better treatment of their members.

In the provision of these goods and services, some situations automatically generate income, either from an input provided or from a service undertaken. In addition to the cost of purchase or sale of a product, the GRO can levy its own cost for doing business on behalf of its members. In all these cases, determining the fee or charge for delivery of a good or service is a key to successful resource enhancement and sustainability. One obvious consideration is the GRO's costs. Groups are for the most part lightly staffed, with few if any permanent, paid employees. Other overhead costs are equally modest, leading in general to modest fees from the GRO's point of view. Yet the goods and services that it provides (such as fertilizer or farm equipment) can be so expensive as to make any additional charge difficult for members to pay.

This leads to two related requirements. The first concerns the need for some form of credit fund. This will permit the GRO to advance members the "inputs" needed to increase their productive capacity until they can sell their product, and to purchase member "outputs" (or some percentage of the total) and market them at the most ap-

Soon the factory was turning out 600 bricks a day. Other members of the community, including women and children, volunteered their labor on weekends to boost production and construct houses in the community.

The coop also has used its bricks to renovate the community center where meetings, sewing courses, and catechism classes are held, and residents built a 7,000-liter storage tank that supplies potable water to the community for the first time. Now the cooperative plans to pool profits from its brickmaking with a small donation from the Catholic archdiocese's social service center to start a restaurant to feed poorer members of the shantytown and to earn extra, steady income by selling prepared meals to workers of nearby factories.

The experience of Jardim Shangri-la vividly portrays the remarkable accomplishments and potential of the Citizens' Campaign. With only limited outside cash donations, a good deal of volunteer labor, complementary institutional partnerships, and a newfound sense of purpose, 16 families are vitally improving their community.

Case study based on John W. Garrison II and Leilah Landim, "Harvesting the Bounty of Citizenship: The Fight Against Hunger and Poverty in Brazil," Grassroots Development, *Vol. 19, No. 2, 1995.*

propriate moment to get the best possible price. Second, the GRO must develop the ability to determine when a so-called income-generating activity has the potential to induce a real return on investment versus when it is responding to an identified and desired social need but has little chance of becoming a profitable and sustainable enterprise. Although this may pertain more to credit programs and the individual loans made to member-borrowers, the principle is an important one for GROs providing services in other productive areas as well.

The terrain of rural development is littered with well-meaning income-generating programs and the failed activities that they spawned. GROs and their members must be willing to separate their social needs from their economic ability to support them. This should not be interpreted as rejecting needed social programs, but rather as protecting both types of endeavors by designing appropriate resource enhancement strategies that address the underlying purpose of each. As discussed in the next section, many social programs and most safety net functions cannot generate adequate funds under the best of circumstances to cover their cost of delivery.

Noneconomic Public Services

Health care and education are considered public services, as are a range of safety net functions. In previous times, government, primarily at the central level, took sole responsibility for the provision of these public obligations. That was before decades of economic mismanagement led to the collapse of southern and eastern economies and the inability of governments to fulfill their responsibilities or impose their will. This created a vacuum in a range of public service delivery functions into which civil society actors at all levels quickly were drawn. While most public services are undertaken at the

MOTHERS' CLUBS, PERU

In Lurigancho, Peru's sprawl of 500,000 people living in straw and mud shacks, Encarnacion Huaman and 13 other mothers had heard that ordinary women in some shantytowns had started *comedores populares* (public dining rooms) to feed themselves and their neighbors. In response to their initiatives, many NGOs contributed food. Huaman's little group banded together to form their own *club de madres*—mothers' club—shared whatever food and utensils they had, incorporated themselves into a community soup kitchen, and began feeding anyone who came to their door.

In a country in which 70 percent of the residents live below the poverty line, with 50 percent in extreme poverty, these self-ignited efforts spelled hope for a massive population. Leftist groups, recognizing the possibilities for furthering their cause, helped the budding enterprises along. But it soon became evident that, try as anyone might to politicize the *comedores*, it was not politics the women were interested in. It was solidarity and survival.

In 1983, when Huaman brought her first handful of potatoes to a gathering, there were 100 such kitchens around Lima. By 1988, there were 1,500 in operation, even though the Shining Path guerillas, anxious to undermine any semblance of organized progress among the poor, had begun rolling bombs through the doors. By 1990, as inflation hit 8,000 percent and Shining Path terrorism continued unabated, neighborhood operations like Huaman's were the only social assistance people had. Today their kitchens provide the poor of Peru with more than 5 million meals a day.

local level, in many southern and eastern countries, particularly in Africa and South Asia, people at this level are least prepared—financially as well as in required skills—to take over many of these functions even when government has agreed to the idea.

There is a qualitative difference between public social services, such as primary education and health care, and those related to maintaining a social safety net, including feeding programs for the poor and disaster relief assistance. GROs must address both. But it is much likelier that members of the GRO and the larger community will be willing and able to pay for some portion of social services. At the local level, it can be expected that GRO members will contribute at least nonfinancial resources to addressing both community social service and safety net needs. Self-help associations and mutual aid societies all over the world have provided their labor and local materials to build schools and health facilities, just as they have in times of drought and natural disaster rebuilt a home or provided crop seed for those affected. The difference is that providing social services is a full-time activity while safety net functions are, in principle, periodic ones.

GROs providing public social services can also count on membership subscriptions and fees, assessments for special activities, and sometimes user fee charges. A parent-teacher association, for example, raises funds from its members and often levies additional charges for a special project such as buying books to stock a new library. Since these groups do not normally manage a school, however, they do not charge user fees, such as

Women's initiatives also led to the establishment of the *vaso de leche* (glass of milk) network. Its 7,500 members distribute a million glasses of milk a day to poor Peruvian children. At first, the women tried to obtain funds from private donations, humanitarian organizations, and so on. Then they acquired milk in bulk and on discount to deliver to the most undernourished children. Within a few years, the effect on the young was so evident that the system became municipal law. Since 1985, official Peru has taken up the task of providing milk to the poor, ensuring that every child up to age 13 receives eight ounces a day; but it is the women in the *vaso de leche* network who organize the distribution. The program has had unexpected benefits, as the women who dispense the milk find out who is sick, who needs vaccinations, who wants access to birth control, and so on.

Some Peruvian economists complain that the government is relying too much on these grassroots social efforts and that poor women are a cowed population providing unpaid voluntary labor. They argue that encouraging these programs does not constitute sustainable development, nor substitute for strong institutions with firm budget commitments. Yet stepping in and subsidizing the poor could strip them of the entrepreneurialism that keeps them alive today.

As the country's leaders cast about for a sensible strategy, one thing should be abundantly clear: the poor women of Peru are the real heroes. Faced with catastrophe, they have shown imagination. In work, they have sought possibility. And in the most desolate communities, they have found hope.

Case study, excerpted, with edits, from Marie Arana-Ward, "Mothers Know Best: What the Poor Women of Peru Can Teach Us," Washington Post, *9 September 1996.*

tuition to maintain and operate their school. This, however, is changing in many rural communities. In Mali, for instance, a new set of laws empowering grassroots communities to build and directly operate primary schools has led to new parent associations to operate them. (See Case Study in Chapter 7.) Thus user fees have been charged for each member-parent with children at the school. The same principle has increasingly taken hold in many communities in the area of health care delivery. Numerous grassroots health committees and associations have been formed and charge for a wide range of goods and services—from drugs and condoms to prenatal care and patient visits.

Slowly a number of new public functions, in addition to those in health and education, are being taken over by emerging GROs in such fields as the management of public housing and feeding programs for the poor. These new public responsibilities are much more likely to take place in urban areas than in rural settings. And given the fact that the urban life is much more money-based and that community ties may be weaker than in rural areas, it is likely that member contributions will be in cash and that earned income strategies will be more appropriate and frequent.

Finding Resources Beyond the Local Level

The capacity of GROs to mobilize resources directly beyond the local level is constrained by their ability to influence those who control the resources, whether public or private. There are, however, a number of institutional actors that GROs have successfully tapped the resources of—local governments, religious organizations, some traditional caste or class associations, businesses operating at the local level, and a range of self-help or microgrant funds.

Although it is still fairly rare in most regions, municipal and local governments have provided GROs with public resources, both financial and in-kind, to undertake a range of social and safety net services, from garbage removal and school management to mobilizing communities for childhood vaccination campaigns and maintaining rural roads. As discussed in Chapter 6, local governments have provided these resources through grants, contracts, and subsidies. Another outside source of funds is "hometown" associations in urban areas. As urbanization has proceeded over the past two decades, these groups based on ethnicity and place of origin have sprung up in many urban centers throughout Africa, Asia, and Latin America. They mobilize resources to finance development activities in their homes of birth.

Other sources include northern embassies, most of which have established small self-help funds targeted specifically at GROs that match locally mobilized resources intended to promote small-scale social development programs. Likewise, northern NGOs and foundations have increasingly attempted to bypass intermediary CSOs and reach grassroots groups with funding for a range of productive and social development programs. Finally, though not often recognized as such, businesses that work at the local level often provide production inputs to farmer or artisanal associations and arrange to deduct the cost of the inputs from the purchase price of the group's output. Tobacco, cotton, certain herbs and spices, and soybeans are among the agricultural produce subsidized in this way, while a range of handicrafts items have also benefited from this type of resource support.

Major Conclusions for Practitioners

The ability of grassroots organizations to mobilize resources is tied closely to their right to participate as legitimate partners in the delivery of public social services. This in turn is highly dependent on governments agreeing to consider a new division of labor, in which civil society also undertakes a range of public functions. (See also Chapter 6.) This holds equally true for the right of GROs to undertake a wide range of productive activities. It is largely up to national governments to pass laws or make policies that permit civil society in general and GROs specifically to undertake what might be called "self-governance"—civil society actors making public decisions concerning their needs and, when appropriate, providing public goods or services with or without government sanction.

As noted earlier, the term public refers here to a well-defined group, whether communities or the members of a CSO, in addition to the general public. The tendency has been for those concerned with improving the enabling environment for civil society participation in sustainable development activities, or in public life, to concentrate their efforts on traditional development NGOs and other formal, national-level civil society actors.

If GROs are going to become true public actors contributing to the economic and social welfare of their members, communities, and larger society, then a wide range of laws on such topics as natural resource management, social service delivery, and economic rights must be passed or reformed. Land reform, decentralization, and local government laws provide the broader legal context within which GROs can address the specific social and economic needs of their members. Movement on both sets of legal requirements is happening far too slowly, however, compared with the proliferation of GROs, their current contributions, and the great potential contributions they have to offer.

One of the continuing myths of development is that the rural and urban poor— the majority in many southern and eastern countries—can neither organize themselves to provide services nor pay for those that are essential to their welfare. GROs have shown that the rural and urban poor can in fact organize themselves, based on problems they have identified, and can cover a significant percentage of their costs from resources mobilized directly from members and their communities. It should also be recognized, however, that many of these services do not lend themselves to recuperating costs, either in part or in whole.

With government's withdrawal from many of its public responsibilities in both economic and social life, GROs by default have had to fill the void. But they are no more likely to be able to cover all the costs of such services than government was. The same can be said for most safety net functions, particularly those that move beyond normal calamities. This is just one of the reasons that groups must look beyond their own members and communities for solutions to complex public problems.

Working Through Civil Society Intermediaries

Ever since the United Nations declared the 1960s as the first development decade, development practitioners and policymakers have looked for ways to involve local communities in the provision of public services. Whether framed as meeting "basic needs" or as addressing the social costs of adjustment, donors and host-country governments have looked at grassroots organizations to implement development programs. Eventually this approach evolved to include GRO participation in project decision-making and even in the fruits of the project.

This concept of development, still very much alive in most parts of the developing world, works against the ability of GROs to address the problems of their communities and to mobilize resources beyond the narrow confines of local operations. One of the principal problems has been the fact that they and the communities they represent have been viewed as the object of other, external actors who make decisions about problems at the local level and how to resolve them. Empowerment means that citizens and their organizations take back their right to both define and set priorities on their problems and then resolve them. The terms and conditions of their relations with external actors are to be negotiated, with the ultimate goal of the GRO being treated as a legitimate and effective partner in sustainable development efforts at the local level and beyond.

A second problem has been the idea of development as a series of discrete, well-defined projects. By their very nature, projects have created hierarchical relationships between those who conceive or manage them and those who are supposed to benefit

AGRICULTURAL COOPERATIVES IN CHILE

The Sociedad de Asistencia Tecnica, Comercializacion y Desarrollo, Sociedes Agricolas del Secano, Ltda. (SADESCA) is a small but dynamic federation of four agricultural cooperatives operating in rural regions of Chile's coastal drylands. About 100–200 families belong to each cooperative. SADESCA was formed because its members felt an acute need to have an intermediary organization of sufficient scale to protect their land rights and to provide technical support in an extremely hostile political and economic environment. A unique feature of the organization is the integration of women into the decisionmaking body.

In 1981, when the organization reconstituted itself from an earlier and larger project, the community-based cooperatives struggled to meet stringent administrative and financial conditions imposed by the national government, which in the 1980s was not particularly positive toward small landowners trying to establish their rights. Legally they could not increase their membership, yet they had to remain solvent in order to keep their charter. To stabilize this precarious situation, SADESCA administered a rotating credit fund so the societies that needed legal assistance could contract for it.

Although SADESCA is relatively young, its activities have had a significant impact on members and their families. Despite the devastating earthquake in the region in 1985, for example, member organizations realized a steady improve-

from them. The best intentions of donors, governments, and even intermediary development NGOs to ensure participation in all phases of a project cycle have done little to mitigate against the top-down view. When grassroots organizations have been formed, it has been primarily to funnel assistance to or mobilize communities to receive project goods or services. As projects normally cover many communities, this has led to the creation of many GROs relating vertically to the project rather than to each other. The more profound impact has been continued fragmentation of the grassroots level—inhibiting the natural growth of linkages among similar groups, their potential federation into more democratic and representative bodies, and ultimately the solidarity and development of norms and networks of community cooperation or social capital.

Traditional grassroots organizations have always provided some type of safety net for the less well off members of their communities. In most cases they still do. As the nature of community problems has changed over the past four decades—through the spread of AIDS, for example, the impact of civil war, and the growth of urban poverty—in large part due to forces outside their control, traditional institutions have often been overwhelmed by the sheer magnitude of the suffering and misery encountered. Thus what once were considered local community problems have increasingly turned into larger public or societal dilemmas in most countries. GROs must be the first line of defense in the public battle to ensure the welfare of all citizens, but it is evident that they must be connected to the larger processes and institutions that have had a role in creating the situation or that can contribute to its resolution.

ment in crop yields, higher-quality meat and wool, and more rational uses of their land and water resources.

Perhaps the most important lesson to be drawn from SADESCA is the need to attend to first things first. In a hostile environment, the federation first attended to their member organizations' legal, financial, and political survival needs. Having accomplished that, they moved on to focus on the development of the institutional capacity of the organizations and to broaden their overall governance to include women in the governing body. This laid the base on which they could broaden their training and educational efforts to become more inclusive of the total family needs at the local community level.

SADESCA continues to function at both the political and legal levels as well as the technical production level. This combination of political and legal activity to lay the groundwork for extended technical and production assistance for small farmers and their families has been possible in part because of the unique role of legal processes in Chilean culture and society. Transfer of this model to another societal environment, without such a value on legality, might be difficult. The blending of advocacy and development activity always raises questions of risk and return, and the strategic question about which needs to come first. This will vary from society to society.

Case study based on Thomas F. Carroll, Intermediary NGOs: The Supporting Link in Grassroots Development *(West Hartford, Conn.: Kumarian Press, 1992).*

As noted earlier, GROs are able to raise a significant portion of their resources to sustain their activities from a combination of member contributions, earned income in the form of fees for service, and occasionally some external funding from local governments, businesses, and foreign donors. While they may be able to serve their members and communities by addressing some problems, GROs must find ways of connecting to the larger worlds of politics and the market that ultimately conditions their social and economic welfare. The answer for doing so lies within the broader realm of civil society itself and in two basic types of intermediary civil society organization— traditional development NGOs with no direct institutional ties to the GRO, and federated bodies that regroup GROs at higher levels of association.

The difference between these two types is fundamental and bears directly on how a GRO relates to the macropolitical and economic context in which it labors, which holds the key to mobilizing additional resources. The difference relates specifically to the role of GROs in the decisionmaking and leadership selection processes of these two intermediary types. Technically, GROs have no legal rights of participation in the internal affairs of NGOs, whereas they are constituent members of federated bodies with formal voting rights. Thus federated CSO intermediaries are directly accountable for their actions and performance to their GRO members, but NGOs are not. Viewed solely as an issue of resource mobilization, whether the GRO works with and through an NGO or federation may not make much difference. But in terms of GROs advancing member and community interests in the broader political environment, the choice is an important one.

Over the long term, the promotion of federated intermediary CSOs is in the best interests of grassroots groups, their members, surrounding communities, and ultimately the larger society. Given that the goal is to increase the autonomy and sustainability of GROs, doing so through federations makes the most sense. It is, however, a long-term strategy; ignoring the important contributions of traditional development NGOs to the political and economic empowerment of GROs would be doing both GROs and NGOs a disservice in the short to medium term. Thus while the focus here is on working through federated intermediary GROs, development NGOs that have promoted GRO solidarity through facilitating linkages and federations are discussed as well. At the same time, resources are limited, and strategic choices must be made about what type of intermediary organization ultimately does the most to promote sustainable development from the grassroots point of view.

Grassroots membership-based intermediary CSOs can take the form of federations, unions, cooperatives, or peoples' movements. Regardless of what they are called, their primary unit of composition is the grassroot GRO, they all provide one or more services that support the missions of their member organizations, their governance structure gives each level of association a right to participate in internal decisionmaking and leadership selection, and when necessary they engage decisionmakers in government and the market. In the case of many intermediary CSOs and particularly peoples' movements, the objective is to change the nature of power altogether—that is, to place citizens at the heart of the political system so that societal goals more accurately reflect the needs, interests, and aspirations of the majority. Thus while the focus here is on the ability of intermediary CSOs to serve their grassroots members, a strong case can be made for promoting their own sustainability, autonomy, and ultimately permanence as a desired institutional actor within civil society.

Membership Strategies

Federated intermediary CSOs in both the South and East as well as the North can have as many as 1 million individual citizen members, usually grouped into several levels of higher association, culminating in the case of a nationwide organization in an "apex" body. While labor unions of this magnitude are found throughout the world, now increasingly peasant federations, cooperatives, credit unions, and more broadly based peoples' movements of similar size are found in locales as diverse as Brazil, the Philippines, and Senegal.

The obvious potential for generating resources from member contributions of cash (fees, subscriptions, or assessments) and nonfinancial resources must be balanced by a number of considerations. First and foremost, most resources collected from individual citizen members must be viewed as being directed toward addressing the purposes for which their GRO was created. Second, depending on the size and scope of the CSO intermediary—whether it extends from the grassroots to the national level or somewhere in between—each of the successively higher units of aggregation will require some level of support and thus lay claim to some portion of fees collected from its members or member organizations.

As a general principle, the farther away from the grassroots community level, the smaller the individual member contributions will be as a percentage of the total resource base of the higher-level representative bodies. Because of the far greater "catchment area" that higher level bodies command, however, membership fees can still constitute a considerable potential resource. The issue of how much or what percent of member fees gets allocated to the next higher level of association must be decided through member votes.

Mobilizing Members' Savings

The principle of mobilizing savings to form the core of the loan program is critical to overall success, particularly for intermediary CSOs that provide credit to their members—whether individuals or member organizations. A distinction should be made between savings used in productive activities (such as marketing) and those that are intended to support social or safety net services on behalf of member organizations. The former should be able to generate enough revenue to cover the cost of managing and administering their distribution and collection. Like a bank or credit union, mobilized member savings grow over time and benefit both the CSO and its members. Savings used to create a development fund to finance construction of, say, a health facility covering several member organizations, on the other hand, would be better treated as resources raised through a special assessment, and thus be considered a membership strategy.

The Federation of Senegalese NGOs, the largest peasant movement—with 19 different constituent federations—has been able to build a fund of more than $150,000 from member contributions, which in turn formed the core of a "guarantee fund" and attracted additional funding from donors. The bank used by the movement eventually decided to become a business partner, based on the organization's capacity to cover the risk associated with the bank's credit loans. In India, the 80,000 members of a women's organization decided to consolidate all their individual savings into a single account, which created a fund of more than $100,000. Based on these savings, the Ministry of Housing arranged a loan for the women's movement for the development of low-cost housing for the poor, which would generate income but also meet an important social need identified by both the government and the group.

In an increasing number of countries in Latin America, Asia, and Africa, federations and people's movements have become so financially powerful in managing member savings—and in a number of cases, other forms of member income derived from their productive enterprises—that they are regularly consulted by government on a range of social and economic policies of relevance to their members and their well-being. Although these financial resources that are productively used by CSO intermediaries translate into power, it must be remembered that individual member organizations—beginning with the GRO—form the foundation upon which this strength is based. When the higher levels of a federation or movement forget the source of their strength, problems begin to emerge in the entire structure.

Earned Income Strategies: Fees for Service

Intermediary CSOs should come into being as needs arise, based on addressing a requirement that no single grassroots CSO can meet itself. This means that it is a ser-

ORGANIZATION OF RURAL ASSOCIATIONS FOR PROGRESS, ZIMBABWE

The Organization of Rural Associations for Progress (ORAP) is a social movement created in southern Zimbabwe in 1980 that currently links some 50,000 families grouped into peasant associations and federations of associations. It has become one of the most important rural social movements in Africa, with an annual budget of some US$2 million. The promotion of local economic activities such as farming, traditional crafts, and social activities clearly demonstrates the movement's impact, although there is still much to be done in terms of acquiring technological know-how and boosting output.

Aware of the implications and the dangers of becoming overreliant on the aid system, and of the system's inability to generate local capital, the directors of ORAP recently drew up a long-term autonomy policy.

Stage One: *Self-Help*—ORAP is well organized and its members have received sufficient training to realize that future success depends on self-help and members' savings. A savings and credit scheme is therefore being promoted at the village, regional, and national levels.

Stage Two: *Flexible and Unearmarked Financing*—ORAP's negotiations with its donors ensure that external financing is elastic and flexible. About 80 percent of this aid is not earmarked for specific projects.

Stage Three: *Creation of Enterprises*—With the RAFAD Foundation's help, a study of possible financial activities was conducted; it found that, thanks to good management, assets enabled three activities to be launched. First, ORAP purchased a garage/petrol station in the regional capital; profit is made from the petrol sales and the garage is used as a depot for ORAP's eight large trucks, donated for the transportation

vice provider to the member organizations that form it. It is from the provision of these services to its members that a CSO must recoup some portion of its costs through a user fee. This obviously is a lot easier to achieve when the good or service provided is used by members in a productive activity or if it supports a social service that members find compelling.

A regional cooperative or peasant federation that supplies fertilizer to district members who in turn supply it to GRO members is a good example of a service supplied by a higher-level organization that can not only cover the cost of the item, but charge a modest fee at each level to cover its own costs of delivery. Because the regional-level CSO can purchase the fertilizer in bulk at a discount, it can sell it to the district level for less than the individual member organizations could, and so on down the line. The same principle holds for a CSO federation working in the health or education field that provides medicines or school books, for example.

The problem facing most intermediary CSOs is in determining how to cover costs related to services that do not provide an essential "good" but rather a desirable "service."

of food to regions in which there is a shortage. Second, a warehouse has been built in the regional capital to help supply the villages and urban areas with building materials and other much needed products; it is managed by an ORAP team. Finally, a farm has been purchased that permits modern livestock breeding and technology transfer to groups of peasants in the surrounding area.

Stage Four: *Creation of a Capital Fund*—The main aim of ORAP's strategy is to use its reserves, already invested in economic activities, to increase its capital so that it can create businesses and grant credit to its members.

Stage Five: *Partnership with the Business Sector*—In 1993, ORAP actively sought ways to establish a source of sustainable income through the business sector. On the advice of the local business sector, ORAP enlisted the help of OXFAM Canada and Christian Aid UK as well as RAFAD. Several business ventures have since resulted, some successful and others less so.

Stage Six: *Creation of a Local Investment Company*—To reduce the number of economic activities and create new businesses, ORAP decided to create a local investment company using the central campaign fund. Contributions are requested from certain investors for specific projects. This company is also open to investors from other Zimbabwean development organizations with the same objectives.

Stage Seven: *Creation of the ORAP Foundation*—All these tools and financial mechanisms require a legal structure to assure coordination and the integration of each tool into a global strategy. ORAP felt that the best way to manage this fund was to create an ORAP Foundation that will provide a legal, fiscal, and financial framework.

For instance, in several Central and East European countries, consortia of NGOs and other civil society actors have created regional service centers where members can send or receive a fax or e-mail, type a letter, or photocopy a document. In short, it provides an office for those organizations that lack one. In some cases, the centers provide a common locus for NGO and GRO program planning and coordination, including developing joint advocacy strategies for policy reform. In most cases, however, the individual members do not have the resources to pay the full cost of the services they are receiving, including the overhead of office rent, utilities, and so on.

Similarly, training and technical assistance services provided by intermediary CSOs present problems for organizations that are engaged in productive endeavors as well as those that perform a social development function. Credit programs throughout the world provide a range of such services to both lower-level CSO financial intermediaries as well as the individual borrowers of the credit. While many CSOs can now cover the costs of their lending operations, the same cannot be said for the necessary training and technical assistance that they require to be successful. Similarly, a federation of community-level parent-teacher associations, while able to cover the costs for books and other learning materials necessary for their members' schools, cannot cover through fees the costs of training members in such areas as curriculum development and school management. Problems such as these require that other sources of finance be found.

Mobilizing Resources from External Sources

Given the functions and responsibilities of intermediary CSOs—serving the internal program and logistical needs of their members as well as representing and advocating members' interests in the larger community—experience has shown that resources generated from within the larger organization seldom cover overall costs. This leads many CSOs to explore a range of strategies described throughout this book—getting access to public resources from government; generating revenue from a number of market-based activities, including corporate philanthropy; and receiving grants from donors. The funds generated from these external sources are used not only to support the CSO's service delivery but also to provide additional resources for its members' own programs.

Major Conclusions for Practitioners

Grassroots citizens' organizations and other civil society intermediary groups are the principal actors involved in this resource enhancement strategy. Their reason for being, however, is to serve and act on behalf of citizens, their communities, and the larger public interest. GROs are the most direct expression of citizen, community, and societal interests, concerns, and aspirations and are thus best placed to act on and advance them. Although their focus is on local problem solving, the solutions are often found well beyond villages and neighborhoods where they work. This includes those state and market actors who make the policies and control the resources that affect social and economic well-being at the grassroots level.

This situation has provided the rationale for the creation of a range of intermediary CSOs that occupy the public space between the GRO—and by extension citizens, their families, and communities—and those who hold power in government and business. The dual role of supporting the program mission of members as well as being their representative and advocate makes intermediary CSOs an indispensable fixture in civil society.

For intermediary CSOs to be effective in these two roles, they must maintain their greatest resource—the democratic and representative nature of their governance structure. As an advocate of member interests, CSOs must first be perceived as being legitimate representatives in the eyes of their members as well as those of government officials and business leaders. In fact, achieving the latter is primarily a function of the former.

Although peasant and women's federations as well as cooperatives and credit unions are membership-based and democratically structured from bottom up in principle, the reality for many of them is far from this ideal. There should be no reason to believe that just because an organization is classified as part of civil society it is by definition democratic. This is particularly true in many southern and eastern countries that have long histories of authoritarian rule, the values and practices of which have permeated associational life to its very roots.

Citizens' organizations at the grassroots level have shown amazing resilience in their adherence to member participation and openness, but the higher up the federated ladder an organization is and the further away from these democratic roots, the more difficult it becomes to exercise broadbased decisionmaking and to avoid personalism and factionalism in leadership selection. This is why intermediary CSOs must work at maintaining their legitimacy, which is the principal currency they have to barter for more concrete resources from external actors.

RESOURCE GUIDE

Bibliography

Carroll, Thomas F., *Intermediary NGOs: The Supporting Link in Grassroots Development* (West Hartford, Conn.: Kumarian Press, 1992).

Edwards, Michael, and David Hulme, eds., *Making a Difference: NGOs and Development in a Changing World* (London: Earthscan, 1992).

Fowler, Alan, *Striking a Balance: A Guide to Enhancing the Effectiveness of Non-Governmental Organizations in International Development* (London: Earthscan, 1997).

Glade, William, and Charles Reilly, eds., *Inquiry at the Grassroots* (Arlington, Va.,: Inter-American Foundation, 1992).

MYRADA, "The Village Reference Book: Inventory of Non-financial and Existing Resource at the Village Level," in Fernand Vincent, *Manual of Practical Management* (Geneva: Development Innovations and Networks, 1989).

Vincent, Fernand, *Alternative Financing Strategies: Volumes 1 and 2* (Geneva: Development Innovations and Networks, 1995).

Vincent, Fernand, and Piers Campbell, *Towards Greater Financial Autonomy: A Manual on Financing Strategies and Techniques for Development NGOs and Community Organizations* (Geneva: Development Innovations and Networks, 1989).

Case Study Contacts

Gabriela Lavickova and Ales Kutak
Center for Community Work
Jagellonska 22
3013 Plzeň
Czech Republic
Tel: (420-19) 22-479
Fax: (420-19) 22-067

Jiri Dusik
Regional Environmental Center for CEE
Ady Endre ut 9-11
2000 Szentendre
Hungary

Thandiwe Nkomo
Executive Director
Organization of Rural Associations for Progress
P.O. Box 877
Bulawayo
Zimbabwe
Tel: (263-9) 71332 or 31009
Fax: (263-9) 72127 or 75661

Concerned Resource Organizations

Boukary Younoussi
Secretary General
**Development Innovations and
Networks (IRED)**
3 Rue d Varembe
P.O. Box 116
1211 Geneva 20
Switzerland
Tel: (41-22) 734-1716
Fax: (41-22) 740-0011

Jane Covey
Director
**Institute for Development
Research**
44 Farnsworth Street
Boston, MA 02210-1211
Tel: (617) 422-0422
Fax: (617) 482-0617

David Valenzuela
Vice President, Programs
Inter-American Foundation
901 North Stuart Street
Arlington, VA 22203
Tel: (703) 841-3834
Fax: (703) 841-1605
E-mail: dvalenzuel@iaf.gov

Horatio R. Morales, Jr.
President
**Philippines Rural Reconstruction
Movement**
940, Quezon Avenue
Kayumanggi Press Building
Quezon City 1112
Philippines
Tel: (63-2) 928-1715
Fax: (63-2) 928-7919
E-mail: hrm@mnl.cyberspace.com.ph

Fernand Vincent
Executive Director
**Research and Applications
for Alternative Financing for
Development**
C.P. 117 Rue de Varembe
1211 Geneva 20
Switzerland
Tel: (41-22) 733-5073
Fax: (41-22) 734-7083
E-mail: rafad@iprolink.ch

Chapter 6

Public Resources From Government

Gonzalo de la Maza, Richard Holloway, and Fadel N'Diame

Civil Society: Legitimate Public Actor

Governments control significant resources that they consider and treat as their own. While government usually controls the largest amount of resources (such as land, finances, and labor) in most southern and eastern countries and is potentially the place from which civil society organizations (CSOs) might get the most help, the history of attempts to tap public resources is poor and the examples few and far between. Indeed, there is little information on public resources allocated to nongovernmental actors.

The Spectrum of Government–CSO Relations

CSOs see themselves as nongovernmental and nonprofit. A large part of civil society actually calls itself NGO (nongovernmental organization). Many CSOs feel uneasy at the idea of getting resources from government because they feel that there is a fundamental difference in values, and that too close a proximity will lead to undesirable results. They would prefer to deal with government only when it accepts their ways of working and comes knocking on their door.

In contrast, another part of civil society believes it is the responsibility of CSOs to engage government, and that what are called government resources are actually public resources. They maintain that these are only held in trust by any particular government, with the country's citizens, present and future, being the legitimate owners. CSOs represent the people, who have every right to call on the government to provide them with public resources.

These two views, on opposite ends of the spectrum, are born from and depend on a mix of attitudes that government has of CSOs, and that CSOs have of the government, based on historical experiences.

The principal experience defining this relationship has been several decades of authoritarian and totalitarian rule in which the distinction between public and government was extinguished, just as market and society, and the resources generated within them, were subordinated to the dictates of an all-powerful state. The net result of au-

CENTER FOR LEGISLATIVE DEVELOPMENT, PHILIPPINES

In 1986, after 14 years of martial law, new democratic elections took place in the Philippines. The Center for Legislative Development (CLD) was established to revive and sustain citizen participation in the formulation, implementation, and evaluation of new policy decisions and to involve the emerging civil society in the redemocratization process.

After assisting a wide array of citizens' groups in their advocacy work, CLD decided to focus on women's groups, given their limited resources. In November 1991, the "Women in Nation-Building Act" was submitted for debate to the House and the Senate. The Center convened a meeting of women's groups and briefed them about the status of the bill and the strategic necessity of organizing and mobilizing for its passage. Women's organizations, realizing the importance of advocacy, established a feminist advocacy initiative at a CLD meeting. Initiatives of Women for the Reform of Law and Society (SIBOL) worked with the authors of the bill to reconcile differences, and legislation was finally passed.

The new law included provisions on women's equality in applying for credit and allocated a certain percentage of official development assistance (ODA) to women's programs. It provided that these funds be allocated to government agencies. CSOs can apply for grants through the National Economic and Development

thoritarianism and totalitarianism as practiced from the end of the colonial era to the fall of the Berlin Wall was that the fundamental values (social capital) and institutional building blocks (citizens' organizations) of an autonomous and legitimate civil society were effectively stunted or killed off altogether.

Various democratic openings during the past decade have significantly changed government and civil society interaction in many countries. India, for instance, with a long history of CSOs, declared in the Seventh Five-Year Plan (1988) that voluntary organizations are partners in development, and it has offered them a range of funding channels. It has also insisted that the government bureaucracy work closely with CSOs. In contrast, few governments in Africa or, to a lesser extent, Asia and Central and Eastern Europe would contemplate giving voluntary organizations access to public revenues, battered as they are by the rigors of structural adjustment and believing as they do that individual CSOs are opportunist, upstart, unprofessional threats to their own credibility.

Wherever CSOs find themselves on the spectrum of civil society-government relations, clearly the resources controlled by governments are potentially important. CSOs' success in gaining access to public funding will to some extent demonstrate government's appreciation of their value and help them increase and diversify their funding sources. The disadvantages will be played out differently in different settings, and will depend greatly on how the relationship evolves. A strategy of accepting public resources from government lets a CSO think about the long-term sustainability of

Authority. The portion of ODA earmarked for women's programs has increased since the enactment of the law, from 18 percent in 1993 to 31 percent by 1997.

Under another initiative, CLD promoted the enactment of local legislation immediately when the new Local Government Code was passed in 1991, devolving important functions to the local level. The Center organized capability-building seminars on policy agenda-setting for legislators and CSOs, which provided an opportunity for the two parties to forge partnerships. In three provinces, CLD facilitated the formation of women's legislative advocacy groups, and in one, women were able to push for the enactment of an ordinance that created the Provincial Council of Women with an appropriation of $10,000.

The Center's activities with mostly women's CSOs led to significant legislative changes at both the national and the local level, which in turn increased the resources of women's CSOs from government agencies. One key for CLD's success is the faith in the possibility of change as opposed to skepticism. Even the organization was surprised by the degree to which they could move women at the village level to get involved. At present they have more than 100 women trainees who have decided to run for the next village elections.

The strategy CLD applies in its activities is the prompt response to new legislation and the timely initiation of legislative change. This was essential to success in the case of both the Women in Nation-Building Act and the Local Government Program.

Case study based on information from Socorro L. Reyes, The Center for Legislative Development.

its work, since government (in one form or another) will continue to exist and thus will continue to be able to fund the work of CSOs.

A government is unlikely to provide resources to CSOs that it perceives as a threat to its tenure or that will undermine its credibility with citizens domestically or with outside donors or international organizations. It is entirely possible that governments can be persuaded by CSOs to help them carry out programs that originated with the CSOs, just as it is possible that governments can be persuaded of alternative policies identified by CSOs. Still, while there may be space for maneuver in their relations with central and local government, CSOs have to accept that gaining access to public resources will be largely on government's terms, at least initially.

Over the long term, there is certainly room to negotiate an expansion of the boundaries of CSO participation in public life, particularly in the making and implementation of sustainable development policies. But for CSOs that see the policies and practices of government as part of the problems they are trying to solve, accepting funding—whether called public or not—would be seen as a danger to their independence rather than a solution to their sustainability.

It is not helpful to be too much of a purist about the contrast between mission-driven activities and income-driven activities. The clever CSO can see the opportunities for carrying out mission-driven activities through work that had not been originally conceived of in that light. There is room for a lot of creative thinking and planning by a CSO for work that fits its mission, even when first-time funding from the government seems to require something different from the main work of the CSO. It is important sometimes just to get a "foot in the door" so that a CSO can demonstrate its program approach and effectiveness.

But if a CSO is twisted out of shape by taking on work it had no intention of doing, simply in order to keep its financial head above water, the group may have problems keeping staff as well as the involvement of those who are interested in its mission. In general, where resources for development purposes are in short supply, competition for whatever does exist will be fierce, and principle is often jettisoned in favor of practical realities, particularly where organizational survival is at stake. This is no less true for northern CSOs working domestically or internationally than it is for their southern and eastern counterparts.

Growing Legitimacy of Civil Society

The diversity of the CSO sector is its strength as well as a manifestation of the different voices and interests within society itself. The issue is how to balance narrow "special" interests, which most CSOs represent, with the larger public good. This is what government claims to do; can civil society do so as well, and in the process claim a share of "public" resources?

CSOs need to promote themselves to government as important organs of society whose inclusion in decisionmaking will lead to better and more successful government policies and practices. To do so, they need to consider how they are going to deal with various constraints to successful collaboration, as described at an Asian Government/NGO Workshop in Hyderabad, India, in September 1991 by the Overseas Development Institute:

- lack of understanding of each other's goals,
- inability of government to identify the types of CSO that might become reliable working partners,
- restrictive government procedures,
- problems of attitude (distrust, and so on) on both sides,
- lack of clear government policy and guidelines on CSOs,
- poor communications among CSOs and between them and government,
- sharp contrasts between the "top-down" working methods of government and the more participatory approaches of CSOs,
- lack of existing linkages between various institutions in the state,
- poor understanding of relative strengths and weaknesses on both sides, and
- lack of CSO accountability to their constituency, or to the public at large, for the ways in which resources are used.

Part of the answer to the issue of CSO legitimacy will require CSOs to invest their own time and resources in educating state and market actors, as well as the public at large, about who they are and why they are valuable assets both individually and as a coherent, well-articulated sector. The World Bank has suggested several reasons why a country should value a strong and independent civil society sector (see Box 1).

Box 1

THE VALUE OF STRONG AND INDEPENDENT CSOS TO GOVERNMENTS

Efficiency: *NGOs can provide goods and services more efficiently.*

Public-Sector "Market Failure": *CSOs can provide public goods and services not adequately supplied by the public or private sectors.*

Freedom of Association and Speech: *CSOs allow this to be carried out in practice.*

Pluralism and Tolerance: *The density and diversity of CSOs and other forms of associational life increase institutional pluralism, providing citizens with more voices and choices.*

Social Stability/Rule of Law: *CSOs provide an essential safety valve for social pressures and energies in a lawful way.*

Privatization of Public Goods and Services: *CSOs can take over more of the services of the state.*

Support for a Market Economy: *The qualities that CSOs enhance (pluralism, trust, local democracy, social stability, rule of law) foster the qualities needed for a market economy.*

In addition to improving the "visibility" of the sector, a concerted effort must be made to improve the enabling environment that conditions civil society's ability to act in the public interest—including laws, policies, and regulations as well as the political institutions that develop and apply them. Finally, and related to the previous two issues, is the way in which civil society takes an active stance in remaking its image and bringing the enabling environment into line with its own needs, including its ability to gain access to the political arenas where public decisions are made.

Today people from countries throughout the South and East are either relearning or learning for the first time the art of voluntary association or how to work together to achieve common objectives, shared interests, or collective aspirations. Civil societies, in short, are not simply born; they evolve and grow as people learn this most basic of social skills and begin generating from within their own voluntary associations the critical norms and values of social capital. At the same time, the leaders of newly emerging democracies are inexperienced and unclear about the potential role and purpose of these civil societies in social, economic, and political life.

To the individuals involved in such associations, and who undertake such activities, the value of civil society is plain to see. To date, however, the aggregation of these many small citizens' actions has not been seen for what it is—a growing third sector, comparable in value and importance to the state and market to which it is now juxtaposed. What is needed in increasing civil society's visibility and values is for the organizations that represent civil society to move beyond the confines of a particular activity or project—as important as these are—to thinking through their role as a critical force in national and local development. In short, civil society and CSOs must become more strategic in their thinking and actions, developing a grand vision for their countries' development and their role in achieving it.

This will require a division of labor within civil society itself. In the case of older CSOs such as labor unions, farmers' cooperatives, and professional and business associations, it often involves demonstrating a definitive break with their previous relations with authoritarian governments and political parties and becoming once again voluntary and autonomous organizations whose purpose is to represent the concerns and promote the interests of their members. In the case of newer CSOs such as community-based citizens' groups, policy advocacy organizations, and human rights associations, it involves clarifying with the public that they perform functions and operate from a set of values that are important for society as a whole, not just small and narrow interest groups.

Finally, as civil society begins to mature, more specialized organizations are needed that serve the "sector" of civil society itself in terms of promoting its visibility, strength, and legitimacy. This will include "apex" organizations or consortia that can develop and institute a code or standard of conduct that ensures an internal source and structure for CSO accountability; that can facilitate civil society linkages, including alliances and coalitions to protect and promote the rights of CSOs as well as those of society; and that can promote intersectoral linkages with institutions in government and business that also want to ensure lasting political reforms that enhance the public interest, including a legitimate role for civil society. (See also Chapter 5.)

If CSOs want to explain their importance to the public, they must start from familiar examples, and not rely on what they consider to be self-evident truths. The question they should be prepared to answer at any time is, What have you done for us—citizens, communities, society—today? The amount of public resources that CSOs are able to secure will be a direct function of how they answer this question and make the answer known to their partners and constituents. The ability of civil society to demonstrate its commitment to civic engagement and the values of philanthropy and voluntarism will largely determine the degree to which the state, market, and society finds it worth providing resources to support the "good works" of individual CSOs.

Overview of Resources Available from Government

Governments are complex, and the ways that they deal with external organizations in terms of resource collection and allocations exhibits this complexity. The sources of government revenue include taxes and other fees levied on individuals and corporations, the sale or rent of government-owned assets (such as natural resources or state-owned enterprises), and grants and loans received from bilateral and multilateral donors and business investors. With pressure coming from international markets and banks, governments throughout the world have increasingly divested themselves of the ownership of a range of "enterprises," from development banks and parastatal marketing boards to medium businesses and heavy industry, but they often maintain a stake in critical markets and major public industries and resources (such as electricity and telephone, land, forests, and extractive industries).

If governments are persuaded to support civil society—or at least elements within it that meet certain "political" criteria—they can sign a contract with a CSO for the provision of goods and services. Or they might make an outright grant to the organization, provide a loan to the group, or subsidize the CSO's work through one of several nonfinancial means. These various forms of support are described at length later in the chapter. There are also important fiscal and legal measures that governments can take to support CSOs, as discussed in the final section of the chapter.

Successful CSOs will act more as entrepreneurs—seeking whatever information they can that will give them an advantage in pressing government for public resources, preferably through grants, but also by competing for contracts where they perceive a comparative advantage over other CSOs or, more often, for-profit firms. Under this strategy, the CSO will have to spend significant time trying to gain valuable intelligence on numerous issues:

- What does the government's overall development policy state about the role of CSOs in general (for example, in terms of program implementation)? Have specific policies been formulated for the concerned program sector(s)?

- Which government agencies have public funds, for what programmatic purposes, and do they have a history of using CSOs in program implementation?

- Who within these agencies is responsible for deciding how public funds will be used and allocated? And how are decisions reached internally (by committee, by an individual, or by a specially constituted review board)?

- What is the origin of the resources (donors or taxes) and what might this mean about how final decisions are made concerning who is eligible to receive "public" funding?

- What is the nature of the program or services to be provided (service delivery or social mobilization, for instance)? Who has previously been responsible for its implementation?

- Which geographic region or regions is the focus of the program? And has a specific target group been defined?

- What is the budget for the program? Has a percentage of the budget been set aside for administrative or operating costs, or does government have a long-standing policy in this regard? What are the government's policies, if any, on charges for overhead and other indirect costs?

- Does the concerned government agency intend to engage the implementing organization by contract or grant? For either one, will the implementing organization be competitively selected? Does the government agency respond to "unsolicited" proposals—that is, to undertake a specific program using government funds?

- Is there a technical or programmatic approach that the government prefers over others? Is it consistent with that of the CSO?

- Does government have a preference for a single or joint proposal for program implementation?

With this information in hand, the CSO will be in a more competitive position for public funds from relevant government agencies.

Scale and Importance of Public Resources

Of the government resources allocated to CSOs, it is likely that the greatest proportion has gone to groups that work in the field of social safety nets (such as emergency relief, food aid, and disaster assistance) and social development (such as health care, primary education, and welfare). Depending on the country, additional major flows have also been noted in the field of conservation, environmental protection, and community-based natural resource management, and also in the development of micro-enterprises and the informal sector.

The sector thought to have received the smallest share of government resources is democracy and governance, meaning the activities of CSOs working on human rights monitoring and protection, voter and civic education, mediation and alternative dispute resolution, oversight of government financial performance, and public policy analysis, formulation, and advocacy. An indicator of civil society's acceptance as a partner of government will be an increase in resource flows to all sectors in general and to the democracy and governance sector in particular.

One way of assessing the importance of government resources to CSOs is to look at the present position of government funding of these groups in the North. Although there is no reason for the South or East to necessarily follow the pattern of the North, it is instructive to note that groups there receive 10 percent of their funding from private philanthropy (of which 90 percent is from individual citizens), 47 percent from earned income (such as fees for goods or services), and the other 43 percent from government (federal, state, and local).

CSOs in the South and East need to consider not just whether they can get access to public resources from government, but what proportion of their budget should come from this source if it does become available.

Benefits and Limitations

In 1993, the Overseas Development Institute carried out a worldwide survey of relations between government and NGOs. The Hyderabad meeting mentioned earlier produced an interesting balance sheet on the benefits and disadvantages of collaboration. It referred specifically to NGOs (self-appointed development organizations set up to help others), rather than any other civil society actors (such as trade unions, cooperatives and credit unions, or professional and business associations), but the results are instructive (see Table 1).

Further benefits and disadvantages may be added from the CSO perspective. On the benefits side, a government grant or contract can lead to closer involvement for the CSO in policy measures. Good CSO programs, when funded by the government, can be scaled up by the government to have much greater impact. (There is, however, a problem here in that the difference in style and process between CSOs and government may mean that a good CSO program, when executed by the government, may not be implemented in the same way.) A last benefit is that government support for a CSO can provide a measure of protection in areas where personal security is a problem.

TABLE 1: Benefits and Disadvantages of Government–NGO Collaboration

A Balance Sheet from Government's Perspective

Benefits	*Disadvantages*
Better delivery facilities for govt services	Govt services shown to be inefficient by NGO's presence and actions
More information available from the grassroots	NGO mobilization work promotes social instability
More interaction with "targets"	Demand for govt services may increase beyond the capacity to meet it
Enhanced cost-effectiveness	NGOs compete with govt for donor funds
Field testing facilities for new technologies	Weakening of govt mandate and credibility
Appropriate training inputs available from NGO specialists	Unaccountability of NGO specialists
More coordination of NGO activities possible; more control of NGOs in general	

A Balance Sheet from the NGO perspective

Improved access to policy formulation	Co-optation by govt and greater bureaucratic controls
Access to specialist research facilities and expertise	The NGO grows to assume a more bureaucratic character
Opportunity to improve govt services "from within" by training	Loss of NGO autonomy and independence
Access to new technologies "from above"	Relegation to mere delivery activities, to the detriment of NGO's wider program
Opportunities for passing on technologies and models for replication or scaling up	Loss of credibility among clients and a tendency to maintain existing social and political conditions
	Substitution by NGO for govt services perpetuates govt inefficiency
	Govt takes credit for NGO achievements

On disadvantages, government tends to support larger CSOs with proven track records, and to ignore smaller groups. Government funding may require the CSO to scale up, which it may not be able to handle. A change in government can lead to a termination of funding. And finally, government support may not be liked by some stakeholders of the CSO.

LOCAL COOPERATION IN GDYNIA, POLAND

The successful collaboration between CSOs and the Gdynia local government was the result of a well-designed strategy of the Civil Society Development Foundation (CSDF), an international CSO working to enhance the sustainable growth of the nonprofit sector in Central and Eastern Europe. In 1994, CSDF promoted the cooperation of the municipality and CSOs in Gdynia, stimulated by the need for more financial resources and more efficient service delivery for local governments in Poland. The strategy CSDF prepared elaborated the benefits of collaboration for the city: a deeper understanding of the needs of communities, deeper evaluation of social problems, access to less expensive and more knowledgeable service providers than local government agencies, and promotion of citizen participation. For the CSOs, the collaboration aimed at ensuring a new source of funds through grants and subsidies from the local government.'

The strategy included a step-by-step program on how to persuade the local government to "buy into" the cooperation—showing that CSOs are important partners, creating clear procedures for cooperation between CSOs and the city, and creating a model of cooperation that can be replicated in other municipalities.

In January 1995, the city accepted the plan and appointed a consultant to the Mayor on CSO issues. The main turning point in the launching of the project took place in April 1995, when CSDF, together with the CSO Coalition and the city, held a meeting with City Council representatives as well as representatives of more than 100 nonprofit organizations. The CSOs elected a Coordination Committee to support activities in Gdynia and a Consultation Commission to evaluate the coop-

Future Trends

There are few hard and objective data on the amounts of resources going from government to CSOs either by sector or by country, but some trends can be observed. Governments are increasingly likely to scale back their work in the social sector, leaving a vacuum that CSOs are most likely to fill. Public resources will be considered less the monopoly of government and more a resource that can be used wherever there are cost-effective and competent citizens' organizations to do the work. Greater acceptance of democracy will increase the political space for CSOs, which is a precondition to greater participation in making and implementation of public policy. External donor funding to governments will decrease, and more of it will be given to CSOs either directly or through the government. An increased tax base may make more money available for public services that CSOs will be able to supply.

There is a growing focus on democratically elected local government as an arena of decisionmaking and resource allocation as a result of decentralization and democratically elected leaders. And donors are beginning to deal with decentralized local governments and to enter into agreements with them for direct funding.

eration project. In June 1995, the Program of Cooperation Between Local Government of Gdynia and CSOs was born. It was enacted into law by the City Council in September, and since then a wide range of projects has emerged.

In October 1995, the first grantmaking session took place, awarding US$70,000 to 20 CSOs. Groups were invited to Council meetings and gained a consultative position in policy decisions. One of the CSOs received a building from the municipality to establish a day care center free of charge. In April 1996, the Gdynia Center of CSOs opened its doors, serving as a meeting place for more than 40 grassroots organizations and providing access to computers and a library. The office was donated by the municipality, and two of the employees are paid by the City. CSOs contributed 10 volunteers, and CSDF supports the maintenance of the Center.

The experience and lessons learned were published in *Together: Cooperation Between Local Governments and CSOs*. The program was accepted and is being recommended by the Association of Polish Cities, the largest organization of city mayors and presidents in the country. Twenty other cities are following the example of Gdynia, including Wroclaw and Krakow.

CSDF learned that the success of the program was based on identifying the common interests of CSOs and the municipality. In the process of program development, the most important step was to gather representatives of both parties and engage them in discussions. The only significant obstacle to the cooperation was the unclear legal regulatory system regarding local government–CSO partnerships. According to the leader of the program, if he could start over again, he would prepare himself much more carefully to answer legal challenges.

Case study prepared by Michal Guc, Civil Society Development Foundation, Gdynia, Poland.

Some commentators on civil society are suggesting that some of the most successful programs in the future are going to be ones that integrate the best elements of all three sectors—government, civil society, and private business. Each of these sectors has a comparative advantage in some part of development, and using all their skills, contacts, networks, and resources makes more sense than having the government give funds only to CSOs. Examples of these tripartite efforts have been written up by the United Nations Development Programme in *Multiparty Cooperation for Development in Asia*. At the heart of the new trend is that greater resources are flowing to a local level rather than the national level. Most CSOs are based at the local level, and local governments seem more willing to fund them to achieve public purposes.

Key Issues

When CSOs start taking funding or other forms of support from the government, a number of operational issues need to be thought through in advance. First, government will start to make more demands on CSOs in terms of accountability. These are legitimate demands of any funder that has been entrusted with public funds and must account for their use, but CSOs are not accustomed to this. In the past, groups have had to be accountable to foreign donor organizations, but not to their own domestic government. In an increasingly open and democratic system, where civil society participates in the making as well as implementation of public policy, government is ultimately strengthened and legitimized. As such, it has the right as well as constitutional mandate to ensure a rule of law and the proper use of public resources.

Governments will therefore legitimately demand:

- *Information:* What does the CSO stand for, what does it do, and where?

- *Governance/Accountability:* Who is in charge, do they do what they say they stand for, are they observing the law?

- *Contribution to Development:* Is what the CSO does publicly beneficial?

- *Management:* Does the CSO demonstrate an ability to manage and account for resources (financial and human)?

- *Coordination:* Is the CSO working within the policy framework formulated by government?

CSOs will be operating much more in the public arena as they take money from government. Political pressure may well lead to the government wanting to police the work of CSOs. To some extent such pressures can be deflected by CSOs agreeing to regulate themselves—developing and implementing a code or standard of conduct—and getting organized to do so. Government will not, however, abdicate its responsibility of accounting for the use of public funds, and may well find space to increase its hold over CSOs by increasing its regulatory demands.

Sometimes governments (and the external donors that support them) have an overly optimistic view of what CSOs can do with additional resources. This gives rise to another key issue in this area. CSOs rarely have a nationwide reach or, more important, perspective. They exist in pockets here and there, and their impact is uneven. As governments look to such groups to take up some of the work in the social sector that they cannot do, there is a great danger that a national perspective will be lost, and that CSOs will do the work only where they happen to have a presence.

Of course, legitimate CSOs thrive because of their close connection to a community or a constituency that they serve, and maybe from which they sprang. So another issue to confront is that greater involvement with government, particularly in a contractual relationship where the CSO may be working on the government's agenda rather than its own, may start to divorce the CSO from its constituency.

As noted earlier, taking government money can lead to a blunting of the essential element of a CSO, which is that it has its own view of the world, not one that comes to it from government or the private for-profit sector. Too great a dependence on government can trade independence for greater funding stability. The ability of CSOs to manage this dynamic tension will determine their ability to survive over the long term. Generally, CSOs should practice a policy of diversity of resources.

Sustainability is likely to occur when intermediary CSOs—traditional development NGOs in this case—are able to establish or hand over their service delivery functions within membership organizations, in many cases their former clients at the local level.

The model that is coming to the fore in many southern and eastern countries is that of primary-level community-based organizations that begin to federate into higher levels of association and that can provide economies of scale in terms of their local members. The long-term objective of gaining access to public funds through governments must be to empower local organizations to manage their own development.

Government Contracts

CSOs are increasingly being contracted by government to manage development projects or the components of larger programs (often donor-financed) or to provide technical or management assistance to government itself. Specialized CSOs have been contracted to manage grant funds targeting other CSOs and community organizations, including poverty programs. Many CSOs have generated revenues by undertaking baseline studies, conducting various kinds of research, or performing evaluations. While such services are normally contracted by line ministries (such as Health, Agriculture, or Labor), there are a growing number of examples of parliaments contracting with a CSO to undertake policy research and analysis, or a Ministry of Justice offering a contract to train its staff in alternative dispute resolution skills. CSOs can also undertake specific technical tasks such as designing a book, making a video, or disseminating public information messages.

By giving a CSO a contract, the government indicates that it wants the organization to execute a program it has already designed, with or without input from other concerned public actors. Many CSOs have voiced concern, however, that they are often asked to implement badly designed programs that would have had a greater chance of success if the CSO had been brought in earlier. This is far more likely to occur with a grant, however, than a contract.

Although the CSO is often viewed simply as the "implementing agent," there may in fact be some room for negotiation over design and implementation issues. When a government contracts a CSO to provide services such as the distribution of condoms, the management of a literacy project, or the delivery of diarrhea prevention messages, it does so in principle because the CSO has demonstrated a technical and managerial capacity in that particular area; in short, the CSO has a successful track record. In many cases, the government will permit and even encourage the group to suggest an alternative "technical solution" to the delivery of the good or service in its bid proposal.

An important reason for "opening" the contracting process to CSOs is the fact that they usually have strong roots or linkages to a particular constituency or client group, and their knowledge and experience with them is rightly viewed as an important asset in mobilizing local participation in the delivery of a required service. And CSOs— whether providing microcredit to entrepreneurs or legal advice to poor women—are considered an inexpensive and efficient means for delivering public resources to those most in need, wherever they may be found.

Sometimes governments consider contracting with CSOs because an external donor has made the use of a certain organization a condition of a grant or loan to the government. This is good for the CSOs that obtain such work, and sometimes provides

MEDICAL ASSISTANCE PROGRAM, YMCA LEBANON

The YMCA Medical Assistance Program in Lebanon was initiated in 1988 to provide chronically ill low-income patients with free medication. Local communities, national and foreign CSOs, and governments contributed to the program. Medication was distributed through local dispensaries managed by local CSOs.

In 1993, after the end of the civil war in Lebanon, soliciting funds for the program became increasingly difficult. The YMCA finally asked the Ministry of Public Health to take over the program. The Ministry responded by asking YMCA to continue implementing the program, pledging to provide significant financial support in the amount of US$1.5 million a year. YMCA still solicits cash and in-kind contributions from foreign governments and CSOs, and clients also pay a nominal fee. But most client expenses are covered by the government contract.

The YMCA's decision to approach the government resulted from both internal and external factors. Many donors were not interested in continuing funding for the program. The YMCA also believed that financing such a program was the responsibility of the government and that CSOs could not continue to shoulder this burden alone.

them with the opportunity to influence government policy, but it can also cause problems when government views such conditions as intrusive and an indirect indictment of its own competence. Still, it does give CSOs the opportunity to prove themselves useful to the government in its development work, and to move beyond the difficult situation of being the "darling of the donors" but undesired by the government.

A number of problems can arise when CSOs are seen as simply cheaper implementing agents than their counterparts in the for-profit sector, when they have little say in the how the good or service is delivered, and when there is a serious mismatch between government and CSO aims and practices. First, the contracted service may fail because of an initial design fault, but the CSO ultimately receives the blame; second, the CSO may end up carrying out the contract differently than originally agreed on to ensure a minimum degree of success, but be penalized by government for a "breach" of contract; and third, the CSO may give up its moral qualms and organizational principles and become one of the increasing breed of nonprofit contractors—a nonprofit in name only.

CSOs that work in many different parts of a country and that have developed a reputation for strength in a particular development sector may have less difficulty positioning themselves with a government, and in particular can approach national governments and line ministries for contracts. CSOs that are much more local and less specific in their focus, in contrast, are less likely to have been identified by an external donor and more likely to have to present themselves as new actors in the local government contracting field. Depending on the extent of decentralization—and the de-

The YMCA had some previous experience with the government, which encouraged them to pursue state funding. Despite this experience, however, the YMCA needed both technical and financial assistance to help solicit the grant. Staff needed to learn how to lobby for the program in Parliament, and new staff had to be hired with public administration and public finance expertise. YMCA members, a network of more than 310 dispensaries and about 75,000 patients, were involved in advocating the program.

Overall, the YMCA's experience with the government is positive. The organization learned that in the long run, satisfying seemingly bureaucratic government requirements is worthwhile. The government's commitment serves as an excellent example to donors of its support for CSO activities, and it helped raise contributions to other programs. To solicit the grant, YMCA had to demonstrate that it was the only organization that could deliver such a service with high-quality standards. Also, the continuation of external support was essential because it encouraged the Ministry to maintain its support.

But the collaboration with the government also had some negative impacts. It pushed the YMCA into political debates, required the adoption of bureaucratic financial and administrative procedures to meet government requirements, and induced hostility from other CSOs who believed they should have received a "share of the pie."

Case study based on information from Ghassan Sayah, YMCA Lebanon.

volution of resources as well as authority—the local government may not have the authority to make decisions on local contracting.

Whether at the national or local level, it is unlikely that a CSO will enter a new and untouched field. There will be people and organizations that have had a previous contractual relationship to government. It will be important that the CSO have an awareness of some of the ongoing dynamics involved in a new contractual situation.

Where central government had previously been handling the task that the CSO seeks to contract, for example, it may not be doing so any longer because it has cut back on staff or budget, because government machinery is unable to perform to a required standard, or because government machinery is corrupt and inefficient. The CSO should be keenly aware that by taking up some of this work from government it is likely taking work and income away from others, who will not be well disposed to the CSO—or to any outsider, for that matter.

In some cases, local government will have previously been responsible for the provision of the good or service. Decentralization in and of itself does not guarantee that contracting improprieties will be any less prevalent among local governments than they were in central government. In fact, where newly elected democratic governments are weak and unable to provide oversight of local government performance, corruption may increase. Thus CSOs wanting to enter the domain of local contracting are likely to find remnants of the previous system or the beginnings of a new one based on kick-back and fraud.

FUNDACIÓN PARA LA JUVENTUD Y MUJER RURAL FUNAC 4-S, COSTA RICA

Clubes 4-S was established as an NGO in Costa Rica in 1960 to provide training and employment opportunities to youth and rural women throughout the country. Its community and small enterprise development programs and seminars reach nearly 10,000 young people and 5,000 rural women each year.

For the first 20 years, the foundation was heavily supported by government grants, primarily from the Ministry of Agriculture. By 1975–76, concerned over threats of reduced government support, Clubes 4-S began to decrease its dependence on government sources.

The foundation started to capitalize on the trend of recent years within many government agencies in Costa Rica to privatize state services. In 1980, Clubes 4-S won a contract agreement from the Social Security Administration, which wished to privatize its hospital clothing manufacturing industry. Clubes 4-S had a group of skilled rural women whom it could readily contract for the work.

Currently, the foundation manages 80 percent of the hospital clothing manufacturing for the entire country, generating approximately 50 percent of its annual operating budget. According to the Executive Director, the large share of

If a CSO offers, for instance, to deliver famine-relief food, build schools, construct rural roads, distribute condoms, carry out inoculations programs, or run local markets—all through a contract with a government agency—it must be aware that it is inserting itself into an existing pattern of obligations and favors. Those who have been put out of work by the CSO's arrival on the scene may retaliate. The CSO must decide if it will pay "dues" to the local government system to get the contracts. If it does not do so, will it seek "godfathers" further up the government hierarchy who will protect it from retaliation?

And there is a reverse "ethical" issue in terms of private firms. Since CSOs normally do not pay taxes, and may in fact receive exemptions on duty for a range of goods related to program implementation, they have an unfair advantage in terms of cost proposals in the bid process, according to local for-profit companies. This has already become an issue in many northern countries where government has disengaged from the provision of welfare services; it is more than likely to emerge in southern and eastern countries as well as the same phenomenon takes place.

Intermediary CSOs that deliver services at the grassroots level often involve community-based organizations in all phases of service delivery with the goal of eventually turning over this responsibility directly to them, or to higher-level associations composed of these base units. The activities of such groups are largely targeted at reaching the poor, who are often geographically isolated and spread out or socially marginalized. As has increasingly been demonstrated, the cost of reaching these individuals with needed goods and services is appreciably more than with other social groups. In short, working with the poor is not a cheap proposition, whoever undertakes it.

business going to Clubes 4-S is due to the government's satisfaction with the lower production costs, higher-quality output, reduced bureaucracy, and rural development benefits offered by the foundation. The government subsequently approached the foundation to coordinate hospital laundry facilities as well as to take over its state-run school uniform production industry.

In 1992, the foundation negotiated a five-year agreement with the Ministries of Agriculture and Education to pay the salaries of all its professional staff. This support amounts to nearly half the organization's annual operating budget.

The Executive Director believes that the government contracts had a positive impact on the foundation's mission, providing dual benefits for the organization. While the garment and laundry ventures contribute to the mission by providing jobs to hundreds of youth and rural women, it has also generated some additional resources for other programs. Learning from this experience, the foundation decided that in seeking "traditional" government and private donor funds in the future, it will identify sources that let Clubes 4-S generate income in addition to meeting other program objectives.

Case study based on Lee Davis, "New Directions in NGO Self-Financing," NESsT, The Johns Hopkins University, Nitze School of Advanced International Studies, Washington, D.C., 1997.

The general lesson for CSOs wanting access to government resources is that they need to make sure that the nature of their work with the poor is viewed by government in this light, and that as a consequence they are not held to the same cost-benefit or effectiveness standards as other CSOs or government agencies that do not work with such social groups. Practically speaking, this must be taken into consideration when they negotiate "performance" contracts (or grant agreements with performance requirements).

Any CSO that enters the world of government contracting must be ready for a new world of paperwork. It must be ready to learn the form and substance of bid documents and corresponding proposal development. No longer will it be evaluated against its own performance or even that of other CSOs; unless a given contract is set aside for CSOs or non-profits, it will be competing against for-profit firms whose survival depends on gaining implementing contracts. It will need to become both strategic and entrepreneurial, including being able to identify whether a sole or a joint bid is most appropriate. Equally important, it must understand clearly from the outset that there is a different philosophy or "bottom-line" involved in performing work to specified performance standards in order to receive payment for a good or service.

The CSO must also be prepared to spend a considerable part of staff time seeking out the information needed to be a successful player in this new world before it can identify the range of contracting possibilities and then target its bids to the contracts that are consistent with its mission and capabilities and that it has a reasonable chance for winning. It may even be necessary, depending on the legal and fiscal environment in the country, for the CSO to set up a for-profit contracting company that will bid on government contracts but pledge the profits to the mother organization.

Another point to consider for a CSO looking to maximize opportunities through government contracting is that as governments shrink in size, the opportunities for government contracts may also shrink. CSOs should not tie themselves into resources that may diminish over the coming years. As is always the case in resource mobilization, safety lies in diversity.

Grants, Loans, and Subsidies

Government Grants

A government makes a grant to a CSO to enable it to carry out something that the CSO has proposed and that is consistent with government policies and programs. As mentioned earlier, such support is unlikely to be for something the government actively opposes, but it may well be something that it does not have the resources to do itself, or does not place a priority on in its own programs. Usually CSOs make proposals to a government department or ministry for funds within certain policy guidelines that a Ministry has already published. In some cases a government may have a secondary objective of supporting CSO initiatives, that is of helping to build and promote the voluntary sector itself so that additional resources are generated and available for future development efforts.

Sometimes the field is large, and the government is prepared to listen to a variety of NGO proposals for different strategies to meet government goals; in other cases the guidelines are narrow and there is little room for the CSO's own ideas. As in all dealings between government and CSOs, there are likely to be two ideas on how, for example, a paramedic program should be run. If there is considerable overlap between the way that the CSO sees it and the way the government sees it, there is little friction. If, on the other hand, the CSO sees the program very differently, it has the opportunity to try and convince the government of the value of its arguments. CSOs should always point out that when the government funds a CSO, it is not just finding another agency to carry out the work, but is buying into an approach and a set of attitudes and values that by definition are different from government.

Governments may operate a grant program in a number of different ways. In some cases the government will cover the entire cost of the activity with no strings—apart from normal progress and financial reporting—attached. In other cases it will provide matching funds in which the CSO contributes some percentage of the cost itself (or from other sources) and the government provides the balance. The ratio of CSO contribution to that of government can vary greatly within countries (from one agency to another, for instance) and between countries. Government may require or encourage a group of CSOs to join together to make a joint proposal, particularly if it requires a range of skills and expertise that no single organization could possess, or if the program has a regional or national scope that cannot be covered by a single CSO. This assumes that the consortium has a similar service delivery approach. On the other hand, governments may want to stimulate competition between CSOs to get the best cost or most innovative approach.

The general principle behind the use of grants to support CSOs is that the government is happy to provide funding to groups to undertake work that promotes the public good and that it is either unable or unwilling to undertake itself. In some cases it may be because government recognizes that CSOs can actually carry out the work better, in terms of the quality of the service and their ability to deliver it more efficiently. In others, it is a simple question of capacity, or lack thereof. One of the greatest challenges for CSOs is to find out what funding the government plans to have available for CSOs; a notable exception to the general lack of information on this is a useful sourcebook from India prepared by the National Institute of Public Cooperation and Child Development.

The true value of grants as a procurement mechanism is that they are in principle supporting the CSO's own program and, in practical terms, often cover core operating costs of the organization and not just a specific program or project that interests the government. Thus a grant is likely to pay for costs such as administrative expenses, staff training and related capacity-building efforts, and on occasion overhead and other indirect costs.

Often grants will be made to CSOs to cover programs in the social service sector that the government is no longer able to undertake itself because of cutbacks in budget or an absence of competent staff. CSOs may therefore find themselves with another ethical problem: are they prepared to take on work, through grants, that allows a government to give up its responsibility for certain basic elements in a country's services to its citizens, such as education, health, and welfare? This issue and debate about the answer is not limited to the South or the East. In the United States and other post-industrial welfare states there is no more hotly contested political issue. Matching a society's values with its willingness to expend resources to achieve them is no less a moral problem for individual CSOs and civil society itself, which when all is said and done are the institutional manifestation of citizen and community voice and choice.

This dilemma is particularly important because governments by definition offer services to a whole country. Primary education, health care, and various kinds of welfare have been designed to be available throughout the country. By contrast, as noted earlier, CSOs are not distributed equally throughout a country. In general, the coverage of CSOs is patchy, a sign of their voluntary nature and dependence on self-identified individuals deciding that they want to form an organization because of some shared values or shared commitment to action with other individuals. Governments would, in many cases, like to provide public services by making grants to CSOs, but are stuck with the political reality that there are not CSOs everywhere present to receive such grants and do the government's work for it.

In many countries, for instance, family planning practices have been handled by CSOs with grants from government, with public funding often coming from external donors. In Thailand, the country was divided into areas where the government provided family planning services and areas where CSOs used grants of public funds to provide them. In Bangladesh, a similar arrangement occurred, but the government urged existing CSOs to expand to take over areas where there was no other CSO coverage. The political reality that the government cannot allow certain areas to remain uncovered by services may mean that CSOs will be encouraged to scale up their operations—taking

LA CORPORACION DE ESTUDIOS Y DESAROLLO NORTE GRANDE, CHILE

La Corporacion de Estudios y Desarollo Norte Grande (Corporation for Studies and Development of the "Big North") is a Chilean CSO established in 1986 in Arica that focuses on rural poverty issues and cultural discrimination in the north of Chile. The organization is committed to promoting local initiatives for citizen participation, innovative regional development plans that are relevant to the local reality, and the economic and cultural integration and exchange of experiences of Andean countries.

In 1991, the organization launched the Entre Todos (All Together) program, financed and initiated by the Fondo de Solidaridad e Inversion Social (FOSIS), a government program initiated in 1990 to support projects focusing on extreme poverty. Entre Todos promoted local participation in decisionmaking and in the implementation of community development projects in rural areas in Chile. Community organizers, with the guidance of the Corporacion, organized the local community and provided leadership training to develop small development projects using a participatory process. This was the first time that the government had supported a program related to local civil participation in Chile.

on much larger areas than they had originally intended. This may well cause its own set of problems for the CSO, including management and accountability concerns.

For traditional nonprofit development intermediaries normally formed by a small group of founder members with the goal of helping others beyond the organization, government grants are not necessarily an instrument for sustainability. The CSO is as vulnerable to a downturn in government funding as it is to a downturn in foreign donor assistance. As a strategy, it makes as much sense for the CSO to spend its time and energy building up the capacity of community-based groups to provide public services as it does to rely on government or build up the NGO's own long-term capacity. The most progressive CSOs see this as part of their mission, as contrasted to NGOs that see themselves as taking over the functions of government as a service provider. The CSO can also have a useful role working with citizens' groups to train them in approaching government, and lobbying for the services they consider essentially a government responsibility.

Loans

Loans are a relatively rare way to provide government resources to CSOs. But in connection with microcredit there is often a situation where government or state-controlled banks recognize the comparative advantage in passing on to CSOs money that they have been loaned for microenterprise development. The recognized skill that CSOs have in savings and credit programs targeting the rural and urban poor and microentrepreneurs contrasts greatly with both commercial and state-owned banks, which are for the most part not interested in small customers. Often loans or

The Corporacion had been implementing local participatory programs before they began Entre Todos. When FOCIS announced its grant "for an innovative project within a public setting," the Corporacion applied, as it needed more resources and the program was consistent with the organization's mission.

The government grant allowed the Corporacion to cover only a minimum of its administrative costs and salaries for necessary professional staff. Most of the grant went to support local organizers and projects. The Corporacion had to leverage support from an international NGO to pay for additional infrastructure and employees. It was able to implement the Entre Todos Program successfully because it could develop and coordinate it alongside other similar projects and finance the costs incurred with international grants.

Despite the fact that the Entre Todos Program was more flexible than other state programs, the government tied the funding to a series of bureaucratic expectations that multiplied with time. According to the Corporacion, the documentation requirements and the unclear regulations were overwhelming and the organization had to learn how to adapt to a huge bureaucracy. It did not have to hire new administrative personnel to satisfy government requirements, but it did have to hire and train new staff for program development.

Case study based on information from Isabel de la Maza.

grants governments have received from international donors languish, and thus they are happy to find a way of spending it. Since the money is on loan, a spread between the rate of repayment from the CSO to the bank and the bank to the international funder is required.

In general, it is fair to say that CSOs are unenthusiastic about loan capital. The only organizations that can be certain of paying back their loans are those that are in turn generating money from their normal work, and this is generally restricted to those involved in credit and small business. The Asian Development Bank, under pressures from its Board to become more involved with CSOs, has tried to entice these organizations with funding made available through loans. In Bangladesh, at least, they had no takers for money available for credit operations from a government loan window, and there were no NGOs in other fields who were prepared to take on a loan.

Gifts and Subsidies

Gifts and subsidies—usually nonfinancial in nature—are most often provided when there is mutual respect and a good working relationship between government and a CSO. The organization may be given some equipment that the government is not using, or the use of a piece of land or a building. In Pakistan, for instance, the government has seconded high-caliber staff to CSOs to work with them and understand how the CSO sector goes about its business. At a much lower level, the government may second a skilled artisan to a locally based CSO to help it with a community project, or a nurse to work in a community-supported clinic. An added benefit of this approach is the good publicity it can garner for government at little or no cost.

THE GET AHEAD FOUNDATION, SOUTH AFRICA

The Get Ahead Foundation is one of the oldest nonprofit organizations in microcredit financing in South Africa. Established in 1984, Get Ahead provides loans to about 8,000 microentrepreneurs in the informal sector annually, and helps create jobs for black South Africans. Forty percent of the foundation's clients are partially or completely illiterate, and 92 percent are women. The foundation has affiliates in 40 areas of the country, those with high unemployment. In February 1996, the foundation split into two nonprofit companies—Get Ahead Financial Services (GAFS) and Get Ahead Development.

Initially, the loan funds of Get Ahead came from local commercial banks. In 1997, the foundation signed an agreement with KHULA Enterprise Finance Limited, a lending institution established by the Department of Trade and Industry in South Africa. The organization currently receives 38 percent of its funding from KHULA. KHULA's mission is to stimulate and aid the development of small, medium, and microenterprises in South Africa. The institution does not lend directly to small entrepreneurs but aids the growing network of

Usually a CSO will have to make the proposal of a gift or subsidy, because the government will rarely be thinking in such terms. The CSO can spot some aspect of resources that is not of high priority to the government, and ask to have the use of it. Usually this will not mean ownership, since very few government departments like to hand over ownership of state property, but it can very well involve "usufruct"—the legal right to use resource for specified times and specified purposes.

In some cases a CSO's approach is based on its previous performance and on government's respect and acceptance of its work; it can ask government to make something available that will allow the CSO to do new work or more extensive work that will benefit the CSO, its clients, and government itself. In other cases a CSO must convince an initially unenthusiastic government that it merits public assistance. It helps a great deal if the CSO is a broad-based membership organization, or has roots deep within a community. The Khet Mujur Samity in Bangladesh, a CSO formed from the remnants of the farmers' front of the Bangladesh Communist Party, was able to persuade the Ministry of Agriculture to provide it with old and dysfunctional government poultry farms, but it required a significant degree of member lobbying to demonstrate the strength of citizens' claims.

The opportunities for CSOs to avail themselves of such resources are growing as governments privatize economic enterprises and scale back in the direct delivery of social and safety-net services. In many cases the rolling back of government has meant divestiture of production units that it once owned. Throughout sub-Saharan Africa, among other regions, there have been and continue to be attempts to sell off state-owned industries under privatization programs. There is likely to be scope

intermediaries, including NGOs, relying on their experience and knowledge of the communities. Capitalized in 1996 by grant funding from the government and from international and domestic donors, KHULA has developed a series of products designed to assist these intermediaries with loans, guarantees, and free technical assistance.

KHULA's lending conditions are competitive with those of the traditional bank sector except for the subsidized interest rate. Get Ahead lends to "stokvels" (small groups) and charges market rates. The average rate of recovery is about 90 percent. Get Ahead intends to provide business loans to individual borrowers by the end of 1997. Currently the program does not sustain itself. The shortfall is financed by international donors. However, the objective of GAFS is to become self-sufficient by the end of 1999 by increasing the client base to 25,000. To meet this goal, Get Ahead would like to transform itself into a microbank by 2000. Get Ahead's brief experience with KHULA is generally positive.

Although KHULA's interest rates are lower than those of traditional banks, they are not as low as Get Ahead expected before GAFS first approached the government.

Case study based on information from Yusuf Sidat, Get Ahead Nonprofit Company.

within such programs for governments to allow CSOs to take up some facilities, as a way to put some capital and property into the hands of civil society. The CSOs can often offer to take over plant or property that is actually a drain on government's limited resources in terms of maintenance and upkeep.

The situation is somewhat different in the case of personnel. Government's loaning of government employees to a CSO can work at two different levels, but both depend on government's appreciation of the work of the CSO sector. At one level, government can make artisans available to help communities organized by CSOs carry out some self-help activities that require the services of, say, a plasterer or carpenter; at another level, government may well want its senior staff to learn more about this burgeoning world of civil society organizations, as happened in Pakistan, or may be interested in implementing staff exchanges so that civil servants learn more about CSOs and CSO staff learn more about government.

One of the "unintended" benefits of the secondment of government personnel to CSO-run programs is that when they return, they come back as ambassadors for the CSO, breaking down the residual suspicion and distrust that governments often have. There is, of course, always the possibility of "negatives" when accepting government officials, including a top-down style of working with villagers, which may run counter to the style of the CSO.

If a CSO requests either goods (such as oral rehydration salts, vehicles, or warehouse space) or services (such as trained personnel on secondment, training, or technical assistance), it should weigh carefully the symbolic value of the subsidized resource versus the trouble or cost that it may ultimately entail—a consistently malfunctioning vehicle, for instance, a piece of land with many contesting claimants, or out-of-date vaccines. The CSO needs to have a clear and precise idea of the terms under which government is providing the subsidy.

Receiving a government subsidy is a valuable way of integrating the work of state and civil society, and while it may not produce income for the CSO, it does reduce expenditures, which is just as valuable as cash in the bank. This is the principal benefit of all nonfinancial resources.

Legal and Fiscal Measures

In most countries, the government controls the legal and fiscal environment that determines what CSOs are allowed to do. Although these organizations usually exist by a constitutionally mandated "right of association," their ability to thrive and achieve sustainability often depends on a series of laws and measures that allow them to be, for instance, legally registered, exempt from taxes, able to raise funds from the public, and permitted to generate funds without paying tax on earnings. Other important measures are those that encourage the public to support their work by providing tax exemptions to those who donate.

These are important "resources" under the control of the government, yet few CSOs consider them in this way. In part, this is due to a lack of knowledge in both the South and East about the enabling and supportive legislation that could support civil society, but in part it stems from the fact that government tolerates rather than actively supports the philanthropy, volunteerism, and self-help that underlie a strong sector.

Without basic or fundamental laws ensuring freedom of association, assembly, speech, and press, not to mention human rights, it is simply impossible to have a civil society that is both voluntarily formed and autonomous from the state and, some would say, the market. Such freedoms are normally codified in a constitution. Even with the wave of democratic transitions of the past decade, many new southern and eastern governments have been less than stellar in ensuring these basic freedoms; those that have tried to seldom follow through with passage and implementation of laws, policies, and regulations that detail the specific rights and obligations accorded to CSOs as valued and legitimate actors in promoting the public good. Civil society's role in ensuring adherence to a rule of law, including fundamental human rights and civil liberties, is one of its most important, particularly where there is little history of government respect for such freedoms and liberties. Promoting and protecting these laws is not the responsibility of any one CSO or subsector but rather of all members, whether formal or informal.

While governments can sometimes be convinced about the value of CSO participation in the provision of public services, it is a rare government that goes out of its way to introduce pro-CSO legislation that encourages greater resource allocations to it. This is especially true where such legal incentives involve a loss to the state of tax revenue. The International Monetary Fund has been pushing governments in exactly the opposite direction by demanding a maximization of tax revenue. In such a climate, ideas concerning tax breaks for CSOs or their supporters get short shrift from international financial institutions and Ministers of Finance.

Box 2

POSSIBLE POLICY INSTRUMENTS TO CREATE AN ENABLING ENVIRONMENT FOR CSOs

Governance: *encouraging public debate and consultation; ensuring the right of association and encouraging the organization of interest groups.*

NGO Regulations: *facilitating and streamlining registration, reporting, auditing, and accounting procedures and requirements.*

Taxation Policies: *supportive legal and fiscal measures on income, local fundraising, philanthropy duties, and imports (a value-added tax, for example).*

Involvement in Policymaking: *providing mechanisms to ensure broad public participation in the policymaking process.*

Project Implementation: *a commitment to consider CSOs as implementers of public programs and projects financed by government.*

Access to Information: *providing CSOs with access to what should be considered public information so that they can act as two-way information channels for their members or clients at the grassroots, particularly about government programs and public resources allocations.*

Coordination: *promoting the need for coordination, including institutional mechanisms within civil society and between it and government.*

Official Support: *made available through a range of procurement instruments grants, contracts, and subsidies.*

Access to Information and Decisions: *of great value to civil society is information about what measures are being considered, what policies are being discussed, and what options are on the table in the government arenas where public decisionmaking takes place; this is particularly important if civil society collectively and CSOs individually are going to be treated as legitimate partners in sustainable development.*

The policy instruments available to government to create an enabling environment for CSOs have been described by John Clark of the World Bank's NGO Unit (see Box 2).

Two fundamental political reforms are essential to CSOs and their ability to gain access to public resources: decentralization and the local laws that are often linked to its conception and implementation. Given the fact that the density and diversity of civil society is greatest at the grassroots level, devolving both the authority for development decisionmaking and the resources required to implement decisions to the lowest level of government is the key. Equally important is the commitment by concerned central state institutions to create local governments that are democratically elected as opposed to extensions of the central state.

THE POPULAR PARTICIPATION LAW IN BOLIVIA

Signed on April 20, 1994, the Popular Participation Law (PPL) in Bolivia "recognizes, promotes and consolidates the process of Popular Participation, articulating the indigenous, campesino and urban communities in the judicial, economic and political life . . . and facilitating citizen participation (of rural communities)." It explicitly recognizes traditional forms of organization and representation.

The PPL organizes the rural sector of the country into municipalities, decentralizing the political authority and calling for a more equitable distribution of public revenues. Allocation of funds from the national treasury for the municipalities are to be based exclusively on the number of inhabitants. As a result, the share allocated to rural municipalities has increased from less than 10 percent to 50 percent.

The participation of CSOs is a critical determinant of the successful implementation of the law because of their extensive experience in working with rural communities. By virtue of the law, each rural community, including indigenous peoples' groups and neighborhood associations, becomes a legal entity referred to as Territorial Base Organization (OTB, from the Spanish). The OTBs select their official representatives for the Municipal Council and participate in identifying projects, implementing programs under contracts, and overseeing the use of funds. The Supervisory Committee appointed by each community controls the activities of the municipality.

With both resources and the authority to use them, local governments will support collaborative relationships including partnerships with local CSOs to address a range of sustainable development problems, including the delivery of social and economic services. And what is little realized is that the greatest potential for alliances across sectors—that is, between state, market, and civil society—occurs between local-level civil society and democratically elected local governments vis-a-vis the central state. If central governments are slow or unwilling to release public resources to decentralized government, local CSOs either directly or through CSOs at higher levels of associations can complement local government lobbying efforts.

Perhaps the most important laws for most CSOs are those that flow from the constitutional right of association by providing them with legal status and with the specific benefits and obligations that it confers. Although all types of CSOs require the protection that such laws of association provide, there has been a particular emphasis on the drafting and passage of NGO laws that provide legal status for traditional development groups, including environmental NGOs and humanitarian organizations. This is obviously important—particularly to donors looking for ways to support their "implementing partners"—but it covers only one subsector of civil society, and a relatively narrow one at that.

Equal if not greater consideration has to be given to associational laws and policies that govern the ability of such CSOs as labor unions, cooperatives and credit unions, professional and business associations, and human rights and civic organizations to under-

OTB representatives are also responsible for submitting the development plan drafted by the communities to the Municipal Council. The PPL gives new authority to municipalities and defines a demand-driven process for directing public resources to rural communities. The Council coordinates and ranks funding requests from the community development plans, and, with the OTBs' input, designs the Municipal Development Plan.

Although the law was initially received with much skepticism, its positive impacts are already clear. Resource transfers to municipalities tripled in Bolivia. Participatory planning has become the main instrument for identifying, setting priorities, and building consensus for the development demands of OTBs and communities. It is the first time in Bolivian history that thousands of campesino communities and indigenous peoples' groups are legally recognized. New forms of local management are now allowing a participation that goes beyond the act of voting.

Still, there are some difficulties with the implementation of the PPL, and the process of citizen participation in defining investment priorities is just beginning. In addition, the PPL has introduced, for the first time, a gender perspective to the municipal planning process—no small endeavor in a nation marked by grave inequities.

Case study based on "Rural Community Development Project, Bolivia," World Bank, 1995.

take the missions for which they were formed. And perhaps most important are laws that govern the degree to which community-based organizations have a right to participate in making and implementing a range of decisions that affect the social and economic welfare of their members and the larger public in their areas of operation.

In this regard, the focus is placed on laws, policies, and regulations that permit local-level CSOs to manage natural resources (such as land, forests, and water), to deliver local social services (such as health and education), to promote economic growth (both jobs and income), and to manage or resolve local conflicts (either social or over resource use). Thus community-based organizations such as grazing and water user associations, cooperatives and credit unions or savings clubs, and parent–teacher associations will all benefit from laws that not only provide them with legal recognition but permit them to undertake what should be considered public functions and thus be eligible to receive public resources.

Finally, associational laws, whether they pertain to NGOs, professional associations, or community-based groups, must allow these and other civil society actors either to federate vertically into higher levels of association or to form horizontal networks and consortia so that the voice of citizens at the grassroots level or their organizations can be heard in political arenas where public decisions are made.

Many governments have deliberately prohibited the formation of what they consider mass organizations because of their potential political power. Although this has normally been aimed at certain social groups (such as ethnic groups, women, or

THE 1 PERCENT LAW IN HUNGARY

In 1996, the Hungarian Parliament passed a new law on personal income tax, under which every taxpayer can donate 1 percent of his or her national taxes to one of about 50,000 CSOs in Hungary. Taxpayers can name any CSO they want to support on their tax returns at the end of the fiscal year. In this way, about US$30 million a year can be channeled directly to CSOs. The law has been a milestone in the development of the Hungarian civil society by increasing the visibility of the sector and changing the distribution of government resources to CSOs.

Although some experts believe that the large organizations that have resources to launch advertising campaigns will benefit most from the new law, many CSOs expect that people will donate funds to small local organizations or to CSOs that they feel close to for personal reasons. A decisionmaking process based on citizen participation will likely channel more resources to smaller CSOs in villages and smaller cities than if a centralized decisionmaking process were in place. In small communities, citizens' decisions will more likely be influenced by personal contacts and informal local networks, which will benefit smaller local organizations. Also, smaller organizations will not have to go through a long grant application procedure or fundraising campaign, which requires special grantwriting skills most do not have.

For larger organizations, the impact will be more indirect. In addition to a small increase in their resources, larger CSOs can capitalize on the positive feedback from the public and increased publicity, which in turn may increase the willingness of their donors to offer more funds.

youth) or economic interests (labor or peasants), it has also been targeted at traditional cooperatives and credit unions as well as parent and student organizations. If civil society is going to be able to promote social development, economic growth, and political freedoms effectively, it must have the right to develop representative organizations that command the support of large segments of the public as a means of gaining legitimacy and clout with undemocratic governments. Equally important, broad-based membership organizations provide a ready-made source of financial and nonfinancial support.

How can government promote the growth of a philanthropic sector where giving and volunteering by individual citizens and business firms become part of the societal norm? As experience from a number of northern countries has shown, a government's fiscal policies can often provide strong incentives for individual and corporate giving and, to a lesser extent, volunteering. Tax laws in particular are important fiscal instruments. Making private contributions of money, time, or material deductible from income taxes can lead to an immediate and tremendous growth in voluntary contributions to CSOs at all levels and for all purposes, as was demonstrated when U.S. tax laws changed in the 1920s. But a country's commitment to its voluntary sector

The law has some negative sides as well. It imposes several costly administrative requirements on CSOs—including advertising and the obligation to publish the use of the funds in newspapers—which particularly hurts smaller nonprofits. The law also does not guarantee that the total of the 1 percent donations will be channeled to nonprofits. If citizens do not name an organization on their tax returns, the money goes back to the central budget. This is a particularly important weakness, since the government has failed to guarantee a certain level of government support to CSOs. In 1996, for example, government grants to CSOs decreased by almost 30 percent. Revenues from the new law will make up for only part of this loss.

Although the civil sector was not deeply involved in drafting the proposal, CSOs welcomed the new law, since it increases their revenues and the visibility of the sector. The Hungarian Nonprofit Information and Training Center established a toll-free telephone service that gives information about any CSO. Free advertisements about nonprofit organizations appeared on the Internet, and paid advertisements were published in daily newspapers.

Despite these efforts, the preliminary results of the National Tax Agency demonstrate that only 27 percent of the population donated the 1 percent to CSOs. This low response rate is partly due to the fact that the law was approved late in 1996 and people did not have time to get information on different organizations. According to most experts, the number will grow every year.

Case study based on Eva Kuti and Agnes Vajda, "In Protection of Biasednessz," unpublished, 1997, and on information from Balazs Gerencser, Nonprofit Information and Training Center, Budapest.

must be constantly renewed, and CSOs must continually demonstrate their worth and, when necessary, defend their interests and benefits.

While the government-initiated fiscal policy just discussed serves as an incentive to increase philanthropic giving, thus generating additional private resources, a second fiscal policy—tax exemptions—works by decreasing the outflow of existing CSO resources. Exemptions on import duties, sales, and income taxes are particularly important for CSOs providing public services that often require material inputs (such as cement, condoms, or pumps) and that depend to a significant degree on external and internal voluntary contributions. Exemptions on taxes for goods and to a lesser extent services can save 10–30 percent of the total costs of a CSO program. Governments are often unwilling to grant exemptions on a wholesale basis, preferring, if they give them at all, to provide them on a case-by-case basis. Governments have used the abuses by a small number of less than honorable organizations as a pretext to deny the privilege to the great majority. Even when the privilege is accorded to a CSO, the bureaucratic requirements, not to mention outright corrupt practices, have made this option far less of a resource enhancer than should be the case.

RESOURCE GUIDE

Bibliography

ANGOC, "Government-CSO Interface in India's Development" (Manila: 1992).

Archer, Robert, "Markets and Good Government: The Way Forward for Economic and Social Development?" (Geneva: U.N. Non-Governmental Liaison Service, 1994).

Clark, John, "The State and the Voluntary Sector," HRO Working Paper No. 12, World Bank, Washington, D.C., 1993.

Commonwealth Foundation, "Non-Governmental Organizations: Guidelines for Good Policy and Practice" (London: Commonwealth Foundation, 1995).

Gary, Ian, *Confrontation, Co-operation or Co-optation: CSOs and the Ghanaian State during Structural Adjustment*, ROAPE 68 (London: 1996).

ICNL, *Handbook of Good Practices for Laws Relating to Non-Governmental Organizations* (Washington, D.C.: World Bank, 1997).

Kandil, Amani, *Civil Society in the Arab World* (Washington, D.C.: CIVICUS, 1995).

Les, Ewa, *The Voluntary Sector in Post-communist East Central Europe* (Washington, D.C.: CIVICUS, 1994).

Overseas Development Council and Synergos Institute, *Strengthening Civil Society's Contribution to Development* (New York: Synergos Institute, 1995).

Overseas Development Institute, *Non-Governmental Organizations and the State in Asia* (London: ODI and Routledge, 1993).

Overseas Development Institute, *Non-Governmental Organizations and the State in Africa* (London: ODI and Routledge, 1993).

Overseas Development Institute, *Non-Governmental Organizations and the State in Latin America* (London: ODI and Routledge, 1993).

Overseas Development Institute, *Reluctant Partners* (London: ODI and Routledge, 1993).

Najam, Adil, *The 3Cs of NGO-Government Relations* (Baltimore, Md.: ISTR, 1996).

Quizon, Antonio B., and Reyes, Rhoda U., *A Strategic Assessment of Non-Governmental Organizations in the Philippines* (Manila: ANGOC, 1989).

NIPPCD, *Financial Assistance to Voluntary Organizations* (New Delhi: 1992).

Salamon, Lester, "The Rise of the Non-Profit Sector," *Foreign Affairs*, Vol. 73, No. 4, 1994.

Serrano, Isagani R., *Civil Society in the Asia Pacific Region* (Washington, D.C.: CIVICUS, 1994).

Tandon, Rajesh, "NGO-Government Relations: A Source of Life or a Kiss of Death?" (New Delhi: Society for Participatory Research in Asia, 1990).

UNDP, *Multiparty Cooperation for Development in Asia and Building Development Projects in Partnership with Communities and NGOs: An Action Agenda for Policymakers* (Bangkok: 1993).

Vincent, Fernand, and Piers Campbell, *Towards Greater Financial Autonomy: A Manual on Financing Strategies for Development NGOs and Community Organizations* (Geneva: Development Innovations and Networks, 1989).

Viswanath, Vanita, and Michael Bamberger, "Issues and Opportunities for Expanded NGO Participation in National Development Policies and Programs" (Dhaka: BRAC/EDI, 1994).

World Bank, *Pursuing Common Goals: Strengthening Relations Between Government and Development NGOs* (Dhaka: World Bank, UPL, 1996).

Case Study Contacts

Socorro L. Reyes
Center for Legislative Development
Room 217 PSS Center
Commonwealth Avenue
Dillman, Quezon City 1121
Philippines
Tel: (832) 927-4030
Fax: (832) 927-2936

Civil Society Development Foundation
ul. 3 Maya 27/31, 81–364
Gdynia
Poland
Tel: (48-58) 218-098

Isabel de la Maza
Borgono 135
Villa Magisterio
Arica
Chile

Yusuf Sidat
Get Ahead Nonprofit Company
227 Minnaar Street
Pretoria
South Africa

Victoria Mwambe
KHULA Enterprise Finance Limited
Headway Hill, Midrand Limited
P.O. Box 1234
Halfway House 1685
South Africa

Balazs Gerencser
Nonprofit Information and Training Center
Margit krt. 58, I/4
Budapest 1024
Hungary
Tel: (36-1) 201-9311
Fax: (36-1) 212-374

Ghassan Sayah
YMCA Lebanon
Delta Center, 3rd Floor
Horsh Tabet, Sin el-Fil
P.O. Box 11-520
Beirut
Lebanon
Tel: (961-1) 490-640
Fax: (961-1) 491-740

Chapter 7

Resources of Development Assistance Agencies

Leslie M. Fox and Ghassan Sayah

The Changing World of Development Assistance

Despite recent trends of indigenous support for development in the Third World, northern countries continue to be a principal source of development assistance for civil society organizations (CSOs) operating there and in Central and Eastern Europe. Northern governments using public tax revenues have financed sustainable development either directly through bilateral programs or indirectly through contributions to multilateral institutions and northern CSOs (N-CSOs), each of which have programs in developing countries and those in transition.

Bilateral and multilateral donors are considered official development assistance (ODA) agencies in the sense that their funding is approved and allocated by representative, publicly elected bodies. Northern CSOs, in addition to being channels for the disbursement of bilateral and some multilateral ODA, have become independent development assistance agents in their own right. Included in this category are traditional development and humanitarian nongovernmental organizations (NGOs), private foundations, professional and business associations, trade unions, civic and human rights organizations, cooperatives and credit unions, environmental and women's groups, and political foundations such as the German *Stiftungs* and U.S. political institutes—in short, the length and breadth of northern civil societies.

Two principal strategies that southern and eastern CSOs can use to obtain resources from development assistance agencies are discussed in this chapter. The first, which might be termed an instrumental approach, assumes a static universe—that is, donors have resources and CSOs want access to them. To accomplish this, a CSO must know as much about a prospective donor—its policies, programs, funding priorities, selection criteria, and so on—as it does about itself. The aims are short-term and tactical: to produce practical knowledge that can be turned into a realistic strat-

177

egy for identifying donors most likely to fund a CSO's programs, and then to develop a step-by-step plan that will lead to the desired outcome.

The second strategy takes a more transformational or long-term and strategic approach—it recognizes that CSOs and civil society in general are legitimate public actors in making and implementing sustainable development policies. (See also Chapter 6.) As such, they are better thought of as partners in helping to shape and formulate these policies, not just instruments of established policy. In this light, CSOs have a right to not only influence the policies of donors, but to call for a restructuring of the broader system of technical cooperation as currently practiced at the national and global levels. This strategy seeks to increase both the quantity and the quality of development assistance resources through the promotion of an innovative set of policies, strategies, and programs with CSOs at the center of the sustainable development paradigm.

Importance and Scale of Development Assistance

Official development assistance increased from roughly 2 percent to 35 percent of total NGO receipts between 1971 and 1994; in terms of actual flows to NGOs, ODA rose from less than US$200 million in 1971 to US$2.8 billion in 1994.

These figures can be misleading, however. First, most ODA going to civil society organizations goes to northern NGOs. There are no hard figures concerning how much then gets channeled from these groups to indigenous southern and eastern CSOs (S/E-CSOs), or how much goes directly from official donors to such groups. Second, ODA figures only pertain to funding made available to traditional development and humanitarian NGOs. There is little or no reporting on funds made available to the wide range of associational types that constitute the broader realm of what is termed civil society.

In spite of these "information gaps," it is clear that ODA has increased significantly over the past three decades in support of sustainable development programs carried out by NGOs and increasingly by other civil society actors. For many CSOs—northern as well as southern and eastern—ODA has become their principal source of funding. In addition, official donors provide significant nonfinancial resources to CSOs, such as technical assistance and training; opportunities to participate in development fora at local and international levels; and, perhaps most important, a commitment to promoting an enabling environment that has facilitated greater CSO participation in national, regional, and international sustainable development policymaking and implementation.

Historically, ODA has had both regional and sectoral emphases. For instance, over the past decade the balance between development and humanitarian assistance has shifted greatly in favor of the latter at a time when overall ODA decreased substantially (particularly since 1992). Official donors have taken great pains to assure southern governments that funds going to Central and Eastern Europe would not affect their own aid allocations. But there can be little doubt that the significant and continuing cutbacks in ODA by most northern governments—coupled with increases in emergency and humanitarian relief—affected sustainable development assistance to the South significantly.

In terms of ODA used for poverty reduction efforts, the U.N. Development Programme (UNDP) has noted that less than one third of this category of aid goes to the 10 most populous countries that are home to two thirds of the world's poor. Nor is ODA focused on what UNDP considers the priority areas of human develop-ment—primary education and primary health care; bilateral donors, in particular, allo-cate roughly just 7 percent of their aid budgets to these areas.

Private contributions from people in the North to N-NGOs involved in humani-tarian and development assistance increased from about US$1 billion in 1970 to US$6 billion in 1994. Again, this figure pertains to resource flows to traditional NGOs, not other development actors in civil society. Citizen philanthropic contribu-tions made available to northern NGOs remained relatively constant in real terms through 1990, and as a percentage of GNP they remained virtually unchanged at 0.02 percent through this same period. The past five years, however, have seen a marked decrease in these private contributions. The principal impact has been to reduce total funding available for N-NGO sustainable development activities, and particularly the flexible funding that citizen contributions—as opposed to more restrictive official donor funding—make possible.

In addition to these general trends, a number of other recent developments di-rectly affect the access of southern and eastern CSOs to development assistance. First, multilateral assistance has decreased significantly compared with bilateral assistance. Since multilateral agencies—particularly the World Bank and U.N. specialized agen-cies—provide a higher percentage of ODA to the poorest countries and for human development objectives, this has had a major impact on CSOs that target poverty reduction in the poorest countries.

Second, ODA from the European Union (EU) has increased significantly in rela-tion to other multilaterals, and even compared with many of its own member coun-tries, and now represents one of the principal sources of funding for northern NGOs and their southern and eastern counterparts. Third, although overall ODA has de-clined in recent years, the percentage made available to CSOs has held steady and may even have increased.

Fourth, over the past five years an increased demand on limited and decreasing ODA resources has come from a range of new countries classified by the Organisation for Economic Co-operation and Development (OECD) as Part I coun-tries—that is, the five Central Asian Republics, Eritrea, Albania, and several other newly independent states.

Fifth, in 1994 ODA stood at US$59.2 billion, of which 38 percent went to Africa, 36 percent to Asia/Pacific, 12 percent to Latin America and Caribbean, and 14 per-cent to the Middle East. Other "official aid" going to Central and Eastern Europe and to the newly independent states amounted to US$7.5 billion. Historical (colonial) ties, geographic proximity, and national interest account for the ways in which funds are allocated by official bilateral aid agencies.

Last, although the "gift-giving culture" and "philanthropic ethos" remain strong in most northern countries, N-NGOs and even those with broad name recognition are find-ing it increasingly difficult to raise funds for sustainable development programs. Although natural disaster and war still bring forth the humanitarian impulse of northern citizens, these supporters too are beginning to feel the impact of "compassion fatigue."

THE CIVIL SOCIETY DEVELOPMENT FOUNDATION, HUNGARY

The Civil Society Development Foundation (CSDF) was created in 1994 to enhance the growth of CSOs and grassroots networks in Central and Eastern Europe by providing nonprofit management training and development assistance.

In 1995, CSDF offices in Hungary and Poland were among the first organizations to receive funding from the European Union's PHARE Democracy Program to build indigenous training capacity in the NGO sector. When the grant was awarded, neither the recipient nor the grantor had much experience in grant administration. CSDF was unprepared for the administrative requirements of EU's large bureaucracy, and could have used training in financial management and accounting to assure transparency and accountability. In its second application to PHARE, the foundation put into the proposal the time and costs of meeting administrative requirements, and hired an administrative assistant to maintain records for PHARE.

The experience of CSDF with the PHARE program is mixed. The grant allowed CSDF to contribute significantly to the strengthening of civil society in Hungary and Poland. But it also meant the involvement of a large bureaucracy

Benefits and Limitations

Autonomy Versus Dependence

Since a significant percentage of S/E-CSO resources comes from external sources, there is a real danger of not only dependency but also the loss of organizational autonomy and decisionmaking power. N-NGOs are the principal channels of nearly all external resources to S/E-CSOs. However, this in not a guarantee in itself that S/E-CSOs will retain as much autonomy over how the resources are used as they would like. This is much more pronounced with resources from bilateral than from multilateral donors.

On the other hand, ODA and assistance from N-NGOs has provided many southern and eastern CSOs with the first significant source of funding to meet the program needs of their members or clients. And depending on the source of funding—for example, directly from development assistance agencies or through southern governments—and the manner in which it is made available to CSOs (such as grants rather than contracts), the assistance can have a truly liberating effect and lead to enhanced performance and autonomy.

Building CSO Credibility or Illegitimacy

Development assistance and nonfinancial resources have improved the institutional capacity of CSOs and hence their effectiveness as development agents. CSOs have increasingly been invited by donor agencies to participate in the formulation of devel-

and serious technical problems that had to be worked out. The long and rigid grant-processing schedule meant CSDF had to make cash-flow plans to avoid shortage of money. Also, the PHARE office wired the money to only one of the regional partners, usually the western one—a real disadvantage for the East Europeans.

PHARE's requirement that Central and East European NGOs work with two West European partner organizations placed serious constraints on applicants that were not well connected and could not identify appropriate organizations. Although the requirement worked well for CSDF because the English and German partners made valuable contributions to CSDF's own projects, it has been changed; now it is possible to include partnerships with other Central and East European organizations as well.

In 1995, PHARE program officers visited CSDF's Summer Institute on NGO Management Training, and CSDF representatives met with PHARE officers in Brussels to present their accomplishments. After PHARE assured itself that CSDF worked well and achieved important results, it approved a second grant. This long-term support is definitely a positive element of the PHARE funding. The organization plans to submit new proposals for the duration of the program, which is to last in Central and Eastern Europe until 1999.

opment programs and strategies, or to take part in donor-sponsored workshops and conferences on national, regional, or global issues and policies.

In all these cases, the net impact has been to increase the credibility and visibility of CSOs with their members, clients, the general public, and even national governments and international institutions. Development agency funding has permitted CSOs to build a track record, which is often a principal criteria used by donors and host-country governments in evaluating funding worthiness.

At the same time, support from development agencies has also led to accusations by a significant number of southern and eastern governments that CSOs are little more than agents of foreign interests—whether official or nongovernmental—in terms of advancing agendas that are not culturally, socially, or politically consistent with the country's values and traditions. This has been particularly true of CSOs that have engaged state institutions over issues of public policy, or in such areas as good governance and human rights monitoring. In short, they have become too "political."

Promoting State–Civil Society Partnership or Competition

ODA has often promoted new partnerships when donors have "suggested" that such funding be used to have CSOs deliver a public service on behalf of overstretched governments. In a time of decreasing ODA, however, with donors increasingly providing direct funding to southern and eastern CSOs to undertake direct service delivery, many host governments have decried such practices for undermining their credibility and capacity to directly provide "public" services to their citizens. Such a "zero-sum" or "fixed pie" mentality has led some governments to argue that the allocation and management of ODA should remain the sole prerogative of official relationships, either through bilateral ties or within the formal decisionmaking processes of multilateral institutions.

Creating Classes Within Civil Society

One of the effects of reduced ODA and "downsizing" of official agencies has been the tendency for donors to make fewer but larger grants to a relatively small number of larger CSOs. Those with a track record in the management of donor funding and with a knowledge of and ability to work well with donors have increasingly received the lion's share of this funding. The net impact has been the creation of a "wealthy class" of CSOs in many countries that now often dominate the policy agenda and establish themselves as the "legitimate" representatives of civil society. The far more numerous smaller, non-donor-funded civil society actors have taken a back seat in the definition of issues and policies relevant to sustainable development in their countries. Thus, donor funding policies and practices influence the evolution, structure, and content of southern and eastern civil societies.

North–South/East CSO Solidarity or Competition

Although the situation today is one of changing roles and relationships, northern CSOs can still be considered the "gatekeepers" of northern public and private funding for southern and eastern groups. This has led to a situation where N-CSOs either are in competition with indigenous CSOs for limited development assistance resources or are forming partnerships with these groups to undertake joint programs. In the first situation, N-CSOs are crowding out their local counterparts and delaying their true participation in sustainable development; in the second, their financial and nonfinancial support is accelerating their participation.

Whether ODA agencies feel compelled to fund their "home-country" CSOs for political reasons or do so because of accountability requirements, the effect is the same; it delays the day when indigenous CSOs become full partners in sustainable development.

Easy Money Versus Hard Decisions

Official donor agencies often waive all or most CSO "matching" or "counterpart" requirements for humanitarian assistance and specially mandated programs (in high-priority countries such as the West Bank/Gaza, for instance, or in specific program areas such as AIDS education). In many cases, donors fund 100 percent of direct costs related to the management or administration of these programs while dropping onerous reporting requirements and rigorous monitoring and evaluation criteria. Such reduced requirements give rise to the notion of "easy money" being available to CSOs willing to implement these programs.

The effect of such special mandates has been to draw many southern and eastern as well as northern CSOs away from their traditional programming expertise into new areas where they may have little existing technical knowledge. Particularly for weaker CSOs without a reliable funding base, these ODA-funded programs can compromise their integrity by altering their basic missions and organizational objectives.

Future Trends

A review of patterns in ODA and citizen philanthropy over the past 35 years indicates a number of emerging trends that are expected to become set over the next several years and continue into the next century. Each of these will directly affect funding available for southern and eastern CSOs.

Although future ODA trends continue to look dismal overall, both multilateral and bilateral funding to CSOs everywhere will likely increase as a percent of overall ODA flows for sustainable development efforts in southern and eastern countries. At the same time, however, the number of CSOs working in sustainable development and thus eligible for ODA is increasing even faster. Traditional humanitarian and developmental NGO intermediaries will be joined by a far larger number of membership-based or popular organizations and a more diverse set of social, political, and economic NGOs with a legitimate claim to development assistance resources.

Most multilateral institutions, with the exception of the EU and perhaps UNICEF, will likely continue to see an erosion of their funding base as OECD governments prefer to allocate the majority of their foreign aid budgets to their bilateral programs and, increasingly, their NGOs.

Bilateral agencies will continue to focus their limited resources on a smaller number of countries—those that demonstrate commitment to economic and political reform—and a reduced number of program areas in each country. They will continue to close country programs and decrease their presence in the developing South and in economies in transition as a result of budget cuts and downsizing. Multilaterals, on the other hand, are likely to maintain their presence, albeit at lower levels of activity. Northern NGOs are likely to take over many official bilateral functions in countries where those agencies are no longer found.

Unless new funding mechanisms are created and policies instituted, the nature of donor funding to S/E-CSOs is likely to continue the current pattern: a smaller number of very large grants for a relatively long duration to the largest and best established organizations.

Traditional private voluntary giving from northern citizens will likely remain stagnant, thus increasing the percentage of ODA as an overall component of northern and, by extension, many southern and eastern CSO resources.

While northern CSOs will continue to receive the majority of bilateral funding, there will be increased pressure by donors to channel a greater portion of this funding to indigenous CSOs.

UNDP and several specialized U.N. agencies that have traditionally provided the most direct funding through centrally designed programs to southern and eastern CSOs will continue to do so. They are likely to be joined by the World Bank and several regional development banks, which may well establish a number of new "civil society" funds and mechanisms.

While northern foundation funding of international (versus domestic) activities will at best remain constant at early 1990s levels, it is likely that the donors will become more strategic or targeted in their support of S/E civil societies, including the promotion and strengthening of the overall sector, philanthropy, and volunteerism.

KATALYSIS NORTH/SOUTH
DEVELOPMENT PARTNERSHIP

Katalysis, as implied by its Greek name, works as a catalyst to foster positive social change among low-income Central Americans. It was founded in 1984 by Robert E. Graham, a development entrepreneur whose vision was to create a real partnership between northern and southern NGOs based on business principles. As an international social enterprise, it is committed to organizational sustainability through cost recovery, building assets, growth in scale, entrepreneurship, and innovation. Today, all Katalysis projects are based on the desires, needs, and direct input of local people and clients who participate in the design and management of development projects.

The Katalysis model works by forming partnerships with established local nonprofit development organizations in Central America. Katalysis currently works in partnership with five such groups in El Salvador, Guatemala, and Honduras that serve fledgling enterpreneurs, primarily women. Its activities include strength-

Over the next several years, there is likely to be a major "shakeout" within northern NGO communities as they continue to move away from a direct and operational role in sustainable development efforts to a purely supportive one, which should translate into increased resources flowing to southern and eastern CSOs.

Emerging Issues

The roles, relationships, and responsibilities of everyone involved in sustainable development in southern and eastern countries are going through profound change and transformation. The pattern of decreased development assistance—both official and nongovernmental—has had the effect of speeding up this process, in some cases heightening conflict and in others promoting collaboration and partnership.

Over the past decade, the types of northern nongovernmental actors participating in sustainable development activities has broadened greatly beyond traditional development NGOs. This has largely been due to the democratic wave that has swept through southern and eastern countries, opening up political as well as social and economic life to an equally broad range of southern and eastern CSOs. This broadened participation has brought an overall increase in private northern resources flowing to southern and eastern CSOs. At the same time, however, it has forced official donors to consider financing a far wider range of northern nongovernmental development agencies. With decreased ODA now the norm for the foreseeable future, official donors have had to become more selective or "strategic" in the types of N-CSOs they support. The reverse side of this coin is that N-CSOs have had to become more competitive for

ening the impact of the partners' community banking and microcredit programs and providing institutional support to ensure each organization's long-term sustainability through training, networking, and resource mobilization.

Katalysis partnerships include many elements that are unique in North-South NGO relationships, including cross-participation in governance through an exchange of board seats, strategic planning by directors and staff across agencies, unusually transparent sharing of financial information, joint fundraising efforts, joint selection of new partners, and organizational and program cross-evaluations. An essential element of the Katalysis strategy is that beneficiaries pay at least a portion of the costs of the services they receive.

In 1994, the Association for Women in Development (MUDE, from the Spanish), a CSO partner from Guatemala, received a grant from corporate donors through Katalysis. This initiative was part of the organization's program to connect donors with partners. According to the Executive Director of Katalysis, there is an increasing need to assist socially responsible U.S. corporations to channel funds to southern CSOs. The direct partnership with MUDE is working well; the Executive Vice President of the donor corporation visited MUDE personally and the grant has just been renewed for another three years.

remaining resources. How official donors and N-CSOs handle this situation will be a major determinant in terms of which S/E-CSOs receive northern funding.

The longer that N-CSOs, particularly N-NGOs, maintain an operational presence in southern and eastern countries, the fewer development resources from the North will be available for southern and eastern CSOs. Although the past decade has seen a reduced role for N-CSOs in the direct delivery of social and economic services in many countries, a significantly large number still operate in this manner. In addition, most northern development resources available to southern and eastern CSOs still pass through N-CSOs. Official donors will need to decide if they are willing to fund southern and eastern CSOs directly, and if so, how to accomplish it. Northern CSOs must determine whether their continued direct provision of services to southern citizens or communities is consistent with the principles of sustainable development.

Identifying Likely Donors

For CSOs to gain access to donor agency resources, they must be familiar with the terms and conditions under which donors disburse funds. This section looks at the current policies, programs, guidelines, priorities, and funding criteria of development assistance agencies.

It would be a mistake for CSOs to believe that all donors are the same. The differences among and between bilaterals and multilaterals are, in many ways, as great as those between official and nongovernmental development agencies. Nor are NGOs

THE NEW PARTNERSHIP INITIATIVE OF USAID

USAID's New Partnerships Initiative was announced by Vice President Gore in March 1995 at the World Summit for Sustainable Development. It is a strategic approach to development partnering designed to increase the capacity of local actors—from civil society, business, and institutions of democratic governance—to work together to solve problems at the community level. NPI moves beyond simple networking to create purposeful coalitions that link community participation to lasting development results.

NPI emerged in response to increasingly complex development challenges coupled with shrinking resources, and to the growing capacity and interest of an expanding array of local development actors to engage in community action to energize development.

All three phases of the NPI process—design, piloting, and mainstreaming—have been characterized by an exceptionally high degree of partnering among USAID bureaus, field missions, and an extremely broad array of external partners. Between March and October 1996, the approach was piloted in 15 USAID missions. An NPI Resource Guide brings together the results of this period of field testing and provides a set of integrated programming tools developed by the NPI Learning Team in the areas of local capacity building, the enabling environment, and development partnering.

and CSOs in the United States and Europe any more homogeneous in their dealings with S/E-CSOs than they are with each other. All these differences are the result of such variables as culture, particularly philanthropic traditions and values; political philosophies and foreign policy considerations; and historical relationships with and geographical proximity to southern and eastern countries.

Bilateral Official Development Assistance

Northern countries devote a small percentage of their public budgets to foreign assistance programs. Funding is normally channeled through a principal aid agency, although it has often been channeled through other state or federal agencies (such as Ministries of Foreign Affairs, Economic Planning, or Finance) and even regional and local governments (sister city programs, for instance). Bilateral aid agencies are responsible directly to public institutions, principally their parliaments or legislatures, which vote their budgets and approve their overall policies, and indirectly to citizens in those countries—the taxpayers.

Most bilateral agencies have only recently begun to develop a comprehensive policy toward strengthening southern and eastern civil societies within a sustainable development paradigm that links democracy and improved governance to increases in economic growth and improvements in social welfare. Many of them have NGO operational policies and guidelines in terms of such issues as criteria for funding, sectors of interest, overheads and administrative costs, and when and with whom to hold

The experience of the NPI pilot missions provided a number of important lessons. First, good partnerships are constructed incrementally. Building collaborative networks—brokering and facilitating relationships—requires time, strategic vision, and an entrepreneurial spirit. In this context, results are critical to the success of the process of institutional and policy change. What matters is what the partners can accomplish together.

Second, where significant resource transfers are the sole focus of assistance, incentives for local participation are hard to sustain beyond the initial resource transfer. Institutional change, in contrast, relies on local capacity building and on incentives generated internally, not externally. The rewards are increased efficiency, better targeting of development efforts, and improved access to benefits. But if results are not evident and real, there are few incentives to sustain participation.

Third, both donors and their partners share a common interest in a clear results framework, and this is greatly facilitated by decentralized programming and implementation. USAID has learned that early involvement of partners, clear agreement on goals, equitable distribution of costs and benefits, effective performance monitoring at low cost, clear delineation of responsibilities, and a low-cost process of adjudication of disputes are critical to an effective process of institutional change and the sustainability of development results.

consultations. Although these policies relate primarily to their own NGOs, they are increasingly being applied to S/E-NGOs and CSOs.

Bilateral aid agencies have begun to narrow both their country and program focus, targeting fewer countries and program sectors in which to work. This is largely due to pressure from increasingly critical northern parliaments and publics to demonstrate greater impact or results with the monies allocated to foreign assistance. As a result, the funding of home-country NGOs as well as those in the South and East is often made contingent on their ability to produce results that are consistent with revised development objectives.

Centrally Funded CSO Programs

Virtually all northern countries have established centrally funded programs for cofinancing activities undertaken by national NGOs (the Joint Funding Scheme of the Overseas Development Administration in the United Kingdom, for example, or the Matching Grant Program of the U.S. Agency for International Development [USAID]). The establishment of these funding mechanisms, which provide for flexible, multiyear financing through relatively large block grants, reflects a donor policy of promoting the autonomy, integrity, and unique character of northern NGOs and CSOs.

Although these programs have traditionally provided funding for direct implementation of N-NGO programs in southern and eastern countries, concerned donors have increasingly conditioned such assistance on the NGO developing partnerships with southern and eastern counterparts. In a number of cases (in the Netherlands, for instance), N-NGOs have served primarily as channels of this assistance by in turn granting funds to their S/E partners.

In the past five years, the range of northern nongovernmental development assistance agencies that have become eligible for cofinancing has increased greatly to include trade unions, political institutes, and business associations. Because most cofinancing programs require the recipient to be registered as a charity, nonprofit, or private voluntary organization in the donor country, the majority of S/E-CSOs are precluded from getting direct access to these bilateral funds.

Often NGOs or CSOs are used to implement special programs or "windows" designed to promote or address a specific sectoral initiative (such as microenterprise or AIDS), a specific concern (perhaps women in development), or a country or region (such as Vietnam) that supports either a development assistance or foreign policy objective of the concerned government. Most funds pass through national NGOs, although a small number are directly open to S/E-CSOs. A number of northern countries have specially mandated and publicly funded programs or institutions that directly target assistance to S/E-CSOs, including community-based organizations. In the United States, this involves public-private Foundations such as the African Development and Inter-American Foundations; in Canada, the Canada Africa 2000 Program; and in Germany, two publicly funded religious development agencies— Miserior (the Catholic church) and EZE (the Protestant church).

Country-Level Program Funding

Most bilateral aid is spent at the country program level. This is also where S/E-CSOs have the greatest opportunity to secure funding directly from bilateral donors.

At the country level, in contrast to funding from the central level, bilateral funding of local CSOs is largely made to advance the donor's objectives, not the CSO's. For a long time, this led to minimal funding of local CSOs. A number of factors mitigate against the continuation of this pattern, providing an opportunity for greater S/E-CSO access to these funds.

First, bilateral donors are now far more likely to involve local CSOs in the development of their country program strategies. As discussed in greater detail later in this chapter, gaining a seat at the table of donor decisionmaking is a first step to gaining increased funding. Second, many donors have now begun to articulate, or at least pay lip service to, a sustainable development paradigm that calls for greater participation of citizens and their organizations in the making as well as implementation of development policies. And finally, southern and eastern governments have proved themselves unable to address the full range of development problems facing their countries, while S/E-CSOs have increasingly demonstrated their capacity to be effective development partners and not just adversaries. This has not been lost on most bilateral (or multilateral) institutions.

Bilateral donors have significantly greater flexibility than their multilateral counterparts to develop their country programs without host-government constraints. On the other hand, there is no question that they are official agencies representing their own governments, and that they operate in the host country through some form of bilateral agreement that requires a minimum degree of government approval of programs.

Box 1

RESIDENT DIPLOMATIC MISSION FUNDS

For a wide range of local CSOs, including community-based organizations, resident foreign embassies provide small-scale funding for many CSO-initiated projects and programs. Such funds have historically provided micro and small grant funding to indigenous CSOs that met certain activity and organizational criteria. The application process is rather painless, especially compared with applying to the official aid agency—with short proposal requirements, a reasonable review and approval period, and a minimum of reporting requirements. The British Head of Mission Gift Scheme and the American Ambassador's Self-Help Fund have provided thousands of micro and small-scale grants over the past two decades to CSOs in virtually every country and region. While most have been for traditional self-help projects in the areas of social development and welfare, increasingly the funds have gone to CSOs working on environmental advocacy, human rights (including women's and indigenous peoples' rights), and conflict resolution.

Bilateral funding of local CSOs is sure to draw notice from the host government, particularly if the amounts are significant and the areas being funded are sensitive ones. As with many of the variables that determine bilateral donor funding preferences toward local CSOs, it is better to identify the policies of each donor in a given country than it is to make a blanket statement concerning a given donor in every situation.

Most direct bilateral funding of S/E-CSOs has been made through grants ranging anywhere from several hundred dollars over three months to several million dollars (or tens of millions in some cases) over three to five years. Although the use of contracts by bilateral donors is not widespread (versus the multilaterals, for example), this funding instrument has been used in a number of situations, including when the nature of the activity involves large sums of money, such as in infrastructure projects; when it requires a high degree of technical sophistication or is organizationally complex, such as in the creation of a local foundation; or when political sensitivities in terms of the host government are evident, such as in support of democracy programs. Recently, perhaps the most common reason donors use contracts rather than grants is to ensure that a high level of CSO performance is achieved and that planned results are produced.

Because of donor accountability requirements and the limited ability to assess and monitor more than a handful of grant applications at any one time, most bilateral funding has been made available to a relatively small number of the larger S/E-CSOs with track records. This appears to be changing somewhat as bilaterals start to use funding mechanisms and instruments to move beyond first-tier CSO funding to a larger number of second-tier organizations with more limited track records.

Although this is more prevalent among multilaterals and northern foundations, a number of bilaterals have begun to develop more responsive mechanisms capable of reaching grassroots organizations. (See Box 1.) The trend toward direct southern CSO funding started in the early 1980s (when eastern CSOs hardly existed), but at the beginning of the 1990s the phenomenon began to take on significance. As noted earlier, it also led many traditional northern development NGOs to question direct bilateral funding of their southern partners.

One way that donors avoid duplication in funding is by joining together in a consortium arrangement, hiring one or more managers to administer funding on their behalf. The first and best known of these new institutional arrangements are the several consortia formed by a number of "like-minded" donors in Bangladesh to fund the programs of some of that country's pre-eminent CSOs. Although this implementation mechanism has been primarily used to fund the largest development CSOs, it also lets hard pressed donors with little institutional capacity manage a large number of smaller grants, which is what is recommended for building a strong and healthy civil society in countries emerging from years of authoritarian rule.

Many bilateral donors have and continue to provide a range of nonfinancial resources to CSOs through their country programs. Much of this support is designed to complement their financial assistance. Thus, technical assistance and training in such areas as proposal writing, financial management and accounting, and performance monitoring and evaluation are areas especially needed by CSOs. This very narrowly defined capacity-building assistance—that is, technical assistance and training provided to enable CSOs to apply for, manage, and report on donor grants—has often been provided directly by donors themselves or contracted out to specialized CSOs and for-profit firms. Capacity-building support that aims to create stronger and more effective CSOs is normally provided through grants or intermediary CSOs that have this as one of their own objectives. (See Box 2.)

Other types of nonfinancial resources include sponsoring CSO personnel at local, regional, and international conferences, workshops, and meetings; making space available for offices, training, or a warehouse; buying or transferring office equipment; and arranging for or providing program-related supplies and materials. Such resources are a good way to pull donors into a CSO's programs without asking for cold cash. And when donor staff become personally involved in arranging for a particular resource, it gives them a high degree of "ownership" in the endeavor. As other chapters make abundantly clear, the greatest and most successful fundraising strategies start with personalizing the good being marketed, and all CSOs need to be entrepreneurial, albeit with a social rather than financial objective.

Multilateral Official Development Assistance

The principal multilateral institutions providing ODA include UNDP, other specialized U.N. agencies, and the international financial institutions (IFIs), including the World Bank and various regional development banks. Also included in this category is the European Union, which as noted earlier has quickly become one of the largest multilaterals, funding CSOs from the North and increasingly the East and South.

Multilateral institutions are directly accountable to their member governments. Their financing comes primarily from the governments that belong to OECD through pledges or quotas that are levied either according to means or through negotiation. In the case of the IFIs, significant funding comes from reserves that are generated from the return on loans made to recipient member governments. These reserves could become a potential source of new funding for CSO programs.

Box 2

THE NORTHERN NGO AS INTERMEDIARY

In the early 1980s, USAID pioneered a new implementation mechanism to address a problem in its Asian programs—how to support the growing number of indigenous NGOs that were being targeted to provide services in a range of social development and poverty alleviation projects. Under what became known variously as a "co-financing" mechanism or "umbrella" project, USAID engaged a U.S. NGO to provide a combination of technical assistance and grant funding to many indigenous NGOs and, in some cases, community-based organizations. The NGO intermediary thus took "fiduciary" responsibility for the use of U.S. development assistance funding, giving local NGOs access to an important source of grant funding and capacity-building assistance.

These implementation mechanisms are now in use throughout USAID country programs. They have been expanded to support a number of regional and subregional programs (such as the Democracy Network Program covering Eastern and Central European countries and the Citizen Participation Network in Central America). Umbrella mechanisms have funded multisectoral programs as well as single-sector objectives. Other donors have adapted the mechanism to their own uses. The EU's PHARE Program supporting Civil Society in Central and Eastern Europe is a good example of how a northern intermediary or in some cases a local foundation has been used to support indigenous CSOs with financial grant and technical assistance.

Given the increasing cutbacks in ODA and the "downsizing" or outright closure of donor-country-level aid agencies, this type of funding mechanism is likely to continue growing. The issue is who and what type of organization will occupy this intermediary umbrella position in the future—northern NGOs or those from the South and East, or perhaps more enduring institutional entities, such as indigenous foundations.

Multilateral agencies, particularly the IFIs, have far less flexibility to fashion deliberate policies toward the support of NGOs and other civil society actors, as they are essentially creations of their members, who are donor and recipient country governments alike. Until recently, many southern and eastern governments did not view NGOs and CSOs as fully legitimate actors in national sustainable development efforts; most multilaterals followed the preferences of their member governments through the late 1980s at least. On the other hand, since the very first "development decade" a small number of U.N. agencies (such as the World Health Organization, the Food and Agriculture Organization, and UNICEF) articulated programs, policies, and strategies that underlie sustainable human development, which is perhaps the strongest endorsement for an increased NGO/CSO role in local, national, regional, and international development efforts. And there can be little doubt that multilaterals—in many cases, even more so than the bilaterals—are now forging new policies toward civil society, including new programs and in some cases innovative financing strategies and mechanisms.

THE CENTRAL AND EAST EUROPEAN BANKWATCH NETWORK

The Central and Eastern European Bankwatch Network was established in 1995 to monitor the activities of international financing institutions in the region, to provide more environmentally friendly alternatives for IFI investments, and to raise awareness and encourage public participation in the process.

The network began with activities in the Czech Republic, Estonia, Hungary, Latvia, Lithuania, Poland, Romania, and the Slovak Republic. The secretariat is based at the Polish Ecological Club, and each national coordinator is a member of a partner NGO from that country. Regional activities are handled by a regional coordinator in the secretariat. There are two meetings a year, at which network strategies are discussed. Good e-mail communication ensures links among all members. Funders of the Network's activities include the Regional Environmental Center for Central and Eastern Europe, the Rockefeller Brothers Fund, and the Charles Stewart Mott Foundation.

A growing advantage of the multilaterals is their presence virtually throughout the developing South and transitioning East. The significant ODA budget cuts in most OECD countries over this period has led not only to downsizing of bilateral aid agencies but to the outright termination of some country programs. Multilaterals are also beginning to feel the pinch of budget cuts and corresponding downsizing requirements as member governments demand restructuring and cost-cutting measures. But their institutional infrastructure at the country level is better protected from severe closures primarily due to the "redundancy" of the U.N. system, which can more easily consolidate specialized agency programs under UNDP or similar arrangements when necessary. And because the IFIs are banks that cover their operating costs through returns on investment, they are obviously better able to justify their extensive presence in their respective regions or, in the case of the World Bank, globally.

Since the early 1990s, multilaterals have been particularly forceful, especially with their official host-country counterparts, in ensuring that local as well as international NGOs and other civil society actors be involved in the formulation of country program strategies or five-year plans. In fact, these regular planning exercises as well as more informal "consultations" have provided a forum where donors have been able to bring their government and nongovernment "partners" together to discuss common problems and interests, thereby facilitating better relations between the two. And paralleling this encouraging progress at the country level has been a similar openness by the multilaterals to gain CSO input into the formulation of their policies at the overall agency level, both as concerns general development and in programs for CSOs themselves.

As with bilateral funding, it is important to make a distinction between multilateral programs funded from the central level and those funded at the country program level. And it is equally important to note that the IFIs, as distinct from UNDP and other U.N. specialized agencies, provide the bulk of their funding through loans to

The idea of creating the Bankwatch Network at the regional level is rooted in the recognition that all the countries in the region have been confronted with similar problems during their transition to a market economy. The major development projects financed by IFIs, as well as the policies of these institutions toward these countries, have much in common and are strongly related to the governments' hopes to join the European Union.

The Bankwatch Network has focused on two main issues considered common for all countries in the region: transportation and energy. National coordinators look in more detail at issues of particular concern within each country. Among other issues, the Network has asked the World Bank to promote more progressive policies and projects, provide adequate and timely information about project pipelines, be proactive on public participation processes, organize national consultations on Bank policies and regional projects, provide assessment money and develop transparent procedures for decisionmaking, and include some money in project budgets for NGO participation activities.

member governments. At the central level, a small number of special funds—with both sectoral and geographic focuses—have been established to support S/E-CSO programs including, in a number of cases, capacity-building needs. While the funds themselves and the individual grants available from them are relatively small, for many CSOs they have been an important source of initial funding. The attraction of such funds is that they are made directly to S/E-CSOs, and are designed to support programs within the policy parameters for which the fund was started. A number of these central funds or programs are cofinanced—that is, bilateral donors match multilateral funds, or more normally provide the bulk of these special programs.

Most multilateral ODA, just like bilateral ODA, is spent at the country level. While there may be a few exceptions, the rule of thumb is that host governments must approve any CSO participation in a particular program or project. This is particularly pronounced in the case of IFIs, whose financing host governments must repay. As noted earlier, multilaterals have been strong proponents of CSO participation in a range of "publicly funded" programs (using donor financing) primarily related to social service delivery, but increasingly so in the areas of income generation, job creation, and natural resource management. And there is little question that in many countries multilaterals—under the banner of either UNDP or an IFI—have played an important role in terms of improving the legal, policy, and regulatory environment that affects the ability of CSOs to participate in sustainable development decisionmaking and implementation. This includes opening up the arenas in which public policymaking takes place to a wide range of civil society actors representing an equally diverse range of social and economic interests.

Publicly financed government-run development programs that use multilateral funding are equally likely to use contracts and grants to engage CSOs, depending on such factors as the type of service being sought, the preferences of a particular government, or donor-mandated requirements. To increase the likelihood of gaining

PARENTS' ASSOCIATIONS IN MALI

Through a partnership between an international private voluntary organization, World Education, and some Malian groups, local NGOs and community organizations were able to contribute to the national debate on educational policy and to implement a program that ultimately led to policy reform. The program grew out of widespread dissatisfaction with primary schooling in urban and rural communities. Despite the schools' shortcomings, communities demonstrated that they cared about their schools and, if given the opportunity, were capable of taking action themselves.

Building on previous experience in Mali, World Education developed a school improvement program that is genuinely community-based. Training and technical assistance were offered to Malian NGOs, which in turn supported the development of active parents' associations. NGO staff train board and committee members so that they can run their organizations effectively and plan and implement school improvements. USAID provided funding for a pilot phase in early 1993, and on the basis of its success subsequently supported broad expansion of the program in Mali as well as in other West African countries.

The success of the program has been due in part to an unusually favorable political environment. The current government in Mali saw an urgent need for educational reforms, and has been willing to engage in a consultative process and allow innovation. Donor agencies were interested in supporting educational reforms and were prepared to fund experimental programs. Both donors and gov-

broader S/E-CSO participation in these programs, the multilaterals have been promoting significant capacity-building components in activities they finance. They have also used a range of mechanisms to provide necessary fiduciary accountability for funding made available to weaker organizations; to provide them with training and technical assistance; and to monitor progress and evaluate impact. In a number of cases northern NGOs have managed an umbrella-type management unit.

Multilaterals frequently contract with S/E-CSOs to undertake a range of services on their behalf, including program or project assessments, designs, and evaluation; studies and research; the delivery of technical assistance and training to a range of stakeholders; and the provision of administrative and logistics functions. Obviously, the CSOs engaged in this regard are highly specialized and capable—in some cases, they might be best described as nonprofit contractors. Such arrangements, although not appropriate for all CSOs, do provide many organizations with a way to sustain their activities.

Northern Nongovernmental Development Assistance Agencies

Northern CSOs

In addition to traditional northern development NGOs, a broader array of northern civil society actors is becoming involved in development. Of particular importance

ernment recognized the potential contribution of NGOs in a sector that had previously been monopolized by the state.

One of the most exciting outcomes of the program is a lively debate about education that is taking place among stakeholders at many different levels. At the community level, teachers and parents have begun to discuss issues such as the curriculum and enrollment of girls and boys. Parents' associations, widely distrusted in the past because of the corrupt practices that took place under the old regime, are now elected. Through the program, they are trained to represent the interests of parents and are now able to engage in dialogue with the school directors.

Increasingly, parents' associations are playing a role in school management—including overseeing the spending of funds raised from community contributions and supplemented with grants for renovations and construction. And the Ministry of Basic Education has begun to consult parents and the NGOs that work with them about proposed educational reforms. One result has been legal recognition of community schools—one of several alternatives to public schools.

World Education also learned an important lesson about the role of an international organization: outside agencies should refrain from speaking for or acting on behalf of local communities, even if this sometimes seems necessary or expedient. Their task is to facilitate a process that allows an indigenous reform movement to emerge among community activists, with support from local NGOs that have strong ties to the communities where they work. Program participants need to speak for themselves and defend the interests of their communities. The end result has been a strong sense of ownership of the program, among both the Malian NGOs and the communities that are building and running their own schools.

are large membership-based organizations and movements such as associations of mayors and governors, trade unions and business associations, professional associations, environmental and women's organizations, and a wide range of civic and community groups. All these can be considered nontraditional northern development assistance agencies.

By definition, civil society organizations come together voluntarily to promote a shared interest, to address a common problem, or to advance collective values. Thus a diversity of N-CSO missions, objectives, and policies relate to their role as sustainable development agents in southern and transition countries. Although it is a bit of a simplification, N-CSOs can be classified into three groups: those that implement their own sustainable development programs at the local level in southern and eastern countries; those that serve in an intermediary capacity, providing technical or management assistance on behalf of official donors (and some governments) to local CSOs (and less frequently to grassroots organizations); and those that have no operational presence in southern and eastern countries and whose organizational mandate is to support the efforts of their CSO partners there.

N-CSOs with operational programs are more likely to enter into contractual or highly structured grant relationships with their local counterparts to implement a component of their program or project, whether financed by an official donor or

THE VIRTUAL FOUNDATION OF ECOLOGIA

ECOLOGIA is a U.S.-based NGO founded in 1989 to provide technical assistance to environmental grassroots organizations. In 1996, the group introduced the Virtual Foundation—the world's first cyberspace foundation for the environment, human health, and sustainable community development.

The Virtual Foundation was developed in response to decreasing international financial support for NGOs in the former Soviet Union and Central and Eastern Europe. It capitalized on the benefits of an already existing global communication network by engaging Americans in individual philanthropy through the Internet. This provides overseas NGOs with access to a vast, untapped source of funding: private citizens, small businesses, community organizations, ethnic groups, and churches. Although these groups and organizations have a strong tradition of local philanthropy, they have had few options for international involvement. Through the Internet, the foundation allows these potential donors to screen projects carefully and fund them directly.

The foundation, managed by ECOLOGIA's office in the United States, posts proposals on a Web site. Another main element of the foundation is Consortium members, who are experienced grantmaking organizations in each region; they solicit and screen local proposals. Donors, who visit the Web site and select pro-

through their own privately raised funding. Such funding is normally highly conditional—that is, tied to specific uses and carrying significant accounting and reporting requirements. This is particularly true when either bilateral or multilateral ODA made available at the country level is used.

But as mentioned earlier, the day of the fully operational N-CSO implementing its own programs at the local level is drawing quickly to an end under pressure from official donors, to some extent from S/E governments, and increasingly from S/E-CSOs. This has led many N-CSOs and the official donors who have funded them to reassess future roles and alternative funding strategies.

While going out of business is one option open to N-CSOs, it is not one that most would choose voluntarily. Thus N-CSOs are starting to adopt more realistic or appropriate strategies to ensure their continued survival in the short to medium term. One of the most interesting has been for N-CSOs to spin off various country programs or projects into autonomous and indigenous CSOs or foundations. The northern group's role then becomes providing some combination of technical advice and management assistance and serving as a channel for both northern voluntary sector and official aid agency support. Whether this strategy is simply a way of perpetuating the life span of a large "multinational" CSO or is truly a movement toward autonomy for indigenous CSOs remains to be seen.

The changing development context has also led many N-CSOs to become specialized either in a technical or sectoral program area or in the field of development management and capacity building. As noted earlier, some have acted as intermediaries managing umbrella-like projects providing a combination of grant and capacity-

jects, may decide to become partners, and to fully or partially fund projects. The Virtual Foundation encourages donors and grant recipients to build long-term cooperation as a sustainable base of support for NGOs from developing countries.

Although ECOLOGIA had previous experience in international partnerships and in use of the Internet, NGOs were initially hesitant to apply for grants from the Virtual Foundation, since it was an untested method of fundraising. However, with some prodding from consortium members and as proposals were funded, NGOs became increasingly interested in participating. Six months after the Project was launched, about 45 proposals had been posted and 13 donations received.

The Virtual Foundation still struggles with how best to advertise the projects to potential donors. ECOLOGIA learned that the organization cannot rely on the Internet as a self-promoting medium. Traditional publicity techniques had to be developed for intensive outreach and promotion. ECOLOGIA also faced legal problems concerning tax deductibility of overseas contributions. The organization developed numerous policies to deal with these issues.

In order to recruit overseas partners, ECOLOGIA plans to provide consulting on how to set up internal Virtual Foundation Web sites for fundraising in developing countries. Web site fundraising in local languages could become a powerful tool for building domestic philanthropy.

building assistance to indigenous CSO communities; others focus solely on providing technical assistance and training in such areas as microfinance, policy advocacy, and community forestry management. Unlike operational CSOs, which normally raise a significant percentage of their budgets from members or the larger public in northern countries, specialized N-CSOs largely depend on grants and contracts from northern foundations and on ODA agencies.

While some have termed such groups nonprofit contractors, there can be little doubt that most of them chose to become specialized and less operational based on their own mandate rather than for survival purposes. In terms of addressing the practical needs of sustainable development, it is increasingly clear that targeting the capacity-building needs of S/E-CSOs and the larger sector itself is consistent with the emerging division of labor among global civil society actors. Many of these N-CSOs have also become lead thinkers as well as best practitioners in the global arena and have contributed to the shaping of a truly international civil society.

The final category of N-CSO is what can best be described as civil society support organizations. Such groups see their mission solely in terms of supporting the development and growth of southern and eastern CSOs and the larger community or sector. Their principal tasks in this regard include mobilizing public, private, and voluntary sector resources in the North and transferring them to the South and East; promoting solidarity between northern civil societies and their southern and eastern counterparts; and increasing the awareness among northern publics of the importance of remaining engaged and committed to sustainable development in general and of the role and needs of emerging S/E civil societies in particular.

THE ENVIRONMENTAL PARTNERSHIP FOR CENTRAL EUROPE

In 1989, several foundations, including the Charles Stewart Mott Foundation, the Rockefeller Brothers Fund, and the German Marshall Fund of the U.S. (GMF), initiated a planning process that led two years later to the establishment of the Environmental Partnership for Central Europe (EPCE). International funding agencies concerned with Eastern Europe urged the consortium to provide small sums and fast and flexible grants to build local capacity and a new democratic leadership and thus assist the region at the community level in its environmental rebuilding efforts.

Since then, some 20 different funders from the United States, Europe, and Japan have joined the consortium and pioneered a cost-effective mechanism across the region to encourage communities to address their environmental problems, increase environmental awareness, stimulate public involvement and participation, train leaders, and promote cooperation between the private, public, and nonprofit sectors. Over the last six years, this experiment has evolved into a model project.

The EPCE has offices in Poland, Hungary, the Czech Republic, and Slovakia. Each is directed by a local leader, has a small local staff, and is governed by a local Board of directors. A regional coordinator connects the country offices with each other and with the neighbors in the West and East. For the first five

Several differences exist between these support organizations and northern foundations. First, they have no permanent source of funding and must raise it from an array of northern contributors, including foundations. Second, they are normally membership-based organizations, composed of either other CSOs or individual citizens. Finally, support organizations actively promote linkages and relationships between the North and the South and East as well as undertake development education programs. While some foundations may do one or the other, they are the exception rather than the rule.

Foundations

As the title of Chapter 3 makes clear, northern foundations provide the venture capital for civil society. Because of the private nature of their funding, mostly generated from trusts and endowments, foundations have provided CSOs from the East and South with flexible funding for innovative types of activities. In fact, many foundation-funded activities in S/E countries have come to mirror programs promoted in northern countries for several decades. This includes encouraging indigenous philanthropy, volunteerism, and foundation movements, which constitute important components of the infrastructure of civil society itself. In addition, foundations have entered into more politically sensitive areas, including providing assistance to increase the capacity of civil society to broaden societal participation in national policymaking, to monitor state performance of public functions, and to promote more open and democratic societies.

years, a Washington Support Office at the GMF provided administrative and program assistance. During 1997, all offices will become independent local foundations. The GMF retains fiscal responsibility for the partnership project.

The EPCE combines a small grants program (up to US$8,000) with technical assistance, training for environmental and other NGOs, fellowships for East-East/East-West exchanges, and efforts to be a catalyst in communities throughout the region. By the end of its sixth year, the EPCE had made more than 1,000 grants (totalling US$4.1 million) and spent US$1.1 million on technical assistance and US$900,000 on administration. Always conscious of their limited funds, the local EPCE offices have focused their grant and technical assistance on projects that strengthen politically influential constituencies and those that will serve as models for other communities.

In 1991, EPCE funders made an initial commitment of three years. It soon became clear that much more time was needed. Reinforced by outside evaluations, the core funders extended their support for another three years, providing additional funds for staff training to develop strategic planning and fundraising capacity. It is expected that several of the core funders will continue some basic support until 2000 to enable the local EPCE foundations to expand their own fundraising capabilities and to continue the regranting program. The most immediate challenge will be to test whether the concept of philanthropy—absent from Central Europe for more than 40 years—can be rekindled, and whether enough local donors will replace western funding sources.

Northern foundation funding that goes to the international affairs category has decreased over the past decade. It also remains a small percentage of ODA and well behind the broad category of northern CSO resource transfers to the South and East. In terms of the share of foundations' overall international funding that goes to southern and eastern CSOs, it far surpasses all other northern donor agencies. Not only have northern foundations provided a considerable amount of funding to a broad range of S/E-CSOs for a wide variety of activities, but many of them have a determined policy of targeting grassroots or community-based organizations as well. This includes foundations with country program offices as well as those without them.

Major Conclusions for Practitioners

The information presented thus far on the policies, programs, and strategies of various development assistance agencies has provided practical information that CSOs will need to identify donors that can best meet their resource needs. The real work, particularly the research, remains to be done. (See Box 3.)

Think Strategically, Act Tactically

For the vast majority of S/E-CSOs, scarcity of resources, particularly financial ones, is an everyday reality. Most groups operate with little more than their members' voluntary contributions of labor, materials, and money. Organizational permanence—

BOX 3

USING A DECISION TREE TO PREPARE RESOURCE REQUESTS

Step 1: *Assess your resource needs in line with your organizational mission and objectives.*

Step 2: *Assess your organizational objectives in line with your current institutional capacity.*

For many CSOs, these two steps may require technical assistance to assess their needs and capacity, the first step in developing a credible proposal. The general rubric under which such assistance falls is strategic planning. Many organizations, both local and international, provide training or technical assistance in this area, and many of them have some funding to provide such assistance for free. The fundamental tenet of all fundraising work is if you ask for help, you are likely to receive it. This is particularly true if a CSO is not asking for funding, but rather capacity-building assistance. If a CSO has done its homework, it should know which organizations, including donors and even government departments, provide this type of support.

Step 3: *If resource needs and institutional capacity are significantly out of balance, reduce and focus your resource needs request.*

Step 4: *Do you have a credible track record in terms of using the resources requested? If not, then you either are not asking for the appropriate resources, or you need to show how the resources would help you achieve your objective.*

Taking a long-term, strategic approach to resource enhancement often means building capacity, and hence a track record, in incremental steps. It can also mean building a long-term relationship with a donor in which a series of increasingly large grants demonstrates your ability to manage funds and achieve results.

Step 5: *If you do have a credible track record, including demonstrated institutional capacity and impact, choose the appropriate donor.*

Step 6: *If you do not know the appropriate donor, conduct a systematic research effort to identify one or more. This takes work and patience.*

Much of the research on donors will involve talking with other local CSOs, as well as civil society support organizations such as umbrella organizations, indigenous

---

paid staff, a functioning office, and fixed assets—is the exception rather than the rule for most CSOs. As a result, their impact is limited and periodic. At the same time, most groups have not gained access to development assistance agency resources. When donor funding does become a possibility, regardless of whether it would contribute to the achievement of a CSO's mission and objectives, there is a reasonable tendency on the part of most CSOs to try to obtain it.

Moving from organizational semipermanence and low impact to being an institutionally effective and capable CSO requires a track record that can often be achieved

foundations, sectoral and geographic networks, and consortia, many of whom provide such services to their members or the larger CSO community. Government agencies, including ministries responsible for coordinating external donor assistance and even local governments, can provide extremely useful advice and contacts. Key multilaterals such as the local UNDP and World Bank missions often are best placed among donors to help CSOs begin the process of researching other donors. And many N-CSOs and foundations see it as part of their mandate to assist their local counterparts in this most important step toward sustainability and autonomy.

Step 7: *Prepare a proposal that matches the resources requested with your institutional capacity and organizational objectives. Explicitly link funded activities to measurable results and the performance indicators that demonstrate achievement of your planned objectives.*

When required, request resources that will enhance your capacity to achieve your organizational objectives. Donors are increasingly willing to entertain proposals to strengthen your institutional capacity, but you must be able to demonstrate the linkage between strengthened capacity and concrete developmental results. Today, more than ever before, donors want to see tangible results from their assistance. "Managing for results" begins with stating in your proposal the results you intend to achieve and the indicators that will measure them.

Step 8: *Negotiate the terms and conditions of your funding from a position of strength, which begins with knowledge of an array of donor regulations and policies.*

Often getting a proposal accepted or approved is only the first step in a longer process that includes negotiating the terms and conditions of your funding. Will you receive funding through a contract or grant? Does your donor cover overhead costs or administrative costs? Is there a "matching" requirement, and if so, is it negotiable? Are funds provided on an advance basis? Or must you spend first and then ask for reimbursement? Are there some costs that a donor will not reimburse? Knowing these policies and regulations beforehand puts you in a stronger position when it comes to negotiating a grant agreement or contract.

with donor funding. It may include "enlarging" the goals and objectives of a CSO to include those being promoted by donor programs to attract the initial funding they need to become accepted "players." Such funding should be viewed as a tactical short-term necessity in a long-term strategy of institutional development and sustainability—not a permanent way of doing business. Otherwise, CSOs turn into chameleons, changing their colors to attract new donors or the revised policies of old ones. The problem with such a tactic is that it can lead to a loss of identity and the uniqueness of mission and vision that distinguishes the CSO from other groups.

Incrementalism Versus the Big Fix

Although there have been a number of technological breakthroughs in agriculture, development in general has been an incremental process in which the results of practical experience have informed and improved future development strategies. CSOs with little or no previous experience or demonstrated track records should not view the resources available from donor agencies as a magic bullet that is going to transform them into prominent development actors.

A grant of US$1,000–3,000 for a CSO with little or no previous track record or permanent organizational capacity makes a lot more sense than one of US$50,000–100,000. Being able to demonstrate solid results in an activity with limited objectives that directly meets the needs of members or clients is the first step toward gaining credibility. And building on this success by asking for resources to establish a limited degree of permanence or to expand successful activity is an incremental approach that fits into a long-term strategic plan.

Building Public Capital

Over the last four decades, building some form of "capital" has been one of the principal strategies of policymakers, although the focus has moved from physical to human and then social capital. In general, building capital has meant raising the quality of stock or resources in one of these areas. CSOs are often held to a higher moral standard in the conduct of their operations than are players in the state or market. The idea that civil society in general and CSOs in particular should have a highly normative dimension centered on notions of integrity, credibility, and legitimacy is a just and accurate one.

In most cases, CSOs have a high stock of public capital—at least in terms of their members or clients—just because they are neither governmental nor market-based. This public capital is the greatest resource that CSOs have at their disposal, and one that should be maintained and even increased. The reaction to a CSO's request for assistance is likely to depend on its perceived legitimacy, including the grounding in local society, and the integrity of its dealings with the larger social and political environment. Funding proposals must be able to demonstrate this larger sense of public capital as well the credibility of the specific request.

Know Yourself First

Southern and eastern CSOs not only need to know the policies and programs of individual development assistance agencies, they must also be brutally honest in terms of knowing what they can reasonably expect to accomplish with additional resources over a given planning period. This requires assessing existing capacities in such areas as strategic planning (such as setting goals and measurable objectives and identifying external factors and actors that affect program success); resource management; and program design, management, and evaluation.

By matching needs with capacities, a CSO can make reasonable decisions concerning its resource requests and be in a better position to approach a donor agency most appropriate to its true resource needs and levels. Knowing your donor as yourself means just that. Being taken seriously by donors means knowing yourself first—your limitations as well as your strengths—and being seen as a credible sustainable development agent.

Changing Donor Policies and Practices

Beyond gaining access to the resources of various development assistance agencies, the time has come for CSOs in the South and East to consider how to increase the overall resources available. The concern here is how to change donor policies, programs, and funding mechanisms to better meet the resource needs of CSOs and the larger civil society.

Broaden the Resource Base

At present, there are essentially two ways to increase resources from northern development assistance agencies. One is to increase resource flows from the known group of agencies. The second is to broaden the resource base itself to include organizations that have not traditionally provided development assistance to southern and eastern countries.

The resources of the existing pool of agencies will only increase if the institutions are able to move beyond the rhetoric of sustainable development and fashion strategies that recognize the critical role of civil society in social, economic, and political development. And then they must find the political will to match this understanding with resource allocations. For official development agencies, this means overcoming the notion that governments are the only legitimate national actor that can allocate and manage ODA resources. Considering that nearly US$60 billion in ODA was transferred to southern developing countries in 1994 and US$7.5 billion to eastern countries in transition, if just 5 percent of ODA went to CSOs it would have a tremendous impact on their ability to reach the poor.

For N-NGOs, a fundamental redefinition of their role in development must take place, in which they move from direct actors in the implementation of development programs to indirect supporters of their S/E partners. This is already happening, as noted earlier, but it needs to speed up. This would release a significant sum of the private voluntary contributions made available by northern citizens to N-NGOs for use in S/E development. Considering that roughly US$6 billion in privately raised funds was distributed by N-NGOs in 1994 in southern countries alone, the potential for increased flows is considerable.

Of course, this discussion only deals with the supply side of development assistance. While this has stagnated and even decreased over recent years, the demand side has increased phenomenally. With the tremendous political changes culminating in democratic and free market systems in the South and East since the late 1980s, associations have proliferated. No longer are traditional development and humanitarian NGOs the only participants in sustainable development in southern and eastern countries.

Today civil societies in the South and East are beginning to mirror those in the North, including truly autonomous and voluntary community and neighborhood associations, trade unions and peasant federations, business and professional associations, human rights and civic organizations, environmental and consumer groups, and nonprofit think tanks and policy institutes. This expanded or inclusive concept of civil society has increased the number of actors with a legitimate role to play in sustainable development activities, especially in areas where a decade ago they had no role—such as policymaking, human rights monitoring, and civic education. Until recently, most of these organizations did not even exist. As legitimate participants in sustainable development, they now have a reasonable claim on northern development assistance agency resources, adding to pressures on the supply side.

One obvious answer—in addition to increasing flows from development assistance agencies—is to broaden the resource base of northern CSOs involved in sustainable development efforts in the South and East. Not only would this increase resources, financial and nonfinancial, for S/E-CSOs, it would promote the notion of a global civil society of citizens' organizations in the North and South/East.

Underlying this strategy is an effort to increase information about and contacts between northern and southern/eastern CSOs. This requires both an educational component and the establishment of institutional mechanisms to facilitate information and contacts. Existing national, regional, and global CSO consortia and networks can run programs of "development" education for concerned governments, international organizations, and the general public about sustainable development efforts of their members. They also act as clearinghouses for the collection and dissemination of information about member activities and partner needs. These roles, and CSOs' capacity to undertake them, need to be better articulated and strengthened.

In practical terms, additional institutional mechanisms need to be developed to link N-CSO interests, resources, and expertise with S/E concerns and resource needs. Official donors and northern foundations are probably best placed to promote true partnerships between nontraditional CSOs in the North and South/East. Interestingly, ODA agencies may have a significant role to play in this regard, particularly in the way they make funding available to CSOs. If official agencies view the promotion of civil society as an important component of sustainable development, they can put their considerable resources behind this objective. Multilateral and particularly bilateral donor agencies can themselves serve as a clearinghouse between N-CSOs and those in the South and East, matching needs with resources. Also, by funding a broader range of CSOs everywhere they will increase contacts and promote greater solidarity.

Participation in Strategy Development and Policymaking

A principal key to increased funding is giving CSOs access to the policymaking and strategy development processes of donors at both the centralized agency and country program levels. In terms of ODA agencies, policymaking takes place primarily at the central level. Increasingly, S/E-CSOs are invited to join donor policymaking processes. Pushing for a concept of sustainable development that treats CSOs as legitimate actors in development strengthens the justification of additional funding for such groups. This must be matched, however, by a demonstrated capacity to design and implement programs and services. Equally important, as noted earlier, N-CSOs and particularly N-NGOs must be pressured to reorient their roles from direct and operational to indirect and supportive. S/E-CSOs have numerous fora to affect the policymaking of N-NGOs.

While advocating for changed donor policies is a longer-term strategy at the regional and global levels, of immediate importance for most CSOs are the country programs of both official and nongovernmental development agencies. This is where most donor funding is spent. And the vehicle for determining its allocation is the country strategic plans that most donors develop on a three- to five-year basis. Increasingly, bilateral and multilateral donors have reached out to local governments, private sectors, and NGOs in addition to host-country central governments. Donors must continue to encourage wide representation from civil society, and a broader range of civil society actors must find a way to join the country strategy development process. It is a lot easier to design yourself into a program strategy from the beginning than it is to try to gain a role after the process has been completed, particularly when corresponding budgets are likely to lock in funding to programs and specific CSOs.

Before development assistance agencies undertake all these needed policy changes, a fundamental revision must take place in their concept of civil society's role in sustainable development. In fact, such changes are beginning to take place, albeit at a slower pace than CSOs would like to see. They require a continuing campaign of advocacy in a range of global, regional, and national fora. This too has been increasing in recent years, as the half-dozen international and numerous regional and national conferences since the Earth Summit in Rio have made clear. And as policies begin to change in favor of greater S/E funding, a corresponding emphasis on a new set of institutional arrangements and funding mechanisms will occur. As described in the next section, a range of new mechanisms and institutional arrangements are being used by donors.

Innovative Funding Mechanisms to Broaden CSO Participation

A major problem facing donors is their inability to fund more than a handful of CSOs. Much of this inability is due to limited staff resources available to assess CSO proposals, to oversee approved grants, and to evaluate completed grants. The result is a concentration of donor funding, and hence power, in a relatively small number of larger S/E-NGOs with whom donors have established a long-term relationship. The long-term impact will be a reduction in the number and diversity of groups that underpins a strong and vibrant civil society. If donors would like to reach out to more— and more diverse—CSOs, several funding mechanisms are available.

A Strategy to Develop Civil Society in Stages

As with the advice to CSOs on how to approach donors, a gradual approach is the best policy, based on the principle of incrementalism. The first step would be to increase the value and effectiveness of the one resource that smaller CSOs have in sufficient quantity—their voluntary or civic spirit. Very small grants to fund activities with a narrowly defined objective that can be completed in, say, three to six months using volunteers would be the first step in such a strategy. Thus the establishment of Microgrant Funds that provide from US$500 to US$5,000 maximum would make it

THE INTERNATIONAL CIVIL SOCIETY CONSORTIUM

The International Civil Society Consortium for Public Deliberation is an international nonprofit association consisting of a number of civic organizations in Europe, Asia, the Middle East, and the Americas. Its aim is to enhance international cooperation in promoting responsible democratic and widely participatory public debate. The process is carried out through deliberative forums ranging in size from small study circles to community-wide public meetings. The Kettering Foundation's International Civil Society Program works in partnership with these organizations, not by providing grants but by offering exchanges of ideas, practices, and staff.

The foundation transfers its ideas and methodologies of public deliberation through a six-month fellowship program at its offices for representatives of member organizations, through the International Civil Society workshop organized every summer with participants from all over the world, and through annual Exchange meetings. In addition, foundation representatives travel to partner countries and work with consortium members to design and implement public deliberation programs.

Each organization that participates in the consortium creates its own programs and networks within its country or region. The Joint East European Center for Democratic Education and Governance is the consortium member in

possible to reach a wide range of CSOs that have never been involved in mainstream sustainable development efforts. Consideration could also be given to funding the activities of larger grassroots organizations.

For a more select group of CSOs that had demonstrated an ability to manage a limited amount of funding, using primarily voluntary labor and contributions, and that had developed a reasonable strategic plan, consideration could be given to funding a longer-term activity, in which building institutional capacity would be one objective. Capacity Development Funds that provide CSOs with financing for both training and technical assistance as well as modest program activities in which a CSO had shown previous success would bring a significant number of new CSOs into sustainable development efforts. Whereas the principal aim of the Microgrant Fund would be to support the activities of CSOs, the purpose of the Capacity Development Fund would be to support the organization itself. Such funds would provide grants in the range of US$50,000–100,000 over one to two years.

Distinct from funding the capacity development of individual CSOs, a separate Civil Society Fund would target the strengthening of civil society itself—that is, building and strengthening its institutional infrastructure. Thus a range of newly emerging civil society support organizations involved in such activities as training, advocacy, representation, information collection and dissemination, financing, and networking would be targeted.

Hungary. It was established in 1991 to initiate civic education programs for schools and NGOs in Hungary.

The foundation's assistance to the Joint Center included transfer of materials, ideas, and expertise; training and fellowships for Joint Center representatives in events organized by the Kettering Foundation, covering all participation expenses; and small grants for publications. All this helped the center to design and implement its own projects, for which it received grants from USAID, the Pew Charitable Trust, and other foundations.

According to the Joint Center, the most significant assistance from the Kettering Foundation was the transfer of the philosophy and methodology of deliberative democracy. "One way or another, it has been the organizing principle of the five programs the Joint Center has been running in the past six years," said a representative. "The Joint Center has had success in receiving funds partly because this philosophy and practice of citizen politics is still somewhat unusual in the democratizing societies in Eastern Europe."

An important result of the personal exchange, according to the Joint Center, has been the opportunity to follow the design and implementation of projects from the beginning until the end. The staff exchange and a continuous personal communication with program managers at the foundation have provided useful opportunities to learn about Kettering's activities, as well as about funders' policies in the United States.

The final component in the incremental strategy would be to establish Sustainable Development Funds whose purpose would be to fund the programs of CSOs that had established themselves over two to three years as effective sustainable development agents. Grants would be used to fund the expansion of existing programs to cover a wider geographic area or to permit CSOs to move into new program areas consistent with their overall mission and objectives. They would also provide a stable and adequate source of funding over three to five years to strengthen and consolidate the CSO's institutional capacity and ability to implement its program. Funding for institutional needs would decrease steadily over the course of the grant, with the intention of increasing other sources of funding. Such a fund would preferably provide financing to S/E-CSOs through block grants, as has been done for many N-NGOs and a small number of large, long established southern CSOs. Sustainable Development Fund grants could be on the order of US$100,000–500,000.

Making such a strategy work will require a new degree of donor coordination in a range of areas. Harmonizing policies toward S/E-CSOs at the country level is the obvious first step. Conducting joint assessments of CSO institutional and program needs is a preliminary requirement to the design and formulation of country program strategies that target CSO participation in sustainable development efforts. The allocation of financing responsibilities among and between donors as well as the types of mechanisms to be used should be decided on during the design stage. Likewise, managing approved programs, monitoring their performance, and evaluating impact will require new and innovative institutional arrangements that can ensure financial accountability, solve implementation problems, and establish and maintain working relations with CSO partners.

CSO Funding Mechanisms

Providing resources under this strategy or in any program wishing to broaden support to a wider range of S/E-CSOs requires finding the right or appropriate mechanism. Some of the following mechanisms have been used in a limited number of cases; others are just being proposed.

- *Donor Consortium.* This could include either official or nongovernmental development assistance agencies. It involves two or more donor agencies joining together in a common management unit to review proposals, assess CSO capacities, administer grants, and monitor and evaluate approved grants. As noted earlier, a consortium arrangement lets donors fund an increased number of smaller CSOs or provide a smaller number of very large block grants.

- *CSO Umbrella Intermediaries.* These could involve a single institution from the North or South/East capable of providing CSO communities with training and technical assistance, grants themselves, and information collection and dissemination. The group would operate more in the capacity of a nonprofit contractor whose only purpose is to provide assistance to CSOs or the larger sector of civil society. It would be contracted with by an ODA agency or by other N-CSOs.

- *Civil Society Foundations.* Rather than donors or intermediaries determining the use of development assistance, independent foundations could be established to undertake a number of important functions related to the strengthening of civil society at the national, regional, or global levels. Among their functions could be capacity building, grantmaking, advocacy and representation, networking, information collection and dissemination, and research. To increase autonomy and sustainability, such foundations could be endowed or donors could make special grants.

- *Dedicated Civil Society Funds.* These would largely be ODA agency centralized funds set up exclusively to support CSOs and civil society at the national, regional, and global levels. They could be used for capacity building for individual CSOs and CSO consortia; for facilitating alliances, networking, and information collection and dissemination; and for increasing participation in policy analysis, formulation. and advocacy. As noted earlier, the multilaterals have established a number of NGO dedicated programs (UNDP) or funds to which NGOs have access (World Bank).

  A few donors (the Inter-American Development Bank and USAID) have been discussing the establishment of dedicated civil society funds, but nothing has yet materialized in this regard. What is recommended here is funds that would not support sectoral program activities but rather improve the capacity of CSOs in a number of more specialized areas (such as advocacy, networking, and research) and promote the visibility, enabling environment, and strategies for CSO resource enhancement at the national, regional, or international level.

- *Partnership, Alliance, and Coalition-Building Funds.* Separate funds could be established to fund N-S/E partnerships or alliances among groups throughout the South. These could promote the sharing of expertise, the forging of solidarity, and the building or strengthening of regional and global coalitions or alliances.

Change Donor Operational Policies

In addition to the constraints imposed by overall donor development policies and strategies, a series of more operational policies and procedures affect donors' ability to provide funding to CSOs even when they so desire. There is thus a need to encourage ODA agencies and the N-CSOs they fund to provide resources within their grants or contracts to build sustainable organizations rather than dependent ones. The procedures that need to change include making it possible to fund capacity building as well as specific programs of interest to the donor agency; covering overhead costs or increasing funding for administration; reducing time-consuming reporting requirements; improving grant selection and approval by including simpler proposal formats, a transparent review and approval process, and published selection criteria; and changing accounting and accountability requirements to allow contributions to some of the innovative funding mechanisms just described.

RESOURCE GUIDE

Publications

Bebbington, Anthony, and Roger Riddell, "The Direct Funding of Southern NGOs by Donors: New Agendas and Old Problems," *Journal of International Development*, 1995.

Bennett, Jon, *NGO Funding Mechanisms: A Guide For Southern and Eastern NGOs* (Oxford/Geneva: ICVA/INTRAC, 1996).

Clark, John, "The State, Popular Participation and the Voluntary Sector," *World Development*, Vol. 23, No. 4, 1995, pp. 593–601.

Fowler, Alan, *Strengthening the Role of Voluntary Development Organizations: Policy Issues Facing Official AID Agencies* (Washington, D.C.: Overseas Development Council, 1995).

Fowler, Alan, and Rick James, *The Role of Southern NGOs in Development Cooperation* (Oxford: INTRAC, 1994).

Fox, Leslie, *Strengthening Civil Society Financing in Development: The Role of Official Development Assistance* (Washington, D.C.: Overseas Development Council, 1995).

Fox, Leslie, *How New Funding Mechanisms Could Be Used to Support Civil Society: A Preliminary Study of Existing Experience* (New York: Synergos Institute, 1994).

Logan, David, *A Guide to Transnational Giving* (London: Director of Social Change, 1993).

The Reality of Aid 1995 (London: Earthcsan Publications Ltd, 1995).

OECD, *Development Cooperations: Efforts and Policies of the Members of the Development Assistance Committee* (Paris: OECD/DAC, 1996).

UNDP, *Human Development Report 1996* (New York: Oxford University Press, 1996).

World Bank, *World Development Report 1996* (New York: Oxford University Press, 1996).

Case Study Contacts

Cathryn Thorup
U.S. Agency for International Development
PPC/DP Room 3637NS
Washington, DC 20523
Tel: (1-202) 647-0600
Fax: (1-202) 647-5189
Web site: http://www.info.usaid.gov/
           pubs/npi/npiresrc.htm

Nilda Bullain
Civil Society Development Foundation
Meszoly u. 4. III/3
117 Budapest
Hungary

Randy Kritkausky
Ecologia
Main Street
P.O. Box 142
Harford, PA 18823
Tel: (1-717) 434-9589
Web site: http://www.virtual
           foundation.org/

Gerald B. Hildebrand
Executive Director
Katalysis North/South Development Partnership
1331 N. Commerce Street
Stockton, CA 95202
Tel: (1-209) 943-6165
Fax: (1-209) 943-7046
E-mail: katalysis2@aol.com

Deborah Witte
Kettering Foundation
200 Commons Road
Dayton, OH 45459
Tel: (1-513) 434-7300

Chapter 8

Engaging Corporations in Strengthening Civil Society

Laurie Regelbrugge

The Mutual Interests of Companies and Communities

Societal structures and norms around the world vary widely, but they are increasingly influenced by a single economic framework—capitalism, a system in which the means of production are privately owned and operated for profit in competitive conditions. As free market enterprise has taken root globally, societies everywhere have begun to look for coinciding expressions of responsibility or citizenship in business operations and policies.

This chapter provides strategies and examples to help civil society organizations (CSOs) learn how to engage the employees and resources of corporations in efforts to build and strengthen civil society. Businesses' engagement with community organizations is a win-win proposition. It is an important vehicle through which corporations can practice their citizenship and responsibilities while benefiting from the relationships.

The focus on corporate engagement should not be read to suggest that corporate action should supersede or replace actions by governments or CSOs themselves. Quite the contrary, these strategies highlight ways that corporations can work constructively with government and civil society to improve community health and well-being. Considering the resource base, mobility, and technical and managerial expertise that companies represent and control, engaging them in efforts to improve the quality of life in communities is strategic both for communities and for the companies themselves. After all, corporate involvement in addressing serious social and environmental problems relates directly to creating and maintaining environments conducive to long-term social stability and commercial success.

Portions of this chapter were adapted from *Global Corporate Citizenship—Rationale and Strategies*, by David Logan, Delwin Roy, and Laurie Regelbrugge (Washington, D.C.: The Hitachi Foundation, 1997). Most of the case studies were gathered in the process of compiling this book.

Business thrives in healthy communities. Companies can play constructive roles in applying their resources, sometimes independently and sometimes in partnership with CSOs and government, to build the healthy communities that ensure long-term business success. CSOs offer rich opportunities for engaging companies more extensively and strategically in community improvement efforts. They work closely with communities in problem-solving, have expertise on the issues, and offer channels through which companies can engage.

There is no single formula for doing this, nor can every company be engaged in the same way. This chapter provides examples of strategies that have worked, and points to some common barriers. The material is relevant for small and large CSOs, and offers ideas for engaging corporations of all sizes, origins, and locations.

What Is Corporate Citizenship?

Although still a matter of considerable debate, there is growing acceptance that corporate citizenship is the practice of a corporation's direct responsibilities—to employees, shareholders or owners, customers and suppliers, and the communities where it conducts business and serves markets.

At a minimum, corporate citizenship means adherence to the laws, regulations, and accepted business practices wherever a company operates. A more expansive interpretation is that it means conducting business in ways that reflect proactive, responsible business decisions in dealings with owners, employees, customers, and suppliers, and with respect to communities, society, and the natural environment more generally. The most successful, long-lived companies take a proactive approach within communities.

Traditionally, many companies could survive with a narrow definition and practice of this citizenship. But the global business climate is changing dramatically. Community needs and expectations are rising, governments' resources are declining, and companies are wielding ever-growing influence over resources. This dynamic global economy is challenging traditional notions and practices of corporate social responsibility and citizenship. Increasingly, corporate citizenship is an issue of competitiveness.

Though the operating conditions for business throughout the world vary, all feature a collection of rights and responsibilities crafted through the interaction of business and government. Civil society is a growing force in policy formulation that influences these rights and responsibilities. In industrial and developing countries (often referred to as emerging markets), societal structures featuring government, corporations, and civil society have become the norm. Since societal conditions affect all three sectors, strategic collaboration offers greater promise of mutually beneficial results than lies in the largely adversarial relations that often exist between these sectors.

As country fortunes and capacities have dwindled and corporate profits have risen, pressure from governments and citizens for broader corporate social responsibility has increased. Anticipating more of this and increased global competition, companies have a vested interest in "strategic social investments," defined as engaging in the development, maintenance, and health of communities and people as a necessary prerequisite for healthy business operations. Strategic social investment means investing in community infrastructure—both social and physical.

Corporate citizenship continues to be defined by many corporate and community leaders as charity. Suggestions that it is or could be something strategic or related to business are not embraced either within corporate operations or by the chief executive officers (CEOs) or other senior executives. Many companies are reluctant to accept the strategic social investment argument, even though they may actively endorse the notion that all companies should engage in charity. These companies seem most sensitive to the stinging question, How can we be giving money away when we are laying off workers? Yet they also have some of the most impressive giving programs in the world. This "charitable" impulse or motivation can be extremely productive for CSOs.

Nevertheless, growing numbers of companies are trying to integrate their social investment and corporate citizenship responsibilities in their corporate structures globally. The experiments are young, and the full ramifications of these efforts are not known. But a strong case can be made for the market motivation. Perhaps the rhetorical, moral, and motivational distinctions of a "charity versus strategic social investment" debate need not be resolved. It is more important that they are revealed as different rationales through which CSOs can effectively engage corporate resources.

Of course, many companies continue to believe that business is their sole focus. And some CSOs worry that engaging companies might overwhelm or undermine CSO efforts, and that corporate agendas would reign supreme to the detriment of the communities in question. Many people worldwide continue to believe in having clear distinctions between sectors, and even adversarial relations, to maintain the integrity of each sector. This sentiment is particularly strong in places where the corporate or government sector has abused its operating privileges. Nonetheless, looking globally at the spread of economic activity, the strategic engagement of companies seems to be an important long-term strategy.

How Much Do Corporations Donate?

The scale of corporate support for CSOs and community improvement activities is not at all clear. While several countries have tried to quantify corporate philanthropy and charitable giving, these data fail to incorporate the marketing, advertising, investment, employment, service, equipment, and volunteer resources that benefit communities. Only highly formalized corporate philanthropy has a good chance of being referenced in statistics. A great deal of corporate action and involvement with CSOs is not yet captured in company, community, or national statistics.

In the United States, corporate philanthropy hovers around US$7 billion annually. In Japan, a 1996 Keidanren study placed corporate giving at roughly US$1.5 billion. The European Foundation Centre estimates that corporate giving in Europe in 1996 stood at US$1.8–2 billion. A study published by the Canadian Centre for Business in the Community listed corporate contributions for 1994 at US$470 million, about 1.4 percent of the contributions to charity. And a 1993 study in the Philippines revealed that 106 companies donated some US$12 million to education, health, disaster relief, enterprise development, environmental preservation, science and technology, and other projects.

In countries with statistics on corporate philanthropy, the largest share of support usually goes to education, with smaller amounts going to human and social services, arts and culture, housing, environmental programs, and recreation. Companies taking tax deductions for their contributions and corporate foundations are required to file tax documents that provide information. In addition, company annual reports may describe community-based activities. Even where such records are maintained, however, there are no uniform data about the full range of corporate support that would provide an accurate sense of just how much—or how little—corporate citizenship is being harnessed in support of civil society.

Corporate Social Responsibility in Transition

In 1994, a United Nations report listed 37,000 transnational corporations (TNCs), of which 24,000 were based in the European Union (EU), Japan, and the United States and were linked to about 177,000 wholly owned subsidiaries. This number is a dramatic increase from the 7,000 TNCs identified in 1975. Taking these three industrial regions alone, the norms for corporate citizenship vary widely.

Just as capitalism is adapted or tailored to a given country's customs, cultural traditions shape a society's expectations, preferred targets or issues, and practice of corporate citizenship. Hence, capitalism and corresponding practices of corporate responsibility or citizenship become a hybrid in each country. These hybrids are also influenced by the company culture and industry. Corporate citizenship has distinctive characteristics in every country and every company.

U.S. companies have lobbied actively to keep corporate taxes low and to minimize regulations. Yet the tax system provides a deduction incentive for charitable activity. This gives companies a tangible reason for investing in civil society organizations. While the financing mechanism has worked well, the structure has reinforced the notion of corporate charity and has not necessarily prompted companies to think strategically and comprehensively about playing a larger societal role.

Generally speaking, European countries have higher corporate taxes and more governmental regulations than the United States does. Efforts to develop an EU-wide protocol for corporate citizenship have been largely unsuccessful to date since the countries retain distinctive business protocols. Nonetheless, some EU-wide policies concerning work force and environmental issues are in force, and these have implications for companies engaging with CSOs. In the EU generally, there is a less formal system for companies engaging directly with CSOs, but instead companies support civil society through paying higher taxes. CSOs receive government contracts to provide services in communities. In this context, the government plays a more central, intermediary role: receiving taxes from companies and extending fees for services to the CSOs. However, direct interaction among corporations and CSOs is on the rise. It is also important to note that there is tremendous variation within Europe.

In Japan, government and business are the society's two primary sectors. Although in the last 10 years interest in building a CSO sector has grown, the tax and regulatory system do not make it easy. The deductions that a company can claim are limited, and both political and charitable contributions are eligible to receive this deduction. As a consequence, most companies use a higher portion of the allowable deduction for political contributions. Other regulations hinder the establishment of

CSOs in Japan, such as the initial endowment requirements. On the other hand, Japanese companies have always been expected to contribute to the health and well-being of employees and communities where they operate. Many communities in Japan have hospitals, schools, libraries, and other facilities and services made possible largely, if not completely, by corporations.

Philippine laws offer several incentives to corporate and private donors. The Department of Finance's Task Force on Tax and Tariff Reforms is considering initiatives to revise the tax system to generate more philanthropic revenues and to alleviate or at least streamline the cumbersome processes that donors confront. Corporations currently can deduct up to 3 percent of their taxable income derived from business operations.

Initiatives are being taken worldwide to build legal and tax systems conducive to the establishment and vitality of a third sector and CSOs. Countries in Eastern and Central Europe, Asia, Latin America, the Middle East, and Africa are seeking to incorporate tax and regulatory policies that would facilitate the establishment and functioning of CSOs. These initiatives seek "enabling environments"—fiscal policies and legislation that support the development and maintenance of a third sector.

The regulations governing the actions of CSOs can also be crafted to restrict, impede, or enable CSO roles in communities. For example, if a CSO is restricted to a narrow set of activities and it is difficult to get authorization to change the mission or activities, the organization will be unable to respond flexibly to changing societal circumstances. If the process of becoming certified or designated as an organization that can receive donations is long and cumbersome, this too presents a barrier to CSO development.

An important part of this reform exercise has to be attention to the financing side. One lesson of a free market system is that incentives are critical in shaping behavior. Engaging corporations in financing CSOs through the traditional mechanism of tax deduction incentives is certainly a prospect for many countries. But this alone will not yield either the scale or the kinds of strategic social investment that have the greatest potential value to communities, largely because of the competing demands and increasing pressure on corporate funds. A responsive, vital third sector depends on two things: the existence of a thriving business sector that can generate resources to support a third sector, and an enabling fiscal and regulatory environment that has incentives for the givers and the recipients to be responsive and effective.

Influences on Corporate Social Responsibility

Although corporate citizenship differs from country to country, the globalization of capitalism and the growth and mobility of TNCs have led to certain key trends in corporate citizenship, each with vast implications for how corporations can be engaged in building and strengthening CSOs. The trends offer CSOs information and insight as to what is possible and what challenges can be expected.

- *Focus:* Corporations are adopting investment and operation policies requiring that all corporate activities serve "strategic" business purpose. Implicit in this approach are short-term, bottom-line results, though there is growing awareness that long-term "positioning" must find expression too. Bottom-line value can be elusive in corporate actions supporting CSOs, but in a longer-term positioning

TATA IRON AND STEEL COMPANY, INDIA

The Tata Iron and Steel Company is based in the State of Bihar in northern India, one of the poorest states, close to supplies of iron, coal, and limestone. It is headquartered in Jamshedpur, founded by the company to support the early iron industry. The steel and engineering businesses combined employ about 250,000 workers, the largest share of whom are in Jamshedpur, the central focus of the company's commitment to corporate responsibility and good citizenship.

Establishing the steel business in a region geographically suited to this production required the Tata family to address numerous social, economic, and technical challenges. Housing, health care, training, and education had to be provided for workers. Addressing these needs has been critical to business success. As in many developing countries, the company had to draw primarily on its own resources to solve these problems. From early on, Tata Steel has maintained high standards of social responsibility both in terms of how it treats its employees and in its support for the community.

The primary focus of the company's social responsibility is first and foremost its employees and their families. By 1912, the company had instituted the policy of an eight-hour working day, 36 years before it became mandatory in India. A welfare department was established in 1917, and free health care and schooling for workers' children were instituted that same year. In the 1920s, a pension

exercise, the social investment field is rife with opportunity for companies. For some, this means engaging with only one or two CSOs for highly specific purposes.

- *Globalization:* The globalization of corporate responsibility is occurring alongside that of business, carried particularly through TNCs to their bases of operation worldwide. The global companies may bring practices that stimulate corporate engagement, or at the very least they can be encouraged to match the participation of local companies. The other factor is competitiveness: companies compete for the most attractive investment opportunities, and having solid corporate citizenship activities is increasingly a factor.

- *Productivity:* Corporations are all being challenged to "do more with less," to complete more work with fewer resources, particularly human and financial resources. This drive for ever-increasing productivity is making companies depend increasingly on partners in many aspects of their businesses.

- *Nonfinancial Resources:* Companies are shifting emphasis in their engagement resources and activities, meaning that they are increasingly using in-kind giving and volunteerism and are decreasing cash contributions and direct financial support. Corporate funds are under extraordinary pressure, and the funds available for strategic social investment will always be severely limited, particularly if these are add-on activities. CSOs stand to gain more value through in-kind giving and volunteerism than companies can provide from funds alone.

scheme was established, along with apprenticeships for young people and holidays with pay. A profit-sharing plan was introduced in 1934, 40 years before the government introduced a similar mandatory scheme.

The company builds and maintains employee housing in the city, provides extensive educational services to employees and their families, and has expanded its basic health care program well beyond Jamshedpur into impoverished rural areas. The company's family welfare program now serves about 700,000 people in the region. Through immunization and family planning programs, it has had remarkable success in reducing the infant mortality rate and slowing population growth.

In 1958, a formal Community Development Program was launched. This organized approach to community development was the basis for an outreach program in Jamshedpur and in villages within 15 miles. The company's approach is one of building self-reliant, self-sustaining initiatives. Where possible, Tata Steel seeks to be a catalyst for change rather than a proponent of a corporate welfare state. The company also fosters the development of independent nonprofit organizations in the city and region.

While there is undoubtedly a degree of paternalism in Tata's approach, this is inevitable given the social and economic conditions. Employees and others depend heavily on the company for their livelihood, but the company has an equally strong incentive, not least of which is reducing costs, to help individuals, families, and communities be as self-reliant as possible.

- *Corporate Vision:* There is closer alignment of corporate citizenship and community involvement actions with business objectives and capacity, so choices are now generally more strategic or corporate-oriented and less "personal." One "personal" variation would be a CEO or board that is passionate about certain issues and influences corporate culture and strategies accordingly. But the era of the highly personalized approach to corporate giving seems to be coming to an end.

- *Bottom-Line Accountability:* Corporate citizenship and strategic social investments are increasingly subjected to a bottom-line measure of accountability. Companies themselves know bottom-line evaluation techniques are not adequate for assessing social investments, yet these are the tools of the corporation and are inevitably used. The challenge, thus, is for CSOs and corporations to work together to develop more accurate tools to understand the real value of strategic social investing and engagement by companies.

- *Global Quid Pro Quo:* The emphasis and distribution of activities increasingly reflects global profits and employment. Philanthropy that was once practiced only in a company's "home town" or country of origin is increasingly being practiced everywhere the company does business. This offers opportunities for emerging markets and any parts of the world that have consumer purchasing power.

- *New Models of Action:* As globalization continues, there are competing trends of homogenization versus hybridization. At best this is a creative tension that characterizes human activity in an age of global contact through communications, politics, migration, travel, and commerce. The forces of homogenization are strong, reflected in a business culture featuring growing similarity of dress, language use, products, and services. But diversity stemming from differing cultures, histories, legal frameworks, and societal values remains a strong influence that tempers the trend toward monoculturalism. The interaction of these forces is leading to commercial and cultural hybrids.

- *Consumer Demands:* As global competition yields price and quality parity, consumers increasingly base purchasing decisions on the socioeconomic, cultural, and environmental distinctions among companies. In this context, firms that adopt environmental or family-friendly policies, for example, can attract more customers.

- *Transnational Competition:* Governments are changing their commercial, tax, and regulatory environments to attract business or mitigate the adverse effects of corporate activity. Although national governments can influence corporate activities within their borders, there is no corresponding body that can effectively or comprehensively regulate global commercial activity or corporate citizenship.

- *Dissemination to Emerging Markets:* Corporate activity and the pace of change continue to be driven largely by the TNCs of industrial countries. But companies in emerging markets, particularly in countries such as South Korea, Singapore, and Brazil, are having an increasing influence.

CSO Strategies on Corporate Citizenship

In considering the range of ways to encourage or force companies to assist CSOs— through taxation, regulation, strategic social investment, and charity (see Figure 1)—the quadrant represented by strategic social investment is probably least well developed but likely represents companies' greatest potential opportunity for building and strengthening civil society. Certainly there remains a role for taxation, regulations, and charity, but CSOs would be well advised to focus their time and resources on engaging companies through strategic social investment. Companies may be interested in this approach since it is closely aligned with business practices and expertise, and because the actions can be controlled somewhat by the company.

When making the case for strategic social investments, ask companies the following kinds of questions.

- *Work Force:* Who are your employees? Who will be your employees 10 years from now, and what kind of training will they need? How much will you have to provide?

- *R&D:* Where will your ideas come from? How will you pay for them?

- *Markets:* What will your market(s) be? Where will they be? How much do you know about the people or companies who will be your customers?

- *Risk:* How stable will your operating environments be? What risks are you most worried about, and how are you acting to minimize risks?

- *Raw Materials:* Where will these come from? What do you anticipate your costs to be? Will resources be available when you need them, and in the needed amounts?

FIGURE 1

How Will Social Investments Be Funded?
WHO MAKES THE DECISION?

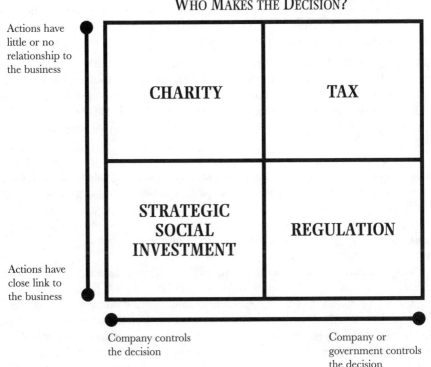

Actions have little or no relationship to the business

CHARITY   TAX

STRATEGIC SOCIAL INVESTMENT   REGULATION

Actions have close link to the business

Company controls the decision   Company or government controls the decision

Source: Logan, Roy, and Regelbrugge, 1997.

- *Government Intervention:* What do you think the tax and regulatory environment will be like in 5 and 10 years, and how is it likely to affect your business?

- *Competition:* What will your competitors be doing, and how will you compete?

- *Venture Partners:* What kinds of organizations and partners will you need to collaborate with to ensure the success of your business? What skills and information will you seek in your partners? How will these partnerships be assessed?

CSOs must be discriminating and creative, even resourceful, in forging partnerships with companies. There is no single formula for success, but rather patterns of behavior that are more likely to succeed. Guilt, government regulation, and pressure are somewhat limited in their effectiveness in getting companies involved in building and strengthening civil society. Efforts that are winning far greater success are those that seek creative, strategic alliances with companies, in which there is a payoff for the company too. While this may not represent charity and altruism in their truest senses, engaging companies in building civil society holds far greater promise if it is not confined to the realm of mere charity.

Three specific strategies for CSO engagement with companies are described in this chapter:

- strategic business interest,
- business/community partnerships, and
- corporate philanthropy.

Although the examples provided favor large, transnational corporations, the same tactics are relevant for small and medium-sized firms in a given locale, scaled accordingly. The strategies are not mutually exclusive, but they can be distinguished by their decisionmaking framework (see Figure 2)—who is involved in the decision, how the decision is reached, how the objectives are established, how performance is assessed, and who is held accountable.

Actions taken out of strategic business interest typically reflect business initiative, and the locus of decision lies within the company. CSOs most often influence these decisions by giving companies ideas or serving as implementing agents. The key is that these efforts are designed to provide tangible benefits to the company, often in the form of visibility or in the action's clear association to central business issues. The value of the community outcomes may be large, but these are not necessarily the driving concerns in the corporate assessment of the activity.

Actions resulting from business/community partnerships feature a collaborative decisionmaking process. The goal is to take actions that are strategic for the company and for the community. In this case, CSOs are formal venture partners and participate in the decisionmaking process. The CSOs may be the "innovators" or implementers, but they are also partners and the action is positioned as such. Strategic business interest and business/community partnerships are points on a continuum of interaction.

Corporate philanthropy and corporate giving programs are formal vehicles for community action. Companies in the United States, Japan, Canada, and some European countries have adopted varying formal structures to pursue specific community-oriented activities. Historically, particularly in the United States, where this practice is well established, corporate philanthropy has been a primary vehicle for the company's charity or charitable contributions. Some corporate philanthropies and giving programs are established within the corporate structure, with company representatives serving as staff and trustees and with activities funded from annual "pass through" funds generated from the company's revenues and profits. At the other end of the spectrum are foundations that are established by companies as independent, nonprofit organizations, often with endowments that generate the returns needed to support program activities, and with outside staff and board members. The decisionmaking process in corporate philanthropy and giving programs can be largely within the company, or external to the company and internal to the foundation.

Consider strategic business interest as one point on a continuum of which self-interest drives business decisions about specific actions. (See Figure 3.) At one end of the continuum are decisions and actions taken with only the self-interest of the company in mind; at the other end, decisions and actions are taken with only the interest of the community in mind. The reality is that businesses are not likely to make many decisions, if any, that have only the community self-interest in mind. The shaded area represents the

FIGURE 2

Levels of Corporate Citizenship

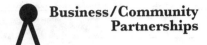

Business/Community Partnerships

PROMOTING THE COMMON GOOD

Actions to support societal health and development. There may be no immediate tangible benefits to the company or its reputation, but actions build the health and vitality of society and the business environment.

EXPANDED SELF-INTEREST
LONG-TERM BENEFITS

Activities that support long-term business success, such as education and training programs, and carry some tangible, yet long-term benefits for the company and its reputation.

IMMEDIATE BENEFITS

Activities beyond normal business that benefit communities and also provide immediate, measurable benefits for the company. Cause-related marketing campaigns and small business initiatives are examples.

COMMERCIAL SELF-INTEREST

Effective business management: adhering to laws; maintaining good relationships with employees, customers, suppliers, investors, regulators, and communities; and responsible research and development.

Strategic Business Interest   **Corporate Philanthropy**

Source: Logan, Roy, and Regelbrugge, 1997.

FIGURE 3

Whose Interest Drives Decisions?

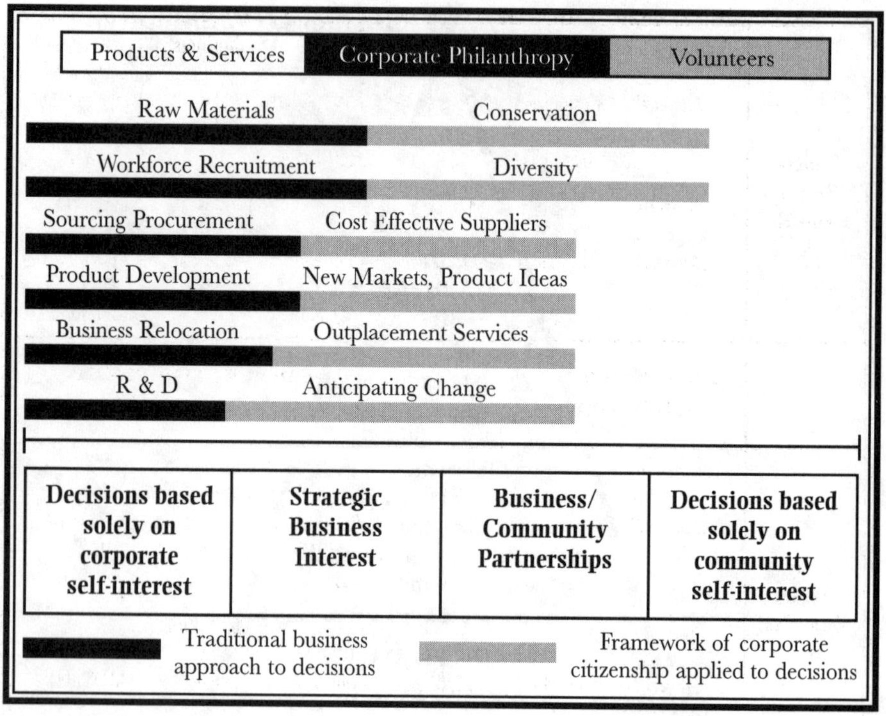

Products & Services	Corporate Philanthropy		Volunteers

Raw Materials	Conservation
Workforce Recruitment	Diversity
Sourcing Procurement	Cost Effective Suppliers
Product Development	New Markets, Product Ideas
Business Relocation	Outplacement Services
R & D	Anticipating Change

Decisions based solely on corporate self-interest	Strategic Business Interest	Business/ Community Partnerships	Decisions based solely on community self-interest

	Traditional business approach to decisions		Framework of corporate citizenship applied to decisions

Source: Logan, Roy, and Regelbrugge, 1997.

kinds of corporate decisions and actions that are easiest to make, where the potential for CSOs to influence is greatest. Although corporate self-interest is the driving element of company decisions, CSOs can influence companies to take community interests into the decisionmaking process as well. The challenge is to try to extend the shaded area so that more business decisions and actions integrate community interests.

Strategic Business Interest

Many companies develop corporate social responsibility initiatives in tandem with or as part of comprehensive business strategies. In these cases, the efforts have several functions: they foster goodwill while advancing business interest, they may provide important demographic research and help develop markets, and they may generate experience and build important networks in unfamiliar places or with emerging issues. Most often these initiatives are selected unilaterally by a company, sometimes even becoming a "campaign" that the company implements throughout its operations.

These initiatives do not translate into "easy money" for CSOs, but they offer valuable opportunities for tapping resources and gaining visibility. Companies spend most of their

FIGURE 4

Self-Interest Over Time

Short-Term Benefits	Infrastructure • *Tata Steel*	Equipment • *Apple, IBM*	Suppliers • *Anglo American*	Packaging • *McDonald's*	Business Consequences • *BP, Bamburi*	Integrated Development • *PBSP*
	Services • *Bell South*	Suppliers • *Aracruz*	Literacy • *Georgetown Steel*	Volunteerism • *Hitachi*	Education • *American Express*	AIDS/HIV • *Levi Strauss*
	Direct Corporate Self-Interest			**Community Self-Interest (Indirect Corporate Self-Interest)**		
Long-Term Benefits	Infrastructure • *AIDS/HIV*	Equipment • *Education*	Suppliers • *Volunteerism*	Packaging • *Literacy*	Business Consequences • *Suppliers*	Integrated Development • *Services*
	Services • *Integrated Development*	Suppliers • *Business Consequences*	Literacy • *Packaging*	Volunteerism • *Suppliers*	Education • *Equipment*	AIDS/HIV • *Infrastructure*

Source: Logan, Roy, and Regelbrugge, 1997.

time thinking about their businesses: how to stay competitive and develop new markets, how to produce and deliver goods and services cost effectively, and what new products to develop. A DuPont executive recently acknowledged that 20 percent of annual global revenue for his division comes from products that became commercial within the last three years. This reflects the importance of investing in R&D, and of having "eyes and ears" in communities that can help keep those product innovations coming on-line.

So, how do CSOs engage companies in building civil society through strategic business interest? Sometimes companies invest in basic social and physical infrastructure. In other cases, they act in highly specialized ways consistent with their products and services. In a matrix, the basic axes might be direct corporate self-interest to community interest, and short-term to long-term perspective and benefits. (See Figure 4.) Most companies are better prepared to think about their short-term direct self-interest than about medium or long-term indirect self-interest. Yet most community investments that are in a company's direct and indirect interest are longer-term: they build the institutions and capacity of communities in ways that reinforce business operations.

BELLSOUTH, UNITED STATES

BellSouth is a telecommunications business within nine states in southeastern United States. The company recently announced a program to provide Internet access and training to 4,000 schools in its operating area. The program involves the donation of school infrastructure and wiring, technology, curriculum material, and teacher training. BellSouth will provide inside wiring kits and volunteers to install the wiring. It will also donate telecommunications services that allow teachers, students, and other school staff to have Internet user accounts. The company's foundation will support teacher training and the production of educational materials to improve instructional effectiveness with the technology.

BellSouth estimates that the initiative will reach 2 million students, 172,000 educators, and 5,400 employee volunteers. It will help build markets and operating networks for BellSouth's products and services. BellSouth has also involved at least one of its suppliers as an in-kind contributor in the initiative. The company is acting to ensure that other companies help address the country's high tech needs. If this succeeds, companies that are competitors and beneficiaries will all contribute to building the infrastructure and providing access.

Engaging companies in wider community development efforts must be considered in light of the companies' interests and capacity. CSOs can play a role in framing the possibilities from the context of the community health and development that are required for successful business operations.

Best Practices

Investing in Infrastructure

Many would describe the situation in which one or a few large companies are deeply involved in the development of the community's infrastructure as a "company town," and examples can be found throughout the world. While it is perhaps more prevalent today in developing countries, the United States, Japan, and Europe still have "company towns" and also have examples of communities that have had to confront the stark reality of life and community development when a company leaves town. Although many oppose "company towns" as paternalistic, establishing them is a corporate engagement strategy nonetheless.

Another example of investing in infrastructure is when a company decides to leave a community. BP Oil, for example, developed an eight-year community involvement program in conjunction with a downsizing and restructuring that would close plants in two communities in South Wales and would affect business for area subcontractors. BP Oil launched two major initiatives that included attracting new businesses to the community through building renovations, a small business loan fund and training schemes, and outplacement counseling for employees. The company established an economic renewal agency chartered as a wholly owned subsidiary to implement the efforts to regenerate the local economy. The programs have attracted 70 businesses employing 600 people, which compares to 700 laid off as a result of BP's closures. In addition, 250 small companies received loans and technical assistance that allowed them to survive and even expand, retaining a total of 1,600 jobs.

The Bamburi Portland Cement Company (BPCC) was featured in the recent *Business as Partners in Development—Creating Wealth for Countries, Companies and Communities*, a publication of The Prince of Wales Business Leaders Forum (PWBLF) in collaboration with the World Bank and the United Nations Development Programme. Since its establishment in 1954, BPCC has played a large role in Kenya's economic development, particularly through producing cement for construction and industrialization. BPCC developed an innovative quarry rehabilitation program, which is now a separate subsidiary called Baobab Farm, that has transformed BPCC's exhausted quarries into a profitable, job-creating forestry, aquaculture, agriculture, and tourist business.

A final example of investing in infrastructure is an education program for employees. Georgetown Steel Corporation, a minimill employing about 730 people that is a subsidiary of GS Industries, discovered that some workers in its Georgetown, South Carolina, facility were not literate. It established a training program for eight nonreaders, but this quickly expanded to include basic writing and math, problem solving, and time management. By now, 484 employees have participated, and 24 people have earned high school equivalency degrees. The program has captured the attention of the federal government, and a portion of the training costs is now covered by a federal grant. It is worth noting that the company action was prompted by an issue that affected a relatively small number of employees. The response benefited those individuals, their families, and many others.

Investing Through Products and Services

Another approach is engagement that is closely linked to a company's products and services. This kind of approach is increasingly being undertaken by companies. Many use their products and services or employee volunteerism as the basis of a large portion of their involvement in communities.

Nonfinancial resources represent the most valuable and sustainable means for engaging company resources in community problem-solving. This is true primarily because corporate resources for things unrelated to core business operations are scarce. Employees, products, and services constitute the business. It is easier for companies to contribute these cost effectively than to allocate scarce funds for financial contributions. Contributions of nonfinancial resources often go unreported, so accurate figures on the scale of these contributions do not exist. Still, they represent the single greatest opportunity to engage companies in community problem-solving from both an expertise and a cost-effectiveness standpoint.

IBM, Apple Computer, and Hewlett Packard, for example, all have programs for donating equipment. Johnson & Johnson donates medical products in areas beset with disaster or poverty, particularly in developing countries. Russia and Eastern Europe in the early 1990s represented new market opportunities for companies; American Express used this as an opportunity to train the work force and develop the service

ANGLO AMERICAN CORPORATION, SOUTH AFRICA

The Anglo American and De Beers Small and Medium Enterprise Initiative (SMEI) was established in 1989 to encourage small business development in South Africa. As a large company, Anglo American relies on small suppliers. Providing contracts to them is as vital a contribution to the economy and society as the creation of regular payroll jobs.

The Initiative helps small businesses win contracts with the Group's companies and, through a fund established with De Beers, invests in the development of promising small concerns. All projects have to meet strict commercial criteria, but SMEI programming and technical assistance help small businesses overcome the many difficulties of dealing with large companies and getting access to credit.

The SMEI is closely controlled by the business and has the active support of the Chairman and the company's Executive Committee. A staff of eight is divided between the Small Business Unit and the investment fund, the Labour Intensive Industries Trust Limited (LITET). LITET never takes a majority holding in businesses. Rather, it seeks to be a minority partner holding

ethic through a program in secondary schools to train young people in hotel and restaurant services and management. The program has direct benefits for the company. It also contributes to work force development and training in free enterprise management relevant to the broader community. American Express's "Travel and Tourism Academies" now offer youth training on four continents.

Another variation in programming related to products and services is investing in suppliers. Aracruz S.A. in Brazil provides seedlings and training to develop the capacity of local farmers to grow and manage forests that help to supply the company with its raw materials.

Regulatory Approaches

There are also times when government regulations influence behavior and offer opportunities for companies and communities to benefit from strategic business interest. In the United States, the Community Reinvestment Act (CRA) is a vehicle for ensuring that banks invest in low-income communities—areas that often appear less promising in a market analysis. (See Chapter 12.) The CRA was intended to be a tool for preventing and reversing the practice of redlining, in which banks would identify areas where they would not make loans or provide regular services based on perceptions or prejudices about the limited profitability of these areas. Decades of redlining have left low-income communities and frequently certain ethnic communities with little access to home mortgages, small business loans, and opportunities to maintain checking or savings accounts. The CRA requires that a bank conduct a portion of its business in these neglected communities. CSOs have played an important role in helping banks direct their CRA funding, and have helped the companies learn that these communities can be and are profitable. The key has been to engage the banks.

10–20 percent. The fund earns fees, dividends, and interest, which help support SMEI operations.

Reef Food Services, for example, was formed in 1990 as a medium-sized venture by four black entrepreneurs. SMEI linked the company with an established catering company. LITET took a 10-percent equity position, 35 percent is held by the partner, and 55 percent is held by the founders. Reef Food Services benefited greatly from its partner's bulk purchasing and training capacity. In 1991, providing food to 1,200 employees in one mine, Reef's services saved the mine roughly $5,500 a month. It now operates in 18 mines and sites, providing food for 18,000 employees. Food quality improvements and other efficiencies have been achieved. The business has annual revenues of $11 million and is securing contracts beyond the Anglo American Group.

When it started in 1989, the SMEI concluded US$1.6 million worth of business. By 1994 it was conducting transactions worth US$34.7 million, involving 155 emerging businesses employing 2,447 people. The total value of its activities since 1989 is US$91 million. Several companies have purchased LITET's equity share, making them fully independent of the SMEI.

Some people feel that a CRA-type tool would be appropriate for other industries too. Critics of a regulatory approach suggest that it leads to minimal involvement that is neither creative nor dynamic. The lesson of the CRA, however, is that there is direct business interest for the banks in areas that were previously ignored or discounted. In the communities that receive new access to banking services through the CRA, fundamental changes begin to occur: people buy homes, and they work hard to maintain them, thereby improving real estate values; microenterprises are established, providing new job and income opportunities; and other businesses move into the areas. While the community improvement does not happen overnight, nor in every case, the bank's direct business interest and broader community interest are served simultaneously.

The CRA originally had a very negative connotation for companies, largely due to its roots in adversarial relations. There has been progress in shedding this image as more companies and CSOs have begun to understand how the CRA can be used proactively as a tool for community development, business, and improved community relations. It is also important to note that many companies are trying to avoid the regulation through ownership and restructuring initiatives.

Managing Future Costs

Levi Strauss & Co. has identified a strategic business interest that reflects a long-term, broad outlook: it launched a worldwide initiative to improve understanding of the causes, consequences, prevention, and possible cures of HIV/AIDS. The company notes that the disease has important implications for health care costs worldwide, and that its campaign can bring greater visibility and awareness to help slow and end the spread of the disease. The company is aware of the potentially high costs in employee medical care and productivity that HIV/AIDS could represent in its business world-wide. It is also aware of the alarming increase in cases of HIV/AIDS among young people everywhere. Engagement is designed to provide information to employees and to increase public awareness. The company has a long-term business interest in keeping young people healthy.

How to Engage Corporations

Companies do many things well. Engaging them around their areas of expertise is of real value to communities. In the past, companies and CSOs have often been adversaries. A context of adversarial relations and suspicions continues to prevail in many parts of the world. If community problem-solving is the goal, the challenge is to get both sectors to move into relationships that bring the values and expertise of each to bear on the problems. A true commitment to improving the health and well-being of people, communities, and the environment must include a cross-sector strategy for collaboration rooted in reciprocal relations rather than extractive actions. The question for CSOs is, How do you engage companies to be responsible citizens in communities?

Think Strategically

Can the CSO provide valuable information, exposure, contacts, services, and experience for the company? Can the company do the same for the CSO? It is important to think about short-term and long-term opportunities, and to be realistic and creative in thinking about how to engage companies. Corporate budgets for community activities are limited. Nonetheless, there are often times that strategic, feasible support can be provided through funding or donations of old office equipment, for example.

For some CSOs, a cause-related marketing venture with a company is a strategic engagement. Proctor and Gamble, for instance, entered a cause-related marketing effort in Italy to promote its Dash soap powder in association with a campaign to build hospitals and schools in Africa. The company developed a campaign with ActionAID, an international development nonprofit, and matched contributions from consumers to fund school buildings and health posts in Ethiopia. Sales volume for the company's product in Italy rose 5 percent, and the charity estimates that 14,000 people in Africa now have access to health care where there were no facilities.

The task of thinking strategically must be based on knowing the CSO's mission, the specific assets the CSO brings to the negotiating table, and the opportunities or needs a company might be able to address.

Do Research

Know the companies you wish to target, and know the community and issues. Many CSOs neglect this critical research, and ask companies for support that is impossible or impractical. Research must be used to formulate initial approaches. It is as important to identify corporations that a CSO would not wish to work with as it is to identify the issues and channels that should be pursued for desirable target companies. If companies already have big initiatives, find out if there are ways to qualify for the benefits or actions of those initiatives.

It is also helpful to research and think about the future directions of the company. Are there expansion plans or new products about to be released? Does the company enjoy a diversified customer/consumer base? Investing in research saves resources, particularly time, for both the CSO and the company.

Identify Self-Interest and Common Interest

This relates to thinking strategically and creatively about opportunities and needs in the short and long term. A CSO cannot assume that a company will have a strategic interest in an effort just because there is a link, superficial or deep, to a product or service base. For example, the fact that Hitachi is a Japanese company that produces electronic equipment does not mean that Hitachi will be interested in all things Japanese or all things electronic or high tech. Research prevents false assumptions that can lead to big mistakes.

Within a universe of "self-interest" ideas, there is a narrow subset that might be feasible. The trick is to identify enough possibilities from a corporate, CSO, and community perspective that one or two might be feasible.

Consider a Broad Range of Resources

We often focus only on money, and thereby neglect far more valuable, feasible ways in which companies can engage in strengthening CSOs and their work. Although equipment donations are not standard business practice in many parts of the world, there is certainly a trend toward increased use of equipment, services, and human resources. In addition to the examples cited earlier, companies can sometimes contribute legal or accounting services, marketing advice or support, photocopying and printing, or even facilities such as meeting or storage space.

Corporate employees can be valuable resources serving on CSO boards of directors, advisory councils, or special committees. Another activity that companies do well is recruit employees and board members. Employee volunteers can also assist with routine clerical tasks or highly specialized technical assistance. Many companies around the world have training programs that can be offered to broader groups of people, such as local teachers or government officials.

CSOs have proved to be effective intermediaries in helping companies engage in social issues, and this pertains to nonfinancial resources and funding—areas where many companies lack the structures for easy engagement.

Communicate, Educate, Inform

Companies have an insatiable appetite for updates and information about initiatives, no matter what level of support has been provided. To engage companies effectively in community-based work, CSOs must provide frequent, regular updates from projects so the corporate representatives can feel confident that a worthwhile investment has been made.

Companies generally want visibility and credit for their involvement. This can serve strategic purposes for the CSO too. After all, companies respond to peer pressure and the need to "keep up" with competitors. If a CSO speaks openly about a company's involvement, it can increase the prospects of other companies getting involved. Chances are the company will even help draft and disseminate press releases and other communication efforts.

Communication is perhaps more important after receiving support than before. All too often a CSO invests heavily in getting support, without much follow-up after the "investment." For companies to remain involved, CSOs must be willing to do the follow-up that "protects the investment." Carefully crafted messages can give top executives and other employees a sense of pride and ownership of the accomplishments. These messages can also be conveyed publicly—corporate representatives can be effective spokespeople for community causes.

Community groups should not assume that a company will know much about a given issue or how to engage effectively. They should make it as easy as possible, by providing education on the issue and "how to" guidance on corporate engagement. CSOs have valuable expertise on community, social, and environmental issues.

Respect and Learn from Cultural Differences

Culture plays an important role in many different ways. Companies and CSOs have different operating cultures, which need to be respected. Companies focus on bottom-line results, and value concrete language and efficiency. They do not want to hear about a project once or twice a year; they want immediate feedback and frequent updates, and agendas of what is to be accomplished, by whom, and when.

CSO operations are less easy to characterize. Some are models of managerial efficiency and effectiveness; others survive without any notable managerial or resource base. Also, the content of a CSO's work—the issues—are often not as clearly defined or discrete as a company's. CSOs should try to understand their own operating culture and those of companies they wish to work with. This will make it easier to develop a relationship. Decisionmaking processes and procedures and channels of communication should likewise be respected.

National or ethnic culture is another important consideration. Transnational corporations are considered "foreign" companies in many places where they do business. Sometimes their operating and societal cultures are different, and their understanding of the expectations and expressions of corporate social responsibility and appropriate involvement may also be quite different. For example, the concepts of philanthropy and volunteerism do not have counterparts in Japan, nor is it customary to solicit money from strangers there. These ideas were quite new to the Japanese executives placed in their companies' U.S. operations. Japanese companies in the United States have learned a great deal over the last 10 years about the U.S. system and the role of CSOs. All countries offer related examples of cultural differences based on national or ethnic norms.

Be Realistic and Start Small

Companies can be extremely helpful in many strategic, valuable ways, but their engagement will require clearly defined limits. It is not realistic to think that companies will provide general, ongoing funding for CSO operations or programs. This is not based on the worth of the CSO program, but on companies' capacity. By nature, most companies are rather conservative in that they like to minimize risk. This attitude is applied to community investments as well. Companies will typical engage in small, cautious ways initially, to gain experience and confidence that the risks are low.

Having unrealistic expectations for a company's engagement going into a relationship is sure to disappoint the company, the CSO, and the community. If a company has a good experience initially, the possibilities for expanding its involvement improve dramatically. It must be considered a relationship, however, in which each party gives and each party receives. A company providing resources will also want something in return, such as visibility or information. Keeping long-term goals in mind is an effective strategy for being realistic early on.

Evaluate and Learn

It is critical to analyze and assess any experience of engaging a corporation. This exercise must help the CSO and the company decide whether an investment is worth the effort. Sometimes an initiative with strategic business interest carries more cost than benefit for the CSO, and possibly even for the company itself. Is it worth the investment? What did we learn? Who benefited, and in what ways? What changed as a result of this investment of corporate resources?

Companies want hard data on the impact and consequences of support. CSOs have to commit to providing this along with qualitative or anecdotal information that enhances the company's knowledge of the issues or outcomes. Assessments serve the CSO well too. It is important to know if the cost of engaging new partners exceeds the benefits. In this respect, the bottom-line analysis that companies do in general operations might help a CSO analyze its operations and make effective decisions about programming options.

Both CSOs and companies can benefit from joint efforts, and both have an interest in understanding the full range and ramifications of these benefits. In the process of engagement, the company will discover benefits and outcomes that are not easily quantified in a bottom-line analysis. Joint efforts require working together to define the indicators of success and the anticipated results. Perhaps the greatest opportunity of CSOs in this respect is to help companies understand community-based activities that serve direct corporate and community interest. Activities undertaken for strategic business interests may not go far enough in engaging companies in community problem-solving, but they are important first steps.

Limitations and Barriers

Many Requests, Limited Resources

Companies are deluged with requests, most of which seek money. They typically have small amounts available for community-related efforts. Increasingly they have very little discretionary funding available. The adoption of stringent cost-accounting techniques means that all financial resources must be allocated to specific business budgets and operating line items. This makes it more difficult for CSOs to get money from companies. Again, adopting a broader vision of the ways companies can engage expands the pool of resources substantially. In-kind resources can be even more valuable than money.

Corporate Structures

Companies around the world have very different structures for dealing with their community responsibilities, and some have no structures at all. Few companies have formal employee volunteer programs or tell local community organizations about the kinds of engagement the company may consider.

Community affairs or community relations departments are often short-staffed. This means that it may be difficult to get to the right person, if there is such an individual. Or the right person may not think about creative ways to consider and even fulfill a request, or the company may have clear policies and structures that inhibit their engagement. CEOs and other executives are typically overwhelmed with the demands of running the business. Besides, targeting the CEO can have the adverse effect of undermining other employees. There is no magic recipe about who to target, but research can help a CSO find the proper path.

Unfamiliarity with CSOs and Specific Community Issues

Companies may know very little about working with CSOs, and will have difficulty choosing from among several that are working on related items. It is important for CSOs to establish credibility that helps a company consider specific requests or involvements. In addition, companies cannot be expected to have expertise in issues unrelated to their business interests, and it may be very difficult for them to consider involvement with such issues.

Time

One of the most severely limited resources is time. A CSO may have only five minutes in which to make its full case. Being concise is important. Yet effective initiatives take time to build. The CSO will probably need to commit far greater amounts of time initially to engage a company and to maintain that engagement. There must be deliberate strategies for getting the company to commit the time of its employees as well, but sometimes that has to come after some initial successes together.

Personnel Changes

Staff turnover is a fact of life in both CSOs and companies. The problem is that often a company's community engagement is not institutionalized in either the company or within the CSO in ways that transfer to new staff easily. One way to overcome this barrier is to get people involved in many aspects of an initiative or project, as volunteers, champions, and "friends" of the CSO. The more people within a company that are involved, the less likely that staff turnover will undermine or eliminate the engagement.

Stereotypes

Stereotypes are held both by companies and by CSOs, and they often lead to rather predictable, self-fulfilling prophecies, with each sector acting accordingly. The stereotypes can be based on philosophy, ideology, organizational approach, culture, or simply the professional or issue-specific knowledge. Fundamental differences of opinion and attitude can be constructive and need not be a barrier.

When companies and CSOs decide to think about the different perspectives they bring to a situation, they often find opportunities for mutually rewarding work. When transcending stereotypes, it remains important nonetheless to consider fundamental differences in determining whether there is a potential relationship. A CSO should not "sell its soul" to engage a company, nor should it believe that such a fate is inevitable.

AMERICAN EXPRESS

In a joint venture that has been in place for several years, proceeds from specific American Express revenue and activities and a portion of its corporate philanthropy are targeted to fight world hunger through the efforts of the nonprofit group Share Our Strength, which regrants these funds to organizations that work in locales around the world on hunger programs. In 1996, American Express pledged to donate two cents from every card purchase up to a maximum donation of US$5 million. The full amount was donated.

This is essentially a case of comparative advantage: Share Our Strength is recognized by American Express as the expert on hunger-related matters, and American Express is the expert on marketing. This partnership uses cause-related marketing as the revenue-generating tool for the funding. The two organizations work together to negotiate the objectives and terms of their collaboration.

Business/Community Partnerships

Business/community partnerships are distinguished from strategic business interest by the establishment of a relationship that supersedes unilateral action by any of the parties involved. These partnerships are characterized by collaboration. The participating parties are involved together in negotiating, planning, executing, and evaluating joint ventures. At one end of the spectrum, a joint project involving a contract between a company and one or more CSOs may constitute a partnership, albeit a limited one; at the other end, a multicompany or multi-CSO partnership may address several issues and have formal operations. Cross-sector collaboration, often including government players, is on the rise as there is increasing evidence that single-sector responses to critical social and environmental issues are inadequate.

Best Practices

There is evidence that corporate social responsibility will increasingly be a determining factor of competitiveness, whether for individual companies or joint ventures. British Gas and the Italian oil company Agip, for instance, outlined a community development program of agricultural training as part of its bid to develop Kazakstan's gas fields, which many suggest probably gave them an edge over the joint bid of BP and Statoil of Norway. Similarly, to improve community relations and its general business image, Petroleos Venezuela (PDVSA), the State petroleum company, sought a business/community partnership with community-based organizations, the Washington-based Inter-American Foundation (IAF), and the Venezuelan government. While PDVSA contributed funds and garnered employee involvement to some extent, IAF served almost as an intermediary in brokering and building relationships between PDVSA and the community-based organizations.

In one well-known case of partnership, McDonald's teamed up with the Environmental Defense Fund (EDF) to design packaging and processes that were more environ-

PHILIPPINE BUSINESS FOR SOCIAL PROGRESS

Several collaborative efforts in the Philippines provide corporate support for the highly active NGO sector. Philippine Business for Social Progress (PBSP) was founded in 1970 by 49 companies to engage corporate commitment in social development and to support programs promoting self-reliance and the sustainable development that is critical to Philippine economic growth and development. The intent was to pool resources in a multibusiness effort to address critical issues facing the nation, ranging from economic stagnation to natural disasters. The businesses pledged 1 percent of the preceding year's profits to support an organization that would have professional staff act on their behalf to address social issues in a significant way.

Today, PBSP has 179 members, including local and multinational companies such as San Miguel Corporation, Shell, IBM Philippines, Nestlé Philippines, and Jardine Davies. Its 1994 budget was US$6.5 million. It is not a philanthropic organization. Its primary mission is to develop economically self-reliant communities. Even assistance given to disaster victims is designed to focus on crisis preparedness and income generation.

PBSP has four programs areas: community organizing, enterprise development, institution building, and technology transfer. It also works to improve the effectiveness of local government and management of services; provides access to credit for small and medium-sized enterprises, particularly in rural areas; supports agrarian reform; promotes environmental protection and conservation; and offers a venue for corporate CEOs to consider business responses to important social issues such as education and the environment. In 1994, PBSP undertook 170 projects in its four priority areas. The organization has also adopted the Area Resource Program approach, which integrates the four areas in single projects to bring comprehensive socioeconomic development to targeted poverty areas.

mentally friendly. Even though it was a limited venture, this shows that business/community partnerships can improve conditions in a community. In this case, McDonald's restaurants around the world are implementing the program, with substantially lowered environmental impacts. EDF, like many environmental nonprofits, was initially skeptical and perhaps even opposed to a partnership with a company, but it has played a valuable role that supports its mission of protecting the environment.

Land O'Lakes, Inc.'s International Development Division is working with U.S. and international nonprofits and the Mexican government to develop a trading arrangement for agricultural and artistic products of indigenous peoples in the Chiapas region. The partnership is intended to influence the organization, productivity, and access to markets of small to medium-sized agricultural producers and artisans, and to help them gain visibility for their products and capture a fair price in a competitive international marketplace. The goal is to create sustainable conditions that increase the economic well-being and self-determination of all people in Chiapas and surrounding states in a way that contributes to cohesiveness and harmony among development participants and community residents.

Sometimes companies are reluctant to participate in community development unilaterally, but prefer to become involved through programs undertaken by industry associations or other groups that can serve as intermediaries. The Prince of Wales Business Leaders Forum was established in 1990 as a forum for businesses to participate in community development efforts around the world. Its goals are to raise awareness of the value of corporate responsibility both to the successful management of international business and to the prosperity of countries and communities worldwide.

PWBLF encourages partnerships among companies, government, communities, nongovernmental organizations (NGOs), and aid agencies as a means of promoting sustainable development. The rationale was to provide the companies with knowledge and techniques through a collaborative forum, and to lessen the risk and exposure of any single company in a community project. PWBLF achieves its goals through a strategy of advocacy, brokerage, and capacity and institution building. The organization researches and communicates good practice from business partnerships in development. It acts as a catalyst, engaging organizations from different sectors to work together on specific projects. And it runs workshops and training programs. The Forum works with member companies from Europe, North and South America, Africa, the Middle East, and Asia Pacific in 17 developing countries.

In the United States, numerous intermediaries feature varying levels of partnership, collaboration, and direct involvement of business. United Way of America and United Way International raise funds from companies and regrant these monies to local social service organizations. Companies and the individual employees who contribute can allocate their contributions to specific qualifying nonprofit organizations. Organizations can apply to become official recipients of United Way contributions, and must meet a standard of accountability and of management and financial information systems to become eligible.

In another example of an intermediary organization, the Ghana Social Marketing Foundation, a private-sector, nonprofit organization with support from the U.S. Agency for International Development, promotes and distributes family planning, health, and HIV/AIDS prevention products through commercial networks in Ghana. The foundation is seeking to develop partnerships with businesses to extend education and sales of contraceptives to the workplace. A report for the foundation by David Logan framed the argument for engaging businesses directly in AIDS prevention activities based on the business rationale. The effort targeted the Employers Association and the Ghana Institute of Personnel Management for involvement in the campaign, and some 50 CEOs subsequently joined the personnel institute in endorsing the action strategy. The Ghana Trades Unions Congress and the government have also joined in the campaign.

How to Establish Partnerships

As with any effort to engage businesses in strategic social involvement, the first step in forging a business/community partnership is identifying an area of common interest. Often a partnership begins with the identification of a very narrow mutual interest. If

IBM

In June 1996, IBM Corporate Social Responsibility Centre and IBM Europe, Middle East, and Africa convened policymakers and specialists in adult training from 17 countries to discuss the social consequences of information technologies. IBM used this conference, "Social Exclusion, Technology and the Learning Society," to shape and launch a Europe-wide program on these issues. According to the conference proceedings:

> *The main aims of the seminar were to discuss the issues that relate to the development of skills of disadvantaged and disabled people; identify how the new technologies can be applied to make training more accessible and effective; and identify the barriers which may inhibit the use of new technologies and how to overcome these barriers.*
>
> *To meet the challenge of these significant technological changes, European governments and societies are focusing on the importance of an adaptable and highly skilled workforce. At the core of the strategy to achieve this is the creation of a "Learning Society" where acquisition of skills becomes a lifelong process and individuals build a portfolio of competencies through continuous education and training. Technology has a key role to play in the attainment of the "Learning Society." It offers the means to*

that venture succeeds, it frequently leads to broader partnership ventures or ongoing activities. A CSO and a company may be interested in a certain geographic region or target population, or there may be a particular topic of common interest.

Once again, research is critical. Successful partnerships are not built on assumptions of common interest, but rather on a definitive intersection of interest and the perception that the partnership or collaboration will add value to the activities of each party.

The second step is to invest in building the relationship, understanding the respective strengths and needs, and jointly exploring possibilities for collaboration. Investing in the relationship is perhaps even more important after a partnership has been established. There are few strong relationships anywhere in the world that are based solely on money. Therefore it is important to build partnerships involving people, exchanges, and assets far more valuable than mere money.

Another important component is to institutionalize the relationship within the participating organizations. Partnerships that are based solely on a few interpersonal relationships do not survive personnel transition and change. In building effective partnerships, it is important to work through the roles and incentives for individuals, but also to establish clear roles and incentives that transcend these personal relationships.

Building effective business/community partnerships requires clear roles and responsibilities for the partners. This is perhaps the most important single component of successful collaboration. When the parties have worked together to establish distinct roles and responsibilities, the resources that are to be committed, and how efforts will be conducted and evaluated, there are few false expectations that lead to irreconcilable conflict.

deliver training flexibly in time and place. It is already facilitating the development of new techniques and tools to transform the pace and process of learning and teaching.

IBM's action agenda emerging from the conference included such actions as supporting or assisting the establishment of information networks in public facilities to acting as a model employer, from supporting programs designed to improve access to supporting or helping with the development of community, private, and public-sector partnerships. The conference conclusions stressed the involvement of those most affected by the consequences of change and working through partnerships.

The expansion and adaptation of education and training to meet the needs of the new structure and nature of work in Europe pose enormous challenges. Creating a "Learning Society" will require major changes in the education system and related social structures and a new relationship between the two. To achieve this will require actions at all levels, which must be based on partnership and the active involvement of those most affected. Working with partners in the not-for-profit sector and other funders, IBM will develop a program of pilot projects. Based on the seminar conclusions, these projects will introduce new approaches to using technology in training for excluded groups, with a view to disseminating the experience across Europe.

Successful collaboration requires time for planning, troubleshooting, performance, reflection, and evaluation. If any party cannot commit to the time required for the collaboration, this must be established at the outset and compensated for appropriately.

Projects and collaborative efforts inevitably face the dynamism inherent in life. Circumstances and conditions, personnel, resources, and opportunities change. Consequently, successful collaborative efforts and partnerships need specific processes for dealing with changes and conflicts that arise. The process must attend to maintaining the relationship and an effective venture: process and content. There must be goals and objectives that help assess performance along the way—benchmarks, as the business world says—and as projects end. All partners should have responsibilities for helping to assess projects, and for communicating these results to the appropriate constituencies.

Corporate Philanthropy and Giving Programs

Corporate philanthropy features formal decisionmaking structures and mechanisms for supporting community activities. While this exists in varying degrees of formality throughout the world, global expectations for its practice have grown along with the fortunes and reach of transnational corporations. In the United States, corporate philanthropy is well developed, and several kinds of formal organizational structures and styles prevail. Corporate philanthropy is also quite common in Japan, Canada, England, and Australia, and is on the rise throughout Europe, Southeast Asia, and

HITACHI

In 1985, Hitachi, Ltd. of Tokyo established The Hitachi Foundation in Washington as a nonprofit philanthropic organization with a mission of promoting social responsibility through effective participation in global society. The foundation's programs seek to build the capacity of all Americans, particularly those underserved by traditional institutions, to address the multicultural, community, and global issues facing them. In pursuing this mission, the foundation engages Hitachi companies with critical social issues through general programming and through special partnership programs with Hitachi facilities.

In 1987, the foundation and Hitachi facilities collaborated to launch the Matching Funds Program (MFP), a program for community action by the facilities. The MFP is implemented through Community Action Committees (CACs), which are teams of local rank-and-file employees who develop strategies to address needs and improve the quality of life in their communities. CACs address community issues by providing donations, volunteers, or in-kind donations of equipment or services. The Hitachi Foundation and Hitachi facilities commit to this community action strategy by making funding and other resources available to the CACs for these activities. CACs can apply to the foundation to use MFP

Latin America. In the early 1990s, Taiwanese and Korean firms began to undertake corporate philanthropy in countries where their business interests were increasing.

Many countries have explicit incentives in their tax systems to encourage philanthropy—that is, companies and individuals can receive tax deductions for charitable contributions. There are also countries that have no incentives for such corporate gifts or have disincentives. Nonetheless, there are CSO efforts in most countries, and governmental efforts in many, to reconsider and even reform tax legislation to promote more philanthropy by individuals and companies. In the United States in the early to mid-1990s, there was a concerted legislative effort to eliminate tax advantages for charitable contributions, prompted by the expected large transfer of family wealth that is beginning to occur due to U.S. demographics. Fortunately for CSOs, these initiatives were defeated, although the idea has certainly not been eliminated. CSOs can promote policies that improve the enabling environment for corporate philanthropy.

The strategies for tapping into corporate philanthropy resources are much the same as for encouraging corporate social responsibility: do research; identify self-interest and common interests; communicate, educate, and inform; respect and learn from cultural differences; be realistic and start small; and evaluate and learn. For a fuller discussion of how to research corporate foundations, see Chapter 3.

Structures

Although specific legal requirements and operating norms vary from country to country, certain similar structures for corporate philanthropy are found in different parts of the world.

funds to match cash grants, in-kind contributions, volunteer activities, and employee fundraising efforts.

CACs identify critical community needs that a corporation and its employees can address—such as education or social services—and then direct corporate resources to address the issue. They also promote employee awareness and community involvement by helping identify and arrange volunteer opportunities, and by eliciting employees' ideas about organizations and projects to support. Finally, CACs have the responsibility for reviewing, approving, and evaluating community action strategies.

The Hitachi Foundation provides initial training materials, including the *Community Action Handbook* and videos, and technical assistance as CACs undertake and operate the program. There is an annual CAC Conference, cosponsored by the foundation and one or more CACs, in which ideas and experience are exchanged, new information is presented, and problems are discussed among participants.

More than 40 Hitachi facilities throughout the United States participate in the MFP. Hitachi facilities in the United Kingdom have also adopted the primary elements of the MFP. The program has succeeded in helping Hitachi understand the diversity of U.S. communities and in engaging the company and employees in deliberate community improvement partnerships.

Historically, CEOs and other senior executives have been driving forces in this area. Often this is because they had discretionary budgets from which contributions could be made or because they played a prominent role in fostering community relations. While executive discretion and desire still wield heavy influence, the pattern of giving in industrial countries seems to be shifting away from the executive-driven choices and toward an approach more integrated with business objectives.

This has advantages and disadvantages for CSOs, as well as within and beyond the company. CEO-driven philanthropy can be a straightforward target: if a CSO's staff, board members, or volunteers have a relationship with a CEO or a relative, the chances for receiving contributions improve. Benefits to the company have often been limited, however, and employees have no stake in these decisions. In addition, this approach does not necessarily address a community's most critical needs.

It is important to stress that communities have benefited from CEO-driven philanthropy and that many CEOs have fulfilled this privilege with deep responsibility. But companies now are demanding greater returns. CEOs and senior executives often maintain discretionary contributions budgets, but corporate funds are increasingly issued through other structures that have targeted strategic internal and external objectives. The internal goals might be to build employee morale and involvement in decisions, while the external ones might be to lend expertise to a critical social problem such as education or health care.

Corporate foundations have been established in many countries, and usually have a special legal status. Many are endowed, meaning that the company has made a financial contribution to establish the foundation that cannot be retrieved, and the foundation uses the investment proceeds and a portion of the principal from these

ICWI GROUP FOUNDATION, JAMAICA

The Insurance Company of the West Indies (ICWI) was founded in 1968. It has subsequently grown, largely by acquisition, to be the leading financial conglomerate in Jamaica. The Group has 15 primary operating companies providing a large range of insurance and banking services. It is expanding rapidly in the Caribbean region, mainly within the financial services field, and several business initiatives have been launched in Asia.

Founded in 1988, the ICWI Group Foundation's mission is to develop "the leadership capacity of young Jamaicans so as to advance the country's economic and social well being." It is dedicated to the promotion of the public good in Jamaica and leadership in its philanthropic effort. It works in partnership with public institutions, such as schools and universities, and nonprofits to create and support innovative programs. In addition, the foundation has a secondary goal of seeking to expand private initiative for development among Jamaicans, their nonprofits, and businesses. It arranges conferences and exchanges, particularly with North America, to promote corporate responsibility and partnership in community action.

funds to make contributions. Tax laws and regulations require specific distribution levels, though some foundations choose to exceed minimum requirements.

As an alternative, some foundations have their operations linked to previous years' business profits. This model is based on a "pass through" approach, whereby a company commits a percentage of its revenues (such as 1–5 percent of the previous year's pretax profits) to the foundation to support charitable causes. The foundation's existence is usually linked to a tax incentive for committing funds in this way. (Japanese companies that have established endowed foundations in Japan and the United States, however, have typically not received a tax deduction and in several cases have had to pay taxes in conjunction with endowing foundations.)

Corporate foundations frequently are tied closely to the company legally and structurally, as is evidenced by boards of directors that have all corporate representatives, operations within corporate facilities, and administration by corporate personnel who have both corporate and foundation duties. In some cases, however, a company establishes and endows a foundation as an independent entity with an independent board of directors and operations. The board of the Hitachi Foundation in Washington, for instance, features one corporate representative on a board of 10. Many corporate foundations select a few board members or establish an advisory council of people with expertise in the subject areas to be supported.

These foundations may review requests cyclically or year-round. Corporate foundation funding priorities are frequently linked to the business area both geographically and substantively. The largest share of corporate philanthropy support is distributed in communities where facilities are located and employees live. Nonetheless, there are many examples of corporate foundations that fund activities with no apparent relationship to business activities, and often foundations have a larger geographic scope than direct business operations.

The foundation has a small endowment of $40,000 but receives annual gifts to fund its activities from the profits of Group companies. The Group is committed to funding the foundation at a level of 0.25 percent of profits. In 1990, the foundation awarded grants totaling US$24,625, but by 1994 spending totaled US$226,401. The operating companies have their own complementary and related programs, but they collaborate with the foundation in community activities.

Educational projects receive 85 percent of the foundation's support. A primary project has been the creation of Jamaica's first Science Learning Centre, which opened in 1991. Based on the campus of the University of the West Indies, it offers hands-on learning experience in science for children and provides support to primary and secondary school teachers in developing their teaching skills. The Centre has its own board and staff, and receives support from the university, other U.S. and Jamaican companies and donors, and the ICWI Group Foundation.

To promote a climate of support for citizen action and greater philanthropic efforts by companies and others in Jamaica, the foundation hosted a 1992 conference on "Good Corporate Citizens—Social Responsibility in the 90s" for companies, foundations, foreign donors, and nonprofits.

Since corporate philanthropy is often linked to overall business image and market development, a broader agenda can help establish name recognition and goodwill beyond the communities in which facilities are located and people employed. Increasingly, corporate foundations work to pull employees into their activities as a natural ally, recruiting them for volunteer programs and soliciting their thoughts on funding guidelines and priorities. Companies have recognized that employee involvement in corporate philanthropy carries many benefits, particularly in improved employee morale and commitment.

Corporate giving programs, as distinct from corporate foundations, are frequently managed by executive offices, community relations departments, or general administration. In many ways they are similar in the funding priorities and guidelines they pursue, yet they are free from the legal codes that regulate foundation activities and they are housed completely within the corporate structure. Some companies have a formula for financing their giving programs annually; others are guided more by the business climate and special circumstances. Many corporate giving programs are built around annual fundraising campaigns like United Way and around employee matching gifts programs, through which companies match the contributions made by individual employees to their preferred charities. Again, corporate giving programs are often aligned with the company's business products and geographic locations.

Many companies offer support for cultural or sporting events, and often these are tied to the activities of employees and their families. Engaging the families of employees is increasingly popular and effective. Often a CEO's spouse or child can help build the CEO's awareness of community issues. At the same time, employees' families provide a wealth of information and resources about community conditions. Often they are the staff or volunteers at CSOs.

Two increasingly popular structures for corporate philanthropy are workplace giving and employee (and retiree) volunteerism. Workplace giving programs allow

WHIRLPOOL CORPORATION

The Whirlpool Corporation is the world's leading manufacturer and marketer of major home appliances, producing goods in 13 countries and marketing products in 140 countries. The Whirlpool Foundation is its primary philanthropic arm, with an average of US$5.5 million in annual grants to programs, primarily in North America and Europe, that support lifelong learning, cultural diversity, and contemporary family life.

The Whirlpool Foundation recognized the need for a better understanding of contemporary family life issues. It created a two-part research initiative that studied women's views toward work, family life, and society, as women are at the core of changes in family life. The research also sought strategic information for the company, allowing it to better serve and understand its customers, product users, and employees, since women are the largest portion of Whirlpool's work force. The first part focused on issues in North America, and the second part, on Europe. The project rationale was to generate data from the research to help guide new grantmaking.

employees to designate a portion of their pretax salaries to CSOs that are eligible to receive contributions through such campaigns. In the United States, CSOs apply for a number in the combined federal campaign and other workplace giving campaigns, and then are eligible to be designated to receive contributions. The rewards for CSOs can be substantial.

Often workplace giving runs in conjunction with employee matching gift programs. In the United States, employee matching gifts provide substantial support for educational institutions, particularly colleges and universities, and for environmental organizations. The Council for Advancement and Support of Education notes from its extensive list of companies with employee matching gift programs to support education that Time Warner, the Washington Post, USX Corporation, and ARCO Chemical Company all match employee contributions to different post-secondary educational institutions, some even exceeding a dollar-for-dollar ratio of support. Some companies also match the gifts of retired employees and employee spouses. CSOs are increasingly doing the required paperwork and application process to tap into these funding programs.

Employee volunteerism has gained in popularity worldwide as corporate budgets have been squeezed and subjected to increasing bottom-line pressure. Some companies provide "release time" for employees, allowing them to volunteer with CSOs during work hours. Or there may be other incentives to volunteer. For example, some companies direct a portion of their giving programs to organizations in which employees volunteer.

The rationale for employee volunteerism is strong. Company employees have many skills to share, and the payoff within the company can also be great. Many companies have documented that employee volunteerism programs make employees more effective in their jobs by enhancing their teamwork skills, productivity, and com-

The research on women was conducted in North America and Europe by professional marketing and social research firms. To ensure that focus-group topics and survey questions provided new insights and data, both studies used guidance and direction from a team of nonprofit NGOs on the most pressing issues of interest to women in the work and family life areas.

The results were issued in two parts: *Women: The New Providers* was completed in 1995, based on a survey of more than 3,000 men and women in Canada, Mexico, and the United States; *Women: Setting New Priorities*, published in 1996, surveyed 7,000 men and women in France, Germany, Italy, Spain, and the United Kingdom.

As a direct result of the studies, 17 percent of Whirlpool Foundation grants in 1996 were directed to women's issues. The public and professional profile of the foundation as a funder concerned about women and family issues was heightened, bringing the organization valuable new partner relationships.

Extensive press coverage raised the identity of the foundation and the visibility of its commitment to women's issues. The media also helped transmit important updated information and insights on women's views regarding work and family life, bringing a new understanding to the public regarding women's realities.

mitment to the company. Employee volunteerism can be an effective way for a CSO and a company to begin a relationship.

Recent Trends

Transnational corporations of any national origin are increasingly shifting corporate philanthropic and social investment funds to global strategy (such as to places where the profits are derived). While U.S. businesses once directed most of their philanthropy to communities within that country, they are now often concentrating their efforts where they are earning profits. Companies of other national origins are also changing their giving patterns and strategies. There is growing pressure to invest in social and environmental causes everywhere a business operates.

At the same time, CSOs that once operated only internationally are now choosing to operate in their countries of origin as well. Many organizations were founded to address poverty or health care internationally or in the most economically impoverished parts of the world. With deteriorating conditions in communities everywhere, these groups are being encouraged to bring their expertise home as well. Many CSOs and private philanthropic funders are recognizing that distinctions between domestic and international programs may not be easy to make. They are increasingly concerned about social or economic deterioration in local conditions, and this leads to pressure to invest locally. Many of these funders are now active in many other places too. Tax and fiscal policies and regulations do affect financial flows. For example, a number of special regulations apply to a U.S. funder that seeks to contribute financial resources internationally, which is why many U.S. funders choose not to work at that level.

CSOs are now building transnational alliances and partnerships, which can increase their visibility and credibility. It can also be a pragmatic approach to the complex and disparate tax and fiscal regulatory environment. Alliances may help small CSOs raise needed funds, or take their work to broader audiences. By the same token, large CSOs can gain local acceptance and credibility through partnerships with grassroots organizations.

The globalization of problems is begging for transnational and even global responses and collaboration, and exerting pressure on TNC and private philanthropy. Problems do not end simply because a national border is crossed. Although transnational problem-solving collaborations of companies, CSOs, and governments are not yet well established (nor would they be easy to develop), the globalization of corporate and private philanthropy provides some prospect for problem solving that seeks to address root causes rather than just symptoms.

Corporate philanthropy seeks increasingly to contribute to the bottom line through such things as product or name recognition, market building, and employee involvement. It also provides a large company with an opportunity for thematic and strategic social investments that can link to a global mission and yet benefit from distinct and culturally appropriate expression in diverse company settings. TNCs are providing more examples of corporate philanthropy programs that have a central goal for the global operations but that are tailored appropriately at the local level. This has been an opportunity for companies to better understand the local operating environments and cultures in places where they operate.

Cross-border giving is extremely difficult and complicated. So even though the corporate philanthropy of TNCs is moving into new places, the legal frameworks of individual countries certainly impede the development of truly global, transnational giving. Some of the efforts under way to address the legal frameworks in which CSOs operate and receive support within countries should be supplemented by attention to multilateral protocols that would facilitate transnational giving.

Corporate philanthropy is under pressure in the context of downsizing, globalization, and bottom-line performance. All these pressures will change corporate philanthropy quite dramatically over the coming years, but they will not eliminate it. Companies could use their philanthropy as R&D to provide important social and environmental information relevant to long-term business success. If companies consider their efforts in this way, instead of seeking comparisons with the results of advertising, for example, corporate philanthropy would likely grow and become more strategic in corporate and community terms. It would benefit from further institutionalization and active support within companies.

RESOURCE GUIDE

Businesses for Social Responsibility
609 Mission Street, 2nd floor
San Francisco CA 94105
Tel: (1-415) 537-0888

Canadian Centre for Business and the Community
255 Smyth
Ottawa K1H 8M7
Canada
Tel: (1-613) 526-3280
Fax: (1-613) 526-1747

The Canadian Centre for Philanthropy
1329 Bay Street, Suite 200
Toronto, ON M5R 2C4
Canada
   Creating Effective Partnerships with Business, A Guide for Charities and Nonprofits in Canada

Capitol Publications Inc.
1101 King Street, Suite 444
Alexandria, VA 22314
   Corporate Philanthropy Report

The Center for Corporate Community Relations
Boston College
Chestnut Hill, MA 02167-3835
   Richard Barnes, *Measurement of Consumer Attraction to Socially Responsible Companies* (1994)

Charities Aid Foundation
48 Pembury Road
Tonbridge, Kent TN9 2JD
United Kingdom

The Conference Board
845 Third Avenue
New York, NY 10022
   David Logan, *Community Involvement of Foreign-Owned Companies* (1994)
   Strategic Opportunities in Corporate Community Activity, a Conference Report (1996)
   Measuring Corporate Community Involvement (1997)

Corporate Citizenship International
1 Russell Chambers
Covent Garden Piazza
London, WC2E 8AA
United Kingdom

Council on Foundations
1828 L Street N.W., Suite 300
Washington, DC 20036
Tel: (1-202) 466-6512
Fax: (1-202) 785-3926
Web site: http://www.cof.org
   Corporate Citizenship in the Asia Pacific Region, Conference Report, Hong Kong (1995)

European Foundation Centre
51, rue de la Concorde
B-1050 Brussels
Belgium
Tel: (32-2) 512-8938
Fax: (32-2) 512-3265
Web site: http://www.efc.be

The Foundation Center
79 Fifth Avenue
New York, NY 10003-3076
Tel: (1-212) 620-4230
Fax: (1-212) 691-1828
Web site: http://www.fdncenter.org
   The Foundation Directory, published
   annually
   National Directory of Corporate Giving,
   published regularly

The Hitachi Foundation
1509 22nd Street N.W.
Washington, DC 20036
Tel: (1-202) 457-0588
   David Logan, Delwin Roy, and
   Laurie Regelbrugge, *Global Corporate
   Citizenship—Rationale and Strategies*
   (1997)

   Daryl Ditz, Janet Ranganathan, and
   R. Darryl Banks, eds., *Green Ledgers:
   Case Studies in Corporate Environmental
   Accounting* (World Resources Institute,
   1996)

   *Redefining Corporate Responsibility in
   a Global Economy, Jobs for the Future*
   (Boston: 1996)

   Lois Vermilya W., Laurie
   Regelbrugge, and Barbara Haase,
   eds., *Quilt Makers: Community Education
   Resources and Challenges* (1996)

Independent Sector
1828 L Street N.W., Suite 300
Washington, DC 20036

**International Center for Not-for-
Profit Law**
1511 K Street, N.W., Suite 723
Washington, D.C. 20005

Keidanren
(Japan Federation of Economic
Organizations)
9-4, Otemachi 1-chome
Chiyoda-ku, Tokyo 100
Japan

**Japan Center for International
Exchange**
4-9-17 Minami Azabu
Minato-ku, Tokyo 106
Japan
   Tadashi Yamamoto, ed., *Emerging
   Civil Society in the Asia Pacific Community*
   (co-published by Japan Center for
   International Exchange and The
   Institute of Southeast Asian Studies
   in cooperation with the Asia Pacific
   Philanthropy Consortium, 1995)

**Mexican Center for Philanthropy
(CEMEFI)**
Mazatlan No. 96
Colinia Condesa
06140 Mexico City DF
Mexico
Tel: (52-5) 256-3739
Fax: (52-5) 256-3190

Philanthropy Australia
Level 3
111 Collins Street
Melbourne, Victoria 3000
Australia
Tel: (61-3) 9650-9255
Fax: (61-3) 9654-8298

The Points of Light Foundation
1737 H Street, N.W.
Washington, DC 20006
   The Points of Light Foundation has
   numerous materials on corporate
   volunteerism

Prince of Wales Business Leaders Forum
15–16 Cornwell Terrace
Regents Park
London NW1 4QP
United Kingdom
Jane Nelson, *Business as Partners in Development: Creating Wealth for Countries, Companies and Communities* (in collaboration with World Bank and United Nations Development Programme, 1996)

The Taft Group
12300 Twinbrook Parkway, Suite 520
Rockville, MD 20852
publications distribution:
835 Penobscot Building
Detroit, MI, 48226-4094
Tel: 800-877-8238

for publications and directories on corporate giving, philanthropy, and nonprofit organizations

Katherine Jankowski, ed., *Directory of International Corporate Giving in America and Abroad* (1996)

Corporate Giving Directory

Foundation Reporter

UNIWORLD Publications
257 Central Park West 10-A
New York, NY 10024
Directory of American Firms Operating in Foreign Countries (features 2,500 U.S. multinationals with 18,500 branches, subsidiaries, and affiliates in 132 countries; 1996)

World Business Council for Sustainable Development
160 route de Florissant
Conches-Geneva 1231
Switzerland

Case Study Contacts

American Express Co./American Express Foundation
American Express Tower
World Financial Center
New York NY 10285
Tel: (1-212) 640-5661

BellSouth Corp./BellSouth Foundation
1155 Peachtree Street N.E.
Atlanta GA 30309
Tel: (1-404) 249-2396

IBM Corporation
Old Orchard Road
Armonk NY 10504
Tel: (1-914) 765-5040

Whirlpool Foundation
400 Riverview Drive, Suite 410
Benton Harbor MI 49022
Tel: (1-616) 923-5580

Chapter 9

Conversion of Debt: A Win-Win-Win Scenario?

Alfred Gugler and Eva Jespersen

Conversion of Commercial or Official Debt

In the years following the break of the debt crises in 1982, a significant number of developing countries were having severe and sustained debt-servicing difficulties and had to undergo repeated reschedulings of their external debt, both commercial and official. It became apparent that the debt crises was not a short-term illiquidity crisis but a case of longer-term insolvency for many countries. The big international banks that had extended huge loans, especially in Latin American, had to get accustomed to the idea that in many cases, and even in a long-term perspective, they would not be repaid in full. In order to reduce the outstanding debt and to spread risks, they started trading debt papers at a discount among themselves, thus creating a "secondary market" for Third World debt. (The secondary market is a sort of "secondhand market" for commercial debt papers, whereby these are traded below the face value.)

The existence of a secondary market or of discounted debt is a prerequisite for a debt conversion operation, which is basically a financial transaction in which an investor exchanges a hard-currency-denominated external debt for a domestic debt payable in local currency by the debtor treasury or central bank. The debt can be redeemed in cash, equity, government debt instruments, or even "in kind," in the form of a protected natural area, for example, in what has become known as a debt-for-nature swap. In the case of a so-called debt-for-equity swap, the investor (a creditor bank or a company) exchanges the foreign-currency debt it holds for shares of a domestic company—that is, it invests the conversion proceeds in a domestic enterprise. Typically, a debt conversion operation implies a more or less significant leverage or multiplying effect, since the debt paper is purchased by the investor at an often substantial discount, whereas the debtor government will redeem it at full face value or at least at a price above the purchase price.

Debt Conversion's Many Winners

Debt conversions may be described as a "win-win-win" situation because the creditor gets some immediate cash payment for an otherwise potentially unrecoverable debt, the debtor saves scarce foreign exchange, and the investor obtains more local resources than in a regular foreign-exchange transaction.

For the investor, the incentive usually is to increase the amount of local resources available for investment purposes, whether this be investments in domestic companies, in environment protection activities, or in poverty alleviation. In the case of major debt conversion programs set up by official development agencies or international organizations, the reduction of the crippling external debt is also a goal.

In terms of strategy, this chapter distinguishes between individual (commercial) debt swap operations, typically carried out by a development or environmental nongovernmental organization (NGO), and larger debt conversion programs implemented by official development agencies or some specialized multilateral organizations.

In the case of individual debt swaps, whether it be debt-for-nature or debt-for-development, the debt paper is usually purchased from (or, in some instances, donated by) banks. The main purpose is not to reduce the external debt in any significant manner— the amounts involved are too small—but to generate additional development resources, to be used for ongoing or new projects of local NGOs. These debt conversions are considered an alternative source of funding for traditional development projects. Typically, these investors try to maximize the leverage effect of the conversion operation in order to get as much additional funds for their partners as possible. Given the small amounts converted, macroeconomic considerations such as potential inflationary effects or additional pressure on the national budget are not a serious concern.

Official debt conversion programs designed by aid agencies are often one component of a more or less comprehensive strategy to reduce the external debt burden of highly indebted developing countries. They mostly deal with bilateral debt—that is, official development assistance (ODA) claims and export credit debt—but may also encompass buy-backs of commercial bank debt. These programs are facilitated by a provision introduced by the Paris Club (see Box 1) in 1990/1991, under which 100 percent of concessional debt (ODA claims) and up to 10 percent (or US$10 million, whichever is higher) of nonconcessional debt can be converted into local currency. (The ceiling was recently elevated to US$20 million for severely indebted low-income countries.)

The amounts involved in this type of conversion are potentially significant; the conversions implemented by the U.S. Enterprise for the Americas Initiative (EAI) and the Swiss Debt Reduction Facility alone, for example, exceed all commercial debt-for-development and debt-for-nature swaps carried out until 1994 by at least 50 percent. Contrary to the small individual debt swaps, these do not as a rule try to maximize the proceeds of the conversion operation, giving due regard to fiscal and monetary constraints in the debtor country.

Help for Civil Society Organizations

Both commercial debt swaps and official debt conversion programs have a potential of enhancing the resources and sustainability of civil society organizations (CSOs).

Box 1

THE PARIS CLUB

The Paris Club is a forum bringing together debtor governments and their official creditors in a unified negotiating framework. It is composed mainly of members of the Organisation for Economic Co-operation and Development, and has a permanent secretariat supplied by the French Treasury.

Its traditional function has been to avoid defaults on loans made by its members by rescheduling officially guaranteed export credits and ODA loans falling due over a period of 12–18 months. In recent years, the Club has developed approaches to reduce the debt service and the debt stock of severely indebted low-income countries (under the Toronto Terms and the Naples Terms) and come up with more generous terms for highly indebted poor countries.

Each debtor country meets individually with all the Paris Club members concerned to negotiate a multilateral agreement. This is followed by bilateral negotiations with each creditor country to agree the implementation of the terms agreed with the Paris Club, a process that can be very lengthy.

The potential may be greater in the case of official programs, because the amounts involved are usually substantially larger than in the case of individual commercial debt swaps, thus providing a critical mass for the establishment of financial instruments like national funds, foundations, or trusts that can enhance sustainability through local decisionmaking and strengthened financial autonomy.

In quantitative terms, debt conversions can play a role as an additional source of revenue for CSOs, but their contribution should not be overestimated. Through 1994, somewhere between US$750 million and US$1 billion worth of commercial debt had been converted into local currency for funding of development projects and programs. This reduced total Third World debt by a mere 0.05 percent. Also, commercial debt swaps for development purposes account for only a little more than 1 percent of the total amount of debt converted. The bulk of the conversions (40 percent) have been debt-equity swaps implemented by banks and international companies. Roughly estimated, these debt-for-development swaps have generated US$300–450 million in local currency, which compared with the total annual ODA flows of approximately US$60 billion (in 1994) was a modest addition to development funding. The biggest investors are National Committees for UNICEF and the World Wildlife Fund (WWF), and the most important intermediator has been the now defunct Washington-based Finance for Development.

There are no precise figures available on the amount of official bilateral debt that has been converted. (See Table 1.) However, official creditors are becoming more involved in debt-for-development conversions. Major official debt conversion programs have been established by Belgium, Canada, France, Germany, Switzerland, and the United States. The amount of official debt converted under these programs can be roughly estimated at US$2.0–2.5 billion.

TABLE 1: Major Existing Debt Conversion Programs, 1995

Major Debt Conversion Programs	Face Value of Debt (US$mn)	Local Currency Generated (US$mn)
Commercial Debt		
Debt-for-nature swaps 1987-94	177.6	128.8
UNICEF swaps 1989-95*	199.2	52.9
Development swaps initiated by Finance for Development 1991-95	175.0	69.2
Official Bilateral Debt		
Swaps under the Enterprise for the Americas Initiative 1991-93	751.8	134.1
Swiss Debt Reduction Facility, Counterpart Funds 1993-95	776.4	189.9

* Commercial and official bilateral debt
Sources: World Bank, *World Debt Tables 1994–1995, 1996* (Washington, D.C.); OECD, *DAC Report 1995* (Paris: 1996); Swiss Coalition of Development Organizations, *Swiss Debt Reduction Facility—A State of the Art* (1995).

As far as qualitative aspects are concerned, the picture is mixed. Regarding the use of the local currency generated, it can be said that a great majority of individual debt swaps carried out by NGOs serve the purpose of enhancing CSO financial resources. Under the Swiss Debt Reduction Facility, about 60 percent of the counterpart fund resources committed to date have funded CSO projects and programs. In contrast, the French Libreville Fund serves in the first place to fund government projects that have to be submitted for approval to the Caisse Française de Développement.

Some debt conversion operations have been used to enhance CSO institutional capacity as well as financial sustainability and autonomy. This has been done by setting up independent and locally managed structures, such as trust funds or foundations. (See also Chapter 11.) But this is feasible only where there is a critical mass of local currency generated by the conversion, which is usually beyond the capacity of NGOs.

One example of such a structure is the Foundation for the Philippine Environment, an environmental trust fund established in 1991 by a partnership among Philippine NGOs and peoples' organizations, the Philippine Government, WWF-US, and the U.S. Agency for International Development (USAID). It is structured as an endowment fund, the resources of which come from several debt-for-nature transactions. The initial endowment was the equivalent of US$10 million. Overall funding comes from a US$25 million commitment from USAID to fund debt-for-nature swaps.

BOX 2

HOW TO LEVERAGE LOCAL RESOURCES THROUGH A DEBT SWAP

A northern environmental NGO buys US$10 million worth of commercial debt on Madagascar from a bank at 48 percent of face value. It will thus pay the bank US$4.8 million. The central bank of Madagascar is willing to convert the debt title at full face value—that is, to pay out the equivalent of US$10 million in Malgache Francs. For the northern NGO, the multiplier or leverage is therefore 2.1 (10 divided by 4.8); in other words, it gets 2.1 times more local currency than in a ordinary foreign-exchange transaction. However, the phrasing of the redemption may lower the real value of the transaction considerably.

The foundation is registered as a private, nonstock and nonprofit corporation, and is governed by an 11-person Board of Trustees with a broad representation from the three major geographic regions (Luzon, Visayas, and Mindanao). Its endowment is currently invested in Philippines Central Bank notes earning interest at market rates. Only the interest income accruing from this investment may be used to fund projects and programs.

Somewhat similar National Environmental Funds have been set up in quite a number of countries. Some have been created through conversions of commercial or official bilateral debt, for instance under the Enterprise for the Americas Initiative. Also in the Philippines, the Foundation for a Sustainable Society, Inc., was set up in 1995 to manage the funds generated by an official debt conversion carried out under the Swiss Debt Reduction Facility.

Most debt-for-nature swaps conducted by WWF, Conservation International, and others have occurred in Latin America. UNICEF, on the other hand, has concentrated on swaps that benefit children in low-income countries. The French Libreville Fund can be used exclusively by Cameroon, Congo, Côte d'Ivoire, and Gabon, while the Swiss Facility has conversion activities in Latin America, Africa, and Southeast Asia (the Philippines). In terms of sectoral allocation, a majority of the overall resources generated by debt conversions have been invested in environmental projects.

Benefits and Limitations

As mentioned, debt conversion operations are often described as "win-win-win" situations. This can certainly be the case if the operation is well designed and implemented, taking into account, among other items, the fiscal and monetary constraints of the debtor government. Debt-for-development swaps could be seen as particularly beneficial to the debtor country as a whole even compared with debt-for-equity conversions, because in the former there is no outflow of profit remittances. Even in these, however, there is a trade-off between maximizing the gain for the NGO receiving the local currency proceeds and limiting the costs involved for the debtor government.

From the investors' perspective, one of the main advantages of debt swaps over traditional foreign-exchange transactions is the multiplying effect (leverage). (See Box 2.) Depending on the purchase price and the debtor's policy regarding the redemption

SWAPPING DEBT FOR NATURE IN BOLIVIA

On 13 July 1987, Bolivia signed an agreement with Conservation International, a private, U.S.-based organization, to reduce its external commercial debt in return for protection and management of natural resources in the Amazon basin. Conservation International agreed to give US$650,000 in foreign debt notes to the Bolivian government and provide the technical, scientific, and administrative assistance to implement the scheme.

The government in turn agreed to provide legal protection to the 135,000-hectare Beni Biosphere Reserve, to create and protect three adjacent zones amounting to an additional 1 million hectares, and to set up a US$250,000 fund to manage the reserve. Of this, US$100,000 would come from the government and the rest from local currency accounts of USAID. This would be managed by Bolivia's Ministry of Agriculture and Peasant Affairs and a local representative of Conservation International.

Numerous lessons were learned during this ground-breaking debt-for-nature swap. One was that legislative and budgetary considerations need to be worked out in advance. Similar agreements are desirable in principle in the future, as this swap supports only one among many nature reserves in need of funding. It is also desirable from the point of view of continuing efforts to reduce commercial debt. The main reservations on the part of the environmental groups and the government, however, concerned the long and costly delays. A clear timetable for implementation should therefore be agreed on in advance and followed as closely as possible, with clearly defined roles for all involved. The delays were probably the most negative aspects of the process.

Still, NGOs gained useful political experience. Although it was left to environmental groups to initially promote the benefits of the scheme, they gained invaluable experience in public relations and established a central role for them-

rate to be paid, the leverage can be quite substantial. (In the case of debt-for-nature swaps to date, the leverage varied between 1.1 and 5.0, with an average of 2.3.)

The transaction is even more valuable for the investor if the debt claim is donated (for example, by a commercial bank). In this case the resources, at least from the investors' perspective, are truly additional, as no money is involved in purchasing the debt paper. The additionality of funds for high-priority programs is, therefore, another advantage of debt conversions. True additionality is only achieved, of course, if debt swap transactions are not used to compensate for reductions in overall program spending for the country concerned.

Furthermore, in some cases debt-for-development swaps may encourage additional foreign-exchange flows to the sectors receiving the conversion proceeds. If, for instance, the donor NGO or government wants to use the local currency exclusively to cover the local costs (salaries, local material, and so on) of, say, a small enterprise promotion program, it will provide additional foreign currency for certain imports (such as machinery)

selves. This was vital, given that many local NGOs are in their infancy, and face powerful and well-organized interest groups. This has probably been the most positive aspect of the process.

Another important lesson was that public education is vital. After an initial bout of bad press, national awareness of the issues was successfully stimulated. While NGOs have a role to play here, the government must take primary responsibility. This might entail making the public aware of the full details of an agreement at the earliest possible stage, with subsequent reports on progress made, both to the public and donors. This would minimize negative press reporting, rumor, and the resulting suspicion that government is acting behind closed doors.

Governments should demonstrate their commitment to such schemes through both words and action. The Bolivian government seem convinced of the importance and desirability of the project, with the Undersecretary for Natural Resources stating "the debt-for-nature decision was one of the best decisions this country has ever taken." But this needs to be matched by action, which includes making sure that the necessary funds are available and disbursed at the appropriate time, ensuring that the necessary legal framework is consistent and properly in place, and doing public education.

Socioeconomic research should be carried out before budgets and legislation are agreed. In Bolivia, it had not been established how much land the indigenous Chimane people within the reserve would need to sustain their traditional way of life as hunter-gatherers. Points like this need to be resolved as soon as possible, to avoid social, environmental, and political difficulties down the line, and delays in project implementation.

To sum up the lessons learned, there needs to be transparency between parties involved and a well-laid plan of action, with tasks clearly demarcated.

Case study prepared by Nils Bhinda, External Finance for Africa, UNICEF, based on Diana Page, "Debt-for-Nature Swaps: Experience Gained, Lessons Learned."

or for technical assistance (experts). In the case of the Swiss Debt Reduction Facility, additional foreign exchange has been provided for feasibility studies and monitoring activities. It is also possible under this program to provide additional balance-of-payments assistance in order to complement the debt relief operation.

Debt conversions may also lead to shifts in debtor-country public spending to socially crucial areas such as health and education. This will have positive effects in countries where these areas are neglected. In the case of Sudan, for instance, UNICEF has benefited from a total of seven debt conversions in which the government reallocated resources to water, sanitation, and health education programs. In the Philippines, legislation allows NGOs to convert debt into local currency at a favorable rate for projects of "high social impact."

In more qualitative terms, debt-for-development conversions allow for innovation and experimentation, because they are fairly new tools and there are not yet any standardized procedures and models on how to implement them. Also, debt conversion

FOUNDATION FOR A SUSTAINABLE SOCIETY, INC.

In August 1995, the governments of the Philippines and Switzerland signed an agreement on the reduction of Philippine external debt. Under this accord, 50 percent of the Philippine government's outstanding export credit debt to Switzerland—amounting to 42 million Swiss francs (approximately US$35 million) was cancelled. The remainder was converted into Philippine pesos. These were then provided by the Philippine Treasury as an endowment to the Foundation of a Sustainable Society Inc. (FSSI), a foundation formed to manage the counterpart funds.

FSSI supports productive activities of NGOs, peoples' organizations, cooperatives, and similar private organizations in the field of agriculture and fishery, as well as in the urban and rural small industries sector. The foundation is in the first place a loan-making institution, but it also provides grants for activities such as technical assistance, feasibility studies, and market research.

FSSI has three interesting features:

- it is exclusively managed by NGOs, and its resources are exclusively being allocated to civil society organizations;

- it is structured as a long-term capital fund—that is, only the interest or the return on investment and part of the loan reflows are used to fund projects and programs; and

- the process that lead to the forging of the agreement was marked from the very start by a close and intensive collaboration between Philippine and Swiss NGOs.

Several important lessons were learned from this experience. First, it is clear that close coordination and permanent communication between organized NGO constituencies in the debtor and the creditor countries are crucial to the success of negotiations between governments. Second, official debt conversions involving the establishment of an autonomous management structure such as a foundation consume a lot of time (two years in this case) and energy, because there are many

proceeds or counterpart funds are "indirect" donor funds coming out of the debtor government's budget or from the central bank. Therefore, some donor governments may be ready to accept or even to push for innovative structures that are more autonomous, locally based, and participatory. Such schemes may, for example, be NGO-managed foundations, trust funds, or similar structures. In the case of the Foundation for a Sustainable Society in the Philippines, for instance, the Swiss Government has accepted that all investment and funding decisions will be taken exclusively by NGO representatives forming the Board of Trustees, while the two governments serve as a nonvoting member and an observer.

Debt conversions do have a certain number of drawbacks and limitations that have to be taken into account. There are problems at the macroeconomic, institutional, and political levels.

actors involved (two governments and two NGO communities) with sometimes differing interests. Thus transaction costs tend to be rather high, and the donor government or NGO must be prepared to pay for the major part of these.

Third, a participatory approach is very important in order for the ownership of the process and the funding mechanism to be created. The southern NGOs should be involved right from the beginning in designing and preparing the scheme. Otherwise there is a risk that they will not stay involved if major difficulties or delays occur. Fourth, it is crucial to have good working contacts with relevant government officials on both sides in order to get access to important information. For instance, the northern NGO may get some important information from its government on the southern government's negotiating position that it can pass on to its NGO counterpart to use in its lobbying work, or vice versa.

There should be no illusions about the outcome of official debt conversions: these are negotiated between two governments, and the final decisions will be taken by these parties. So the results may be different from the scheme initially proposed by the NGOs. Thus it is all the more important to have strong NGO networks on both sides with a high capacity to advocate their positions in order to reach the best result possible.

One of the most positive aspects of this process was the excellent collaboration between the two NGO communities, which were both very motivated and committed to the common cause. Another positive point was the broad and inclusive consultation process among the Philippine CSOs, including those who are critical of debt swaps and cooperation with the government. This inclusive process allowed broad participation in FSSI's Board of Trustees and especially in its membership.

One negative aspect was the pressure of time during the negotiation period, which did not allow for sufficient consultation of the participating NGO representatives, since decisions had to be taken very quickly. This is a major drawback of this type of official debt conversion, where as a rule NGO representatives are not permitted to sit at the negotiating table.

At the macroeconomic level, there is the potential inflationary impact of debt conversions. But as noted earlier, the scale of debt-for-development swaps is so small that this impact is marginal. If the scale of official debt conversions were to increase substantially, compensatory monetary measures would be needed. Potentially, conversion rates at or close to face value, especially in the case of large-scale official debt conversions, can offset efforts to reduce the budget deficit and thus conflict with structural adjustment targets. Already, the International Monetary Fund (IMF) is often advised of possible debt conversions and takes these into account in its budget negotiations. It may be advisable to seek the understanding of the IMF for major debt conversions.

At the political level, debt swaps have sometimes been criticized for leading to a loss of sovereignty on the part of the debtor country. In the late 1980s, some Latin American countries—fearing the growing policy influence of northern environmen-

DEBT REDUCTION IN ZAMBIA

Zambia's commercial debt-for-development swap took place in July and September 1994. This case is particularly interesting as it was conducted under the Debt Reduction Facility of IDA, and involved the buyback of a large amount of commercial debt by the Government of Zambia—one of only two operations to include a carefully integrated debt-for-development option. The result of the operation was the reduction of Zambia's eligible external commercial debt of US$240 million by 83 percent, which amounted to a 45-percent reduction in its total commercial debt. The swap also helped participating NGOs enhance social-sector projects in the fields of health, environmental preservation, education, low-income housing, and micro-enterprise development with increased local currency funding.

The swap was facilitated by the Debt for Development Coalition Inc. (DDC, subsequently renamed Finance for Development Inc.). Its responsibilities included designing, marketing, coordinating, and implementing the deal in conjunction with the government, its advisors, and IDA. One role of DDC was to match creditors willing to participate in the first option with NGOs. Participants were narrowed down by the fact that only two creditors were willing to donate their debt, and by the inability of all but 14 of the shortlisted NGOs to purchase the debt.

Overall, no major difficulties were experienced with the swap. All NGOs received the disbursements they were entitled to, and none pulled out of the deal. However, one group did not program their funds for a while, and the option enabled one to program funds before or after closing.

In any similar debt-for-development swap, the following issues should be considered:

- The limited time available between the government's invitation to creditors to participate and the closing date meant that many NGOs did not obtain all the debt they wanted.

tal organizations in this sphere through debt-for-nature swaps—used the word "eco-colonialism" to express their concerns.

One major drawback of debt conversions is their complexity and the risks involved. The political and economic context in a debtor country can change very quickly. This can, for instance, mean that an operation that has been in preparation several months cannot be completed due to a change of government or a shift in central bank policy (such as suspension of the debt conversion program).

In addition, there are a number of aspects that limit the scope of conversions of both commercial and official debt:

- Significantly rising secondary market prices for commercial debt papers make swaps less attractive because the leverage is reduced.

- Major budgetary and monetary constraints in countries that are undergoing economic stabilization and reform programs do not allow for large-scale debt conversions.

- Interaction between the government and NGOs was very open. No interaction took place with the IDA donors, however, as they were not involved in the implementation of the operation. DDC communicated with several donor agencies on behalf of the NGOs, and explained the option to them.
- Many NGOs did not have the available funds, yet were initially accepted to participate. Pre-eligibility screening of NGOs looked only at whether they were operating legally in Zambia, not whether their programs were funded or not, so as not to preclude debt donations. As it turned out, the level of donations was very low. This could be explained by the huge loss to creditors of 89 percent on principal, and the write-off of all interest accruals. Although DDC explained to NGOs that it was unlikely many creditors would be willing to donate, the outcome of allowing any NGO to participate was to encourage even the smallest and poorest to seek funding. An alternative could be to open the option only as an enhancement to NGOs with funding already in place. Any donated debt could then be used by an NGO chosen by the Government.
- The option was designed to enhance funding for projects that had already been approved, and only the major NGOs created new projects to be funded by the swap. Thus projects funded by the swap were not created and funded by the option.
- IDA funds were not available for hard-currency imports. With the closing of the deal and the crediting of IDA funds to the escrow account, NGOs gained control of the money. The program allowed escrow funds to be used for imports, but not in Zambian Kwacha.
- The development funds received by Zambia were additional: motivated by the 50-percent premium, UNICEF, CARE, and World Vision raised additional funds.

Case study prepared by Nils Bhinda, External Finance for Africa, UNICEF.

- With ODA budgets shrinking everywhere, there is little room for additional funds from these sources for debt conversion activities.
- There is no market for official debt claims, so it is difficult to determine the "right" price to be paid to the export credit agencies and the holders of the unguaranteed part of the debt.
- With its maximum amount of US$20 million per country, the amount of Paris Club (export credit) debt that can be converted is still rather limited.
- Only a few debtor countries have a legal framework for conversion of commercial debt that would allow for standardized and quick procedures.

A critical issue is how to protect the local currency proceeds against erosion of value. If the local money cannot be spent within a short period of time, one option is to have it disbursed in several installments, indexed to a hard currency. Another possibility is to invest the cash received in Treasury Bills or similar government debt instruments, in equities, or even in real estate, provided that the income derived from these investments is higher or at least equal to the inflation rate.

A Trend Toward Official Debt Swaps

Although interest in debt-for-development swaps has increased in recent years, the scale is still limited. Debt-for-nature swaps originating with NGOs have slowed considerably over the past two years, probably due to rising secondary market prices in Latin America following the conclusion of Brady operations. (The Brady Plan was proposed in 1989 for the highly indebted middle-income countries, particularly in Latin America; it provided for the restructuring and reduction of commercial debt, with financial support from the World Bank and the IMF.) Due to some of the limitations just mentioned, it is expected that commercial debt conversion activities will stagnate or at least slow in the years ahead. This trend might be reinforced by the fact that the Washington-based Finance for Development, which facilitated a number of debt conversions over the last five years, went out of business (although some of the staff have resurfaced in other debt swap entities).

On the other hand, there is reason to believe that there might be an increase of official debt conversions in the future. There already are several such programs under way, and a number of other countries—such as the Netherlands, Norway, and Austria—have shown some interest. Also, some southern countries, such as Peru, are actively promoting this type of conversion in the Paris Club.

With the approval of the Highly Indebted Poor Country Initiative by the governing bodies of the IMF and the World Bank, affected countries may for the first time receive some relief of their multilateral debt, once their other debt has been rescheduled as much as possible. Earlier, the World Bank's soft-loan arm (the International Development Association) had provided considerable amounts of money for commercial debt buy-backs that have, for Bolivia and Zambia, included a swap component. Country-level implementation of the Highly Indebted Poor Country Initiative may provide opportunities for debt-for-development swaps.

In terms of program implementation, there seems to be a shift taking place from direct project funding to more participatory forms of debt conversions. One example is the establishment of environmental trust funds or foundations (the concept of the "second generation" of debt-for-nature swaps, developed by WWF). Similarly, under the Enterprise for the Americas Initiative, a number of National Environmental Funds have been set up, with administrative councils consisting of representatives from both governments and from the national NGO community. The Swiss Debt Reduction Facility, too, follows the concept of locally based, broadly composed counterpart funds that define their funding policy independently.

There is growing recognition among the development community that sustainability of development effects can only be achieved if there is enhanced ownership of the funding structure by the CSOs involved, along with financial autonomy. Ownership—in the context of debt conversions—can be improved through participatory approaches, getting interested NGOs and other CSOs involved in designing the debt conversion scheme and participating in decisionmaking. Financial autonomy

Box 3

CAPITALIZATION FUNDING FOR FINANCIAL INSTITUTIONS

To capitalize a financial institution (for example, a credit NGO) means to provide it with seed capital or to provide funds that allow it to broaden its existing capital base. The ultimate goal of capitalization is to build a self-sustaining institution. This implies that the capital base is strong enough and that the capital is invested in a way that generates sufficient income to cover the institution's operating costs.

Capitalization funds can be used in three different ways:

- *for investment—the aim here is to maintain the real value of the funds and to generate a reasonable cash flow to cover a portion of the operation costs;*
- *for a loan fund—a certain percentage of the capital can be allocated to this purpose, although a loan loss reserve from noncapital funds is required to protect the principal; or*
- *as a guarantee fund—part of the capitalization funds can be used as partial collateral, which allows the institution to negotiate favorable terms (with a commercial bank, for instance) for a leveraged credit line for its customers.*

---

can be enhanced through setting up locally managed trusts and foundations that use only the return on investment for funding projects and programs.

A major remaining question is whether debt conversions represent just an alternative source of funding development projects and programs, or whether they could also be used in an innovative way to promote institutional and financial autonomy of participating CSOs and thus reduce dependence on northern donor sources, whether they are public or private. In promoting financially self-sustaining CSOs, a debt conversion can contribute to reducing a whole NGO sector's dependence on outside sources. This is, for instance, the case with environmental NGOs that get funding from National Environmental Funds. It would seem that in the face of shrinking ODA budgets and increased uncertainty about the continuation of existing programs and credit lines, promoting the financial autonomy of CSOs is a possible solution.

Creating new institutions such as foundations or trust funds may not be feasible in connection with a small debt swap, and in some cases it may not even be desirable, because it could kill existing structures that are less "supply-driven." In such cases, a debt swap might, for example, support existing financial institutions such as credit cooperatives, self-help banks, credit guarantee facilities, and so on. An interesting and innovative use of local currency proceeds is to capitalize such financial institutions and thus enhance their sustainability. (See Box 3.)

Commercial Debt Swaps

Swaps involving commercial debt are significantly different from official debt conversion programs in at least three ways:

- there is no official leverage on the debtor government to comply with a debt swap agreement,
- the debtor country may not have the experience or the institutional capacity to readily proceed with a conversion, and
- the debt will not necessarily come from a domestic creditor and the price of the debt will be fixed in the market or through negotiations with the creditor.

These factors make undertaking commercial debt swaps rather more time-consuming and uncertain endeavors. A special case of commercial debt swaps is those organized by the World Bank, which have some similarities to government programs.

As discussed in this section, the nature of commercial debt swaps suggests that they should be a certain size—possibly at least US$3–4 million—to justify the efforts involved. They may be most likely to succeed for activities or programs that have high government priority and that can absorb the local currency generated through the conversion over a relatively short time (one to three years).

Commercial debt swaps are dominated by debt-for-equity swaps, and a few countries account for the bulk: Costa Rica, the Philippines, Panama, Bolivia, and Ecuador, which by the end of 1992 accounted for 90 percent of all debt-for-development or debt-for-nature swaps according to *World Credit Tables* (1995). The field has, however, broadened somewhat over the past five years.

Most commercial lending to developing countries is secured by public guarantees; debt incurred on purely commercial terms makes up some 10 percent of total world debt owed by developing countries, whereas guaranteed commercial debt accounts for about one third. For low-income countries, guaranteed commercial debt (when not fully serviced) will be covered by Paris Club restructuring, and may therefore be covered by official debt conversion programs; for other countries, guaranteed commercial debt may also be available for swaps.

Of unguaranteed long-term obligations to commercial banks, severely indebted low-income countries—most of which are in sub-Saharan Africa—owed about US$4.5 billion, while middle-income countries owed some US$50 billion. Some of this debt (mostly London Club debt) is valued and traded in the secondary market. For some countries, however, the number of creditors and the actual size of the debt are too small for a market to exist, and price setting must be agreed through negotiations. The latter is also the case for debt owed to countries in the Middle East, countries of the former Eastern bloc, and Latin American countries, which offer potential for debt swaps.

Why Get Involved?

The low market value of some commercial debt (down to 8–10 percent of face value) and governments' willingness to redeem debt at levels above the market price (multiplying 1.2–2) can provide a premium of local currency for local development activities. The moral and political considerations concerning the involvement in commercial debt swaps are discussed in Kaiser and Lambert (1995).

What is in it for the creditors? Banks and other commercial entities may want to get bad debt off their books, and many may already have made provisions to write it off but can still recuperate a small fraction of the debt through trade. Losses on debt can also be modified through tax credit for donations of the debt to nonprofit, local charitable entities. According to *LatinFinance*, since February 1987 the U.S. Department of the Treasury has through Revenue Ruling 87–124 permitted tax deductions for debt donated to a U.S.-based charity equal to the debt's "fair market value," taking into consideration the local currency issued as a result of the conversion. Similar provisions in other countries and more recent changes need to be verified with the appropriate authorities. Tax deductibility for loan loss reserves may in other cases act as a disincentive for selling debt.

Kaiser and Lambert caution that "NGOs should make sure that the creditor's consent to sell is motivated by the opportunity to limit damage and not by the chance to make a net profit" (1995, p. 51).

What is in it for the debtor? On the one hand, debtor governments can save foreign exchange through converting debt it is servicing into local currency contributions to local development programs. On the other hand, a debtor government may have reservations about the trade of debt that it gives low priority to (having decided not to repay). Debt-distressed governments do not service all their debt, and often a political decision lays behind what debt does get serviced. Debt owed to the international financial institutions and major private trading partners is given the highest priority in order to maintain access to funding from these sources. Bilateral creditors and creditors no longer seen as useful trading partners (such as the former Soviet Union), in contrast, have little or no priority.

The World Health Organization also suggests that governments may be hoping to obtain large debt reductions through negotiations with their creditors, and may therefore be reluctant to enter into smaller swap deals that would indicate a willingness to make concessions in exchange for debt reductions (Genberg, 1992). There may also be a fear that debt-for-development swaps will drive the price of debt up in the secondary market and thereby make other (commercial) conversions less attractive.

Generally, the degree of debt servicing and the market value of the traded debt reflect poor economic and budgetary conditions in the debtor country. These conditions will also affect domestic economic conditions, most notably through high inflation, and may affect the ability and willingness of the debtor government to meet its obligations under a debt-swap agreement.

The primary risks are that inflation and devaluation will reduce the real value of the agreed government redemption (although different model agreements can help secure a maintenance of value, depending on local conditions), and that the government will change budget priorities or suspend or change the debt conversion program. Programs have a better chance of succeeding if the government partners involved—resource ministries, the ministry of finance, and the central bank—give high priority to the selected activities and these have a relatively good capacity to absorb the generated local currency quickly.

Even as important a donor as UNICEF, which holds some leverage with collaborating governments, has seen a few of the swaps benefiting it subjected to renegotiations following devaluations in the collaborating country or facing protracted delays in availability of counterpart funds.

It is highly desirable but rarely feasible to determine that government resources for the redemption of the debt are in addition to existing resources. Legislation for debt swaps, experience with debt conversions, and budget line items for funding debt conversions should give some assurance about the ability of the government to meet its debt-swap obligations and its interest in doing so.

Practical Steps

The same basic rules about the identification of projects apply to both commercial debt-for-development swaps and official conversion programs, but for swaps it may be particularly important that the activities considered have high priority with the government in order to increase the probability it will meet its obligations, have a substantial local currency component, and can be implemented as a stand-alone component. The fact that negotiations can easily take 6–18 months needs to be factored into the planning of activities.

The initial investigation can be undertaken by the interested donor NGO and its local counterpart by contacting commercial banks in the donor country or through contacts with the ministry of finance or central bank in the debtor country. As suggested earlier, there may be cases where commercial banks are willing to donate their outstanding credit to the donor NGO.

In cases where the debt is traded, or where only debt held by commercial entities in other countries is available, it is strongly recommended that a broker who specializes in discounted debt be involved in arranging the purchase. Kaiser and Lambert do not recommend this kind of operation for small inexperienced NGOs, and suggest that only larger groups with a well-established financial division should consider this type of conversion (1995, p. 47).

What often happens is that creditors inform brokers about their interest of trading debt, and the brokers in turn seek buyers. Brokers will negotiate the trading of the debt and can help obtain authorization from the debtor government as well as assist in negotiating the redemption and payout or maintenance of value during the course of the agreement.

A number of entities have by now established themselves as experts in debt swaps. (See the Resource Guide at the end of the chapter.) Commercial banks with international business may also have experience in trading debt (but less experience in negotiating with counterpart governments). Citibank, for example, was used as an agent for the swap of Bolivian debt to finance the protective management of the Beni Biosphere Reserve by Conservation International, and ING Bank has been used as an agent by the Dutch National Committee for UNICEF. Some brokers are experts in particular regions or with particular creditors, but it is a competitive business.

The brokers are usually not philanthropic; they expect to make a good income out of the transaction, although some are "nonprofit." They usually ask a fixed share of the face value of the debt negotiation upon success, depending on the extent of the services (1–2 percent), but there would be no harm in trying to negotiate a *pro bono* service.

Once suitable debt has been identified and a project and partner identified, it is necessary to obtain an authorization from the debtor government to formally make an offer to the creditor and proceed with the conversion. The debtor government will require information about the investor (the donor NGO), the beneficiary, and the activities (including a detailed budget) to be funded through the debt conversion, as well as a statement on how they fit with the government's development priorities.

The government needs to ensure that the proposed debt conversion is covered by existing agreements, will not conflict with agreements with the IMF concerning public resources, and is not being considered for debt swaps by other partners and for other purposes. Granting the authorization may take a long time.

In some cases, especially where the debt is not traded in the secondary market or where a special, favorable price is offered, the creditor may want to offload the entire bad debt it holds on a debtor country. The magnitude of the debt—or rather the price being asked—may exceed the funding or absorptive capacity of the investor or beneficiary. Brokers will often have contacted a number of NGOs active in debt swaps; alternatively, the investor may establish such contacts, which will allow a number of interested NGOs to join a pool for a debt swap. The piecing together of a joint swap may add time and complications to the negotiations.

The price will have significance for the leverage that the swap will produce. As a general rule, the price should not exceed 50 percent of face value. National Committees for UNICEF have on average paid 15 percent for debt converted into local currency for UNICEF programs.

A certain element of discretion may be required surrounding the purchase of debt in order not to drive up the price, but the broker should be able to indicate an approximate price close to the average secondary market price. And the investor should generally set an upper margin in order to avoid sudden unexpected price rises that may substantially lower the proceeds of the deal.

According to Konrad von Moltke, an important decision concerns the actual purchaser of the debt. In some instances it may be appropriate for the investor in the creditor country to acquire the debt (for example, if the debt originates in the same country as the investor, which is often not the case) and then donate it to the partner in the debtor country. In others, it may be possible to donate the necessary resources to permit direct acquisition of the debt by the beneficiary organization. As a third alternative, von Moltke suggests that debt may be donated directly to the beneficiary, acting as an agent for the investor. The factors governing the choice of actors are mainly financial and tax-related, although accounting considerations may enter for the investor. The broker must be able to lay out the consequences of all relevant alternatives.

At the same time that debt is identifyed and purchased, contractual negotiations are needed between the investor, the debtor government, and the beneficiary. The lower the price (and thus risk), the better the chance that the government will agree to a redemption in local currency that provides for substantial leverage on the invested funds. There have been many cases where governments have agreed to redeem the debt at face value in local currency. But some governments will agree to a redemption that allows for a certain premium. As a rule of thumb, the multiplier should be at least 1.3 in order for the efforts of the conversion to be worthwhile for the investor (relative to the opportunity cost of the invested resources). The actual structures of the deal, particularly the efforts to preserve the real value (vis-à-vis the invested foreign currency and the time horizon), are important determinants of the actual multiplier.

ENVIRONMENTAL FOUNDATION OF JAMAICA

The Environmental Foundation of Jamaica (EFJ) was the result of debt reduction agreements in August 1991 and January 1993 between the governments of Jamaica and the United States. Under these and follow-up agreements, 77 percent of Jamaica's debt originating from food aid (PL480 debt) and its USAID debt was cancelled—a total of US$405 million. The remaining 23 percent was restructured for quarterly payments by the Jamaican government into a fund controlled by the EFJ. Over 20 years, this will amount to US$21.5 million.

The debt conversion came about through the efforts of U.S. environmental NGOs. It was included in the 1990 Enterprise for the Americas Initiative of President Bush that was designed to promote hemispheric trade and investment, to which the burden of debt servicing was seen as an obstacle.

The EFJ Board of Directors has nine members—six seats for NGOs, two for the two governments, and one for a representative of the University of the West Indies. An interesting feature of the EFJ is its membership—some 59 NGOs and community-based organizations. More than half participate actively in selecting a slate of Board representatives (from which the Minister of the Environment appoints the Board), guiding policy, advising on project selection, and monitoring the work of the Board and the Secretariat.

This collaboration among NGOs works well in spite of its novelty and initial differences in age, size, and degrees of organization. The older development agencies were fairly well organized, while the newer, smaller environmental groups that were just trying to get their act together took the lead on debt con-

For longer time horizons, the impact of inflation will reduce the purchasing power of the agreed amount of redemption. There is also a question of the long-term ability or willingness of the government to honor the commitment. As a general rule, it is advisable to design programs that can absorb the funds within three to four years. A range of alternatives has been used in debt swaps depending on the particularities of each conversion, including:

- The investor/purchaser retains the debt in its original form, denominated in hard currency, until local currency is required and then swaps only a tranche for a set period of implementation. Each tranche is swapped at the exchange rate prevailing at the time of the conversion and in accordance with a prearranged schedule.

- The investor/purchaser exchanges the debt title for promissory notes denominated in a hard currency and then exchanges for local currency in tranches according to an implementation schedule.

- The investor/purchaser exchanges the debt instrument for local currency bonds or other financial instruments linked to the U.S. dollar or another hard currency with maturities that correspond with the needs of the project.

version. More difficult and challenging was the collaboration with the governments. NGOs in Jamaica, in the absence of any legal, regulatory, or policy re-
straints, learned that it had to be done and could be very useful, but also that collaboration had to be approached carefully and critically.

The object of the EFJ is to provide grants toward the conservation and sustainable management of Jamaica's natural resources. Priority is given to projects
involving local community management and capacity building of NGOs and
community groups. A set amount of funds also goes to child development and
child survival projects that have an environmental dimension.

From August 1993 to July 1996, the foundation approved 219 projects, for an
average annual total of US$1.5 million, a figure that was expected to top US$2
million in 1996–97. At the same time, effective management of income by professional investment firms has brought the EFJ's resources to more than US$12
million. This has gone into an endowment fund established in 1997 to ensure the
continuity of the foundation after the debt conversion payments cease. EFJ is also
seeking to diversify the sources of funding in order to build up the endowment.

For the NGO community and their umbrella organizations, the EFJ has been
a valuable experience. Grasping the opportunity for collaboration on several
fronts and showing patience and persistence, the NGOs have asserted control of
the foundation, put it on a sound footing, and kept it faithful to its mandate. Yet
its leaders remain aware of the need to establish sustainable funding and of the
difficulty—with limited funds—of having significant impact on massive environmental and developmental needs.

Case study prepared with the assistance of Horace Levy, Board Member, EFJ.

Official Debt Conversion Programs

Programs for the conversion of official bilateral debt are often part of a donor government's efforts to reduce the overall external debt of highly indebted countries.
Instead of simply cancelling the debt they are owed, some governments prefer to convert it into local currency to fund local projects they are implementing or to set up special funds that should benefit domestic NGOs and other civil society organizations.
On the other hand, an export credit agency may wish to improve its financial situation by selling "bad" debts to the official development agency or another investor.

As noted earlier, two types of debt fall under this category of debt conversion.
ODA debt is concessional debt usually owed to the official development agency or
some other government institution; according to Paris Club rules, 100 percent of outstanding ODA claims can be exchanged for local currency. Export credit debt, in contrast, is initially commercial debt incurred at market conditions and guaranteed by a
government's export credit agency. It becomes official debt once it has been rescheduled in the Paris Club.

While ODA debt is exclusively owed to the government, export credits usually
have an uninsured part, the so-called tail, which has to be bought back from the "tail

holders"—suppliers and banks. Since there is no real market for this type of debt, it is not easy to determine the "right price" to be paid to the tail holders. Typically, the prices paid for the "tails" have been close to secondary market prices for commercial bank debt.

Several countries have established major debt conversion programs. One of the largest is the Enterprise for the Americas Initiative launched by the U.S. government in 1991. Under this program, ODA debt (food aid and USAID loans) owed by Latin American and Caribbean countries has been partly forgiven. The interest on the reduced debt is paid in local currency into a special fund. Since 1991, the United States has signed EAI agreements with Argentina, Bolivia, Chile, Colombia, El Salvador, Jamaica, and Uruguay. These agreements will endow the EAI local funds with approximately US$150 million that will be used for environmental and child survival programs. Due to a lack of budget authority, the program is presently on hold, but it is expected to be restarted after new legislation has been passed by the U.S. Congress.

Switzerland also set up a special facility in 1991 to reduce the official bilateral, commercial, and multilateral debt of highly indebted countries. To date it has signed 18 bilateral debt reduction agreements covering about US$750 million of export credit debt. In 11 cases, counterpart funds in local currency have been established for a total amount of approximately US$190 million. In almost all funds, NGOs are associated with project selection, and a majority of the fund's resources are allocated to CSOs. Another 10 countries are "in the pipeline"—that is, the Swiss Government has bought back the bilateral debt but cannot, for the time being, negotiate it for governance reasons.

In 1992 the French government established the Libreville Fund, consisting of nonperforming ODA loans totalling FF 4 billion (approximately US$700 million) for Cameroon, Congo, Côte d'Ivoire, and Gabon. This program will cancel debt in exchange for financing of projects and programs in the environmental and social spheres designed by the respective governments and implemented partly by NGOs. Use of this fund was suspended with the devaluation of the CFA franc in early 1994, but it resumed in September 1995. To date, conversions of a little more than one fourth of the total amount have been approved by the French government.

Germany, Canada, and Belgium also have substantial conversion programs, and some others have been involved in individual debt conversion operations.

Official debt conversion programs are relatively complex and can involve various public and private players at different levels. If such programs are to be used for CSO resource enhancement, they should include at least two actors from both the creditor country (Development or Finance Ministry, possibly the Export Credit Agency [ECA], and an NGO) and the debtor country (Ministry of Finance or Central Bank and CSOs). In any case, the basis for the conversion and the use of the proceeds will be an agreement between the two governments. This, of course, reduces the scope for CSOs, whose influence crucially depends on their ability to lobby their respective governments.

In other words, unlike in a commercial debt swap, a CSO cannot decide whether or not it wants to carry out an official debt conversion because it cannot do it alone. It can, however, decide if it wants to put energy (and money) into pushing its government to engage into this kind of operation, or whether and in what form it wishes to participate in an existing program.

Since an official debt conversion is not a purely technical and financial procedure but also has a political dimension, there is no clear-cut sequence of steps to be taken by a CSO.

The following steps and actions may be required for a northern NGO:

- identify eligible debt (ODA and export credit debt) owed by the countries the NGO is interested in;

- lobby the government to make available additional money or push for budget appropriations in order to buy back or cancel the relevant debt;

- propose an appropriate mechanism for buying back or taking over debt held by the national ECA (guaranteed part of export credit), and possibly push for a change of legislation in this sphere;

- propose an appropriate mechanism and an adequate price for the buyback of "tails" held by the suppliers (unguaranteed part of export credit);

- contact partner organizations or networks in the countries concerned and discuss with them different options for managing and using debt conversion proceeds;

- consider contracting partner CSOs or local consultants to investigate potential institutional frameworks for managing these resources and to come up with recommendations;

- present these proposals to the creditor government and lobby for their acceptance; and

- in case of acceptance, consider supporting the creditor government in negotiating the proposed solution with the debtor government and consider helping implement it in collaboration with southern partners.

When an official debt conversion scheme is already in place but CSOs on both sides are not sufficiently involved, the northern NGO may want to:

- lobby its respective government to include CSOs in decisionmaking bodies of existing local structures or consider the establishment of more autonomous new structures (trusts or foundations) with greater CSO participation;

- lobby its government to at least allocate more resources to CSOs; and

- advise their partner organizations on how to receive funds from such funding mechanisms.

CSOs in the debtor countries may have to take the following steps:

- assist northern partners in identifying eligible debt by getting in touch with their central bank or Ministry of Finance;

- inform northern partners on any existing guidelines regarding conversion of official bilateral debt;

- investigate existing funding mechanisms and evaluate their track record and results;

- propose existing mechanisms to manage the conversion proceeds or design new institutional frameworks for managing the funds and formulate proposals for the northern partner;

- lobby their own government to get the proposed solution through in the bilateral negotiations;
- set up or assist in setting up the negotiated institutional structure; and
- assume a role in any new funding mechanism.

RESOURCE GUIDE

Bibliography

Bouchet, M.H., *Les Conversions de Créances "Club de Paris": Les Expériences des Pays de l'OCDE en Matière de Conversionde et d'Abandon de Créances*, Séminaire CNUCED, Geneva, 27/28 January 1994.

Debt for Development Coalition, Inc., *Debt for Development Conversions in the Context of the Debt Reduction Facility for IDA-Only Countries*, prepared for the Project Finance Group of the World Bank, Washington, DC, 1993.

Genberg, Hans, "Debt for Health Swaps: A Source of Additional Finance for the Health System?" technical paper, Macroeconomics, Health and Development Series No. 3 WHO, Geneva, 1992.

Gerson, Noel, and Diana Page, "Debt for Nature, Three Case Studies," *LatinFinance*, No. 16, undated.

Griffith-Jones, S., and P. Mistry, *Conversion of Official Bilateral Debt*, Vol. 1, UNCTAD, Geneva, 1994.

Griffith-Jones, S., *Official Debt Marketization*, UNCTAD, Geneva, 1993.

IUCN, The Nature Conservancy, and WWF, *Report of the First Global Forum on Environmental Funds*, IUCN, Gland, Switzerland, 1994.

Kaiser, Jürgen, and Alain Lambert, "Debt Swaps for Sustainable Development—A Practical Guide for NGOs," IUCN, SCDO and EURODAD, 1995.

Saravanamutto, Neil, and Christopher Shaw, "Making Debt Work for Education," Association for the Development of African Education, 1995.

Spergel, B., "Environmental Funds," WWF, Washington, DC, April 1995.

Von Moltke, Konrad, "Back to Nature: Five Basic Steps," *LatinFinance*, No. 16, undated.

World Credit Tables, "Creditor-Debtor Relations from Another Perspective, 1994–95," EURODAD, 1995.

World Bank, *World Debt Tables 1996*, Washington, DC, 1996.

Consultants for Debt-for-Development Swaps

Anne Auriault
Agence E4 International
81, Rue des Archives
F-75003 Paris
France
Tel: (33-1) 4887-3778
Fax: (33-1) 4887-3811

Anne Guillaume-Gentil
**Association Conversion de dette
pour le Développement et l'envi-
ronnement (ACDE)**
6, rue Talleyrand
F-75007 Paris
France
Tel: (33-1) 4550-4678
Fax: (33-1) 4753-0673

Frans van Loon
**ING-Bank
Emerging Markets Department**
P.O.Box 1800
NL-1000 BV Amsterdam-Zuidost
The Netherlands
Tel: (31-20) 563-5138
Fax: (31-20) 563-5853

New York Bay Company, Ltd.
61 Broadway, Suite 1417
New York, NY 10006
Tel: (1-212) 344-5450
Fax: (1-212) 344-5575

Helmut Reuschle
**New York Bay Company, Ltd.
(European Office)**
Chemin de la Dôle 20
CH-1295 Tannay
Switzerland
Tel: (41-22) 776-3910
Fax: (41-22) 776-7349

Owen Stanley Financial
21, Bd de la Madeleine
F-75001 Paris
France
Tel: (33-1) 4455-8740
Fax: (33-1) 4296-4090

Christine Parniere
c/o Capricorn Development
Partner Ltd
21 rue des Templiers
F-78850 Paris
France
Tel: (33-1) 3054-4948
Fax: (33-1) 3054-4501

Institutions with Experience in Debt Conversions

Conservation International
1015 18th Street N.W., Suite 1000
Washington DC 20036
Tel: (1-202) 429-5660
Fax: (1-202) 887-5188
E-mail: m.guerin-mcmanus@
conservation.org

Carlos Quenan
Epargne sans Frontières
32, rue Peletier
F-75009 Paris
France
Tel: (33-1) 4800-9682
Fax: (33-1) 4800-9659

P. Enrique Gonzales Torres, S.J.
Fondo para la Asistencia,
Promoción y Desarrollo, A.C.
(FAPRODE)
Temistocles No. 33 Col Polanco
11560 México, DF
Mexico
Tel: (52-5) 280-3022 or 281-1166
Fax: (52-5) 281-0583
E-mail: faprode@mail.internet.com.mex

Jürgen Kaiser
Initiativkreis Entwicklung
braucht Entschuldung
c/o Kindernothilfe
Düsseldorfer Landstrasse 180
D-47249 Duisburg
Germany
Tel: (49-203) 791-728
Fax: (49-203) 778-9118
E-mail: 101515.1753@compuserve.com

Jerry Quigley
MEDA Trade and Consulting
155 Forbisher Dr., Suite I-106
Waterloo, Ontario NZV 2EI
Canada
Tel: (1-519) 725-1725
Fax: (1-519) 725-9083

Rudy de Meyer
NCOS
Vlasfabriekstraat 11
B-1060 Brussels
Belgium
Tel: (32-2) 539-2620
Fax: (32-2) 539-1343

Pedro Morazán
SÜDWIND
Lindenstrasse 58-60
D-53721 Siegburg
Germany
Tel: (49-2241) 53617
Fax: (49-22410 51308

Richard Helbling, Alfred Gugler
Swiss Coalition of Development
Organizations
Debt-for-Development Unit
Postfach
CH-3001 Bern
Switzerland
Tel: (41-31) 381-1714
Fax: (41-31) 381-1718
E-mail: scalition@igc.apc.org

The Nature Conservancy
1815 North Lynn Street
Arlington VA 22209
Tel: (1-703) 841-4865
Fax: (1-703) 841-4880
E-mail: ggreen@tnc.org

Frank Joshua, Anne Miroux
UNCTAD
Development Finance Unit
Palais des Nations
CH-1211 Geneva 10
Switzerland
Tel: (41-22) 907-1234
Fax: (41-22) 907-0057

Alain Lambert
World Conservation Union (IUCN)
Rue Mauverney 28
CH-1196 Gland
Switzerland
Tel: (41-22) 999-0001
Fax: (41-22) 999-0020
E-mail: all@hq.iucn.ch

World Wildlife Fund
1250 24th Street N.W.
Washington DC 20037
Tel: (1-202) 778-9544
Fax: (1-202) 861-8324
E-mail: barry.spergel@wwfus.org

Funds and Foundations Created Through Debt Conversions

Dr. Terrence W. Thomas, Executive Director
Environment Foundation of Jamaica
25 Haining Road
Kingston 5
Jamaica
Tel: (809) 960-2848
Fax: (809) 960-2850

Eugenio Gonzales, Executive Director
Foundation for a Sustainable Society, Inc.
Unit E., 46 Samar Ave. corner Sct. Albano St.
1103 Quezon City
Philippines
Tel/Fax: (63-2) 928-8671

Donna Z. Gasgonia, Executive Director
Foundation for the Philippine Environment
77 Matahimik St., Teachers Village
1101 Quezon City
Philippines
Tel: (63-2) 927-9403 or 927-2186
Fax: (63-2) 922-3022 or 931-6243
E-mail: fpe@gaia.psdn.org

María del Carmen Rocabado, Acting General Manager
Fondo Nacional Para el Medio Ambiente (FONAMA)
Edificio Mariscal Ballivián, Mezzanine
Calle Mercado No 1328
La Paz
Bolivia
Tel: (591-2) 392-367 or 392-370
Fax: (591-2) 391-774

Chapter 10

Establishing and Operating Microcredit Programs

M. Pilar Ramirez

New Opportunities for Financial Autonomy

For the world's poor, microcredit programs have been called a "development revolution" in terms of poverty alleviation and income generation. As a documentary by the Ecumenical Church Loan Fund points out, "small credit programs are ample evidence that the poor are creditworthy and that they usually do not seek charity but a chance to improve their situation. Most of the poor of the world never get that chance, because they don't have access to credit."

According to Women's World Banking, more than 500 million of the world's economically active people run micro and small enterprises. Yet to finance their businesses, fewer than 10 million of them have access to anything but moneylenders. Nontraditional specialized intermediaries that focus on financing low-income entrepreneurs reach less than 2 percent of this potential market.[1]

Microcredit programs established and operated by private, nonprofit organizations are ingenious ways by which the poor of the world now have access to affordable financial resources. A 1996 survey by the World Bank found that 206 institutions had about US$17 billion in outstanding small loans to more that 13 million individuals and groups as of September 1995.[2]

The programs considered in this chapter are those that aid enterprises of up to 10 employees, although usually fewer; the enterprises include the part-time activities of individuals to raise income, family-oriented businesses, and very small companies that hire workers. Many of these programs also offer their clients technical assistance and training in a variety of skills useful to the income-generating activity. Examples of this include training courses in management and productive techniques, marketing, product design, and improvement of quality. This chapter will address solely the financial side of these programs; the other services just mentioned are usually managed separately.

Starting a Program

Typically, a microcredit program begins as a development solution to problems related to lack of cash. These programs have generally been started by private social development institutions in the absence of private and public formal sources of credit for low-income populations. In many cases, the programs have learned from indigenous credit and savings schemes or from other informal sources of financing that people in poverty have traditionally devised for themselves.[3]

The establishment of a microcredit program is no simple matter. In addition to having some basic knowledge of credit methodologies and procedures, the implementing organization must take care of other issues before initiating a program. Knowledge of the sector that will be receiving the loan is the first priority. The sector's previous experience with credit, if any, must also be taken into account. Understanding the formal financial and legal context, as well as the informal one, is also important.

Of course, there may be sectors of the poor—perhaps the "poorest of the poor"—who will not benefit from credit at all but need other types of support. The impressive results of some microcredit programs coupled with a justified donor impatience for poverty eradication have perhaps led to overenthusiasm on microcredit as a blanket solution. This in turn can distort facts and create false expectations that will be harmful in the long run. Microcredit programs initiated by civil society organizations (CSOs) must be very clear at the outset about the "target group" they expect to work with and if credit is the best way to support that group.

Finally, and most important, inflation in most countries requires these programs to adopt measures that maintain the value of their funds. Many programs—if not most—in the South work in two currencies: the local one and U.S. dollars. In order to maintain the value of the funds, loans can be made in U.S. dollars or in local currency with a value maintenance clause pegged to the dollar. Repayment schedules, principal, and interest are made in U.S. dollars or local currency, adjusted by its depreciation in terms of the dollar.

Many microcredit programs already operate in different parts of the world, and it is tempting to copy whatever has worked elsewhere. This may not always be effective, however, and those organizations that have been ready and willing to experiment and innovate according to their particular social and cultural context are today better positioned in the field.[4]

Enhancing Organizations' Resources

In addition to providing aid to the recipients of funds, microcredit programs have also turned out to be a successful resource enhancement strategy for the CSOs that establish and operate them. In the process of consolidating and expanding microcredit programs, many CSOs have demonstrated not only increased ability to ensure the continuity of the credit services provided, but also effectiveness in resource management and enhancement for their own growth and institutional strength.

As a resource enhancement strategy for the implementing organizations, microcredit programs are similar to earned income in that they engage the market, involving the trade and exchange of goods and services. In this case, credit is the service offered, for which the clients pay by way of interest. As the service rotates through repayments of the loans and the interest, the original pool of funds increases, allowing for new loans and more "earned income" from the interest charged. Successful microcredit programs are those that take advantage of economies of scale in loan disbursement and collection. These gains in efficiency allow for greater resource enhancement up to a certain scale of operations. At some point, institutions need to consider whether becoming larger is worth the increased management burden and risks.

Of course, not all microcredit programs make this transition. In fact, many of these programs (such as village banking) do not evolve beyond a rotating-credit status with a limited and fixed amount of funds. In addition, programs that operate mainly on subsidized funds (grants or soft loans) may find that since these funds are harder to obtain today, there is worry over the continuity of the credit services. So thousands of programs around the world are not able to grow into strong and sustainable operations because of inadequate lending methodologies, inefficient management of loan portfolios, insufficient funds, lack of institutional capacity or credibility, or a greater orientation toward education than toward economics.

For those that do succeed, programs have moved along a continuum from being totally dependent on donor funds to increased levels of self-sustainability (at which point income equals or exceeds expenditures). The evidence of success includes increased amounts of financial resources, growth of equity and investment capacities, expansion of operations, autonomy and independent actions, and an unprecedented capability to influence the making and changing of national and international public and private financial policies.

If microcredit programs are to become a valuable CSO resource enhancement strategy, they must incorporate early in the course of their operations specific measures aimed at precisely that: resource enhancement for full self-sustainability. This means simply adopting an entrepreneurial stance toward the activity. The three basic components of this approach—the strategies discussed in greater detail later in this chapter—are efficiency-oriented credit operations, the capacity to obtain new financial resources, and savings mobilization.

Establishing and operating microcredit programs requires foremost an approach to social development that will be efficiency-oriented at the same time that it preserves the service-oriented mission of the CSO. Since most CSOs are nonprofit, it takes a particular kind of organization and membership to combine these apparently opposite prerequisites. Such are the CSOs that are showing the resource enhancement capacity of microcredit programs—a capacity to increase their outreach, attain financial self-sufficiency, and in some cases also provide nonfinancial services in the areas of education, health, management training, housing development, and so on.

The program that has received the most coverage to date is the Grameen Bank in Bangladesh. With 2.1 million borrowers and US$1.8 billion disbursed in very small loans as of December 1996, it is also by far the biggest microcredit program.[5] Another notable example is the Centro de Fomento a Iniciativas Económicas (known as FIE) in Bolivia, which since it was launched in 1985 has made more than 75,000 micro loans (averaging US$670 each) for the equivalent of US$50 million to more than 17,000 active borrowers.[6]

CENTRO DE FOMENTO A INICIATIVAS ECONÓMICAS, BOLIVIA

Founded in 1985 by five professional Bolivian women as the first nonprofit organization offering microcredit services to the so-called urban informal sector, the Centro de Fomento a Iniciativas Económicas (FIE) was initially supported with small grants, as seed money, from northern donors and from

Oxfam America and Diakonia of Sweden. In 1987, FIE was approved for an Inter-American Development Bank small projects division soft loan for the equivalent of US$500,000, to launch the credit program on a broader scale.

Between 1988 and 1990, institution building was the priority: perfecting FIE's individual lending methodology, acquiring knowledge of the clientele, improving the loan officers' performance, perfecting the software for loan portfolio control and daily performance indicators reports, and planning for sustainability. In 11 years, the organization grew from a staff of eight in La Paz to a working team of 136 and a presence in seven of the nine departments in Bolivia.

FIE has loaned out the equivalent of more than US$50 million to date, with average loans of US$670 each, to more than 17,000 active clients. More than two thirds of its clients belong to the microproduction sector, usually in the area of manufacturing (clothing, furniture, simple machinery, processed foodstuffs, and so on), while only 20 percent is solely dedicated to commercial activities (street vendors). In most other microcredit programs, the ratio is the other way around. Women participate in almost 80 percent of the loans, and 30 percent are loans exclusively for women.

These two efforts offer exciting proof of CSOs' ability to design and implement a mechanism with a concrete and clear twofold result: the development and growth of very small economic activities, providing income and employment for millions of the world's less privileged sectors, and the financial sustainability of the CSO to ensure the expansion and continuity of the service offered. Few development initiatives have shown such a capacity.

Benefits and Limitations of Microcredit Programs

This strategy has the potential of enhancing resources many times over and of ensuring the sustainability and continuity of a CSO. Mobilizing financial resources creates more money, which in turn stimulates the broader economy. Effectively managed microcredit programs have shown this potential. In addition, and perhaps more significantly, the strategy has the possibility of building equity. With more available resources and an equity base, the implementing organization has increased leverage capacity, independence, and autonomy of actions and lobbying power from and within civil society. This is no small achievement for CSOs that are usually initiated

Self-sustainability was a goal from the very beginning. Effective management of the loan portfolio, with improvements in information gathering and in the credit technology and loan collection practices and incentives, showed a financial growth that could help FIE qualify for market rate loans from local commercial banks. And it became clear that increased outreach and sustainability could only be achieved through working with funds from the local commercial market. This required not only an excellent performance by FIE's loan program, but also the ability to fulfill the guarantee requirements of commercial banks.

FIE's management moved to obtain the financial support of international guarantee funds, such as RAFAD and the Union of Swiss Banks, and to negotiate loans from commercial banks in Bolivia. To obtain these loans, FIE's associates mortgaged their personal properties. In addition, FIE was able to convince socially minded individuals and institutions to make long- and short-term savings deposits in the banks willing to lend money to FIE. The banks then agreed to on-lend these funds to FIE.

For CSO-initiated microcredit programs in Bolivia, this was a first. The show of confidence in its low-income clientele and the risk-taking entrepreneurial capacity of the CSO proved successful on an unexpected front: the Ministry of Finance and the Superintendency of Banks, with prodding from donors, for the first time begun accepting microcredit NGOs as part of the broader financial system that public investment policy must take into account.

As the new financial laws in Bolivia allow NGOs to transform themselves into regulated financial institutions, the latest development is the creation of a new financial entity: FIE Private Financial Fund, consisting of FIE, the Fundación Johnson (a family cultural and educational Bolivian foundation), the Swiss International Cooperation Agency, and three private individual investors.

with few start-up funds and with the dedication and commitment of its individual members as its only resources.

All this would not be possible if there were any doubt about the ability of clients to repay the loans. It is an undeniable fact now that lending to the poor makes excellent business sense. Loans given in affordable conditions to the poor show excellent repayment rates, and when economies of scale are exploited in order to make the operations cost-effective, the activity is profitable. The benefits are therefore twofold and reinforcing: as more clients receive more loans and repay them, the pool of funds available for the implementing organization increases, allowing it to give out even more loans. In the process, the CSO is capitalized and strengthens its equity base.

Yet the limitations of the strategy are also many and significant. To begin with, not every CSO has the capacity to establish and operate a microcredit program of the characteristics just described. The CSO needs entrepreneurial vision and wisdom combined with a strong determination to find ways of solving problems of lack of access to credit for the people it has decided to support. It takes a membership and working team with some knowledge of credit operations, cost recovery, and profit, as well as a stubborn conviction that exclusionary rules have to be changed (such as the poor not

SHRI MAHILA SEWA SAHAKARI BANK, INDIA

The Self Employed Women's Association (SEWA) is a trade union formed in 1972 to improve the lives of poor, informal sector women workers. Any self-employed woman in India can become a member of SEWA by paying a membership fee of at least 5 rupees a year. As a membership-based organization, SEWA has spawned numerous self-help initiatives, including a cooperative bank.

The clients of SEWA Bank are all self-employed women. SEWA clients have low incomes, little or no savings, no assets, and no direct access to raw materials. Access to financial services is a major problem for poor self-employed women such as hawkers, vendors, home-based workers, manual laborers, and service providers. Because they do not save, emergencies and obligations often force women to borrow heavily from informal moneylenders. However, they are unlikely to have the experience or self-confidence to obtain credit from a formal financial institution.

At the same time, the institution's regulations and procedures rarely meet the needs of a woman seeking a loan. Therefore poor self-employed women often depend on informal moneylenders, contractors, and wholesalers who charge exorbitant interest rates. This often starts a downward spiral of increased indebtedness, perpetuating poverty.

In response to this constraint, in 1974 some 4,000 SEWA members established a cooperative bank owned by shareholding members, to provide credit to

being able to offer collateral for loans) and that risks must be taken to show that these rules can be changed (through, for example, accepting as collateral what the poor have and value).

As the credit program grows and the leverage capacity for obtaining new sources of funds increases, the need for more accountability and specialization in its operations and management may be seen as a limitation for the CSO. The organization must operate in a manner that is completely professional, highly competitive, and accountable to the public it serves and the state in whose laws and regulations it operates. This definitely will mean a loss of autonomy and freedom of action, and will require a willingness to be externally controlled, overseen, and supervised, which was usually not the case before.

Traditional financial sources for these programs—the international development agencies and bilateral assistance agencies—have begun to change their policies in the direction of microcredit programs that are part of networks of similar CSO programs. They have done this, understandably, in an attempt to reduce their administrative costs. It is less costly to approve, supervise, and monitor a large financial operation (loan or grant) to a multimember organization that distributes and controls the funds than it is to support many individual grants or loans. Lack of access to these international funds is clearly a limitation for many small programs that are not part of a microcredit network, or that choose not to join one.

Another limitation comes as a result of the strategy's success. With increased financial growth, it can be tempting to forget the original founding mission of the CSO and

self-employed women and reduce their dependence on moneylenders. SEWA bank borrowers are required to buy 5 percent of the loan amount in bank shares when receiving a loan and to open a savings account. The women are therefore the bank's shareholders, and they hold annual shareholder meetings. The bank is supervised by the Reserve Bank of India, which determines the interest rates on loans and savings deposits, the proportion of deposits that can be loaned, and the areas of operations.

The members of the bank elect the Board of Directors. The Board consists of 15 members, 10 of whom are trade leaders. All major decisions are made by the board, including sanctioning all loans advanced. The sources of capital for SEWA Bank are savings deposits, share capital, and profits that are plowed back into the institution. SEWA Bank currently has approximately 60,000 depositors and 6,000 borrowers.

Between 1974 and 1977, SEWA Bank concentrated on attracting deposits from self-employed women and served as a guarantor to enable depositors to obtain loans from nationalized banks that are required to lend to the poor. In 1976, SEWA Bank started to extend loans to its depositors from its own funds and gradually withdrew from the credit arrangement with the nationalized banks.

Case study written by Craig Churchill, Microfinance Network.

devote more time, energy, and activity to credit operations that enhance resources quicker and in greater quantities. This may mean leaving original clients and working with a more profitable clientele or type of service (that is, middle-class clients or consumer loans), focusing solely on the organization's benefit and self-interests.

If microcredit programs are to reach their full potential as a resource enhancement strategy for CSOs, they must become part of the broader financial system; they must go "from creating good projects to creating healthy financial institutions for the poor."[7] This means a change of focus from "small is beautiful" programs to big and continuously growing programs that address the needs of low-income entrepreneurs and that are financially self-sustaining. This large-scale lending, which is crucial for self-sustainability, cannot be accomplished through subsidies from grants. The organization must therefore become a true resource enhancer and build accordingly—build on existing resources with new ones from the national and international financial system, and incorporate savings as an indispensable component.

Developing along these lines would entail a dramatic transformation for the CSO implementing the microcredit program, but one that many consider necessary and right. The transformation is from being a small nonprofit operation catering to a limited "target population" to being a financial intermediary operating within the legal framework that governs financial institutions in each country. This raises issues of regulation and supervision that many CSOs have never had to deal with. It also requires some internal "soul searching" to see if the organization in fact can transform itself without renouncing the original mission and vision of service to others. Deciding whether to go ahead with such a transformation will be a most difficult decision for most organizations, but one filled with many new and exciting challenges.

Key Issues Under Debate

Several main issues regarding microcredit programs are currently being debated, sometimes at the urging of practitioners and other times due to concerns of the international agencies supporting the programs. These debates help focus and clarify the field for all parties. The five issues discussed in this section are incorporating savings into microcredit programs, interest rates to be charged, group versus individual lending, the enabling environment and legal context, and nonprofit organization versus financial institution.

Savings

The debate about savings centers on the cost-effectiveness of incorporating such a component into microcredit programs as a source of new funds for future loans. Some participants advocate offering a savings facility along with the credit service, for the sake of the program's sustainability; others caution against doing this, pointing out the risks, the costs involved, and the know-how needed to do it well.

The discussion in this case is not about the many small programs that use and require savings deposits as a condition to granting loans, as collateral building for loans, or as another type of requirement in that direction, as these do not require public supervision. The savings component under debate is one that qualifies as financial intermediation of public funds, in which protection of depositors is a major concern of regulatory authorities.

Interest Rates

For years the debate centered on the ethics of programs charging interest rates that covered their costs—rates that are usually higher than those charged by formal, commercial financial institutions. People often ask whether "the poor" should instead be serviced through subsidized (lower) interest rates, or pay no interest at all. But the negative experiences of largely subsidized rural credit programs and of credit programs run by nongovernmental organizations (NGOs) that were also subsidized, combined with the success in so-called expensive programs, have made it clear to practitioners and funders alike that what the poor really need is access to credit and continuity of credit services.

In addition, as Jorge Muñoz shows, other loan attributes—such as duration, size, speed of delivery of funds, contingency clauses, repayment flexibility, and collateral substitution—are also important to this clientele. Therefore, the cost (interest rate) of obtaining the loan may be a secondary consideration for these borrowers. Access and continuity depend on program growth and sustainability, and this in turn depends, for the most part, on income gained from interest rates. In other words, "maximizing benefit to poor people."[8]

This does not mean, of course, that interest rates can be as high as the programs want them to be or consider necessary, or can make up for any inefficiencies. Microcredit programs must do what is necessary to lower operating and financial costs, be able to charge the lowest possible interest rates, and still ensure the program's sustainability. In addition to not burdening the clientele with unnecessarily high interest rates, offering a lower rate may be the only competitive edge some microcredit programs have today.

Group or Individual Lending?

For most practitioners, group or individual lending is not an issue because the program's credit delivery procedures are structured one way or the other for reasons the programs considered valid and appropriate from the start. In fact, some programs would not have been possible at all without group lending. Such is the case of the Grameen Bank in Bangladesh.

"Group lending" is a way to circumvent the problem of poor people's lack of collateral. Borrowers are typically asked to form small groups (usually with three to five members, although sometimes more) to obtain a certain sum of money as a loan, which is then distributed among the group members. Each person then acts as guarantor of other members of the group. If any one person fails to pay his or her part of the loan, the entire group must cover for that person. The members of the group are in this manner collectively liable for each member's loan, and the group's access to new loans is conditioned on full and prompt repayment.

Different forms of group lending have different requirements, such as that the members of a group have to be unrelated by family ties, or that they have to have their businesses in the same area. Many programs have preset amounts of loans for groups to begin with, along with upper ceilings of loan amounts. A group might, for example, be given a first loan of the equivalent of US$100, and when that is repaid, the group then qualifies for a second loan of US$150, and so on.

"Individual lending" is simply lending to the person who requests the loan, who is expected to offer the guarantees that the program requires. It is individual-based in that it is tailored to the borrower's needs and particular economic activity, seeing each case separately and acquiring information about the borrower through direct inspection, visits, and interviews. Individual lending assumes that the costs and risks entailed in lending to this clientele are not a given but a function of the "credit technology" used.[9] In addition, programs may or may not have preset amounts for beginning a lender-client relationship. Some begin with small amounts and short terms for the loans to build a credit history of their clients. In others, the needs of the client are reviewed and an amount is decided on the basis of the cash flow of the economic activity the person wants the loan for.

At first glance, group lending has several advantages. Gathering information on clients is costly; it requires analyzing the client, the business, any previous performance as a creditor, and so on. Relying on the support, knowledge, and guarantee of two or three or more individuals from a group makes this information gathering less necessary. In addition, other forms of collateral become unnecessary, and loans can be processed relatively quickly. The costs of processing and managing these loans is also less than in individual lending because each group is registered as one client, and responsibility for collecting each one of these loans rests with the group, not the lender. In effect, the transaction costs of evaluation, monitoring, supervision, and

KENYA WOMEN FINANCE TRUST

Established in 1981 as an affiliate of Women's World Banking, the Kenya Women Finance Trust (KWFT) aims to strengthen women's participation in the economic mainstream. It focuses on clients who have little access to formal lending institutions and seeks to strengthen their position by lending to women owners of microenterprises. As of March 1996, KWFT had successfully disbursed close to the equivalent of US$1 million in 4,068 individual small loans that averaged US$225 per loan.

Although KWFT started in the early 1980s with several donors providing grants, that support dwindled by the end of the decade due to poor performance. By 1990, general mismanagement had resulted in a relatively high number of nonperforming loans. Operations had largely ceased, and donor confidence was badly eroded.

KWFT subsequently restructured, with a new board of directors of professional women, and introduced a group-based credit methodology similar to that used by the Grameen Bank in Bangladesh. The *Uaminifu* Scheme adopted in 1993 seeks to wholesale a unit loan to existing groups, which then retail loans to their members. This eliminates some of the expenses of group formation and loan administration, strengthens the groups, and improves KWFT's outreach. In addition, other changes have been introduced to ease administration and increase efficiency; these are related to group size, loan repayment period, frequency of meetings, and the loan review process.

Performance has greatly improved and KWFT has been able to tap support from new sources of funding such as the Ford Foundation, the International Fund for Agricultural Development, the Belgian Survival Fund, and Barclay's Bank of

enforcement are shifted from the lender to the borrower. It is, therefore, a quicker and cheaper way for lenders to reach more borrowers.

Programs such as those that operate on the village banking methodology or the Grameen Bank model are reaching groups, especially of very poor women, for whom the collective provides many social as well as economic benefits. This may be the only way for financial resources to reach these women and at the same time support and strengthen their natural organizations (which in some cases are CSOs in themselves), allowing them to learn how to engage with the formal financial world.

On the other hand, some theoreticians and practitioners have consistently defended individual lending over group lending for several reasons. First, group lending assumes a homogeneity of needs, wishes, priorities, consumer habits, and practices of borrowers. This stance toward the clientele may not foster individual self-respect. The preset amounts and scaling up of loan amounts assumes that everyone in the group has identical financial needs for their economic activities.

Second, the clients of microcredit programs already face many more requirements and limitations to opportunities than clients with higher incomes. Having to join with

Kenya. This support from grants and subsidized loans allowed the loan portfolio to expand, which in turn increased income from interest. Improved earnings are in line with KWFT's drive for sustainability.

KWFT has developed a reputation among Kenyan women, especially rural women, as a reliable and quick source of credit. Since lending is KWFT's core business, the strategy is to keep administrative costs down and link the growth in lending to the availability of funds. Sustainability is closely related to lending capacity and the level of repayment rates. Small loans are expensive to administer, and KWFT knows it can only survive as an institution by charging competitive interest rates, lending to many women, and maintaining a high repayment rate.

As part of its capacity-building strategy, KWFT realizes that it needs to develop capital funds to cover operational costs and fund innovations and to leverage its activities with other institutions. An example of this is a collaborative arrangement with Barclay's Bank of Kenya, where KWFT facilitates larger loans to individual women. These loans are partially guaranteed by the Trust and the bank; the client provides collateral to guarantee the balance.

KWFT tries to be innovative, making modifications based on an analysis of feedback from clients and others. It is committed to the ongoing training of personnel and to improvements in its management information system. To a large extent, the remuneration and training policies will determine the organization's ability to sustain a program of financial services delivery. Retaining qualified staff entails matching the remuneration policies of competitors. This is only possible because KWFT knows that it must be highly efficient in its lending operations.

Based on an excerpt from Jennifer Riria-Ouko, Managing Director, KWFT, "Kenya Women Finance Trust: Case Study of a Microfinance Scheme."

other individuals who will exert yet another form of social control ("peer pressure") may be experienced as additional burden.

Third, group lenders may face two types of constraints. They have no individual loan product to offer their best clients, who may demand larger individual loans to avoid the transaction costs and risks of group lending. And other members of a borrowing group may not want to be jointly liable for a larger-than-average loan required by one of the group's members, even if the lender is willing to grant it. So group lenders may lose their best customers to individual lending programs, which can better satisfy their loan demands.[10]

A fourth concern is that the small loans this clientele usually requires encourage programs to seek alternative collateral as guarantee, to accept what the client values and has to offer as guarantee (that is, something that would be difficult for the borrower to replace if it were seized), and then to see if these forms are backed by lending laws. For a loan of the equivalent of US$500, a cosignatory or a personal guarantee from a third party may be enough and accepted by the laws of the country. In Bolivia, for instance, telephone lines until recently were valued commodities; a telephone line worth the equivalent of US$1,500 would be legally offered as collateral, and the telephone company collaborated in these transactions. Programs must make the effort to recognize new forms of collateral that still satisfy each country's legal requirements.

Fifth, individual lending that requires the program to handle all the information gathering on the client and the business through direct inspection is undoubtedly costly at the beginning. But with time, the program and the staff handling loans acquire valuable information, know-how, experience, and contact with the clientele—all of which is missing in group lending. This important information in the long term can offset the costs of obtaining it. The program can convert this experience and knowledge in the screening process into cost savings, introducing this knowledge into procedures that become routine, leaving the program better prepared to innovate and react flexibly to clients' particular needs.

The Enabling Environment and Legal Context

Democratic liberties for civil society participation in activities that further the common good is, of course, the first requirement for any CSO-initiated microcredit program, and is a matter of concern in a region such as Latin America that is finally consolidating its democracies and defining the role of citizen action.

The economic activities supported by microcredit programs depend foremost on macroeconomic stability and controlled inflation. (ACCION International, for example, did not begin its operations in Bolivia until the hyperinflation period was well under control.) In addition, openness on the part of the government to the nonprofit sector entering the financial arena with services for low-income groups is important. Many worthwhile programs have suffered setbacks because of a lack of understanding from government offices that deal with NGO activity, in terms of supporting the so-called informal sector, landless farmers, poor women, and similar groups. Lack of information in governments on the economic contribution of these sectors to income and employment generation has been a particularly difficult obstacle. Finally, "nonprofit" is still identified with charity in some circles that have decisive effects on access to operating permits, licensing, government funds, and so on.

With these problems in mind, the changes that have occurred in the past 10 years within governments, donor agencies, the private banking sector, and the like have nonetheless been encouraging. The story is one of very slow approaches, trying to reconcile NGO microcredit activity and the financial world. The issues that have been tackled have contributed to changed points of view in what is considered the "real money" world, which is proving to lead to exciting projections.

Foremost are changes in the legal environment, which is important for the existence of programs and for their ability to scale up operations, become self-sufficient, or transform themselves for financial intermediation. (CSOs must be authorized to lend money and charge interest before starting a microcredit program; this may not be possible under some nonprofit legislation.) As unregulated financial entities, microcredit institutions were free to adapt their operating methods to service their target market. This produced robust specialized financial institutions, creative delivery methods, and the extension of the financial services market. Bank regulators are now being asked to develop coherent guidelines that will further the growth of the microfinance sector while protecting the interest of small savers and supporting the integrity of the financial sector as a whole.

For these institutions to succeed, they must operate in regulatory environments that allow them to incorporate two critical elements: positive interest rates and savings facilities.

Interest rate deregulation is a matter of priority, so programs can charge full-cost interest rates, both from the government's financial policy side and that of the donors. The lending policy of a successful microcredit institution is based on the use of positive interest rates on the understanding that subsidies are unnecessary to the entrepreneur and damaging to the institution's sustainability. Interest charges are calculated to cover the full cost of lending operations, including a surplus for financing further loans. Because such institutions effectively extend the lending market, it must also be understood that they charge significantly higher interest rates than the "traditional" banking sector. This is a function of economies of scale in loan size and the high transaction costs of administering microloans. If countries have usury laws that apply to microfinance institutions, they will undermine this important segment of the financial market.

While the vast majority of microcredit programs are not legally permitted to accept deposits, a small number are authorized to do so and others may have experimented in this direction. In low-income communities, there is an enormous demand for voluntary savings services with real interest rates. Many programs want to be able to provide this important service, not only to assist their clients but also as a resource enhancement strategy, in order to establish a stable source of capital for lending activities. The regulatory environment should encourage a broader range of financial services for this low-income clientele. Of course, any effort to allow microcredit institutions to mobilize savings must ensure that the deposits of low-income persons, who certainly cannot afford to lose their life savings, are sufficiently protected.

This opens up another issue—that of risk—about which regulators are particularly apprehensive. Microcredit institutions have many risk features in common with other financial institutions. Yet many of the regulatory features that have been adopted to address the risks of standard commercial financial institutions simply do not apply to those dealing with microfinance. Nevertheless, microfinance institutions have their own risk profile, and leading institutions in the field have demonstrated that these risks can be managed effectively over many years. The design of appropriate regulation for these institutions is based on an understanding of these risks and effective measures to mitigate them. Donors are aware of this, and in some cases technical assistance is being provided to help regulatory authorities move in this direction.

Financial legislation must also contemplate facilitating the transformation and transition from a nonprofit microcredit program to a financial institution, and these regulations must reflect government policies toward agricultural and industrial development of microproduction, income and employment generation, gender policies, and poverty eradication. In nearly all cases the strongest motivating factor to shifting services from an NGO to a regulated financial intermediary is the organization's desire to ensure its long-term financial and institutional viability by substantially increasing access to borrowed funds, either by accepting deposits, by entering the interbank market, or by opening

TSPI DEVELOPMENT CORPORATION, PHILIPPINES

Tulay Sa Pag-unlad, Inc. (TSPI) was founded in 1981 by a group of Christian businessmen who were concerned about worsening poverty in the Philippines. In 16 years of operations, TSPI has grown from a quiet undertaking to an industry leader—from a fledgling NGO to a US$4-million breakthrough, and from a seven-person office to a 150-person organization.

With technical support from Opportunity International, a U.S.-based private organization, TSPI spent its first year identifying board members, developing a shared vision, and establishing initial operating systems. It began lending operations in February 1982 with a focus on a direct credit program geared toward income generation and job creation among small entrepreneurs in Metro Manila. By 1985, TSPI started to replicate the success of its pilot program by setting up six NGO partners in other urban areas around the country, and providing them with wholesale loan funds. In 1991, the organization diversified its programs and broadened its target market to include women microentrepreneurs, mass transportation workers, and market vendors.

TSPI's most successful direct lending product is the Sakbayan loan to self-formed groups of six motorized tricycle drivers to buy new vehicles. In Manila, tricycle taxis are one of the primary means of public transport. Taxi drivers can

access to credit lines. While access to additional funding sources can be a powerful incentive, other considerations can arise.

To facilitate the creation of regulated microfinance institutions and to accommodate the unique characteristics of these programs, several jurisdictions have established specialized categories for microfinance. These create a regulatory framework for such institutions that limits their functions compared with those of a commercial bank, but that generates appropriate standards for these organizations to enter the formal financial system. Such categories for specialized microfinance institutions are only necessary in two situations. First, if the institution mobilizes savings from the public, then the bank superintendent has a responsibility to ensure that deposits are properly managed. Second, if the institution has access to public funds, there is a need to supervise the use of public resources.

Nonprofit Organization or Financial Institution?

Expansion of lending activities in order to reach more and more clients is the goal of microcredit programs that want to have an impact on poverty eradication and improvement of the living conditions of the low-income majorities with whom they work. As programs begin to grow in outreach capacity, it becomes evident that continued expansion will only be possible with increased access to funds. Nonprofit programs have access to donor funds on a limited basis. After a certain level of growth, donors are reluctant to continue supporting these programs through grants or even low-cost loans. There are other priorities to attend to, and other worthwhile programs to support.

earn a good living if they own their own vehicle. Using the group and the vehicles as collateral, TSPI's Sakbayan loans enable taxi drivers to buy their own vehicle and go into business for themselves.

TSPI has also been able to increase its impact significantly through its intermediary lending operations. By supporting credit programs, local associations, and cooperatives, TSPI has expanded its reach to areas where it does not have a direct presence. Partnerships have been forged with more than 30 institutions, with a combined outreach of more than 30,000 borrowers. These intermediary institutions have received no-lending or institution-building funds from TSPI for their credit operations.

In 15 years, TSPI has disbursed US$11.3 million to more than 12,000 small and microentrepreneurs through its direct lending programs. By the end of November 1996, TSPI's direct lending portfolio had nearly 7,000 active clients (76 percent women) and US$3.5 million. The repayment rate for all programs is 97 percent. Renamed TSPI Development Corporation in 1995, the organization has achieved financial sustainability and recently launched a Bank Project to create a regulated financial institution that is dedicated to serving low-income communities.

Case study prepared by Craig Churchill, Microfinance Network.

Full financial intermediation—being able to deliver both credit and savings—seems to be the way to fulfill the goals of expansion and impact on any significant scale, and many of these CSO programs are working toward this. This has stirred the NGO development community, especially in the South, because it touches directly on issues that have long concerned them: growth and autonomy, donor dependency, neoliberal economic policies, structural adjustment policies, alternative development, the for-profit financial sector, and so on. At the same time, few can ignore the many new advantages and challenges that come with full financial intermediation. Besides the obvious—new sources of funds (public funds channeled only through financial institutions and through savings mobilization)—the transformation allows the institution to venture into many new financial products that its clientele has never had access to (such as savings, money transfers, insurance, retirement plans, smart cards, and social security systems).

As noted earlier, becoming a financial institution for microcredit operations means transforming the nonprofit essence into a profit-making entity that is still dedicated to a mission of service and common good. Many in the field feel this is an impossible proposition and an unnecessary one. They call on governments and donors alike to recognize the merits of the current microcredit programs because of what they are (essentially nonprofit), and to allow them to intermediate between savers and borrowers without having to change their essence. In addition, it poses serious questions on the issue of growth and the direction of that growth for the CSOs. Must credit NGOs necessarily grow to fulfill their missions?

ALEXANDRIA BUSINESS ASSOCIATION, EGYPT

The Alexandria Business Association (ABA) began its activities in 1983 as a committee of the Alexandria Chamber of Commerce. Its initial objectives were to provide support for the private sector, promote the interests of businessmen, and provide networking opportunities. The committee was instrumental in giving voice to the private sector by representing the interests of local businesses to the government.

This concept soon developed beyond advocacy to encompass community service. Members began contributing time, money, and efforts toward constructing and upgrading hospitals, schools, and various social institution in poor areas of the city. These new activities necessitated the formation of an independent entity. The Alexandria Businessmen's Association was founded and registered in March 1988 as a private nonprofit NGO with a 15-member managing board elected by the 300 members. (In 1993, the name was changed to Alexandria Business Association.)

USAID was impressed with the focus and direction of ABA, and entered into a formal relationship with the organization in April 1989 to implement the Small and Micro Enterprise Project in metropolitan Alexandria. USAID provided financial and technical services to ABA, which in turn provided financial services to businesses in Alexandria that did not have access to credit from the formal banking system. The credit program was initiated in January 1990, and achieved operational self-sufficiency by January 1992—two years earlier than expected. It has continued

One significant reason behind this position is the fear that the transformation may gradually mean forsaking the original mission. Legislation for the transformation requires entering a universe of "shareholders," "percentage of shares," and "renewed capital contributions"—a process that necessarily influences the internal balance of power and decisionmaking. The partners that a CSO picks for the transformation must be selected carefully, seeking individuals or organizations that share a vision of society and a mission for the new institution. This brings with it important issues such as ownership and good governance—ensuring the rule of law, improving efficiency and accountability, and developing effective and transparent administrative structures. In addition, the new institution must now face new costs such as those incurred in order to comply with banking laws, reporting requirements, personnel with new qualifications, and so on. These are not insignificant matters for organizations that have been created in the nonprofit sector.

Efficiency-Oriented Credit Operations

No matter how socially driven CSO-initiated microcredit programs are, they must be established and operated as if they are commercial enterprises. Even though the CSO will necessarily be not for profit, its guiding principles must be of cost recovery, capitalization, and full pricing—in other words, efficiency-oriented quality financial services to ensure full self-sustainability and to build an equity base. As Robert Schmidt and

to cover all its costs, as well as to expand, since early 1992. ABA is now generating profits that it reinvests as retained earnings.

ABA was an ideal organization to initiate the microcredit program because it combined business know-how with an institutional commitment to small and micro enterprises. ABA has tailored its lending methodology to meet credit needs of these entrepreneurs. It offers small loans with few prerequisites, flexible loan repayment conditions, and hands-on technical assistance. ABA has eight branches in Alexandria, and in 1996 expanded its activities to provide credit in another region of the country. This is a major strategic step to develop decentralized operations, and eventually to become a national organization. ABA also provides training services to microcredit programs in Egypt and the Middle East.

In seven years, ABA has issued more than 60,000 loans valued at US$50 million to more than 25,000 borrowers, with a delinquency rate below 1 percent. To expand its focus and development impact, ABA is also innovating to extend credit to urban-based female microentrepreneurs in Alexandria.

ABA believes that the key to success in microfinance is networking with other communities and organizations that are devoted to implementing healthy microcredit programs. It also relies heavily on performance-based staff incentives to reward both loan quality and outreach.

Case study prepared by Craig Churchill, Microfinance Network.

Claus-Peter Zeitinger put it, "a credit technology can be called 'efficient' if it makes it possible to reach the target group better and do so at a lower cost to the lending institution than would be possible with other credit technologies."[11] In the long term, this means that increased sustainability leads to a broader outreach, thereby fulfilling the CSO's mission better.

Different types of microenterprise clients have different characteristics and demands.[12] A microcredit program that is successful must be able to service these differences in ways that are tailored to the clientele, such as client-appropriate lending, understood by quick, simple, and convenient access to small loans, often short-term, that are renewed or increased based on repayment record; the use of collateral substitutes or alternative forms of collateral; an emphasis on character-based lending for smaller loans; and simple cashflow and project appraisal for larger and longer-term loans. It also means gender-responsive loan collection techniques and incentives to pay that may include flexible office hours and collection schedules, repayment amounts tailored to clients' needs and cash-flow patterns, incentives through increased credit eligibility and ease of loan processing, and so on.

Microenterprise clients usually require very small loans and processing in a very short time, which raises the costs of the programs. The programs must therefore be able to manage small transactions efficiently, with high productivity, as measured by variables such as loans per loan officer and operating costs as a percentage of average annual portfolio.

KENYA RURAL ENTERPRISE PROGRAM

The Kenya Rural Enterprise Program (K-Rep) is a private microfinance institution registered as an NGO. Its mission is to facilitate poverty alleviation by developing systems and institutions that will enable poor people to organize their lives financially. K-Rep's activities include microfinancial services, research and evaluation, information dissemination, and consulting services. K-Rep has one of the most extensive resource centers for microfinance in Africa.

Recently, K-Rep has established a commercial bank that will assume its microfinance operations. This will be owned by K-Rep, the International Finance Corporation, Shorebank Corporation, Triodos Bank, and possibly the African Development Bank. The decision to create a bank was based on the realization that NGOs lack the capacity to serve as effective financial intermediaries. In part this is because the corporate image of NGOs elicits skepticism in the minds of the community, clients, the government, and particularly other institutions in the financial markets.

Second, NGOs have limited legal capacity to explore other financial instruments and products such as savings mobilization. K-Rep commissioned a study in 1994 to determine the best institutional form to support its continued expansion. The study looked at different types of institutions, such as credit unions, nonbank financial institutions, and commercial banks under the banking act. It recommended the commercial bank as the best form, given its capacity to provide a wide range of financial services.

The government's bank supervision division had limited exposure to microfinance and no experience with an NGO owning a bank. And the banking indus-

Efficiency means keeping an eye on the quality of the portfolio, and maintaining arrears low enough that late payments and defaults do not threaten the ongoing viability of the institution. Successful microcredit programs show rates of arrears as low as 3–4 percent.

Microentrepreneurs need access to financial services that are sufficient and timely, and that will be there when they need them. These programs recognize that poor entrepreneurs are able and willing to pay what it costs an efficient lender to provide sustainable financial services. This means having appropriate pricing policies, and offering loans at rates that are able to cover the full costs of efficient lending on a sustainable basis (after a reasonable start-up period). Interest charges should be set to cover the costs of capital (at the opportunity cost, including inflation), administration, loan losses, and a minimum return on equity.

Programs must aim for steadily reducing dependence on subsidies. Operational efficiency—defined as covering all administrative costs and loan losses with the revenues obtained from the clients—is usually achieved first. Financial self-sufficiency—defined as covering all administrative costs, loan losses, and financial costs at nonsubsidized rates from client revenues—usually takes longer. International experience shows that programs can achieve both during a period of 10 years.

try in Kenya had been severely hit by a significant number of bank collapses, which made the bank supervisor even more wary of new ideas. So K-Rep worked with highly placed and respected individuals to secure the attention of decisionmakers, and to garner political and media support for the idea of establishing a bank. Once this was accomplished, it embarked on an education process for the bank supervisors, providing them with information about successful regulated microfinance institutions elsewhere in the world.

Finally, K-Rep organized an exposure visit for the Deputy Governor and the Director of Bank Supervision of the Central Bank of Kenya to see BancoSol in Bolivia. This visit was instrumental in shaping their understanding of the vast potential, as well as the inherent risks, of microfinance.

In discussing the K-Rep bank with the bank supervision division, some of the key issues raised were ownership (with K-Rep allowed to be a shareholder of the bank as long as it did not hold more than 25 percent of the shares), governance (with K-Rep required to have at least three bankers on its management team), security, lending methodology, and the overall relationship between the NGO and the bank.

During the course of these negotiations, the bank supervisor agreed to consider special legislation for microfinance institutions to create a new regulatory category. K-Rep intends to become a full commercial bank, in part because it wants to challenge the thinking of the financial sector regarding the acceptance of low-income communities as a legitimate market. K-Rep's efforts appear to be opening the door for other microfinance institutions in Kenya.

Case study prepared by Craig Churchill, Microfinance Network.

Capacity to Obtain New Financial Resources

In terms of process, having the capacity to obtain access to new financial resources requires at least two phases: the start-up or institution building, and then consolidation and expansion of activities toward full self-sufficiency.

For the institution-building phase, CSO-initiated microcredit programs will require a significant amount of nonrefundable funds or grants. The financial resources obtained in this condition become the organization's equity base and will allow it to initiate its activities. These funds, usually obtained from donor agencies such as the the the Inter-American Development Bank and U.S. Agency for International Development (USAID), substitute for the investment contributions of shareholders placed in any enterprise. What the CSO membership can usually afford to contribute as "assets" is time, professional expertise and experience, and a vision of development. The funds therefore allow the CSO to experiment with its credit methodology—to build on the lessons learned, and on its errors—in order to design the efficiency-oriented credit operations the microcredit program requires.

How long the program operates on donated funds is not really a matter of choice as a result of the strategic plan the CSO adopts if it aims to become fully self-sufficient and expand its outreach capacity. Nonrefundable funds are scarce and usually available for small credit operations that are just beginning. The trend toward sustainability argues for working with subsidized funds only until the program is able to show an equity base that allows it to reach a break-even point, as evidenced by its financial statements. In this phase, therefore, it is important to recognize that a significant portion of the program's operating costs must be subsidized because operation revenues will be insufficient to cover costs. As the program increases its operations and as revenues from the interest paid also increase, the subsidized components decrease.

Once the break-even point is reached, in order to ensure full self-sufficiency and expand the impact through the volume of its operations, a second phase in the process begins—obtaining access to new financial resources. This will require opening up to new and different sources of funds, with the difference that the majority of these funds will now be "refundable" and will entail financial costs. This means borrowing money, usually at market rate conditions, from either local commercial banks or specialized agencies within international cooperation institutions or individual investors.

To be able to do this, the microcredit program will usually be expected to show the technical and financial capacity to borrow, as well as a level of sustainability that qualifies it for these loans. Requirements vary, of course, but in general this also means convincing the lending institutions that the organization is solvent enough or can present sufficient guarantees to obtain the loans. It also means having the legal capacity to do so. In most countries, international cooperation funds that go through central banks must be disbursed to the final clients through intermediary financial institutions. Some countries have legalized NGOs to do this in order to qualify for these funds. World Bank funds in Bolivia, for example, can be used by private financial funds, a provision of the banking law that allows microcredit NGOs to transform themselves into intermediate financial institutions.

Rapid expansion and growth have been possible for microcredit programs that have been strongly supported by powerful partners or sponsors. These sponsors have been country-specific international cooperation agencies, national private enterprises, governments, or private foundations—sponsors that have selected certain programs to support and lobby for, buffering any problem or obstacle that may arise. For programs operated by local NGOs, grassroots organizations, or community self-cooperative groups without a powerful sponsor, however, the road to growth, expansion, and sustainability has been quite different. Their stories are seldom heard precisely because they lack external support accompanied by public relations activity.

The difficulties have inspired new initiatives, and some CSOs have been started with the express purpose of supporting microcredit programs to help them qualify for local or international funds. One example of this is the RAFAD Foundation in Switzerland, created to make access to bank credit easier for southern development CSOs by introducing a mechanism of guarantees to southern banks on behalf of these organizations. As an international guarantee fund, RAFAD covers in part or totally the risks taken by local banks when guaranteeing loans for microcredit programs. Organizations seeking to leverage new financial resources from commercial banks are being effectively supported by RAFAD. Another approach being used is convincing lending institutions to accept the microcredit program's loan portfolio (or parts of it) as guarantee, since in most cases this is the only "asset" the CSO really has. Lending institutions such as the Ecumenical Development Cooperative Society in the Netherlands (founded as a development bank by the World Council of Churches in 1977) are beginning to adopt this approach.

International cooperation agencies that have been following the results of microcredit programs have been pointing out that grants for equity are of strategic importance in enabling organizations to build a capital base for increased outreach and sustainability. These grants for equity, or capitalization, can be used to generate investment income, build the loan portfolio, and leverage funds from local banks. They also let institutions mix the costs of grant funds with those of commercial sources during the period it takes to build efficient operations and reach efficiencies of scale. Organizations that are making these equity grants available are notably USAID, the Swiss Agency for Development and Cooperation, and Belgium Cooperation.

Because the strategy has shown cost-effective development results in terms of poverty alleviation and income and employment generation, governments are now adopting policies and initiating programs to support CSO microcredit programs. Obtaining access to government resources is therefore a natural part of this strategy.

Savings Mobilization

Microcredit programs throughout the developing world have been mobilizing savings from their borrowers in various ways and for different purposes: as part of the credit requirements, as forms of loan guarantees, for education/human development, to encourage capitalization of the microenterprises, and so on. The interest here in terms of enhancing resources for civil society is in the ability of these programs to mobilize savings as a source of capital for the credit fund. In this sense, having access to savings is viewed as a financial resource enhancer through which the program can expand its lending capacity.

As noted earlier, the CSO interested in this substrategy must be aware of the legal framework and any regulations on savings intermediation. These are usually very specific as to the type of organization that can seek out savings from the public: only credible institutions that are financially sound and have the legal authorization to intermediate these funds.

Many practitioners and development experts advocate incorporating a savings component in microcredit programs. They have seen that the clientele these programs service, especially people living in rural areas, have many more demands related to money than just credit. Some of these needs include having safe places to keep their money, easy access to these money deposits, safe cash transfers when buying or selling or when sending money to relatives in urban areas, and a safeguard against severe economic vulnerability. In most countries where microcredit programs operate in rural areas, there are no formal, commercial institutions offering such services. And even when commercial banks are found in rural areas, low-income sectors are not part of their regular clientele who can qualify for the services they offer. A savings facility in a microcredit organization they are already familiar with and that presumably they trust seems to be a natural next step in the mission of these programs.

BANCO SOLIDARIO, BOLIVIA

In 1987, PRODEM was created as a joint venture between prominent members of the Bolivian business community, who provided seed capital and leadership, and ACCION International, a U.S.-based NGO that provided the technology and methodology. This included providing small short-term loans for working capital to solidarity groups of four or five entrepreneurs.

With initial funding from USAID, the Calmeadow Foundation, and the Bolivian private sector, PRODEM began lending in 1988. Its early success opened the doors to new funders and larger grants. By the end of 1991, PRODEM was financially self-sufficient. It had 11 branches, 116 employees, and a loan portfolio in excess of US$4 million, yet it had not made a dent in the demand for financial services from the informal sector. As an NGO, PRODEM was unable to gain access to sufficient financial resources to keep pace with the demand, and was restricted from providing additional services to its clients, most notably savings.

In response to these limitations, the directors of PRODEM decided to create a commercial bank, with PRODEM as the largest shareholder. PRODEM could then focus its attention on developing financial products and delivery systems for

At the same time, others caution CSOs about considering this option. Becoming a savings collector, even when this is legally possible and economically feasible, changes the nature of the microcredit program in a way that is obvious. But its risks and costs may not be that apparent. Whereas before the clientele stood at the receiving side of the relationship, as depositors they are in a better position to demand of the program certain services and conditions. Issues of trust and credibility also become reversed. The clients must now be the ones to trust and choose the savings program over others in more formal or "credible" financial institutions. They need to know whether their money will be safe, whether they will be paid the highest interest rate possible, whether they will have access to their money when they need it, and so on. For the CSO, the question is whether incorporating savings does, in fact, enhance the program's income.

It will be important to consider also the type of savings the program will seek. Will it be the credit program's clients who are targeted to trust the program with their savings, which may be many in number but usually small in amount and for very short-term periods? Or will the program seek out wealthier clients (or institutions) for fewer but larger and longer-term deposits? These are serious issues to consider when thinking about mobilizing savings. Uninformed decisions may put a credit program's viability at risk, no matter how successful it is.

As Schmidt and Zeitinger point out, a savings program can be considered "successful" if success is merely measured in terms of the number of savings accounts and the volume of voluntary savings obtained from small savers; this tends to be what is reported in the literature.[13] When the cost of running these savings operations is considered, the activity may not be that successful. On the other hand, aiming for a few

rural areas. So Banco Solidario, or BancoSol, was established in 1992 as the first private commercial bank in the world solely dedicated to the microenterprise sector. Today, BancoSol has more than 70,000 customers, representing 40 percent of the banking costumers in Bolivia—an impressive outreach for a bank that has been in existence for only five years.

PRODEM now owns slightly more than 30 percent of BancoSol. Other shareholders include Profund, the Inter-American Investment Corporation, and local Bolivian investors. BancoSol introduced a voluntary savings service in all its branch offices in mid-1994. Approximately 25 percent of BancoSol's loan portfolio is funded by savings mobilization.

Both BancoSol and PRODEM rely on market pricing. The bank has an excellent loan repayment. Without BancoSol, Bolivian microentrepreneurs would depend on moneylenders who charge exorbitant interest rates.

BancoSol can be described as both a development organization and a profit-seeking commercial bank; it aims to succeed by combining both these goals. Profit levels have fluctuated since 1992 from a low of 5 percent to a high of 18 percent return on equity.

Case study written by Craig Churchill, Microfinance Network

big savers may be less expensive, but it too has its risks. If the funds are easily withdrawn, the institution could run into serious liquidity problems for both its credit and its savings programs. Although savings are considered the sustaining half of local finance, credit and savings are not two sides of the same coin. Each requires its own methodology, financial technology, and information system.

Bank Rayat of Indonesia's (BRI) unit bank savings program, designed after extensive fieldwork and research of local financial markets and the views of the clients of those markets, has pointed the way for many CSO-initiated microcredit programs that look to incorporate a savings component. Four main principles guide BRI:

- liquidity, or the possibility of unlimited number of withdrawals from the savings accounts;

- convenience and security of the deposits;

- a mix of banking instruments and services to meet varied local demand; and

- a set of deposit instruments offering different proportions of liquidity and returns.

When effectively applied in combination with a credit program, this can simultaneously meet client demand and allow institutional profitability.

Nevertheless, it is wise to remember that as an established government-owned bank, BRI presented the new microsaver with many advantages in the area of credibility and security of the deposits. This initial "guarantee" is definitely not the case with CSO-initiated microcredit programs, a necessary caveat when reading about the success and growth of BRI's savings program.

Major Conclusions for Practitioners

Establishing and operating microcredit programs is not an easy undertaking. Even when CSOs have the financial resources to begin operating, the credit technology best suited for the particular context and clientele has to be tried and tested. This takes time, a committed and highly motivated staff, and sufficient operating funds to allow for trial and error in designing the credit program. The risks of failure are many, and failure can be more harmful to the supposed "beneficiaries" than if nothing were done. The CSO behind the program that fails is also affected, further jeopardizing many worthwhile programs. CSOs are advised, therefore, to consider this seriously before setting out to establish a microcredit program.

On the other hand, if done effectively, these programs offer many concrete and evident rewards. The loans are repaid because the economic activities supported flourish, and there is evidence that the individuals, families, and groups involved directly benefit from the program. Borrowers return for new loans, and subsequent visits to the microenterprises reveal growth in production, increased volumes of sales, additional cash income for the family, and some improvements in the house or workplace. All of this occurs at a relatively low cost when compared with the quantities of "development aid" funds whose impact continues to be questionable.

For CSO-initiated microcredit programs that are already operating, it will be important to keep up with the trends in the field and to make adjustments, depending on what direction they want to take. Having access to information and to consultants with expertise in the field is an investment well worth considering. Programs certainly need to find out for themselves what works in their specific contexts, but they also need to avoid making mistakes that have already been addressed in the literature.

Some of these problems were discussed in the December 1996 issue of *Nexus*, a newsletter published by the Small Enterprise Education and Promotion (SEEP) Network.[14] It described the performance problems and crises in three microcredit programs: in Colombia, where an affiliate of ACCION renamed itself Corposol in 1993 and established a commercial finance company, which by July 1996 was on the verge of collapse; in Tanzania, where the Mennonite Economic Development Associates (MEDA), a group credit program started in 1994, discovered in April 1996 that one third of the clients were fictitious; and in El Salvador, where the Foundation for International Community Assistance (FINCA) found that fictitious clients were also used by a branch office and a local bank to divert US$914,000 in 1994.

The article includes the following useful summary of the lessons learned:

1. A rapid pace of program expansion was common to all three programs. Driven to achieve self-sufficiency and/or increase profits, they all had a vested interest in growth fueled by varying degrees of pressure from donors, staff and clients to expand. While no accepted formula can determine the appropriate pace of growth, it is critical to assess management's capacity to keep up with it . . . .

2. Methodological Diversification: Corposol was the most ambitious in its pursuit of new products and services. But expansion through new products that

are not fully understood by staff undermined the foundation upon which ACCION affiliates have been able to grow so successfully: their proven, well developed lending methodology. MEDA, too, found its staff sought new clients by deviating from the solidarity group method and venturing beyond their geographical boundaries.

3. The need for better systems of financial management and internal control is obvious especially given that reputable external auditors did not detect any problems in two of the three cases . . . .

4. The issue of governance, while different for each of these institutions, underlies the other problems noted above. Both ACCION and FINCA grappled with how to be most effective in their position as northern apex institutions guiding a southern affiliate: ACCION . . . now states that true effectiveness [on the Board] requires the political will to risk an organization's affiliation with the network when fundamental issues are at stake. FINCA now negotiates agreements with donors that explicitly state terms of its long-term assistance to affiliates to ensure the development of sound local institutions.

MEDA is slightly different because it both works with local partners and implements programs itself. While MEDA started the Tanzania program, management there was focusing on setting up a local institution to take over. Its lack of attention to, and physical distance from, the Mbeya branch operations was a large part of its downfall. MEDA now opts for staying close to operations and getting them right before engaging in the intensive process of institution building.

These themes raise interesting challenges for the field. The initial, and often northern, reaction to instances of fraud is a collective cry for greater control. Yet given the persistent challenge to minimize the high transaction costs of making very small loans to the poor, how far should programs go to protect their funds? How sophisticated should they get? The appropriate balance needs to be found.

At the same time, [management information systems] cannot be a panacea. Equally important is building local responsibility for program integrity and performance, requiring greater investments in human resources. If programs continue to hire less expensive, unqualified people and rely on [management information systems] to detect and correct their errors, some predict that fraud will simply become a cost of doing business.

Finally, the costs of these preventive measures need to be factored into the timeframes for achieving self-sufficiency that are increasingly being articulated as expectations or standards to which programs must adhere.

Notes

1. Women's World Banking Global Policy Forum, "Missing Links: Financial Systems that Work for the Majority," New York, 1994.

2. World Bank, "A Worldwide Inventory of Micro-finance Institutions," The Sustainable Banking with the Poor Study, Washington D.C., July 1996.

3. Dale W. Adams and Delbert A. Fitchett (eds.), *Informal Finance in Low-Income Countries* (Boulder, Colo.: Westview Press, 1992); Robert Peck Christen, "What Microenterprise Credit Programs Can Learn From the Moneylenders," ACCION International Discussion Papers, Document No. 4, 1989.

4. Ibrahima Bakhoum et al. *Banking The Unbankable: Bringing Credit to the Poor* (Washington, D.C.: The Panos Institute, 1989).

5. Jannat E-Quanine, Deputy General Manager of Grameen Bank, International Conference on the Social Economy in the North and South, Oostende, Belgium, private communication, March 1997.

6. Information taken from FIE's microcredit program financial statements.

7. Maria Otero and Elizabeth Rhyne, eds., *The New World of Microenterprise Finance: Building Healthy Financial Institutions for the Poor* (West Hartford, Conn.: Kumarian Press, 1994), p. 5.

8. Richard Rosenberg, C-GAP Occasional Paper No. 1, Consultative Group to Assist the Poorest, World Bank, Washington, D.C., August 1996.

9. Reinhart Schmidt and Claus-Peter Zeitinger, *The Efficiency of Credit-Granting NGOs in Latin America* (Frankfurt am Main: IPC, 1994), p. 47.

10. Sergio Navajas, Richard L. Meyer, Claudio Gonzales-Vega, Mark Schreiner, and Jorge Rodríguez-Meza, "Poverty and Microfinance in Bolivia," Rural Finance Program, Ohio State University, 1996.

11. Schmidt and Zeitinger, op. cit. note 9, p. 71.

12. This discussion is based on Donors Working Group on Financial Sector Development, "Micro and Small Enterprise Finance: Guiding Principles for Selecting and Supporting Intermediaries," Washington, D.C., 1995.

13. Schmidt and Zeitinger, op. cit. note 9.

14. "When Performance Falters: Lessons From Three Cases," *Nexus* (Small Enterprise Education and Promotion Network, New York), December 1996.

RESOURCE GUIDE

Bibliography

Adams, Dale W., and Delbert A. Fitchett, eds., *Informal Finance in Low-Income Countries* (Boulder, Colo.: Westview Press, 1992).

Adams, Dale W., Douglas H. Graham, and John D. Von Pischke, eds., *Undermining Rural Development with Cheap Credit* (Boulder, Colo.: Westview Press, 1984).

Adams, Dale W., and J.D. Von Pischke, "Microenterprise Credit Programs: Déjà Vu," *World Development*, Vol. 20, No. 10, 1992, pp. 1463–1470.

Bakhoum, Ibrahima et al. *Banking The Unbankable: Bringing Credit to the Poor* (Washington, D.C.: The Panos Institute, 1989).

Bebbington, Anthony, "Crisis y Caminos: Reflexiones Heréticas Acerca de las ONG, el Estado y un Desarrollo Rural Sustentable en América Latina," NOGUB-COTESU, La Paz, Bolivia, 1996.

Berenbach, Shari, "Regulation and Supervision of Microfinance Institutions: Experience in Latin America, Africa and Asia," Microfinance Network, forthcoming.

Binswanger, Hans, John McIntire, and Chris Udry, "Production Relations in Semi-arid African Agriculture," in Pranab Bardhan, ed., *The Economic Theory of Agrarian Institutions* (Oxford: Clarendon Press, 1989).

Bornstein, David, *The Price of a Dream* (New York: Simon and Schuster, 1996).

Christen, Robert Peck, "Financial Management of Micro-Credit Projects," ACCION, 1995.

Christen, Robert Peck, "What Microenterprise Credit Programs Can Learn From the Moneylenders," ACCION International Discussion Papers, Document No. 4, 1989.

Christen, Robert Peck, Elizabeth Rhyne, Robert C. Vogel, and Cressida McKean, "Maximizing the Outreach of Microenterprise Finance: An Analysis of Successful Microfinance Programs," USAID Program and Operations Assessment Report No. 10, Center for Development Information and Evaluation, Washington, D.C., 1995.

Donors Working Group on Financial Sector Development, "Micro and Small Enterprise Finance: Guiding Principles for Selecting and Supporting Intermediaries," Washington, D.C., 1995.

Gonzales-Vega, Claudio, Mark Schreiner, Richard L. Meyer, Jorge Rodriguez, and Sergio Navajas, "BancoSol: The Challenge of Growth for Microfinance Organizations," in Hartmut Schneider, ed., *Microfinance for the Poor?* (Paris: OECD, 1997).

Hossain, Mahabub, *Credit for Alleviation of Rural Poverty: The Grameen Bank in Bangladesh*, Research Report 65 (Washington, D.C.: International Food Policy Research Institute, 1988).

Krahnen, Jan Pieter, and Reinhard H. Schmidt, *Development Finance as Institution Building: A New Approach to Poverty-Oriented Banking* (Boulder, Colo.: Westview Press, 1994).

Malhotra, Mohini, "Poverty Lending and Microenterprise Development: A Clarification of the Issues," GEMINI Working Paper No. 30, May 1992.

Muñoz, Jorge A., "Rural Credit Markets and Informal Contracts in Cochabamba, Bolivia," Ph.D. Dissertation, Food Research Institute, Stanford University, Stanford, Calif., June 1994.

Navajas, Sergio, Richard L. Meyer, Claudio Gonzales-Vega, Mark Schreiner, and Jorge Rodríguez-Meza, "Poverty and Microfinance in Bolivia," Rural Finance Program, Ohio State University, 1996.

Nelson, Candace, Barbara MkNelly, Kathleen Stack, and Lawrence Yanovitch, "Village Banking: The State of Practice," The SEEP Network, New York, 1995.

Otero, Maria, *A Handful of Rice: Savings Mobilization by Micro-enterprise Programs and Perspectives for the Future*, Monograph Series No. 3 (Washington, D.C.: ACCION, 1989).

Otero, Maria, and Elizabeth Rhyne, eds., *The New World of Microenterprise Finance: Building Healthy Financial Institutions for the Poor* (West Hartford, Conn.: Kumarian Press, 1994).

Patten, Richard H., and Jay K. Rosengard, *Progress with Profits: The Development of Rural Banking in Indonesia* (San Francisco, Calif.: ICS Press, 1991).

Rhyne, Elizabeth, and Linda Rotblatt, *What Makes Them Tick? Exploring the Anatomy of Major Microenterprise Institutions*, Monograph (Washington, D.C.: ACCION).

Robinson, Marguerite, "Rural Financial Intermediation: Lessons from Indonesia," Harvard Institute for International Development, Cambridge, Mass. 1992.

Rosenberg, Richard, C-GAP Occasional Paper No. 1, Consultative Group to Assist the Poorest, World Bank, Washington, D.C., August 1996.

Schmidt, Reinhart, and Claus-Peter Zeitinger, *The Efficiency of Credit-Granting NGOs in Latin America* (Frankfurt am Main: IPC, 1994).

Schmidt, Reinhart, and Claus-Peter Zeitinger, "Prospects, Problems and Potential of Credit-Granting NGOs," *Journal of International Development*, Vol. 8, No. 2, 1996, pp. 241–258.

Schmidt, Reinhart, and Claus-Peter Zeitinger, "Critical Issues in Small and Micro-business Finance," mimeo, IPC, 1994.

Vogel, Robert C., "Savings Mobilization: The Forgotten Half of Rural Finance," in Dale W. Adams, Douglas H. Graham, and John D. Von Pischke, eds., *Undermining Rural Development with Cheap Credit* (Boulder, Colo.: Westview Press, 1984).

"When Performance Falters: Lessons From Three Cases," *Nexus* (Small Enterprise Education and Promotion Network, New York), December 1996.

Women's World Banking, *Building Strong Credit and Savings Operations: Vol 1* (New York: 1993).

Women's World Banking Global Policy Forum, "Missing Links: Financial Systems that Work for the Majority," New York, 1994.

World Bank, "A Worldwide Inventory of Micro-finance Institutions," The Sustainable Banking with the Poor Study, Washington D.C., July 1996.

Yaron, Jacob, "Successful Rural Finance Institutions," World Bank Discussion Paper No. 150, 1992.

Credit Programs

Alexandria Business Association
52 El Horeya Avenue
Alexandria
Egypt
Tel: (20-3) 483-4062
Fax: (20-3) 482-9576
E-mail: aba@brainyl.ie-eg.com

Banco Solidario
Calle Nicolá Acosta No. 289
Plaza de San Pedro
Casilla No. 13176
La Paz
Bolivia
Tel: (591-2) 392-810
Fax: (591-2) 391-941
E-mail: bancosol@utama.bolnet.bo

FIE (Centro de Fomento a Iniciativas Económicas)
Calle General Gonzales No. 1272
Casilla No. 7524
La Paz
Bolivia
Tel: (591-2) 322-933
Fax: (591-2) 322-850
E-mail: fie@wara.bolnet.bo

Kenya Rural Enterprise Program
Ring Road, Kilimani
P.O. Box 39312
Nairobi
Kenya
Tel: (254-2) 718-301
Fax: (254-2) 711-645
E-mail: krep@arcc.or.ke

Kenya Women Finance Trust, Ltd.
Muchai Drive off Ngong Road
P.O. Box 55919
Nairobi
Kenya
Tel: (254-2) 712-823
Fax: (254-2) 723-883

SEWA Bank
Sewa Reception Centre
Opp. Victoria Garden
Bhadra, Ahmedabad 380001
India
Tel: (91-079) 550-6477
Fax: (91-079) 550-6446

TSPI Development Corporation
2370 Antipolo St., Guadalupe Nuevo,
Makati
P.O. Box 12690, Emerald Avenue
Pasig, Manila
Philippines
Tel: (63-2) 631-5721
Fax: (63-2) 892-8389
E-mail: tspi@cnl.net

Additional Contacts

Consultative Group to Assist the Poorest
Secretariat
The World Bank
1818 H Street N.W.
Washington, DC 20433
Fax: (1-202) 522-3744
E-mail: CProject@Worldbank.org

Ecumenical Development Cooperative Society
Gert van Maanen, General Manager
P.C. Hooftlaan 3
3818 HG Amersfoort
The Netherlands
Tel: (31-33) 463-3122
Fax: (31-33) 465-0336
E-mail: office@edcs.nl

MicroFinance Network
733 15th Street, N.W., Suite 700
Washington, DC 20005
Tel: (1-202) 347-2953
Fax: (1-202) 393-5115

Microfinance Training Program
Economics Institute
1005 12th Street
Boulder, CO 80302
Tel: (1-303) 938-2500
Fax: (1-303) 492-3003

Research and Applications of Alternative Financing for Development
1, rue de Varembé
P.O. Box 117-1211
Geneva 20
Switzerland
Tel: (41-22) 733-5073
Fax: (41-22) 734-7083

The Small Enterprise Education and Promotion Network
C/O PACT
777 United Nations Plaza,
New York, NY 10017
Tel: (1-212) 808-0084
Fax: (1-212) 682-2949
E-mail: seepny@undp.org

Women's World Banking
8 West 40th Street
New York, NY, 10018
Tel: (1-212) 768-8513
Fax: (1-212) 768-8519
E-mail: wwb@igc.apc.org

Chapter 11

Building Indigenous Foundations That Support Civil Society

S. Bruce Schearer

This chapter addresses an approach to resource enhancement that applies to a small number of civil society organizations (CSOs) but that benefits many: the building of grantmaking organizations that provide funds to other CSOs. It is included here because many groups have the potential to become grantmaking organizations, and the chapter may help them think about the possibilities available to them. Also, many CSOs that do not wish to become grantmaking organizations may want to help stimulate the creation of new foundation-like organizations in their countries, since they could potentially benefit from grants from such entities.

Types of Foundations and Their Sources of Income

Private grantmaking foundations exist in large numbers in some countries, and not at all in other countries. Across the world, they take a wide variety of forms. Some, like the Ford Foundation in the United States, control billions of dollars of assets that they invest to earn profits that in turn supply the money they use to make grants. Only a handful of foundations in the world have assets in the billions of dollars, which allows them to give away hundreds of millions of dollars in grants each year. Beyond these mega-foundations, many hundreds of large private foundations have assets above US$100 million and give out tens of millions of dollars annually. Examples of these include the Charles Stewart Mott Foundation, the Sasakawa Peace Foundation, and the Aga Kahn Foundation.

But while these large foundations often dominate the public consciousness, small foundations give as much or more in the aggregate because there are so many more of them. Tens of thousands of small private foundations base their grantmaking on earnings from assets. A small foundation with assets of about US$20 million typically earns enough income to make US$1 million in grants annually. Smaller ones with US$2 million in assets can give on the order of US$100,000 in grants, based on earnings of about 5 percent.

FUNDACIÓN PARA LA EDUCACIÓN SUPERIOR, COLOMBIA

Fundación para la Educación Superior (FES) was founded in 1964 to help a public university meet its cash flow and program expenses. Given that government disbursements were habitually late, the university was forced to borrow from local banks at high interest rates. At the same time, funds received from foreign foundations were deposited in local banks without earning interest. These donors advised the university to set up a mechanism to promote donations from alumni and the local business community. The president and trustees selected 12 prominent civic and business leaders in Cali to establish a private foundation and an office for fundraising and development.

To start up, each founding member gave FES a modest contribution and the Ford Foundation provided a seed grant, while the Rockefeller and Kellogg Foundations agreed to channel their donations through FES and allow the foundation to use the earned interest. FES became independent in the early 1970s and its reach broadened. A Vice President for Social Development was established to make grants, conduct research, and create seed programs outside the original university.

One especially interesting form of endowed foundation is the community foundation, which in the United States, the United Kingdom, and some other countries is built out of numerous capital endowment funds provided by many donors. Each mini-endowment is invested to earn profits, which then are distributed as grants in accordance with the designated purposes of each fund. Often community foundations also raise money from other sources—grants from other private foundations or corporations, or gifts from individuals—to increase the amount they can give away through grant-making programs. In addition to making grants, community foundations often operate programs. The East Tennessee Foundation, for example, makes grants and provides technical assistance to local nonprofit organizations.

Clearly, if more private grantmaking foundations with capital endowments could be established around the world, they would constitute an important additional source of financing for civil society.

But accumulating capital for endowments is a difficult, often lengthy process. The New York Community Trust, for instance, was founded more than 70 years ago with less than US$25,000, which it steadily augmented though investment earnings and additional contributions; today it owns and administers US$1 billion in assets in more than 1,000 individual funds.

Because endowment building is usually slow, it is important to also consider foundations that do not rely on earnings from capital assets in order to give their grants. Instead, regular annual flows of income from one or more donors are the source of revenues for their grantmaking. Many family foundations, for example, rely on annual contributions from family members. The Philippine Business for Social Progress (see case study in Chapter 8) receives contributions from the pretax profits of Philippine corporations each year for distribution in its grantmaking programs. It also uses the funds to leverage

The "take-off" as a financial institution began in 1975, when the government allowed FES to operate as a type of financial entity that could seek monetary resources in the capital market and make loans, which could then be linked to capital accumulation to increase its earning capacity. Today, FES has evolved into a new corporate structure, controlled and owned by Fundación-FES, that operates seven primary financial endeavors. Its leaders apply principles of business efficiency to the foundation—team work and horizontal communication are encouraged. The total capital for the corporate group is US$42 million.

FES's programs provide financial support to NGOs and research organizations in the form of donations directly and to Permanent Endowment Funds. These typically consist of money earmarked for a specific purpose, which FES matches with a 50-percent contribution and serves as financial manager for. In 1994, there were 400 such funds, worth nearly US$22 million.

FES's programs focus on health, education, economic and social development, environment, children and youth, and civil society support. To date, FES has distributed more than US$50 million in grants.

Case study prepared by John Tomlinson, The Synergos Institute.

resources from international donors. Similarly, the IBM Foundation is supported by donations from the IBM corporation each year. These examples show that regular commitments of income can be a valuable source of foundation financing.

Another type of foundation relies on income earned from its own business activities. The Fundación para la Educación Superior (FES) in Colombia, in addition to relying on income from an endowment, operates a group of financial services companies to generate additional grantmaking revenues. Fundación Social, also in Colombia, owns businesses worth US$4 billion and uses the profits earned by these companies to make its grants (see case study in Chapter 2).

"Operating foundations," in contrast to those described thus far, do not make grants, but instead use earnings from any capital endowments and revenues they may receive from other sources to undertake their own programs. This kind of foundation essentially acts like a well-endowed nonprofit organization. The Kettering Foundation in the United States, which works to address the problems of communities, politics, and education, and Fundación Carvajal in Colombia, which supports community development and microenterprise programs, are examples of operating foundations.

These examples demonstrate the many types of foundations and the wide variety of financing mechanisms they rely on. This profusion of models has been made even more complicated in recent years by the emergence in southern nations and in Central and Eastern Europe of nonprofit grantmaking organizations that incorporate a variety of foundation-like features. These mixed models generally obtain their funding from a variety of sources, including endowments (usually small), grants from other organizations, earned income, and contributions from businesses or individuals. In some cases the groups are called "foundations," "trusts," or "funds"; sometimes they are called "foundation-like organizations"; and some of them prefer to be designated as nongovernmental organizations (NGOs). (In Latin America, the term "fundación" encompasses a variety of organizations, from NGOs to foundations.)

Many of the mixed models receive funds from official foreign aid agencies or private foreign groups, which they then "intermediate"—that is, pass on in smaller grants to other CSOs in their own countries. They often also receive funding from national governments to be passed on in grant programs. In some instances, they use debt swap proceeds as the source of their grantmaking revenues (see Chapter 9).

These mixed-model foundation-like organizations typically conduct programs as well as provide grants. Most of them act as conveners of civil society groups and as networkers within the sector and between it and other sectors of society. Many provide technical assistance as well as catalytic funding for innovative approaches to social and economic problems. Throughout Africa, Asia, Central and Eastern Europe, and Latin America and the Caribbean today, these mixed-model organizations number in the hundreds.

This chapter is concerned with all forms of grantmaking foundation-like organizations. They will be referred to here as civil society resource organizations (CSROs), since they mobilize and make resources available to civil society. The CSROs discussed in this chapter exhibit the following characteristics:

- They are indigenously owned, governed, and operated.
- They are private, nongovernmental, and nonprofit.
- They mobilize resources that they channel to other civil society organizations.
- They provide grants and often other forms of assistance.
- They are sustainable because they have a dependable stream of income from an endowment or other sources.

Importance and Potential Impact of CSROs

The core strategy presented in this chapter is to use a foundation-like CSRO as a mobilizing mechanism to obtain resources that can then finance parts of civil society in different countries. CSROs offer a powerful rationale around which to organize people and institutions to identify resources, pursue them, acquire them, and, once they are obtained, put them to use for grantmaking purposes.

The power of the rationale comes from the multiple strategic functions performed by CSROs as intermediary institutions:

- They serve as mechanisms for channeling resources to civil society.
- They mobilize resources that might not otherwise be available to support the sector or address society's needs.
- Most CSROs realize that the relatively small scale of their grantmaking forces them to strive for catalytic action that will leverage the capacities of their recipients rather than merely support them. Thus they actively invest in capacity building and institution strengthening of their recipients so they will be more independent and better able to use grants effectively.

- CSROs typically serve as a bridge between large numbers of NGOs and communities on the one hand and donors and policymakers on the other.

Because they need to mobilize financial resources for their work, CSROs are usually sophisticated organizations with a wide range of contacts and working relationships, among them ties with donors, government agencies, the business sector, and foreign groups. At the same time, they are extremely knowledgeable about, well connected to, and accepted by NGOs and community-level CSOs, since they fund these groups. As indigenous intermediaries rooted in their own countries, they can play a uniquely valuable role in mobilizing civil society participation in national development and policymaking processes.

The special contributions CSROs can make to national development have been well established. In southern countries and in Central and Eastern Europe, where CSROs are emerging but still small in number, they are beginning to have a major impact. In Mexico, the Mexican Rural Development Foundation is a major provider of guarantees for credit to rural farmers, working in 27 states. In Mozambique, the Fundação para o Desenvolvimento da Comunidade has built capacity in dozens of NGOs as the number of such organizations has grown from a handful five years ago to several hundred today. In India, the Self-Employed Women's Association provides a variety of financial, economic, and social services to its 150,000 members, most of whom are poor, self-employed women. Philippine Business for Social Progress has benefited 1.6 million Filipinos through grants totalling US$45 million for 3,000 projects. And in Colombia, FES has distributed more than US$50 million in grants in fields including education, health, income generation, and preservation of the environment.

Establishing new CSROs or substantially strengthening existing ones can have a great impact in many southern nations and in Central and Eastern Europe. These organizations are needed because of the dearth of funding available to CSOs in many different fields of effort—education; health care; environment; science and technology; programs supporting women, children, and families; human rights; civil society strengthening; agriculture; and community development. In each of these areas and others, there is a need for strong independent intermediary funding and capacity-building organizations to help existing CSOs carry out their missions and play a bigger role in national development processes. A well-developed "infrastructure" of such intermediary organizations already supports civil society in northern countries. If similar intermediaries can be created elsewhere, civil society will receive a tremendous boost.

Benefits and Limitations of This Approach

Civil society organizations of all kinds benefit from the establishment of grantmaking organizations devoted to funding projects in areas in which they work. They themselves can become the recipients of such grants, and overall funding in their area increases.

For organizations with the potential to become a CSRO, the benefit can be huge—they can greatly expand the scope and impact of what they are able to do in their area of work. In addition, the stability that sustainable financing provides often allows

THE FOUNDATION FOR THE PHILIPPINE ENVIRONMENT

The Foundation for the Philippine Environment (FPE) was legally established in January 1992 through the efforts of environmental and development NGOs in the Philippines and the United States and the governments in each country (principally the U.S. Agency for International Development and the Philippine Department of Environment and Natural Resources). The process included extensive civil society consultations in the Philippines: eight formal regional consultations, and national conferences of eight major NGO networks. In total, more than 300 NGOs and two dozen academic institutions were engaged in the process.

The founders of FPE also consulted widely with international actors and conducted a study tour on philanthropy, funded by the Ford Foundation, to expose the new organization's initial governing board to U.S. organizations with expertise in foundation formation, governance, and grants management.

It took more than three years to create the endowment—from the beginning of negotiations between the governments in 1991 to the 1994 turnover of the completed debt swap to the World Wildlife Fund and the Philippine Business for Social Progress, which led to the creation of FPE. Foreign assistance of about US$18 million was used to purchase debt valued at about US$29 million. Currently, FPE's endowment is worth US$23 million.

FPE has been careful not to compete for funds with Philippine NGOs, viewing itself as a fund facilitator. It turned down an opportunity for funds from Switzerland that it felt might better go to other organizations.

In 1993, FPE disbursed more than US$1.5 million in grants through a variety of mechanisms that include responses to proposals and pro-active grants on issues the foundation deems of importance. FPE also acts as a fund facilitator, generating additional financial resources and providing financial linkages between donors and Philippine NGOs and peoples' organizations.

Case study prepared by John Tomlinson, The Synergos Institute.

CSROs to operate in a more strategic manner, freed from the distraction of short-term fundraising.

The principal limitation of the CSRO approach is the difficulty inherent in establishing sustainable streams of income. Usually this requires building a new institution or substantially upgrading the financing of an existing institution to play a grant-making role. In rare instances, a source of funding to establish a CSRO may be readily available—for example, through the donation of a large endowment grant by a wealthy individual or the commitment a well-endowed northern private foundation. But usually no such easily attainable large-scale funds are in sight, and those who wish to build a CSRO need to find the resources to make the enterprise possible, as described in the next section.

PRONATURA, DOMINICAN REPUBLIC

The Integrated Pro Nature Fund (PRONATURA) was created in 1990 as a coalition of CSOs and government organizations in the Dominican Republic dedicated to the conservation of biodiversity and natural historical heritage and natural resource management. Government representatives may not sit on the board.

The funding has come from debt-for-nature swaps and from donors, including the MacArthur Foundation, U.S. government agencies, The Nature Conservancy, and the Global Environment Facility's Small Grants Fund. The fund is currently operating as a sinking fund, in which its assets and investment earnings are expended over time.

PRONATURA supports projects that address sustainable development issues. It also helps strengthen member institutions and beneficiaries by assisting in project planning and implementation. And it has supported the use of electronic mail by environmental groups in the Dominican Republic.

Its work is well integrated with national environmental plans and the work of environmental NGOs in the country because of the inclusion of government and NGOs in the PRONATURA General Assembly.

Case study adapted by John Tomlinson, The Synergos Institute, from Ecofondo, Regional Consultation on National Environmental Funds (NEFs) in Latin American and the Caribbean: Final Report and Profiles of the National Environmental Funds *(Bogota: 1996).*

Another closely related limitation is the need for highly committed and effective leadership to launch and guide the effort, along with managerial capacity to help sustain it. CSROs are not likely to be built successfully without such leadership, and this limits how widely the approach can be used. The ongoing challenge of carrying out two different functions simultaneously is another drawback: balancing effective resource development with program delivery.

Finally, the time frame required to establish a CSRO is very long—many years in most cases, and in some instances decades. The need to combine good relations with diverse constituencies with a strong measure of autonomy requires careful planning and broad consultations. The task of building sustainable financing, often preceded by earning credibility with donors, can also be time-consuming.

How This Strategy Can Be Applied

The core strategy for building a CSRO is to use the fundamental rationale for the organization to serve as a mobilizing vehicle for assembling the finances, people, and other support needed. This has five basic ingredients:

- deeply committed and talented leaders who want to devote themselves to this task;
- familiarity with similar experiences elsewhere;

- knowledge about the sources of financing that might be tapped;
- good contacts and access to a wide range of "stakeholders" and sectors of society, potential resources, and key political actors and policymakers; and
- a compelling vision, rooted in local realities, of why the CSRO is needed and what role it will play, along with a comprehensive plan for launching it.

The first element—a founding person or group with a deeply felt social purpose—is usually the starting point for creating a CSRO. This core of deep commitment is the wellspring that makes it possible to start up a new CSRO. Usually it also provides the initial vision that ultimately determines the character and structure of the CSRO.

Broad political and professional support is essential; any key actor that opposes the initiative may be able to block it or at least seriously restrict its development. Such broad support usually requires the extensive involvement of different actors in developing the vision, which helps to instill in them a sense of ownership and participation. This approach can sometimes run into conflict with a strong founder's desire to advance his or her own deeply held goals, but the payoff in the long run is enormous.

Once the leadership and sufficient national support are in place, the process often proceeds in stages, beginning with a concept paper, moving to a detailed vision statement and then a well-developed case statement, and finally concluding with a full-blown feasibility study and launching plan.

The remainder of this section covers the basic elements that need to be addressed in any such plan.

Mission and Program Focus

Without a well-articulated mission and program focus, it is unlikely that the plans for the CSRO will get off the ground. The initial vision must be turned into a clearly articulated vision and mission statement that will be persuasive to pertinent groups both within the country and outside, along with a pragmatic implementation plan that is similarly convincing to others and achievable. The vision and mission need to be deeply connected to national needs and circumstances in a way that will speak to all the groups that could be affected by the new CSRO.

Justification

The case must be made for the mission of the CSRO requiring an endowment or other source of a sustainable income stream. What distinguishes it from an ordinary NGO? For example, many national environmental funds were created out of recognition that environmental problems require long-term solutions that can easily be undermined by shifts in donor priorities. Another rationale is that indigenously controlled funding mechanisms, freed of shifting donor interests, can be more responsive to local needs. Another is that sustainable development requires sustainable supporting institutions.

Sometimes there is a need for a long-lived but not necessarily permanent funding mechanism. One approach to be considered in such cases is a sinking fund in which not only interest but also a portion of the principal is spent each year until the fund is exhausted. The benefit of this approach is that larger-scale programs can be supported for a given endowment size. The drawback is the limited life of the CSRO.

The Aaron Diamond Foundation, which works on culture, education, health, and human rights in New York City, is an example of a sinking fund.

Scale

The program scope, intended impact, and size of assistance that the CSRO is to provide are important elements of the feasibility/implementation plan. They can vary tremendously from place to place. An organization in a single locality, such as Slovakia, will be different in scale than one intending to serve an entire nation or large political area. But differences in scale do not just include the size of an organization in terms of its overall budget and staff—they also include the scale of the support offered. In the Slovakian case and in the emerging Community Foundation for the Western Region of Zimbabwe, very small grants can be powerful catalysts for large numbers of people in specific neighborhoods or villages. The critical factor is to define an institutional scale that is both consistent with the mission and realistic with regards to resources available.

Legal Nature

Depending on the local legal environment, CSROs typically incorporate as trusts or foundations. Sometimes an organization might be incorporated with two legal identities at the same time. And in Colombia, FES became a financial intermediary—a legal status unique to that country—which enabled it to generate significant financial resources. These experiences suggest that when creating CSROs, all legal options should be investigated thoroughly, and creative approaches may be most effective.

Governance Structure

Two basic governance models are most frequently used by CSROs—a membership body that elects its own representatives to the board and a self-perpetuating, founder-selected board. In some instances, a mixture of the two has been used. In any case, consideration must be given to what sectors of society are represented. This is particularly true for CSROs whose founders come principally from one sector. If the existing network of founders is well rooted in the business community, for example, a challenge can be finding ways to incorporate more grassroots civil society participation. If the founders are from the NGO community, on the other hand, the challenge may be getting people with good business or government connections involved in the organization.

The complexity of the governing body must also be considered. Some CSROs use specialized committees (such as executive, operational, advisory, regional, and professional). Although there is no evidence that a simpler board structure will hinder the effectiveness of a CSRO, more complex structures can facilitate active board involvement in specialized tasks. They can also encourage wider participation of external constituencies in the organization's work. For CSROs that want active boards, subcommittees on specialized tasks can be effective.

Staffing

Staffing the organization raises similar issues. Most CSROs require staff with expertise on the business and the sales side—with experience and skills in resource generation

HEALTHY CITY FOUNDATION– COMMUNITY FOUNDATION BANSKÁ BYSTRICA, SLOVAKIA

The Healthy City Foundation–Community Foundation Banská Bystrica began in 1993. It grew out of an earlier foundation in Banská Bystrica, Slovakia, that went through an organizational crisis and survived through rebirth as a community foundation.

Initial funding for the organization came from the city government, which was persuaded that a community foundation would serve the public interest. Other important support for the foundation has come from foreign donors such as the Mott Foundation and Rockefeller Brothers Fund, the Environmental Partnership for Central Europe (a CSRO operating in Poland, Hungary, and the Czech and Slovak Republics), and local corporations and individuals. Sup-

and management, that is, and in public outreach and communications—as well as on the social side, with experience relating to project development and management and to the programs of the civil society sector.

Financing

A realistic financing plan is essential to provide a blueprint of how the CSRO will operate. It needs to provide detailed projections of income over at least a five-year period from all anticipated sources. It needs to estimate yearly expenditures over the same period for management and administrative costs, as well as for program costs, including grantmaking. The next section describes some ways to develop such a plan.

Financing CSROs

Like all civil society organizations, a new CSRO must rely on four sources to form a sustainable income stream:

- earned income, including fees, other self-generated income, and investment earnings;
- contributions from domestic foundations, businesses, and individuals;
- domestic government subsidies and payments, including grants and contracts; and
- foreign aid from private and official agencies, from private businesses, and from individuals overseas.

The way to tap into these income sources is described in depth in the various chapters of this book. This section highlights some of the most promising sources for starting a CSRO and for providing an existing one with sustainable funding.

port from Mott and the Environmental Partnership has taken the form of challenge grants.

The foundation's budget is small—about US$30,000 per year—and it has an endowment of some US$50,000. It is estimated that an endowment of US$500,000 is needed to support its programs completely and sustainably.

The foundation provides support to local CSOs that are working to improve the quality of live in and around the city. The amounts given are often small—less than US$300. Its program areas include environmental, neighborhood, rural, women's, and youth programs. The youth program is particularly innovative in that a program advisory committee has been established from high school volunteers. Together with the foundation's 500 Friends of Banská Bystrica fundraising campaign, the youth program is helping rebuild a sense of civic engagement in the area.

Case study prepared by John Tomlinson, The Synergos Institute.

Each potential source needs to be researched in depth to formulate an achievable financing plan for a CSRO. The founders need to conduct careful "market" assessments to ascertain just how much and what kind of resources they are likely to be able to attract from different sources. They need to gauge over what period funding is likely to become available, and under what conditions or constraints.

It will be extremely unusual for a CSRO to be able to rely on a single source or donation to create a large enough endowment to finance the desired program. Much more likely is the possibility of obtaining some initial core financing to start up operations and make some initial grants. These funds will then need to be expanded through additional fundraising, which will generally be of two kinds: for capital funds to establish an endowment or credit facility, and for intermediation funds given by external donors annually or as large program grants to be used for the CSRO's grantmaking.

It is important to include at the outset plans for how to "grow" the initial, often small endowment and ways of earning income. A number of groups have used these strategies successfully—such as the FES endowment built from proceeds of financial services described earlier. Since both endowment growth and the successful establishment of income-generating activities are slow processes, it is vital to begin them early.

Once the initial market research on all possible sources of financing is completed, the potential size of the new CSRO and its likely scale of program and impacts can be envisioned. Experience with a number of emerging CSROs indicates that this is a precarious stage. On the one hand, a clearly articulated vision, mission, and profile of value to be added to the country's existing civil society programs must be in hand in order to conduct good, in-depth market research of potential funding sources. On the other hand, a good sense of the probable size and impact of the new CSRO is necessary in order to build this profile, but this is difficult to estimate in advance of the market research that will yield some of the estimates of likely financial support. This "chicken-and-egg" problem has slowed the emergence of many CSROs. There is no easy solution to the problem, but it can best be overcome by becoming familiar with

THE KAGISO TRUST, SOUTH AFRICA

The Kagiso Trust (KT) grew out of the European Special Programme for the Victims of Apartheid in 1985. Through dialogue between the European Community and South African organizations, particularly churches, this indigenous development entity was created in 1986 to serve as a conduit for ODA from Europe to South Africans, bypassing the apartheid government.

KT funds its operations through grants from official international donor agencies and foundations. Its financing rose from just US$1.5 million to US$58 million in 1992. Between 1987 and 1994, the trust channeled approximately US$200 million from external donors to projects in South Africa. The European Union has been the largest donor, followed by the Japanese, Canadian, and Scandinavian aid agencies. Now it faces an uncertain future, as the end of apartheid means that international donors are increasingly channeling their resources directly to the democratically elected South African government.

The trust is exploring the creation of an endowment with local and foreign funds from development agencies, foundations, and corporations. It has registered

the experience of other emerging CSROs and by drawing lessons from how they have solved this problem.

Among the most promising sources of initial core funding for new CSROs are the following:

- *Proceeds from a debt swap or purchase.* In countries with outstanding public or private debt that is not being repaid because of economic limitations, it is sometimes possible to persuade a foreign government's aid program or one of the large multilateral institutions such as the World Bank, UNICEF, or the Inter-American Development Bank (IDB), to purchase some of the debt and negotiate with the national government to put a portion of the savings in the form of counterpart funds into an endowment fund. This has been the case for PRONATURA, the Foundation for the Philippine Environment, Fundación Esquel Ecuador, and a number of national environment funds established through the Swiss Debt Reduction Facility (see Chapter 9 and Bless-Venitz, Gugler, and Helbing).

- *Initial capitalization grants from northern private foundations.* Once a new CSRO has produced a vision, case statement, and initial track record, major northern foundations may be willing to make large, one-time capitalization grants to help establish an initial endowment. The CSROs supported by the Ford Foundation and the International Youth Foundation (IYF) are examples discussed in the next section.

- *Funding from governments and foreign aid agencies.* National environmental funds have been established in at least 20 countries with financial capital or property being provided by national government departments, often supplemented with grants from foreign aid agencies such as the Global Environment Facility. The Interagency Planning Group on Environmental Funds has aided this. This informal collection

as a charitable organization in the United States to encourage contributions there. But prospects for building the endowment remain uncertain.

To earn income, the Kagiso Trust recently created an investment company to support its work and simultaneously address other vital issues such as job creation, skewed wealth distribution, and infrastructure development. One example of this is Kagiso's purchase of a major publisher of school texts, to address the need for new textbooks in post-apartheid South Africa. Another recent avenue for funding is proceeds from a national scratch card lottery, which in 1995 provided more than US$130,000 a month.

Program areas include community-based institution building and development, primary health care, AIDS awareness and prevention, microenterprise development, and education and training. Applying to the trust for a grant has been complicated and time-consuming, as applications need to be approved by not only KT staff and board but also the head of the EU's development ministry and other EU officials. Consequently, beneficiaries of KT have expressed frustration at the long delays in receiving money.

Case study prepared by John Tomlinson, The Synergos Institute.

of more than 20 organizations, including development assistance agencies, private foundations, NGOs, and environmental funds, serves as a forum for exchange of information and experience, as a mechanism for coordinating services and technical assistance for environmental funds, and as an advocate of environmental funds as an innovative approach to conservation and sustainable development.

- *Implementation of an aggressive earned-income strategy.* With very small amounts of start-up funding from an individual founder, foundation, corporation, or other source, a new CSRO can deliver services or products for which it charges fees, and it can invest such income so that it grows into a sizable initial corpus of capital.

Among the most promising mechanisms available to a CSRO for translating an initial round of start-up financing into an ongoing sustainable stream of income are the following:

- *Matching philanthropic gifts.* Challenge grants, such as those provided by IYF to its partner foundations, can serve as a powerful incentive to other donors to invest in the CSRO. Sometimes the prestige associated with joining a well-known donor can be an additional incentive.

- *User fees and other sustained sources of earned income.* Fees for financial services and other businesses can generate significant revenues. CRY in India (see case study in Chapter 2) has demonstrated that the public too can be an important source of income—its greeting card sales both raise money and help educate the public about the plight of poor children in that country.

- *Intermediation of foreign aid donor funds.* CSROs are well placed to act as intermediaries. Due to their very nature as supporters of indigenous civil society, they typically have strong connections to indigenous organizations and initiatives that are

THE PUERTO RICO COMMUNITY FOUNDATION

The idea of establishing the Puerto Rico Community Foundation (PRCF) began at a forum sponsored by the National Puerto Rican Coalition (NPRC), a nonprofit organization led by Puerto Ricans living in mainland United States. Several U.S. foundations—including the Carnegie Corporation and the Ford, MacArthur, Mott, and Rockefeller Foundations—welcomed the idea of a foundation that could be a local intermediary for their grantmaking. They provided technical assistance, which helped the PRCF start operations quickly.

The PRCF "started big," with more than US$500,000 in grants in the first year. They believed that this would increase the foundation's visibility and encourage both donations and inquiries about grants. One of the businesses active in the discussions, Schering-Plough, identified another major source of funding: U.S. corporations that received tax credits for investing in manufacturing on the island. These benefits were under attack in the U.S. government. By supporting the community foundation, these corporations hoped to demonstrate their commitment to Puerto Rico, thus enhancing their standing in Washington.

The founders had hoped that significant funding would also be available from local corporate and individual donors, but local donors have lagged behind.

difficult, often impossible, for foreign donors to develop. At the same time, they also have well-developed grantmaking and administrative structures that help ensure that foreign aid funds are well used. When CSROs have a strong public reputation and good connections with policymakers, it makes them attractive to both public and private foreign aid organizations. Fundación Esquel Ecuador's role as an intermediary, for instance, is something that was not anticipated by its founders but today is an important source of financing for the organization.

- *Creation of donor-designated funds.* Really a sub-category of intermediation of foreign aid funds, this approach can attract donations to CSROs by allowing them to take direct advantage of their grantmaking infrastructure. In some cases, such as the U.S. Agency for International Development's support for the Foundation for the Philippine Environment, the donor-designated fund can be the main portion of a CSRO's grantmaking. In others, such as the Community Foundation for the Western Region of Zimbabwe being built with contributions from hundreds of villagers and the Puerto Rico Foundation's family funds, each donor-designated fund is an important piece in a larger whole.

These tasks are quite complex and require considerable research both outside the country and within. This takes time, and it often must occur at the outset, before agreement about the vision and basic structure of the CSRO are reached. When key stakeholders, including any organizations that may be supplying resources, have not yet committed to the still ill-defined venture, it is difficult to assemble the required human or financial resources to move ahead intensively with this initial research. Hence, the first step of eliciting and building strong agreement among key stakeholders is critical.

Two reasons for the relatively less successful local fundraising are that large local corporations prefer to give money directly to charities close to their communities and they are already leading sponsors of United Way.

In 1986, the Foundation began accepting earmarked grants from other donors, which it administers. It also manages nine donor-designated family funds to attract individual donors. Those donors benefit from the PRCF's local expertise in grantmaking.

Much of the discussion among the founders of the PRCF concerned board composition. U.S. foundations and the NPRC wanted large numbers of community representatives, while business leaders stressed the importance of including recognized business people in order to raise funds. The founding board was mainly composed of business and professional leaders; grassroots leaders were gradually added.

The PRCF has five priority areas: economic development, community development, art and culture, health, and education. It also contains an autonomous Permanent Fund for the Arts with its own program director and separate grants budget. In addition to grantmaking and grant intermediation, the PRCF directly sponsors programs, including the Institute for the Promotion of Philanthropy.

Case study prepared by John Tomlinson, The Synergos Institute.

The Role of External Donor Partners

Many existing CSROs in Africa, Asia, Central and Eastern Europe, and Latin America and the Caribbean have been established with assistance from outside groups. A number of private northern foundations and nonprofit groups are interested in strengthening development activities in southern countries or Eastern Europe by providing funds to help establish indigenous grantmaking organizations. These groups, in cooperation with local individuals and organizations, have taken the initiative to begin formation of CSROs in a number of countries. If they can agree on the vision and goals, initial funds in the form of planning grants are usually provided by the foreign donors.

One example of international support for building CSROs is the work of the Ford Foundation in New York. In the mid-1980s, based on experience in supporting new community foundations throughout the United States, the foundation decided to test this approach in other places. Over the next several years, it identified local groups interested in pursuing this goal in Puerto Rico, India, and Senegal, and began the long process of working with them and supplying resources to create new CSROs. The result is the National Foundation for India, the Puerto Rico Community Foundation, and the West African Rural Foundation.

Established in 1992, the National Foundation for India's mission is to promote equitable, sustainable, and culturally appropriate development. Its programs focus on areas of broad national concern, including poverty, population, equity, employment, and national integration. Support for the foundation has come from the Ford and Rockefeller Foundations and from Indian businesses, including the Tata trusts, the National Dairy Development Board, the India Bank, and others.

Box 1

Partner CSROs of the International Youth Foundation

Children and Youth Foundation of the Philippines

Children and Youth Foundation of Slovakia

German Children and Youth Foundation

Fundación Esquel Ecuador

Human Resources Trust (South Africa)

Irish Youth Foundation

National Council for Child and Youth Development (Thailand)

Polish Children and Youth Foundation

The West Africa Rural Foundation (WARF) developed from a program to support local organizations begun in 1989. Operating in Gambia, Guinea, Guinea Bissau, Mali, and Senegal, the foundation helps create and promote participator management systems for rural development through grants, training, technical assistance, and publications. International support has come from the Ford Foundation and the International Development Resource Centre in Canada.

Similarly, in the late 1980s, the International Youth Foundation—with major financial support from the W. K. Kellogg Foundation—began an ambitious program of establishing grantmaking institutions around the world devoted to addressing problems of youth. By 1996, IYF had helped launch or strengthen eight such CSROs (see Box 1), and it continues to pursue this goal in other countries.

International donors, as well as large environment and conservation CSOs in the United States and Europe, have also played a strong role in helping create CSROs to address national environmental issues. Dozens of these national environmental groups have been established throughout the world in recent years (see Box 2).

For many of these environmental CSROs, national government has also played a central role as partner. Governments clearly have access to resources to help establish CSROs when they perceive it to be in the public interest to do so. It is a challenge to CSROs in other fields of development to make equally persuasive cases to appropriate branches of government for public contributions to their programs.

During creation of a CSRO, formal agreements typically will be made among the stakeholders about the mission, governance, and bylaws of the organization. Often the financial strength of foreign donors or government partners gives them great bargaining power in negotiating these initial agreements. Here the challenges are ensuring that one stakeholder does not dominate the initial agreements and keeping sufficient flexibility in the bylaws to permit the resolution of conflicts that may arise later due to limits imposed by the original agreements. Careful and lengthy negotiations may be the only way to address these issues.

One of the most helpful decisions a new CSRO can make is to invest in establishing a wide range of linkages and connections with other CSROs and with northern

Box 2

EXAMPLES OF ENVIRONMENTAL CSROS AND
THEIR MAJOR DONORS OR SUPPORTERS

Activities Conservation Trust *(Madagascar)—U.S. Agency for International Development and Conservation International*

Conservation of Forest Trust *(Sri Lanka)—Norwegian Agency for Development Cooperation*

Corporación ECOFONDO *(Colombia)—Canadian International Development Agency and Enterprise for the Americas Initiative*

Environmental Foundation of Jamaica—*Enterprise for the Americas Initiative*

Far Eastern Biodiversity Conservation Fund *(Russia)—U.S. Agency for International Development, World Wildlife Fund*

Fundo Brasileiro de Biodiversidade *(Brazil)—Global Environment Facility and private sector*

Indonesia Biodiversity Foundation—*U.S. Agency for International Development*

Mgahinga and Bwindi Impenetrable Forest Conservation Trust *(Uganda)— Global Environment Facility and U.S. Agency for International Development*

PRONATURA *(Dominican Republic)—Puerto Rico Conservation Trust, MacArthur Foundation, U.S. Agency for International Development, The Nature Conservancy*

Table Mountain Trust Fund *(South Africa)—World Wildlife Fund*

---

private foundations from which it can gain experience and various forms of support. This is a costly action for an emerging CSRO with little disposable income for such outreach activities, but it is an investment that will greatly enhance its chances for success. One way to accomplish this is to build the activity and its financing into the start-up budget. This will make it an integral part of its institutional development.

Some Conclusions and Pointers for Practitioners

In-depth case studies of the process of establishing CSROs along with organizational development analyses of the studies provide some important lessons for those interested in creating a new CSRO. (See also the Synergos Institute paper series.)

First, this is not a path for the fainthearted. The establishment of a new institution of this scale and complexity is an arduous, long-term process. Not only must the founders assemble the necessary financing, they must build an effective organization and establish it securely in an often challenging national political and professional environment.

The initial choices made by the indigenous founders with regard to sources of financing and external partners have extremely profound long-term consequences that should be carefully weighed. For example, if the CSRO is created with a foreign partner playing a major role, unforeseen shifts in the fortunes or priorities of that partner can expose the CSRO to risk or pressure to change course. If the national founders fail to stay with the CSRO because of such pressures, the CSRO can lose its local credibility and legitimacy. In any case, the loss of foreign funding can put the very existence of the CSRO at risk.

By relying on significant outside assistance, founders of a new CSRO automatically require it to deal with—and please—two constituencies: foreign donors and partners, and indigenous recipients and colleagues. This can cause tensions within the CSRO and force it to design its programs and operations in ways it might not otherwise have chosen. With narrower options and decreased flexibility, it can be less well equipped to face changes in its environment in the coming years. By recognizing these dangers at the outset, the founders and partners can seek to keep their programming structure open, to diversify their financing structure, and to build a deeply rooted national governance mechanism.

The alternative of relying mainly or exclusively on domestic funding to start a new CSRO has the advantage of greater autonomy and usually the disadvantage of scarcer resources. Striking a balance that allows for the participation of external donors within a framework of maximum autonomy and indigenous ownership of the CSRO is clearly the most desirable course.

In the final analysis, the most important ingredient for success of a CSRO is not its financing, governance, or organizational capacities, although each of these is essential, but rather the value it is able to add to the efforts of its "clients." At a minimum, these "clients" are the principal actors in the field in which the CSRO works, including the recipients of its grants. If there are donors who provide the CSRO with ongoing funding, they too are "clients." Unless the CSRO is perceived by its national clients as fundamentally serving their needs in a significant way, it will not be a successful institution, nor will it contribute importantly to national life. And unless it is perceived by its donor clients as meeting their objectives, it will lose their support.

Future Trends and Issues

A number of organizations have made a commitment to helping local groups establish CSROs not as donors but as civil society partners. They hope that by adding catalytic resources in countries where they are most needed, they will be able to stimulate the widespread growth of CSROs. In addition to the donor role being played by about a dozen major foundations in the United States, Europe, and Japan, private nonprofit support groups like the Council on Foundations, the Asia Pacific Philanthropy Consortium, the Group of Asia Philanthropies, PACT, the Swiss Coalition of Development Organizations (in some of its debt conversion activities), the Synergos Institute, and the Interagency Planning Group on Environmental Funds are playing important technical support and resource mobilization roles. This trend may be strengthened through further coordination between these groups and interested donor agencies in the future.

A critical issue for the future is the degree to which major bilateral and multilateral development agencies will support and join in this effort to catalyze the formation of

CSROs as a strategy aimed at deepening local ownership of official development programs and engaging the civil society sector more fully in them. Although a number of development agencies, including the World Bank, the United Nations Development Programme, the IDB, the U.S. Agency for International Development, and the Swedish International Development Agency have been looking at this question, progress has been slow. Since such agencies provide on the order of US$50 billion yearly for national development activities, their entry as a partner into this arena could dramatically accelerate the pace and impact of current efforts.

Closely related is the future role of national governments in either supporting or resisting the establishment of domestic CSROs in southern countries and in Central and Eastern Europe. Of all the issues raised in this chapter, this is perhaps the one with greatest potential impact because of the vital importance of a supportive enabling environment of policy, law, and collaboration.

Ten years ago, CSROs outside the wealthy northern countries were a rare phenomenon. Today hundreds exist, and it is very likely that this number will grow to thousands over the next few decades. The quality and scale of these new development actors and their success in addressing pressing needs will be determined by whether they are fostered by the interplay between the public, private, and civil society sectors.

RESOURCE GUIDE

Bibliography

Barrientos, Andrea, *Building Community Philanthropy in the Caribbean* (New York: Center for the Study of Philanthropy, 1996).

Bless-Venitz, Jutta, Alfred Gugler, and Richard Helbling, *The Swiss Debt Reduction Facility: A State of the Art* (Bern: Swiss Coalition of Development Organizations, 1995).

Council on Michigan Foundations, *Community Foundation Primer: An Outline for Discussion and an Initial Organization Start-up Kit* (Grand Haven, Mich.: 1997).

Ecofondo, *Regional Consultation on National Environmental Funds (NEFs) in Latin American and the Caribbean: Case Studies on In-county Resource Mobilization* (Bogota: 1996).

Ecofondo, *Regional Consultation on National Environmental Funds (NEFs) in Latin American and the Caribbean: Final Report and Profiles of the National Environmental Funds* (Bogota: 1996).

Hamrell, Sven, and Olle Nordberg, eds, "Autonomous Development Funds," *Development Dialogue*, 1995:2.

Interagency Planning Group on Environmental Funds, *Environmental Funds: A New Approach to Sustainable Development* (Report by the Interagency Planning Group of a Briefing on 26 April 1995 in Paris for Interested Members of the OECD/DAC Working Party on Development Assistance and Environment).

Machel, Graça, Horst Kleinschmidt, and David Winder, *Lessons from African, Asia and Latin American Experiences with a View to Enhancing Regional Cooperation* (Summary Report of Southern African Grantmakers Conference, Maputo, Mozambique, 1996).

Mikitin, Kathleen, "Issues and Option in the Design of GEF Supported Trust Funds for Biodiversity Conservation," *Environment Department Working Papers*, No. 011 (Washington, D.C.: World Bank, 1995).

Overseas Development Council and the Synergos Institute, *Strengthening Civil Society's Contribution to Development: The Role of Official Development Assistance* (Washington, D.C., and New York: September 1995).

Pierce, Stephen D., "Grassroots Development and the Issue of Scale: The Colombian Case," *Grassroots Development*, Vol. 19, No. 2, 1995.

Robertson, Philip S., *Foundation-like Organizations (FLOs): The Future of Sustainable Development*, unpublished paper for Johns Hopkins School of Advanced International Studies, Principles of NGO Management Class, 1996.

The Synergos Institute, *The Process and Techniques of Foundation-Building: Experience from Eight Organizations in Africa, Asia and Latin America* (New York: 1996).

Vincent, Fernand, *Finance Autrement: Les Associations et ONG de Développement du Tiers Monde* (Geneva: Development Innovations and Networks, 1994).

Yamamoto, Tadashi, ed., *Emerging Civil Society in the Asia Pacific Community* (Tokyo and Singapore: Japan Center for International Exchange and Institute for Southeast Asia Studies, 1996).

Organizations

Oscar Rojas
Vice President for Social Development
Fundación para la Educación Superior
Apartado Aero 5754
Cali
Colombia
Tel: (57-2) 882-4502
Fax: (57-2) 883-4706

Amita Kapur
Honorary President
Child Relief and You (CRY)
Community Facilit Complex
DDA Slum Wing (Bharat Char)
Bapu Park, Kotla Mubarakpur
India
Tel: (91-11) 469-3109/3159
Fax: (91-11) 463-2302

Lic. Bernardo Barranco Villafan
Director General Adjuncto
**Fundacion Mexicana para el
Desarrollo Rural, A.C.**
Bahia de la Concepción No. 14
10. y 20. Pisos
Col. Veronica Anzures
11300, Mexico, D.F.
Mexico
Tel: (52-5) 260-0980
Fax: (52-5) 260-7412

Atty. Donna Z. Gasgonia
Executive Director
**Foundation for the Philippine
Environment**
No. 77 Matahimik Street
Teachers' Village
1101 Quezon City
Philippines
Tel: (63-2) 927-9403/927 2186
Fax: (63-2) 922-3022

Ms. Aurora F. Tolentino
Executive Director
**Philippine Business for Social
Progress**
3/F Philippine Social
Development Centre Magallanes Cor.
    Real Street
Intramuros, Manila
Philippines
Tel: (63-2) 527-7741
Fax: (63-2) 527-3740

Horst Kleinschmidt
Executive Director
Kagiso Trust
18th Floor, Total House
209 Smit Street, Braamfontein 2001
South Africa
Tel: (27-11) 403-6319
Fax: (27-11) 403-1940/1941

Ms. Ethel Rios de Betancourt
President
**Puerto Rico Community
Foundation**
Royal Bank Center, Suite 1417
Hato Rey, San Juan
Puerto Rico 00917
Tel: (1-809) 751-3885
Fax: (1-809) 751-3297

Chapter 12

Tapping Social Investment Through the Market

Malcolm Hayday

There is a whole network of institutions that lie between the state and the individual—from voluntary organizations and hospitals to quasi-autonomous nongovernmental organizations (NGOs) and firms. The insistence that the choice is either the state or the individual wholly neglects this institutional infrastructure and the importance of the social capital it generates. Rather, the aim must be to nurture and sustain them.

This chapter considers the role of socially directed private capital as a sustaining force for NGOs and the importance of locally generated finance to the development of long-lived institutions. As Anne Heidenreich, an NGO practitioner from Kenya, has pointed out: "Different people have different things in mind when they speak of financial sustainability: does it mean NGOs managing on their own without donor support? or managing the funds they receive so well that donors continue to support them? or investing the funds they receive now so that they can live off investment earnings later?" For many NGOs, the latter may be the most realistic goal.

Self-financing for some NGOs is difficult while northern NGOs and donors are reluctant to provide funds as endowments, or for investment, or for enterprise. If NGOs cannot derive finance from their own communities, they are linked to the successes of faraway communities that bear no relation to their own. Specific attempts have been made in various parts of the world to acquire resources and to manage them effectively. These often involve the participation of intermediary vehicles—sometimes NGOs; other times, for-profit or banking-type organizations.

From Tithing to Social Investment

Social investment is not new. As early as the fifteenth century, banking institutions in Italy were set up to lend small amounts of money at minimal interest to relieve suffering and distress among the poor. Most of the funds that formed the lending pool were derived from charitable donations, although in some cases the bank paid interest on deposits and made loans to the wealthy, using the income to subsidize other activities. Three hundred years later, Benjamin Franklin set up a fund in Philadelphia and another in Boston that were administered as loan pools to young artisans starting up their own businesses. And throughout the world, religious tithes for the common good have been present throughout time.

What is a relatively new phenomenon today is the more formal access to private capital through the market for socially beneficial purposes. Private capital may be made available through institutions, through market instruments, or directly from individuals. But its source is invariably the philanthropic impulse or savings of citizens.

All organizations pass through a number of life-cycle stages. These may be characterized as moving from start-up to establishment to operational viability and then to financial viability and maturity. The analysis can also be made in terms of self-sufficiency. The lowest level operates with a large amount of subsidy or donated funds—this may include advocacy groups with no identifiable earned income or those whose objectives require them to operate deficit services, such as free education or advice. Here, dependence on donations remains high. At the next level, grants may be required to meet core operating costs but services are being developed that can repay loans on "soft" terms. At the third level, grants are sought only for specific projects or as start-up capital for new developments. The highest level is achieved when internal cash flows, member/supporter savings, and borrowed funds can support the organization's activities. It has to be conceded that few civil society organizations (CSOs) have reached—or would even wish to reach—this fourth level.

Nonetheless, loan and social investment funds show that over and above the existing grant and donation streams, resources exist that can enhance CSO development. And because these require levels of commitment and responsibility, they can lead to greater independence and so promote sustainability.

Development is an asset-based process. Long-term, broad-scale community development relies on core economic principles familiar to any private-sector business. The values may be different, but the tools are the same. Successful organizations require access to or development of assets and resources (capital), and the investment, management, and use of assets to generate revenue and wealth. Similarly, if the wealth or welfare of a community is to increase, the community must be able to identify and use its assets. All communities, even the economically disadvantaged or isolated, possess or have access to assets that can be used to advance their development. Sustainable development does not result from subsidized programs driven solely by social or economic goals; it must be capable of creating both economic and social wealth. But communities can be constrained from such development through a number of factors, including lack of finance.

Yet it is important for CSOs to recognize that social investment is not a revenue source in its own right; it is one element of a finance continuum—with grants at one end and purely commercial finance and moneylenders at the other. It is a resource to enable organizations to generate income in other ways, often without the strings that can accompany a grant. Social investment will be more relevant to and important in some sectors than others. Areas such as education, health care, social welfare provision, and reintegration of marginalized groups may require substantial expenditure on capital assets such as schools, clinics, hostels, and training programs, which in turn may generate income.

In 1991, Lester Salamon and Helmut Anheier at The Johns Hopkins University in Maryland launched a 13-country study of the nonprofit sector. The countries were selected to represent different levels of development, government spending, and religious and cultural traditions. According to conventional wisdom, what sets NGOs apart from their counterparts in the public and business sectors is their reliance upon private charitable giving as the principal source of support. In fact, the study revealed that on average only 10 percent of nonprofit income originated with private philanthropy in the seven countries for which comparable data were available. And that 47 percent of all nonprofit income comes from service fees and sales, with the other 43 percent from government.

This finding reflects the market context within which many NGOs operate and the growth in demand for their services among people able to pay, either on their own or with public-sector help. Consequently, earned income accounts for 64 percent of total nonprofit revenues in Sweden, 60 percent in Japan, 57 percent in Hungary, 53 percent in Italy, and 51 percent in the United States. Only in France and Germany does fee income lose its primary position, as the public sector accounts for 68 percent of the income of German NGOs, and 59 percent for the French. The lack of data made it difficult to extend the reach of this study, although further work is now under way.

The study also considered the challenges that lie ahead. If the sector is developing alternative sources of income to buttress its relationship with the state, then the preservation and expansion of a meaningful level of private support is essential in providing the zone of autonomy crucial for the health of civil society. The exact level of private funding required is difficult to specify. It is unrealistic to expect that private support will constitute all or even most of NGO income. At the same time, the study suggested that a level much below 10 percent is probably insufficient to provide the financial cushion that a healthy civil society sector requires. As it turned out, only three of the countries examined in depth—the United States, the United Kingdom, and Hungary—had levels of private giving that exceeded this minimum range. Significantly, the countries with the lowest levels also had the least generous tax incentives for such activity. Here, social investment can go some way to restoring the balance.

The Benefits of Borrowing

Research in the United States has shown that more than 70 percent of charitable nonprofits there borrow, and that the percentage increases with asset size to 93 percent for groups with assets of more than US$1.5 million. Although the share is much lower in the United Kingdom, even quite small organizations with assets in thousands of dollars equivalent have borrowed from time to time. Indeed, research there in 1996 suggests that borrowing is proportionately more prevalent among smaller organizations than among the largest ones. By and large, it is also done efficiently—that is, the benefits outweigh the cost. The organizations' cautious approach and cultural reserve encourage borrowing only where there is a real need or a recognition of its beneficial role in capital creation, and where there is every prospect of being able to service the debt.

Productive borrowing is where the expected return from borrowed funds exceeds the cost of borrowing. This may be a short-term bridge facility to counter the temporary mismatch of income and expenditure flows or receipt of a grant, or it may be to facilitate diversification into related areas of activity, although this only makes sense when the new activity is consistent with the overall mission. Other examples include borrowing to expand service levels or to facilitate new fixed asset acquisitions such as computers or a building, which can help consolidate operations and so achieve economies of scale.

Borrowing can also achieve intergenerational equity. Cash outlays on a building project require the present generation to pay for items that benefit future generations at the expense of current programs. Borrowing enables the costs to be shared. And it enables a project or activity to go ahead now rather than having to wait until sufficient cash has been raised—by which time the demand may have changed. Equally, it can extend the life of a project that may have only a finite grant support. A donor may have funded a pilot program or a service for, say, two years, during which time it proves itself. Borrowing may enable the project to become permanent.

Any borrower must give some thought to the repayment schedule, to business planning, and to financial discipline. If properly structured, this will create a savings pattern that can be maintained after the loan has been repaid, creating an internally generated cash flow and self-sustaining resource. In turn, this appeals to social investors who see their involvement as enabling organizations to find long-term solutions rather than applying a bandage to problems.

While a loan will have predominantly financial disciplines, it does enable an organization to develop its own strategy rather than be led by the requirements of donors or grants with strings. It is evident, for example, that as a number of European Commission grant programs have been refined and developed, the beneficiary organizations have also changed (not necessarily consciously) to be in a better position for continued grants. In doing so, they may well have shifted from their original mission and from the needs of their beneficiary group.

Borrowing is a risky business and is not suitable or sustainable for all organizations. Equally, too much money—particularly in one lump sum—can cause problems. The U.S. research into borrowing activity also identified a number of factors limiting access—perceptions of risk, lack of understanding of CSO culture, lack of "hard bankable assets," the regulatory environment, and the often small size of transactions. These factors may be viewed differently by social and commercial investors.

As noted earlier, it is likely that the impact of social investment will vary between social enterprises (high) and advocacy groups (low) as well as between professionally run (high) and volunteer-led groups (low). It is not clear whether geographic imbalances also occur. Social investment is an established activity in North America; it is becoming better known in Europe, although it is still a niche activity. Examples exist elsewhere, but whether these are typical or isolated cases is not clear.

Future Developments

James Robertson has noted that there is a "possibility that a 'third sector' consisting of enterprise with mixed economic and social objectives will emerge alongside the conventional public and private sectors as a major feature of the 21st century economy." He expects this will lead to a "financial third sector" as well. This will require new institutions that can help people channel their savings into investment for social and environmental wealth.

Writing in *SOSVA Post* (India) in July 1995, the editor V. Srinivasan suggested:

> When the voluntary sector is being hailed as the fourth sector of development, after government, private and co-operative, it is imperative to evaluate the support it enjoys. Simply exhorting the sector will not bring about its development, only positive support can. The voluntary sector is singularly bereft of an institutional infrastructure the other three enjoy. There are no training, research, financial or promotional institutions that work exclusively for the voluntary sector. To add to the difficulties, the inherent nature of the NGOs prevents efficient and effective utilisation of whatever services are available. There is thus a need for a whole range of institutions serving the voluntary sector.
>
> NGOs currently are funded by government, funding agencies or the community. Apart from paucity of funds, one of the major problems is the delay in sanctioning and disbursement of grants. While some of the delay can be laid at the NGOs' doorstep for not complying with procedural requirements, governments long drawn procedures are a major stumbling block in what should be fairly routine grant releases. Most NGOs operate on shoe string budgets and any delays in receiving grants means slowing down or even abandoning the project. The morale of the personnel working on the project is severely affected leading to attrition. This constant uncertainty also prevents well qualified professionals from joining the sector. While this reduces the efficiency of the NGO, the ultimate sufferers are the constituents.
>
> The NGO could borrow money from banks or other financial institutions to tide over the gap, but this is never as simple as it sounds. The NGOs are neither able to proffer adequate collateral for loans taken nor make the interest payments. The costs of processing these loans are also often high.

Srinivasan's solution to this problem of barriers to access to mainstream finance was to propose the establishment of a financial intermediary that understands the sector—in this case, a bridge loan fund. The problem of barriers to access is not unique to India; it is relevant to CSOs everywhere.

As the pressures upon these organizations grow, new mechanisms and new institutions are required to intermediate between social investors and organizations. With money center banks continuing to redline areas and even whole countries, and becoming global in an investment sense but not in terms of retail banking, this is given added impetus. Some of these intermediaries will begin as NGOs, such as BancoSol in Bolivia, the Association for Sarva Seva Farms (ASSEFA) in India, or even the Charities Aid Foundation (CAF) in the United Kingdom. (See Chapter 11.) Part of their funding will come from people and companies who choose a balance between risk-adjusted financial returns and the social impact of the investment. The social impact can increase as the financial returns decrease. Some people are prepared to substitute altogether the benefit of the common good for private gain.

Box 1

CHECKLIST FOR CSOs SEEKING SOCIAL INVESTMENT

What do you want the money for? Where are you in your stage of development? Would a grant be more appropriate to your need?

Will it enable you to help you do your job more effectively and efficiently? Increase the reach of your program? Develop a new activity?

Are your trustees/managers of like mind in this and how to finance it?

Have you prepared a business plan? Does it include a sensitivity analysis? What if certain assumptions change?

Have you got the right skill mix at board and staff level to deliver the program?

Do your beneficiaries want it?

Can you manage the program?

What impact will it have on your current programs and beneficiaries?

Have you approached the formal credit sector? What did they say? Why?

Do you know that while a loan or social investment will enable you to do things, it also carries commitments? Can you meet the terms of the loan or investment?

Have you asked for enough? Too much? Too little?

Do you have the same values as your lender or investor?

If you are asked to report certain milestones and financial information, do you have systems that allow you to do so?

If the loan or investment is from an external source, are there any restrictions on repayment?

If you miss a repayment, what are you going to do?

What sort of relationship do you have or will you seek to build with your lender or investor?

What lessons can you learn or have you learned?

Has it achieved what you set out to do and what your beneficiaries needed?

Was it achieved within budget?

What experiences can you share?

In a time of unmet need, social investment is attracting greater attention. Whether the World Bank and initiatives such as the Consultative Group to Assist the Poorest can relate to these financing needs by providing some form of credit enhancement in a citizens' world bank, as suggested at the end of this chapter, remains to be seen.

If CSOs are to pursue a strategy of sustainability through social investment, some key considerations need to be taken into account. (See Box 1.) First, there must be a benign environment that encourages such investment, and mechanisms through which the investment can flow. While the investment may initially be from an external source, local partners need to be developed to ensure that the project can be taken forward locally. In general, institutions that act as intermediaries for social investment require an environment in which governments and other official agencies recognize the contribution of CSOs to social cohesion and in which savings and banking legislation does not inhibit the development of a financial infrastructure to support them.

The CSO itself needs to demonstrate financial competence and that it has people within its management who have business acumen mixed with social responsibility (people increasingly known as social entrepreneurs), capable of delivering the project or program. In this way, the organization demonstrates responsibility and earns the trust of the investor.

The organization must be willing to be transparent in all its dealings with investors— something hidden may destroy trust. Although investors will let the organization set its own goals and manage its business, they expect it to be accountable to them for the use of their funds. A change of program or shift of emphasis in, say, the beneficiary group requires explanation if the trust of the investor is to be maintained. This becomes even more necessary when the investors are local and may be providing their support for very specific, local reasons.

In any lending or borrowing activity, mistakes may happen, losses may be incurred. The organization must be able to demonstrate to funders that it has learned the appropriate lessons and is prepared to share these—both good and bad—with others so that examples of best practice can emerge to the benefit of all civil society organizations.

Mobilizing Private Capital for Socially Beneficial Purposes

The underlying assumption of social investment is that mobilizing finance for the common good in addition to or rather than for personal gain can benefit society. Why should this be so? If development is an asset-based process, it requires tools familiar to any for-profit business. Yet the commercial banking sector does not provide the financial infrastructure necessary to ensure that a healthy civil society can thrive. Rather, it falls to investors who think about more than just money to support the development of such an infrastructure.

While there has been little empirical research into the effectiveness of social investment vis-à-vis commercial investment where the two coexist, recent research for the European Commission has shown that jobs are created or preserved and that actions are undertaken that may otherwise not have occurred. Furthermore, the cost of such job creation may be markedly lower. There is evidence from around the world that commercial investment has been withdrawn from whole areas of population. In North America and Europe, commercial banks seeking cost efficiencies through the closure of branches and the substitution of automated teller machines leads to credit being available to the individuals, companies, and organizations who can fill in credit-scoring application forms correctly. It is not a flight of fancy to assume that this process will lead to more people and organizations being denied access to formal credit. This "redlining" makes regeneration and development difficult if not impossible, and can make it

A U.S. BANK–CSO RELATIONSHIP

In the United States, relationships of mutual gain are growing between some banks and activist community-based organizations. One of the most remarkable examples is between groups in Pittsburgh, Pennsylvania, and the National City Bank (NCB, formerly Integra Bank). Over a decade, the 32 neighborhood organizations that form the Pittsburgh Community Reinvestment Group (PCRG) have developed with NCB a written agreement that formally details their relationship in more than 50 pages, describing their mutual commitment and processes of exchange.

The relationship developed with the support of the Community Reinvestment Act. The community groups and the bank first made contact in 1988, because of a bank merger. They negotiated their first memorandum of understanding (MOU), which included a commitment by the bank to invest US$109 million in PCRG members' neighborhoods. The MOUs include lending goals, and are renegotiated every two years. The 1996/97 agreement stated that "past achievements plus future goals exceed(ed) $1.4 billion."

PCRG and the bank have collaboratively created products with design and marketing features that are particularly appropriate for low- and moderate-income individuals. In addition, they jointly work to support neighborhood development;

much harder to create the initial impetus for locally generated savings and activity that is so important to sustainability.

In recent times, social investment has re-emerged through two paths—as a result of legislation and as a positive decision by people and institutions. Microfinance, particularly when combined with increased access to basic social services, is playing an increasingly important role in the relief of poverty. The role of microfinance is considered in Chapter 10; this chapter refers to some of these initiatives but looks at how CSOs and microfinance funds themselves can mobilize social investment.

At a macro level, the World Bank is the biggest source of market-based loans for development. It is funded mainly by borrowing from governments and the international capital markets. While investors are providing a major source of development funds, it is likely that they are more interested in the fact that the World Bank is a AAA risk on which they earn a low but safe return than they are in how the funds are used.

Community Reinvestment Through Legislation

In the United States, a few institutions have used legislation as an opportunity to contribute more fully to community development. They address the transaction costs by working with and through intermediary organizations such as community development loan funds. These "enlightened" few recognize that the federal government is devolving community programs of all types and that the public—the banks' customers—are demanding bank support at the local level. They see that the debate about poverty alleviation and rebuilding communities is moving on from charity and welfare to providing the support necessary to encourage self-sufficiency.

for example, if the bank has foreclosed on an abandoned house, it may turn it over without charge to the local community organization for redevelopment.

The relationship grows partly out of organizational symmetry, with a major internal division of the bank having responsibility for a market area almost identical to that of PCRG members. PCRG undertakes a variety of activities, including research into bank lending patterns and neighborhood investment, that it makes available to the bank. The 1995 MOU provided for the bank to pay PCRG US$55,000 annually for general operating support. PCRG member organizations also receive support from an intermediary that receives donations from the city, foundations, and banks.

When asked whether the bank is being too generous with the community groups, bank representatives point to the numerous business benefits of the relationship that have led it to become the primary bank for 60 percent of Pittsburgh households. And in response to queries about co-optation, PCRG and its members point to the importance of accountability to local residents and having open processes for election. Both parties stress the importance of transparency of interactions.

Case study prepared by Steve Waddell, Program Director, Institute for Development Research, Boston.

This means that some CSOs are moving into community development lending and need business-disciplined investment to help them grow. As these organizations become larger and more like social businesses, they need investment to help them increase their long-term financial capacity, so that they do not have to rely on government funding or annual operating grants. In this way, commercial banks can help CSOs accomplish things that the banks cannot, or at least have not thus far.

The federal Community Reinvestment Act (CRA) has encouraged—even required—banks and other financial institutions to invest in communities, and therefore in civil society organizations, which they would otherwise not choose to do, partly because of perceptions of risk but also because of the costs involved in such transactions. The act requires the Federal Reserve Board (one of the regulators) to evaluate a bank's performance in helping to meet the credit needs of the communities from which it derives its business.

It is clear that the participation of many banks—particularly foreign ones with U.S. branches—is limited to the minimum required to comply with the CRA. One Canadian bank was questioned about its role in community finance; although there is a strong element of philanthropy in Canada, this had not motivated the bank. It was required by the CRA to do something. Feelings of altruism or being a good corporate citizen, a guest in another country, did not play a part in its decision.

After the merger of two major U.S. banks, Chase Manhattan and Chemical, the new group made a five-year community investment commitment of US$18.1 billion nationwide, not just in the CRA areas. Admittedly that figure includes US$13.5 billion of affordable mortgages to low-income groups, but it also includes US$3.4 billion in loans and investments to assist small businesses and community-based CSOs,

ABYSSINIAN DEVELOPMENT CORPORATION

Created in 1987 under the auspices of the Abyssinian Baptist Church in Central Harlem, the Abyssinian Development Corporation (ADC) has developed more than 300 units of housing for low- and moderate-income families, the elderly, and the disabled. In addition, ADC advocates for improved delivery of municipal and social services.

The Nonprofit Facilities Fund has provided two loans to support ADC's work. In 1992, NFF provide a loan that allowed ADC to purchase new computer equipment and move from a less than 20-square-meter office to one that is 10 times bigger. In 1993, ADC used a second loan of US$200,000 to complete construction of a Head Start center that had been stalled due to delays in funding. This center now serves 100 preschool children from low-income and formerly homeless families. Both loans have been repaid, which helped ADC establish a successful credit history and attacked one of the premises of commercial banks that such lending is inherently more risky.

US$1.2 billion in loans and investments for affordable housing and commercial and economic development, and US$70 million in philanthropic initiatives directed at smaller community-based CSOs.

The CRA has been instrumental in introducing substantial amounts of funding for community development in general and for CSOs in particular in the United States. It has also aided the development of financial intermediaries capable of providing "banking" facilities for these groups. One such is the New York-based Nonprofit Facilities Fund (NFF). NFF has long-term loan funds from the Ford Foundation, CRA qualifying money from banks, and funding from social investors. As its name implies, NFF provides loans and advisory services to CSOs for facilities projects. Its New York Area Program serves all nonprofit subsectors in the city, while its Cultural Facilities Fund Program serves arts and culture organizations in other parts of the United States.

Established in 1980, NFF found it difficult to generate a sufficient scale of activity until 1991, when the Federal Reserve indicated that NFF loans could be included as part of a bank's CRA rating. This enabled NFF to make five loans in 1991, 12 in the following year, and 15 by 1996. In total, NFF has made 145 loans totalling approximately US$15 million. Average loan size is US$145,000, with loans ranging from US$5,000 to US$600,000. NFF reaches out to NGOs by running grant-aided workshops on a range of issues, such as "Managing Risk in Developing Community Facilities" and "Expanding Child Care Opportunities," as well as through newsletters, publications, an active Board, and word-of-mouth recommendation.

With better child care centers, community theaters, office space, and computer equipment, community development corporations can do more to empower and revitalize communities. Finance is a key ingredient in the mix of resources required to achieve this, and NFF has built relationships with a number of these regeneration vehicles.

The lessons learned from NFF's work include that borrowing can work. The second lesson is that the lender needs to have a very clear mission—to fund the development, building, or refurbishing of facilities. It knows its market, which is also geographically defined. It provides technical assistance in the form of workshops and capacity-building programs. Such programs help to manage risk by better preparing an organization not only for borrowing but also for managing the facility and understanding its fit in that organization. The borrower benefits from this. A sound business plan and management acceptance of responsibility for the facility ensure that it is central to the organization's activity and does not get neglected.

Although the CRA has evidently been successful in galvanizing private-sector investment for social benefit within the United States, it has not been taken up by other free-market economies. Nor have participating banks sought to extend the social investment skills they have developed to other countries, preferring the traditional grant-aided form of corporate philanthropy. It would appear that these banks do have assessment skills and investment products that could be of benefit in other communities, and that CRA-type encouragement should be considered where banks and other institutions do not already recognize that a soundly resourced civil society is a mark of a mature world. All charities and voluntary agencies thrive only in a climate that encourages such activity.

Intermediate Organizations Harnessing Social Investment

In the United States and in other parts of the world, a growing number of intermediary organizations are able to harness investment for social rather than private benefit. One network—INAISE, the International Association of Investors in the Social Economy—has in its membership many examples of the differing instruments that can be developed to attract social investment. INAISE has 40 members in 16 countries. Many are located in Europe, but some are found in Zaire, Costa Rica, South Africa, New Zealand, and Japan. And some European members also work in third countries.

None of the members of INAISE are big enough to operate at the same level of activity as large commercial banks, although some have certainly achieved self-sufficiency. Banking status brings with it capital requirements that may be onerous and the need to demonstrate a track record—which is impossible in a start-up. This is important for protecting the depositor, but it may be at the expense of supporting the very organizations some social investors wish to reach. Intermediaries may therefore follow other paths to achieve the same end.

The Latin America Development Fund (FOLADE), for example, is a regional finance organization that has some 22 NGO members in 14 countries of Latin America. Its purpose is to support a broad section of the people who have no access to traditional bank finance but who are capable of meeting repayment obligations. It seeks to attract local and international social investment.

Investors in Society is one of the newest of these intermediary initiatives and is unique among the members of INAISE in that it serves only CSOs and nonprofits. It was founded in 1996 by the Charities Aid Foundation—a U.K. registered charitable trust whose purpose is to increase the substance of charity. CAF had recognized that:

the market does not meet [needs] because unmet need provides no commercial return; and governments are limited in what they can take from the market's earnings for this purpose, among so many others. So, beyond government, there is only unremunerated effort to confront unmet need. That effort has to be made and resources have to be given to support it. For people, there is this obligation: to organise the entry of earnings, by whatever route from their origin in markets, into support of voluntary effort.

CAF's response was to capitalize a social investment fund that could then attract interest-free exempt deposits and donations from private individuals, companies, and other organizations, including commercial banks, to lend at low rates of interest to CSOs. The interest charge covers operating costs, loan loss provisions, and the technical assistance necessary to minimize risks. Such a fund also recognizes that in the United Kingdom the financial pressures on personal life-styles have led to changing patterns of life-cycle cash flows. As a result, while some people naturally want to make grand gestures to charity, reality suggests that it is foolish to completely give away assets during life. A loan can also work harder than an outright donation. For a company, a loan allows it to use its balance-sheet strength rather than take the expense of a donation through its profit-and-loss statement.

NGOs Working with Commercial Banks

Other ways of harnessing private capital include the use of existing mechanisms, particularly the banking system. CAF is exploring with U.K. banks ways to leverage the strength of their balance sheets for social good as well as financing exclusion projects through the commissions that are generated by investment funds.

In France, ADIE and its local partners screen micro projects to be funded and carry out all of the technical support. If they are approved by a joint ADIE–Credit Mutuel credit committee, Credit Mutuel will fund and manage the loans. And in Belgium, Netwerk Vlaanderen was set up in 1982 as a solidarity fund so that like-minded people could use money for social purposes rather than personal economic gain. It also seeks to develop new attitudes to money. Together with the now privatized savings bank, ASLK-CGER, it has developed a savings account, *Krekelsparen* ("cricket savings"). In return for generating savings for ASLK, Netwerk receives commissions that can be used for social exclusion projects. The savings themselves are invested ethically. Netwerk also benefits from an ASLK line of credit.

Use of Capital Markets

A further development has been the adaptation of capital markets instruments for social investment purposes. While the United States has state-backed bond issues for civil society purposes, there are several investment schemes in France where either the interest on the investment or part of the capital is applied for these purposes.

At least four new funds to make investment leading to job creation use Fondation France Active and its subsidiary finance company, Societe d'Investissement France Active, as intermediaries to manage these investments and to assist the development of community enterprises. Between 1987 and 1994, almost 240 million French francs (more than US$40 million) had been raised. The support of the trades union movement was critical in promoting the funds among the compulsory savings committees required under French employment law.

SHARED INTEREST

Shared Interest is a special form of cooperative lending society registered in the United Kingdom in 1990 under a cooperative law drafted by Christian socialists in 1852. It enables U.K. depositers to provide business credit for Third World cooperative and nonprofit enterprises. The Shared Interest vision is of an alternative to the capital-driven company, an alternative based on fair trade and mutual service in meeting human needs rather than on the open-ended accumulation of profit. The more than 4,000 investors are also members and shareholders.

Shared Interest helps to fund the whole cycle of production, from the purchase of raw materials, through trade finance, to long-term loans for equipment and buildings. In 1995 it launched a five-year zero coupon loan stock, guaranteed by the Co-operative Bank. This was the first time that a mainstream bank in the United Kingdom had been directly involved in a social investment of this type. Shared Interest has raised in excess of £10 million (approximately US$17 million).

A number of initiatives, including that by CAF, started with donor funding either from a group of individuals or from a foundation or other institution. In the United States, charitable trusts and foundations have used program-related investments (PRIs) to extend their support for civil society organizations. (See also Chapter 3.) PRIs can include loans, loan guarantees, equity investments, asset purchases, and linked deposits when made for charitable purposes. Although not used by all trusts, PRIs have amounted to more than US$700 million since their introduction more than 15 years ago.

Some foundations have also been seed funders of initiatives in third countries, such as Nigeria. Here, notwithstanding the crisis in governance, civil society is making a major effort to address the critical issue of enhancing the productive capacity of both the urban and rural poor, particularly women. Easing the access of the poor to credit is at the heart of the strategy to make economic development more sustainable.

Similarly, in the United States, community development loan funds recruit and lend capital around values of social justice, seeking to balance the interest of both individuals and communities. They look for variety in both the number and type of investors they attract. Five types of investor account for more than 93 percent of all loan capital in these funds, with the three largest being to individuals (27 percent), faith groups (23 percent), and foundations (with 20 percent).

An extension of this idea is exemplified by the Calvert funds, one of the leading sponsors of environmentally and socially responsible mutual funds in the United States, managing more than US$1.2 billion in responsibly invested funds. In late 1995, Calvert introduced Targeted Community Investment Notes, which let Calvert investors target savings at community development funds working in disadvantaged areas. These note instruments have been established for the sole purpose of bridging the gap between the world of investment and the passion for building a better world. They are in addition to the allocation by Calvert of up to 1 percent of the Calvert Social Investment Fund's assets for high-social-impact investments, whose experience and track record they are able to call on in enacting due diligence. Although focused

SELECTED PROJECTS SUPPORTED BY INAISE MEMBERS

Tabora Beekeepers is a cooperative of 2,500 beekeepers in Tanzania. They needed hard currency to buy the imported drums required to ship their honey to Traidcraft, a fair-trade organization in the United Kingdom. As Traidcraft had already paid them the maximum advance allowed, it introduced them to Shared Interest, in which many of its own supporters invested. After due diligence, Shared Interest provided a loan that the cooperative was able to repay from the sales proceeds when the honey reached Traidcraft.

Loca Labora is a producer of organic vegetables and spices in Belgium. It also provides catering and related services. It trains excluded people such as the long-term unemployed and the disabled. As Loca Labora does not benefit from core grant funding, it needed an alternative source of funding to develop its facilities and programs. This related to Netwerk Vlaanderen's mission, and it was able to help Loca Labora by providing low-interest prefinancing facilities, which could be repaid as cash flowed from the group's activities.

Instant Muscle is a U.K. charity that seeks to help unemployed and other disadvantaged (socially excluded) people enter employment or self-employment. Among other things, it runs Job Clubs on behalf of the Employment Service. In setting up new clubs, it needs to invest in resources and facilities before it receives payment, yet as a nonprofit it has not been able to build reserves to fund this internally. The banks were not interested. Investors in Society, founded by the Charities Aid Foundation, could help because the service met a social need and was viable at a preferential rate of interest

A small group of monks cares for terminally ill people, including AIDS sufferers. The monks decided to settle on a farm in northern France that provides a peaceful environment for these people. They needed a sympathetic lender who would understand the financial dynamics of the group and therefore how repayment could be arranged. INAISE member NEF was able to provide a loan to help with the purchase.

predominantly on need in the United States, up to 20 percent of available funds can support overseas projects, when risk can be identified and controlled.

Major Conclusions for Practitioners

The defining characteristic of many civil society organizations has been their lack of a secure resource base. There is a need for appropriate capacity building programs to strengthen NGOs' ability to both manage the resources they have and acquire additional resources. Many programs overlook these issues and concentrate instead on internal constraints, such as poor management or accounting systems and lack of reporting mechanisms. Although these are important, skills that help NGOs manage their resource dependence are also important, especially for NGOs in new democracies—since they have a unique window of opportunity to gain outside support that may close once the transition to democracy has been accomplished and donors withdraw. The need for private investment resources then becomes more acute.

As noted, private capital can be mobilized for socially beneficial purposes through legislative means (such as the CRA) or through a wish to do something. That impetus may have two driving forces. On the one hand, it may come about from the need to obtain credit that is not available in the formal finance sector; on the other, it may be driven by like-minded individuals who sense that the generation of social wealth is at least as important as the accumulation of personal financial wealth.

Market research in the United Kingdom has established that while people will continue to make donations, they can also be encouraged to "invest." Such investors will want to take CSOs seriously if they are to put capital at their disposition. They will want to channel their funds through acceptable and trustworthy intermediaries capable of monitoring their exposure and accountable to them. This is not about replacing charitable impulse and philanthropy; it is about extending it to meet changing circumstances.

Whatever their legal form, all these organizations share the common attribute of creating products and services that allow them to mobilize private savings for socially beneficial purposes, whether directly or on the back of the strength of a major bank's balance sheet. They also share the values of their contributors.

It seems that there are three key criteria to their success:

- Social benefit—An acceptance that it is not unreasonable to sacrifice a small part of financial investment return if it can lead to the creation of social wealth, including jobs.

- Connection—There is a clear link between investment in the funds and investment in social wealth creation in the region or area from which the funds came.

- Transparency and reputation—There is an openness about how the funds are collected, which is reinforced by the reputations of the savings organizations promoting the funds.

What is clear is that if such intermediaries are to be self-sustaining they need to bring the strands together. (See Box 2.) This can be achieved if the intermediary has a clear objective, such as to support CSO development, yet can provide comfort to investors, perhaps through partnership with existing financial institutions—where these are trusted—or through the use of existing financial market instruments. Transparency of action and connection between sources and application of funds are also essential components.

Guy Dauncey has noted that when a community's savings are controlled by a banking, savings, or investment institution whose commitment is to its own profit line and not to the well-being of the community, the community finds it hard to gather together its own resources to finance its development goals.

Yet it would be wrong to be euphoric about the role of social investment. Tapping into philanthropic contributions, let alone social investment, may be difficult in new democracies. The legislative and tax structures are not developed sufficiently to encourage giving or investment or to facilitate NGOs' acceptance of such funding. The economy in countries in transition is often marked by a decline in the middle classes and a widening gap between the haves and the have-nots. In Central Asia, for

Box 2

CHECKLIST FOR CSOS CONTEMPLATING ACTING AS INTERMEDIARIES

Why? What is your vision, and is it common to all stakeholders?

Does the legal, fiscal, and political framework allow your collective vision to be realized in whole or in part? If in part, will this prejudice what you are seeking to achieve?

Strategic planning for viability

Have you got the management and resources to deliver the plan?

Appropriate pricing, including accounting for inflation

Savings mobilization

Develop suitable products

Efficient operations

Be accountable; be transparent

Risk management

Human resource development—in-house and among borrowers; develop capacity to manage credit

Client support services

Share experience

Is it achieving the vision and meeting your plan? Are these still shared?

What are you learning? What have you got wrong? What have you got right?

What are you prepared to share with others?

How do you measure viability?

Are you moving toward viability?

What relationships are you building with the formal credit sector?

Are any of your customers passing into the formal credit sector?

---

example, NGOs would need to draw on the wealth generated by the 5 percent of the population who are benefiting from the transition. Such countries may also be characterized by low levels of confidence in government, which may mean that money is stored outside the country rather than reinvested within it.

Social investment is still at the margin when compared with need. It is not mainstream—and perhaps it never can be if it is to remain innovative. It is not yet ingrained in people's savings and investment habits. It is a revolution that is still too quiet. Most social investment institutions are small; many are no doubt undercapitalized and underresourced.

In established markets, social investment institutions are not always encouraged. A recent attempt to establish a bank in France to tackle social exclusion issues failed because the formal banking sector would not admit it into the deposit insurance fund. Yet shortly afterward some of the largest French banks were reporting losses far in excess of anything that could be contemplated by such a bank. Similarly, the Bank of England appears at best agnostic to the need for a sector-specific banking institution in any sector—let alone one that supports CSOs, which it does not particularly understand. On the other hand, the transformation of some microfinance initiatives into banking institutions shows what can be achieved when regulators and lawmakers are sympathetic to the ends being achieved. (See Chapter 10.)

Linking Private Capital to Local Finance and Sustainability

Community development is typically undertaken at a local level, but it is worth remembering that it takes place within a broader global market context today and is influenced by many external forces. Communities can position themselves to better anticipate and respond to changes by bringing together the various components of the community to work collaboratively. If a community's savings are deployed locally, there is a greater incentive to support sustainable community development because people have a sense of participation and local ownership.

Again, there is nothing new in this. Savings and credit cooperatives originated in the German *raiffeisen* in the 1840s. They provided people of modest income, excluded from the formal banking sector, with a place to save money together and make loans to each other at moderate rates of interest. Throughout the Industrial Revolution, the financial cooperative movement expanded to meet the economic need of its members. In the early 1900s, savings and credit cooperatives spread to Canada and the United States, and by the second half of the twentieth century they were found in all corners of the world.

Credit unions are associations of people who share a common bond that creates a degree of trust sufficient to serve as a guarantee for a loan. The members save in a collective account and lend their accumulated capital to each other up to specified limits. Worldwide, there are more than 200,000 such groups. In Ireland, 460 credit unions serve 20 percent of the population, while in Canada some are as large as banks. With some notable exceptions, they are as conservative as banks and have put deposit protection above innovation. But a radical pioneer is the VanCity Credit Union in British Columbia, which has developed a seed capital fund for young entrepreneurs and community initiatives as well as an ethical growth fund. Yet the importance of credit unions should not be downplayed. A recent World Bank report found that credit unions represented 11 percent of loans sampled in a wide survey of institutions offering microfinancial services.

Community Development Banking

The outstanding example of local community banking is South Shore Bank in Chicago. Its primary purpose is neighborhood development and renewal. In 1972, Shorebank

Corporation was incorporated as a regulated bank holding company. South Shore was a previously affluent part of Chicago with good, architectural-quality housing stock that had nonetheless experienced a continuing cycle of economic decline. The bank was soon included in the group of businesses on the point of failure. A consortium of voluntary-sector and church organizations came together with individuals to take forward the idea of a bank with mixed financial and social objectives. It was designed as a model of a permanent development financial institution that could renew neighborhoods and do so profitably.

It now has a group of operating companies providing a variety of financial products, and it has expanded into other rundown areas. It is also developing the world's first environmental development bank in the Pacific Northwest, seeking to match the wishes of environmentalists with the needs of communities who inhabit the area. Commercial banking includes working capital, refinancing, equipment purchase, plant acquisition and expansion loans, and asset-based loans. Real estate banking covers single and multifamily mortgages, housing rehabilitation, and refinancing loans. For nonprofit and community organizations, Shorebank provides a range of banking services and loans. It also handles retail and personal banking services for individuals.

Shorebank has also worked with the European Bank for Reconstruction and Development to share its skills in small business lending in Poland and Russia. After three years, the Polish program was sufficiently advanced to be able to turn it over to local control.

Shorebank has steadily increased the participation by local depositors, thereby retaining local funds for local needs while also attracting capital and deposits from around the country. However, it is fair to concede that the profile and growing "affluence" of the area have not been reflected in the rate of growth of the local deposit base. Marketing savings products to socially responsible individuals across the United States has ensured deposit growth. A key issue for the future will be whether Shorebank can break out of this "virtuous circle" to attract mainstream deposits as well as social investment. Measurement is also an issue. Hard measures of social outcomes are not easily developed, while soft measures of "community" can be observed.

A Community Investment Fund

A different approach was adopted in Scotland, where Scottish Community Enterprise Investment Fund (SCEIF) was formed in 1989. It emerged from the community business arena in response to a perception that commercial banks did not understand businesses or organizations run by unpaid directors with values other than personal profit. The banks wanted to tie the directors into the business through personal guarantees, which was seen by those involved as an unrealistic request when they were already seeking to provide services needed by the local community. The lending climate was one where community businesses were seen as a social experiment run by worthy people but destined to fail.

SCEIF was a response to this problem, and it set out to raise US$320,000 to lend to community businesses that could not raise funds elsewhere. These funds were to be used to help the businesses create or protect employment in disadvantaged areas. SCEIF now operates with its funds fully lent to 17 community businesses in Scotland. Although it is a closed-ended fund, the bedrock of SCEIF is the support of a range

SELECTED BANKING INTERMEDIARIES

Credit Populaire Zairois (CPZ) was created in 1987 by consumer and production cooperatives in the North Kivu region of Zaire in order to obtain access to finance readily available from commercial banks. Following authorization by the central bank, CPZ began operations in 1989. Deposits are obtained from members and others for lending to social housing and nutrition projects, environmental projects, and microfinance activities. However, the very uncertain economic and political climate has been a limiting factor in CPZ's ability to develop its services.

Banque Alternative Suisse (ABS) was started in 1990 by a working group of like-minded organizations. Lead contributors include World Wildlife Fund Switzerland, the Green Party, Network for Self Management, Christian Peace Service, and other NGOs. They encourage the participation of individual investors, and in 1994 there were more than 17,000 shareholders. ABS supports projects in the environment, housing, education and culture, health care, and women's projects and businesses.

Eko-osuuspankki (Eko) is a Finnish cooperative bank owned by members drawn from individuals and organizations. It is in the capital-raising phase now, and in the interim operates under the umbrella of another Finnish cooperative bank. Here the public can target their deposits or savings in a number of different ways, including farming, ecological products, social purposes, education, and fair trade.

Triodos Bank was founded in the Netherlands in 1980 and now also has branches in the United Kingdom and Belgium. It specifically seeks to invest in sustainable development. Triodos offers a range of savings accounts; some of them make it possible to direct funds to a particular project or sector, while others allow the investor to forego a level of return in favor of the borrower. From a strong European base, Triodos is increasingly active in financing projects in developing countries, including small financial institutions serving micro and small businesses, solar energy projects, and fair trade.

of individuals and institutions motivated to support their local communities largely through a sense of social responsibility. This was realized through a share issue rather than deposits, which would have raised regulatory issues.

The main shareholder groups are: individuals, 215 out of 291; community businesses, 39; local authorities, 16; commercial businesses, 11; charitable trusts, 5; churches, 3; 1 university; and 1 trade union. Individuals are not only the most significant category, they provide the bulk of the funding. Most community businesses appeared to be motivated by a sense of the importance of the strong within their movement helping the weak. Legislation requires that the funds committed by the local authorities be allocated within their geographic areas of benefit.

Three issues affect the sustainability of this fund. The first is the existence of willing shareholders. Like many of these institutions, including Shorebank, there is no ready market for the shares, and a seller must be matched with a willing buyer before funds can be realized. The second concern is the ability of the fund to revolve its credit base from borrower to borrower. To date, SCEIF's record has been positive, with less than 1 percent of its book nonperforming. The third issue is the level of administrative overhead the fund can sustain. By developing back office partnerships to outsource some of these activities, SCEIF has arrangements in place that effectively deal with this.

SCEIF was the first loan fund of this kind in the United Kingdom, and it has learned from its experience. The most significant lesson is that the legal structure was wrong, which has led to a decision not to expand the fund, at least in its present form. Limiting the size of the fund provides a barrier to the economies of scale that can be achieved. It was only when SCEIF funds were fully loaned out that it moved into surplus, and it still carries the start-up costs.

Village Banking

The Association for Sarva Seva Farms is one of the largest rural development organizations in India, working in six states and approximately 1,500 villages. Like many development agencies, ASSEFA seeks to foster self-reliance among those it works with, viewing its own involvement in any one area as catalytic and temporary—with withdrawal taking place once local institutions are strong enough to be self-sustaining. Defining exactly when and how to do that has proved more difficult. Groups go through cycles of increasing confidence, cohesion, and control followed by conflict and possible collapse or a sense of renewed cohesion and growth. It has been argued that only after surviving several such cycles can a group be considered self-reliant.

ASSEFA finance for the village councils has taken the form of grants for collective activities (such as the establishment of a day care nursery or employment of a night school teacher) or loans to village members for a specific purpose (such as crop loans to finance cultivation costs or for irrigation projects and livestock purchase). The latter is provided on credit terms, primarily to avoid undermining values of self-help and self-reliance. Since ASSEFA's presence in any area is intended to be temporary and demand for such assistance invariably exceeds supply, loan repayments can be used to build up a revolving fund that can remain as a source of loans for the village after ASSEFA has withdrawn. (See also Chapter 10.)

The Sarva Jana Seva Kosh, People's Welfare Bank (Kosh) was established by ASSEFA as a step in the process of enabling each village to establish its own independent, democratic, and sustainable system for recycling the funds that until then had been allowed simply to accumulate in a savings account held by ASSEFA on the village's behalf. Once the idea was implemented, other proposals about its role and mode of operation emerged.

The Kosh is registered as a profit-making company limited by guarantee and as a nonbanking finance company subject to direction by the Reserve Bank. It is owned by a body of shareholders who each have a capital stake of one rupee.

One function of the Kosh is to encourage savings, and to this end it can collect individual deposit accounts but not collective accounts, such as that of the village council. As a nonbank financial institution, it is also required to cover deposits with investments in a recognized bank. This means that it cannot leverage the deposits for unsecured lending. A second function is to provide shareholders with access to credit on more attractive terms than might otherwise be available. The initial source of capital for this is the repayment of the original ASSEFA assistance. This limits the potential size of the fund. Interestingly, the village council body—not the Kosh branch manager—is responsible for deciding who should get loans. This is motivated by ASSEFA's belief that this will foster participation and a sense of ownership among shareholders.

In 1993, a study of the Lathur branch of the Kosh found that various stakeholders did not share the same vision of the Kosh. One view was of a permanent organization providing financial services to shareholders, some of whom had been beyond the reach of any other formal financial institution. In this way, poor clientele can be reached by delegating loan appraisal, monitoring, and recovery to voluntary village institutions, thereby substantially reducing the transaction costs. Yet a second quite distinct view also emerged. This was that the Kosh should not be a permanent institution at village level at all, but a means to establishing each village council as a fully independent financial institution. The danger is that if this idea is prematurely implemented, it could lead to a rapid erosion of the capital or its monopolistic control by a small minority within the village council.

While these tensions had still to be resolved at the time of the study, there had been impressive growth in the number of shareholders, value of savings, revolving funds, and loans outstanding. If the Kosh is to be truly sustainable, however, it must be able to lend the deposits to the benefit of the communities rather than having to place them with banks unless these deposits lever direct bank lending.

Community Initiatives Based on Traditional Ways of Saving

In Nigeria, there is a strong tradition of credit and savings that has for centuries supported informal-sector activities. These include *esusu* (revolving credit associations) and regular savings collections, as well as the mutual aid program in which members assist each other through the extension of cash and in-kind services.

During the 1980s there were organized public-sector efforts to expand development finance flows to microenterprise for investment and working capital. In addition, a number of NGOs have adapted traditional practices to create community development finance initiatives (CDFIs). Founded often by visionaries, CDFIs are now moving to the institutional stage of development and the need to build skills in financial intermediation management. They generally adopt a multisectoral approach that allows them to address a whole range of social needs by using microfinance as an entry point to promote social development messages.

The CDFIs offer both credit and savings facilities to people—generally female micro entrepreneurs—who lack access to the formal financial sector. To enhance savings mobilization, most CDFIs have linked credit access to savings deposited. Savings are beginning to be an important factor in the growth of loan funds, contributing between 10 and 50 percent of loanable funds. Two organizations in Nigeria, DEC-Enugu and COWAN, have begun to link clients to the formal banking sector. This has been facilitated by loan guarantee arrangements designed by the groups. In DEC-Enugu, a system for graduating borrowers to the formal banking sector after five years has been developed. Initially, they can access credit from a commercial bank with a loan guarantee from the DEC Finance Trust set up for that purpose. COWAN uses funds from a donor and members' savings deposits to guarantee loans from the United Bank for Africa for its members. Under this arrangement, COWAN is able to leverage twice the amount of the guaranteed funds.

CDFIs are able to build strong relationships with their members and clients at a local level by going out at least once a month to meet beneficiaries at their places of work and residence. FADU, the largest CDFI, has built a membership of almost 300,000 in its eight years of existence. The membership of COWAN, the oldest CDFI, has grown from 50 in 1982 to more than 78,000 in 1996, while others typically range from 3,500 to 50,000. The growth in domestic savings activity is essential for the longevity of these institutions. The CDFIs have managed to draw on the traditional savings and credit practices as well as to use outreach methods that reduce the likelihood of client alienation in environments with particular cultural values. By using female officers in Islamic communities, for example, CDFIs such as DEC-Bauchi have facilitated the involvement of women in purdah in microenterprise activity.

CDFIs face a number of challenges that need to be overcome if they are to meet the needs of the informal sector. Included here is a high dependence on donor provision of loan funds. The importance of private capital and savings mobilization cannot be overemphasized if the programs are to attain sustainability, especially if donor priorities change. The portfolios are still too small in relation to need. Governance and skilled management will become increasingly important issues as CDFIs grow. They must also be able to demonstrate to donors, contributors, and savers that the impact and reach of their programs can be measured. The success of DEC-Enugu and COWAN in engaging the formal financial sector must be extended, otherwise a self-perpetuating cycle will not be broken. Social development programs and other nonfinancial technical assistance will require ongoing grant funding and should not expect to be covered by operating surpluses.

A further challenge for CDFIs is to build links with the formal financial sector and to devise ways of leveraging the amount of finance necessary to diversify the funding base and to expand the loan portfolio. One response has been the establishment in 1993 of the Community Development Trust Fund in Nigeria to serve as an intermediary to facilitate the scaling up of CDFI activity. Its objectives are to promote linkages between the formal and informal financial systems through credit guarantees, to support grassroots development institutions to improve their management skills and generally strengthen their organizational capacity, and to develop and maintain a sectoral database.

The Community Development Trust Fund provides portfolio refinancing facilities to retailing CDFIs and lends directly itself. It assists with institutional capacity building and supports older CDFIs through loan guarantee facilities. These services are currently extended to 21 CDFIs. The emphasis on capacity building recognizes the need to create better service delivery processes and to attract higher caliber staff. There is also a need to network and share experiences—good and bad—as well as to minimize areas of overlap. Finally, the Nigerian CDFI market needs to develop self-regulatory mechanisms if it is to continue to develop in an innovative and non-bureaucratic way.

A 1997 report on community development finance in Nigeria suggests that the future viability of the sector—and by implication, of civil society—depends on a continuing donor role in providing a strong institutional framework. But this must be tempered by a higher level of relationship between CDFIs and organized private capital through the use of credible intermediary institutions. Although these are important, by far the greatest challenge concerns the need for CDFIs to become more business-like. To attract private capital, especially at the local level, to gain the respect of the formal financial sector, and to win official encouragement, they need to show more clearly how they alleviate poverty through the use of measurable indices of outreach and service delivery. In social programs, this is not always easy to achieve.

Developments in Countries in Transition

Although these examples may have elements that could be translated in the context of the countries in transition, none address what is happening in countries where there is a real need to build a sustainable civil society. Many of the financial intermediation initiatives are directed at microfinance, such as Fundusz Mikro in Poland, the Nachala Foundation in Bulgaria, and Yednannya (Unity) in Ukraine. They are not yet providing finance or introducing social investment to CSOs. If some of these initiatives do build stronger communities, however, that could lead to more local resources becoming available to support civil society organizations.

One interesting development has been Bise, the Bank for Socio-Economic Initiatives. Established as a joint stock bank in Poland in 1990, Bise's objective is to support economic restructuring policy rather than act as a commercial bank. As it does not take deposits from the private sector, it is not a mechanism for the harnessing of social investment for public benefit per se. But from the start, Polish government organizations have been partnered by the French Caisse Centrale de Credit Cooperatif and the Credit Foncier de France, which have introduced both external private capital and banking know-how about small and medium-sized enterprises and about community sectors.

Bise specializes in term lending, but also provides money management services and consultancies, particularly for foundations and associations. There is now an ISE family of companies, which includes the Foundation for Socio-Economic Initiatives that has developed capacity-building programs to support projects aimed at stimulating business activity in local communities.

Although Bise does not appear to be financing CSOs on a commercial basis, it has done so through a grant program that is an integral part of its activities. Projects supported have included a primary school near Bilgoraj (the work was started with funding raised by villagers and then completed with a grant from Bise), the NGO fund at the Stefan Batory Foundation, the Child's Heart Foundation for special care children in Wejherowo, and the intensive care ward at a children's hospital in Warsaw that Bise has supported since 1992.

The Inter-American Foundation has suggested that "economic stability and basic conditions for generating genuine wealth seem to be prerequisites for mobilizing significant local resources for development." In the first instance NGOs in the new democracies may have to engage with the corporate sector or even state-owned businesses to generate financing for civil society development. However, as confidence grows and a middle class develops, NGOs must be able to adapt to accommodate these sources as well.

Many of the microfinance initiatives in the countries in transition are targeted at building a new middle class rather than serving the very poorest. If they are successful, it will be interesting to see whether the private savings that this new class will generate can be harnessed with the objectives of banks such as Bise.

Major Conclusions for Practitioners

In their own ways, these examples show different types of intermediary institutions, some of which have sought to harness local savings while others have benefited from external capital and the banking know-how that came with it. Why are local resources necessary? True financial intermediation takes place between net savers and net borrowers without dependence on external funds.

But this will not always be possible. A marginalized community may not have adequate seed capital to start a savings initiative. It may require external funds by way of grant or outside social investment to have sufficient capital to get under way. Over time, this should allow it to build and then strengthen its own saving capacity to become a self-sustaining organization.

Longevity is not solely a function of ability to raise locally generated deposits, however. An organization must also have the ability to lend at market rates (however determined) and to control loan delinquencies within acceptable norms. This is particularly relevant to microfinance institutions. Poverty is not a practical common bond for a self-sustaining financial organization. Assessment of the borrowing needs of CSOs or microenterprises can require both time and investment in active account management. When placed alongside the relatively small size of individual loans, this leads to high transaction costs. These make it difficult to maintain a sustainable institution based solely on lending operations. There is a clear need to attract people and organizations with the capacity to be net savers, as well as those who have a realistic capacity to save. These contribute to a savings pool from which borrowers may have access to credit—unless regulations divorce the two activities, as in the Kosh.

In spite of these constraints, these and other innovative mechanisms can help CSOs move away from the project cycle of existence and toward financial sustainability, where core costs are covered and the organization can exercise control over its activities. As noted earlier, organizations pass through various stages of development as they move toward sustainability. And the highest level is achieved when internal cash flows, local savings, and borrowed funds—that may in part or wholly be represented by social investment—can support the organization's activities.

The funding needs of CSOs are large and growing. Where investment is hard to get, it is natural that organizations will turn to government or charity for support, often in the form of a grant. Unless this support is geared to securing a graduation to other forms of financing in due course, two issues arise: the amount of grant or aid is limited and geographically uneven, with supply subject to economic and political pressures. Although a grant may kick-start the project or the organization, there can be no guarantee that support will continue. Further, such funding will not provide the track record and experience in dealing with finance necessary to develop the organization's full potential.

Being able to recognize the stages of development of an organization better positions supporters to understand the nature of an NGO's relationship with donors, beneficiaries, and the community in which it operates. Many NGOs in new democracies, for instance, are struggling with the first stage of starting up their activities; few have been able to acquire the resources necessary to finance expansion of their activities. When they have, they are often driven by donors' plans and priorities. Capacity-building assistance is required to allow them to maximize creative financing strategies. Early-stage development requires the mobilization of resources, while later-stage development, as in Scotland, requires mechanisms to let CSOs and community businesses finance the capitalization of resources.

So how do civil society organizations graduate from grant and aid dependency to attracting social investment and building local cash flows? The response is not simple. Indeed, there is probably no single correct answer. Some find it at least an uphill, if not impossible struggle.

The problem right now is that capital is unevenly distributed around the world. Grants and external social investment are needed to establish and support fledgling organizations, or to scale up existing operations. The flow of this "capital" must be controlled to avoid it becoming a hydrological tube that drowns the very organizations it is seeking to nourish. While they depend on these sources, CSOs can never progress to self-sustainability. To do so, they must build local partnerships and relationships. At one level, this will be through the ability to attract local savings or investment to help finance their activities; at another, it will be the ability to generate income locally from services or products that allow them to build internal cash flows to service indebtedness and finance expansion.

A second-generation American from the Ukraine or an expatriate Indian living in Canada or an Australian living in London may all feel a sense of social responsibility to the land of their forbears. But outside of the immediate family circle, there may be no ready way of establishing trust about which organizations to support, nor a cost-effective way of holding them to account or measuring the effect of the "investment." The scale and the diversity of need and resource is beyond the compass of existing social investment organizations.

The time is perhaps right for a citizens' world bank, which could be the grit in the oyster that turns global social investment, drawn together by existing savings mechanisms, into effective support for local CSOs by being able to make key lending and investment decisions while remaining accountable to its investors. Such an institution would also be in a position to provide technical assistance to organizations to help them build the confidence and knowledge necessary to create local relationships central to their prospects for longevity.

As groups seek to fund an increasing number of entrepreneurs in the countries in transition who will help to form a new middle class, it is necessary to ensure that the infrastructure of a civil society is also soundly resourced. An institution of such scale must not, of course, be allowed to undermine the efficacy of credit as a tool in the relief of poverty or in the building of a civil society. Nor must it exclude the very organizations and people it was designed to serve. Rather, if it can establish some form of collateral enhancement through, say, one of the arms of the World Bank, it should develop a capability to support innovation and to take the risks necessary to ensure a vibrant civil society in all parts of the world.

RESOURCE GUIDE

Bibliography

Awolowu-Dosumu, O., N. Amah, K. Samuel, and V.N. Ahuchogu, *Community Development Finance in Nigeria* (Lagos, Nigeria: Malthouse Press, 1997).

Brophy, M., "Citizens World Bank," unpublished paper. 1995.

Copestake, J., P. Bragman, and S. Michael, *Report on a Review of the Sarva Jana Seva Kosh* (Friends of ASSEFA, 1993).

Dauncey G., "Alternative Banking and External Investments" in Reigier and Ford, eds., *Banking for People* (Berlin: De Gruyter, 1992).

Federation du Credit Mutuel Mediterraneen, *Sud Developpement*, Marseille, France, quarterly.

Getubig, I., J. Remenyi, and B. Quinones, eds., *Creating the Vision* (Asian and Pacific Development Centre, 1997).

Green, E., *Banking, An Illustrated History* (New York: Rizzoli, 1989).

Hayday, M., "New Sources of Borrowing for Charities," in *Charity Finance Yearbook 1997* (London; 1997).

Hudock, A., "From Transition to Consolidation," paper prepared for the Johns Hopkins University School of Advanced International Studies, 1997.

Hughes, P., "Scottish Community Enterprise Investment Fund," working paper for INAISE research, 1996.

INAISE, "Member Profiles," Brussels, 1996.

Inter-American Foundation, "'95 in Review," Arlington, Va., 1995.

Loffredo, F.A., and M. Zagaria, "Give Solidarity a Credit!" Fores-Mag, Napoli, Italy, 1996.

Ministry of Rural Development, "Poverty Eradication and Microcredit," Kuala Lumpur, Malaysia, 1997.

National Association of Community Development Loan Funds, "A 5-year profile of the Membership of NACDLF," Philadelphia, Pa., 1991.

Nigam, A., and M. Mohiuddin, "Give Us Credit," based on the findings of *Microcredit: Lessons Learned from UNICEF Experience* (New York: UNICEF, 1997).

Nonprofit Facilities Fund, "Columns," the NFF newsletter, New York, 1996.

Otera, M., and E. Rhyne, *The New World of Microenterprise Finance* (Intermediate Technology Publications, 1994).

Renz, L., and C. Massarsky, "Program-Related Investments," The Foundation Center, New York, 1995.

Robertson, J., "Future Wealth, Future Work and the Social Economy in Europe," address to the Developing Social Wealth, INAISE Conference, Birmingham, 1995.

Unwin, J., *Lending Money* (London: The Baring Foundation, 1997).

Vincent, F., *Alternative Financing of Third World Organisations and NGOs* (Geneva: IRED, 1995).

Organizations

Bise Bank
ul. Krolewska 27
00-060 Warsaw
Poland
Tel: (48-22) 827-6639
Fax: (48-22) 827-7824

Calvert Foundation
4550 Montgomery Avenue
Bethesda, MD 20814
Tel: (1-800) 727-5578
Fax: (1-301) 654-2960

Charities Aid Foundation
Kings Hill
West Malling
Kent ME19 4TA
United Kingdom
Tel: (44-1732) 520-000
Fax: (44-1732) 520-001
E-mail: inquiries@caf.charitynet.org
Web site: http://www.charitynet.org

CTM Cooperazione Terzo Mondo
Via Macello 18
39100 Bolzano
Italy
Tel: (39-471) 975-333
Fax: (39-471) 977-599
E-mail: CTMBZOO @ link-Bz.com-
        link.apc.org
Web site: http://ines.gn.apc.org/ctm/

The Foundation Center
79 Fifth Avenue
New York, NY 10003
Tel: (1-212) 620-4230
Fax: (1-212) 691-1828

Hivos (Humanist Institute for Cooperation with Developing Countries)
Raamweg 16
2596 HL The Hague
The Netherlands
Tel: (31-70) 363-6907
Fax: (31-70) 361-7447
E-mail: hivos@antenna.nl
Web site: http://www.dds.nl/~hivos

International Network of Alternative Financial Institutions
International Secretariat
IDESI Nacional
Calle Las Perdices 122
San Isidro, Lima 27
Peru
Tel: (51-1) 221-7232
Fax: (51-1) 422-5213
E-mail: postmaster@inafi.org.pe
Web site: http://www.rcp.net.pe/inafi

International Association of Investors in the Social Economy
Rue d'Arlon 40
B-1000 Brussels
Belgium
Tel: (32-2) 230-3057
Fax: (32-2) 230-3764
E-mail: aries-inaise@geo2.poptel.org.uk

International Labour Office Enterprise and Cooperatives Development Department
PO Box 500
CH-1211 Geneva 22
Tel: (41-22) 799-6070
Fax: (41-22) 799-7691

International NGO Training and Research Organisation
PO Box 563
Oxford OX2 6RZ
United Kingdom
Tel: (44-1865) 201-851
Fax: (44-1865) 201-852
E-mail: intrac@gn.apc.org

International Development Resource Centre (IRED)
64 Horton Place
Colombo 7
Sri Lanka
Tel: (94-1) 695-481
Fax: (94-1) 688-368

IRED Nord
Via Tacito 10
00193 Rome
Italy
Tel: (39-6) 320-7849
Fax: (39-6) 320-8155

Nonprofit Facilities Fund
70 West 36th Street
11th Floor
New York, NY 10018
Tel: (1-212) 868-6710
Fax: (1-212) 268-8653
E-mail: info@nffny.org

Opportunity International
360 West Butterfield Road
Elmhurst, IL 60522
Tel: (1-630) 279-9300
Fax: (1-630) 279-3107

Opportunity EE and CIS
Dapontegasse 2
A-1030 Vienna
Austria
Tel: (43-1) 715-2589
Fax: (43-1) 715-2588

Stichting Doen
Van eeeghenstraat 70
PO Box 75621
1070AP Amsterdam
The Netherlands
Tel: (31-20) 573-7333
Fax: (31-20) 675-7397

Triodos Bank NV
Prins Hendriklaan 9-11
PO Box 55
3700 AB Zeist
The Netherlands
Tel: (31-30) 693-6500
Fax: (31-30) 693-6555
Web site: http://www.Triodos.com

World Bank Sustainable Banking with the Poor
ASTHR/AGPRW
1818 H Street, N.W.
Washington, DC 20433
Tel: (1-202) 458-0277
Fax: (1-202) 522-1662
E-mail: ccuevas@worldbank.org

Chapter 13

Mobilizing Civil Society's Resources: A Shared Responsibility

David Valenzuela

Participatory democracy and the active involvement of citizens in defining public policy and contributing to the betterment of society require a strong and diverse civil society. This is at the heart of making democratic forms of governance function in an effective and accountable manner, while remaining responsive to citizens and providing them with space for individual or collective initiative and creativity. For civil society to exist, there must be citizens interested in organizing and belonging to organizations, freedom to associate, and public policies and societal norms that set the scope and parameters for organizations to form. Also essential, however, is a secure and independent source of revenue to sustain them.

As noted throughout this book, civil society organizations (CSOs) around the world have used a variety of strategies to generate resources to sustain their work. International assistance has been an important source of financing in the developing world and newly democratic countries, as have member contributions, grants from public and private entities, and income generation mechanisms such as the sale of goods and services. Increased attention is now being given in these countries to building local philanthropic habits and institutions and establishing organizational endowments to foster and sustain civil society initiatives. In most countries of the world, however, fledgling CSOs still face the challenge of securing a long-term, stable resource base while maintaining their autonomy and independence.

The resource enhancement or funding strategies of civil societies in northern countries with strong democracies can serve as important models. But innovative and locally generated resource enhancement alternatives rooted in individual cultures need to be developed. The growth of a strong civil society will depend on the ability of its members and citizens to secure local resources to create and sustain their organizations.

Grants and loans from international donors will continue to play an important, albeit diminishing, role in southern and eastern countries. Debt swaps, where possible, could provide a unique opportunity for securing large amounts of funds to establish endowments or related grant-making facilities.

Governments are increasingly open to providing contracts or grants to CSOs, often as a result of a competitive procurement process. This source of funding, with the inherent risks of political manipulation, is likely to grow in importance for CSOs in the South and East as governments "downsize" and seek new ways of providing services. In Latin America and elsewhere, there is a strong move toward decentralization and transfer of resources and functions to local governments, which in many areas are turning to CSOs to extend their service delivery capacity, to help in planning, and to be a direct link to local communities and constituencies.

As economic reform and privatization continue to generate greater market activity around the world, private-sector institutions are also becoming engaged in social and community development activities. CSOs' relations with the private sector are therefore another area of significant activity and priority, as is their direct engagement in the market.

The preceding 11 chapters offer insight into concrete strategies and give examples of CSO resource generation around the world. As mentioned in the Foreword, however, *Sustaining Civil Society* is not intended as a handbook or a "how-to" training manual. Instead, in addition to providing the illustrative examples of other CSOs, it is intended to challenge CSO leaders to question and critically examine their current resource status and begin the process of determining how to best combine and apply these varied approaches into a comprehensive strategy for long-term financial sustainability—as well as how best to affect the policies and decisionmaking processes that influence their work.

Defining a Strategy for Financial Sustainability

Perhaps two obvious conclusions can be drawn from this compendium: First, no single resource enhancement strategy can serve as a silver bullet or panacea for civil society. Second, no single recipe for CSO financial sustainability exists. There is no single combination of multiple strategies, sequence of steps, or preconditions that can be established, nor any single formula for replication from one organization or context to another. Local cultural, economic, historical, political, and social as well as organizational realities are simply too diverse. Instead, the variety and diversification of these resource generation approaches is imperative to the sustainability of CSOs and to their capacity to act effectively as autonomous and independent voices in society.

Sustainable CSO financing relies on a diverse base of funding sources so as to minimize an organization's dependence on any one source and its vulnerability to shifts in fund availability and donor preferences. A strategy to accomplish this consists of diversifying sources of income along several dimensions: tapping both public and private sources; using primarily local sources, although potentially also national and international ones; and applying different types of resource generation approaches (contracts, grants, sales, fees, dues, and so on).

Sustaining Civil Society aims to help CSOs in the sometimes daunting process of understanding these various and diverse strategic resource enhancement methods. By illustrating the wide variety of tools at the disposal of CSOs, it is hoped that the book helps begin a process of critical examination. CSOs and their supporters must take a more "holistic" approach to resource generation, recognizing that responsibility for sustaining their work is shared with other sectors of society. Such an approach begins with a fundamental redefinition of the traditional perceptions and relations of civil society with other sectors of society—the state and market. While the need for autonomy is essential for a healthy public life, the delineation between the three sectors has become increasingly artificial, and the need for cooperation and partnership is clearer than ever in light of increasingly scarce resources and the recognition that no single organization or sector can meet myriad expanding social needs.

A truly holistic and sustainable strategy to resource generation consists of a dual-level approach, addressing the organizational sustainability of CSOs themselves as well as the external environment that surrounds them. First, financial sustainability depends on the institutional capacity of CSOs and their ability to plan, manage, and evaluate their activities effectively. Second, it depends heavily on an enabling environment. The legal, policy, and regulatory environment largely dictates CSOs' relative ability to leverage and mobilize resources. The institutional sustainability of CSOs and thus their financial sustainability is therefore a shared responsibility of all sectors.

The Need for Multisectoral Partnerships

Although this book was designed to focus on defining effective strategies for mobilizing resources to sustain CSOs, it would be impossible—if not negligent—to ignore the critical role CSO relations with other sectors play in determining the effectiveness of these strategies. Defining sustainable resource mobilization strategies requires a recognition of the larger environment in which civil society exists. In so doing, it becomes clear that the responsibility for ensuring a vibrant and effective civil society is shared between CSOs, the public sector, and private institutions.

Not only is the resource base of international donors shrinking, but the magnitude of needs throughout the globe is growing. While myriad innovative possibilities exist for enhancing resources, is it realistic for civil society to assume the burden of development in the wake of the failure of the state? With the dramatic growth in corruption in many regions of the world, widespread disillusionment with government at all levels is understandable. Yet is the mosaic of civil society institutions a realistic alternative?

Successful cases of sustainable development point to a different approach—one based on a balanced partnership between civil society and the state and market, especially at the local level. A new relationship is needed between citizens and state, where each performs a vital role. The goal of sustainability hangs in the balance of this relationship. What is needed is a new compact in which governance becomes the instrument that leads to the partnership between organized citizens and their democratically elected governments. For this balance to work, democracy, participation, decentralization, the rule of law, equity, and social investment are all required.

The challenge for civil society is to strive to achieve these conditions in order to reach this new balance.

Sustainability may be akin to a complex ecosystem in which the survival of the whole depends on the individual parts, and vice versa. Individual resource enhancement strategies are an important part of the solution. But the fuller answer may lie in the equilibrium and interaction of mutually interdependent and complementary stakeholders. Local government in the developing world has been a key missing link in the achievement of that equilibrium.

In highly successful societies, local governments sustain the essential services required for people to live satisfying lives. Yet this task cannot be performed adequately without the full participation of the organized community and the active involvement of the private sector. Poor localities also depend on central government to equalize services and opportunities for all citizens. Employment generation requires economic development, which in turn depends on an enabling environment, entrepreneurship, and investment. The task of economic development—like democratic governance—is a shared responsibility for all stakeholders in a community. These same stakeholders must also ensure a healthy environment, access to health and education, recreational and cultural activities, adequate shelter for all citizens, and so on.

If an entire nation is to move forward as one, sustainability must start at society's base: among individuals, their families, and, most important, their communities. Civil society and its organizations are the intermediaries that connect these base units of society to one another and the larger society. This is the essence of the overall strategy of shared responsibility.

Resource enhancement strategies are part of a symbiotic relationship of local stakeholders. Local governments must have a resource base to provide services and foster the enabling environment for social and economic development. Civil society partners mobilize citizen participation, foster policy dialogue, present innovative solutions, and extend the capacity of local governments as recipients of grants and contracts. The private sector is no less important in this ecosystem. Its job is to become a full partner in the process, as well as to provide leadership in generating the goods and services for the sustenance of everyone.

Although this multisector partnership might appear to be logical, it is far removed from the reality in most developing countries, which are deeply rooted in authoritarian traditions that have bred low levels of human trust and impeded collaboration beyond the confines of the extended family or ethnic group. Enlightened governance is nothing less than the task of cooperation and consensus building to undertake actions for the common good.

While individual CSOs must define a strategy to sustain themselves, the sustainability of the whole of civil society requires a complex fabric of cooperation and interdependence among all its subsectors. National and local governments, the private sector, philanthropic organizations, citizens, and foreign donors all play a role in this process. Few private organizations in the South and East—or in the North, for that matter—are able to sustain themselves solely on the contributions of their members. For these organizations, the road to sustainability, independence, and fulfillment of their institutional mandates requires a diversified funding strategy.

Groups of organizations can partner to share resources or can contract with each other. As noted in Chapter 5, grassroots citizens' organizations and intermediary non-governmental organizations (NGOs) and federations are traditional allies. The incorporation of new actors, such as private business organizations and local governments, can broaden both the partnership and the resource base. Countries with weak civil societies have revealed a reluctance of civil society members to join forces in cooperative action; in this case, there is a deficit of social capital rather than financial resources. Ultimately, the individual and collective strength of civil society depends on the willingness of its members to cooperate with one another, and to reach out to other stakeholders in the state and market.

Role of the Private Sector

The private sector and the countless institutions related to it are key and indispensable counterparts of a strong civil society and a vibrant democratic system. Emerging markets in the South and East are testimony that a strong private sector is the engine of economic growth and job creation. The private sector has an enormous stake in, as well as sharing significant responsibility for, the existence of social harmony and basic freedoms that only democracy can provide. Strong economies have experienced a parallel growth of civic institutions as they seek to strengthen the rule of law and democratic freedoms.

Throughout the world, there is growing awareness on the part of the private business world that social investment and justice are fundamental elements for sustainable economic growth. Without strong and sustained investments in education, economic development goals are likely to fall short for lack of a qualified labor pool. Education is considered the highest-yielding investment for both individuals and nations. Similar returns can be expected from a healthy labor force.

In many nations of the South and East, the move to privatize is swelling the ranks of the private sector and attracting unprecedented levels of foreign investment. At the same time, as governments curtail spending and struggle to bring their macroeconomic houses in order, they are faced with reduced capacity to tend to the social investment needs of their populations. This has forced the private sector to reassess its own role in addressing issues of poverty and environmental degradation. Private-sector think tanks are offering their own solutions to these problems and, increasingly, their resources.

Among the vestiges of the cold war is a lingering distrust between civil society organizations and the private sector and government. Often, the private sector viewed some CSOs as being ideologically opposed to free markets and the profit motive. CSOs, in turn, considered that private business did not necessarily play a socially responsible role. Since the collapse of state socialism as a realistic alternative for social organization, civil society and the private sector have been finding common ground in their commitment to democracy and the importance of market-driven economic development. As CSOs become more accepting of the market and the need to maintain macroeconomic balances, the private sector is demonstrating growing awareness of the problems of inequality and the need for a greater commitment to social investment.

Role of Government

In many regions of the world, local governments are increasing their involvement in formulating and implementing social and economic policy. The extension of democratic forms of governance to the local level, coupled with growing municipal revenues and responsibility for basic services, is offering unprecedented opportunities for local civil society's cooperation with municipal authorities. Creative mayors have realized the importance of CSOs in reaching broad constituencies to foster participation in resolving local problems. They have come to realize that grassroots citizens' organizations and intermediary NGOs can be powerful allies in the struggle to reduce poverty and foster local economic growth. Equally important, they can also make good allies in approaching central governments that are reluctant to devolve authority or resources to the local level.

When central governments curtail their programs to adjust to fiscal realities, they are obliged to transfer responsibilities to local governments. When this is accompanied by an expansion of democratic practice and the election of local officials, the momentum for further decentralization increases, along with the demand of citizens for better and more responsive local government. With or without new resources, democratically elected local authorities are under growing pressure from their constituencies to act in the public interest.

The bulk of civil society activity is focused on local issues. Hence, effective decentralization to the local level of essential services for people offers enormous opportunities for CSOs to become engaged in the critical matters that affect people's daily lives. Obviously, decentralization alone does not necessarily lead to good governance. A strong (as opposed to large) central government is necessary to ensure an equitable distribution of national resources and to establish and maintain national standards for education, health, environmental quality, administration of justice, and so on. For the same reason, decentralization also needs a strong national civil society to maintain focus and vigilance over critical issues affecting the whole of a country.

Decentralization is a global trend that can have a far reaching impact on the role of civil society and the consolidation of democracy. While it remains an infant proposition in much of the South and East, still in the stranglehold of strong centralist traditions, decentralization is creating a new dynamic at the local level that promises to redefine the relationship between the individual and the state. Local elections and performance demands on local officials are creating new space for citizen participation in defining priorities that have a direct bearing on their daily lives. In most countries, the transfer of resources and revenues generally lags far behind the delegation of responsibilities from the central to the local levels. Nevertheless, localities in many countries have seen their income levels increase dramatically.

Still, it is a practical reality that elections alone cannot guarantee effective government. The challenge that lies ahead is to develop new traditions of local governance and democratic practice where none existed. In this respect, CSOs are critically important to ensure effective programs and participation, sound fiscal management, and accountability.

Local government funding of civil society programs offers great potential for the sustainability of services. As the resource base of municipal governments grows, there is a great temptation to emulate central governments in building bureaucracies and imposing programs from the top. It is of paramount importance for civil society to resist such moves to ensure that local governments develop participatory methods and rely on partnerships with civil society and the private sector to carry out their mission.

Role of Donors

There is a growing realization that development assistance from the North is diminishing dramatically. Many countries in Latin America and in Central and Eastern Europe have seen official development assistance practically disappear. Although external funding has been of critical importance for many CSOs, it has also constituted a mixed blessing. Oftentimes, resources are accompanied by preconceived notions of what program priorities should be. Most donors have carefully crafted ideas to go along with the funds they are willing to make available. Not infrequently, the package of funds and ideas also includes expert consultants, eager to influence the outcome of programs.

Even the most enlightened donors have difficulty avoiding the problem of dependency among their beneficiaries. Sustainability of programs and organizations, following the withdrawal of external assistance, has been a major unresolved problem for both donors and recipients. They share the notion that success means doing without the other, while maintaining programs and services for the ultimate beneficiaries. Donors are constantly challenged by their overseers to demonstrate that the programs they support can have a life of their own, while grant recipients dream about achieving self-sufficiency, with the freedom and independence that entails.

The issue of sustainability has plagued donors, large and small, in the same manner that it has frustrated CSOs and grant recipients anxious to escape dependency. As resources for international development assistance diminish, there is a growing realization that self-sufficiency and sustainability must come from locally generated capacities to build coalitions and mobilize resources. However worthy or tempting a project for basic human services may be, it can lead to frustration and failure unless it has a clearly defined plan for future sustainability. The basic problem is that sustainability remains elusive.

As a rule of thumb, however, the closer the delivery of goods and services is to those requiring them, the greater likelihood that they will be sustained over time. This is particularly true if local community-based organizations are able to participate in the formulation of the service delivery policy and its implementation, and can receive government sanction, including resources, for this. This is a logical extension of the decentralization principle discussed in the section on the role of government.

The well-documented incapacity of most governments in the South and East to address poverty and foster sustainable development has contributed to the emerging role of civil society. Bilateral assistance programs and multilateral donors have joined U.S. and European foundations in praising civil society actors as the preferred way to "get the job done." In many cases, funds have more effectively reached the intended beneficiaries. The wells were dug, condoms distributed, food rations given, and micro-credits extended while the funds lasted.

But shifting donor priorities, budget cuts, and debates about foreign assistance have severely shaken the confidence of southern and eastern CSOs and their northern partners, casting doubt on program sustainability. Wild swings from feast to famine for southern and eastern CSOs are not uncommon, as donor funds migrate from priority to priority. During times of plenty, CSOs have been known to replace or overshadow local and provincial governments in resources and, hence, power. When the funds dry up, so do the programs. And people go back to basic survival or subsistence patterns. However difficult it may be to tackle the sustainability question, donors can no longer afford to treat this matter lightly.

A New Order?

In closing, beyond the practical utility of this book for CSOs struggling to secure a resource base to carry out their work, it is essential to maintain a clear focus on the ultimate meaning of these endeavors. Without doubt, a worldwide movement is afoot seeking new directions and paradigms to conquer poverty and injustice and to bring dignity and hope to humankind. At the threshold of the twenty-first century, far too many in this global community still live in poverty and despair. The gap between rich nations and poor ones is widening, while income distribution is as skewed in some countries in the North as it is in the South and East. In an age of breathtaking technological marvels and achievements, development strategies have been woefully inadequate to the task of arresting environmental degradation, halting war and violence, and fostering sustainable social and economic development in most of the world.

The end of the cold war has closed a chapter of world history that pitted opposing political ideologies against each other, obstructing the emergence of new alternatives to development. The growth of civil society in much of the South was held hostage by authoritarian regimes that were often supported by the North for being anti-Communist, by socialist states supported by the Communist nations for suppressing capitalism, by populist governments supported by demagogic rhetoric and false promises, and by statist systems of all stripes supported, until recently, by much of the North and the multilateral lending institutions in the name of stability. Fledgling democracies in the South and East still have little understanding of the meaning of citizen participation. Fragmented political parties vie with each other to manipulate the system for the spoils of power and to impose their solution on a passive citizenry.

From this blur of opposing forces, in which people have been the object of the grand visions of others, a new people-centered paradigm seems to be emerging through the growth and assertiveness of civil society. The collapse of social and economic models centered on the state and the gradual deepening of democracy are opening new spaces for the organizations of citizens, anxious to offer their voices, energy, creativity, and resources to help bring hope to much of the world. Advances in global communication have played a critical role in propagating the cause of civil society.

The billions of dollars contributed by northern donors to emerging CSOs and grassroots organizations in the South and East over the past three decades—much of it during times of little hope for better days amidst dictatorships and failed utopian regimes—appears to have borne unexpected fruit in the form of the exponential growth of social capital and civic organizations. From Asian hamlets to African villages and Andean communities, it is possible to encounter organized peasant cooperatives, mothers' clubs, cultural groups, NGOs, youth organizations, and small enterprises seeking a part in the marketplace. From the endless squatter settlements of Lima to the favelas of Rio and the slums of Calcutta and Lagos, people are organizing not only for survival but to forge a better future.

The expansion of civil society in much of the world is also testimony to the irrepressible emergence of new forms of citizens' organizations seeking to lend their voices and creativity to the search for solutions to the problems of conflict, hunger, environmental degradation, corruption, and lack of opportunity. These voices have rallied to express themselves at U.N. conferences in Rio, Cairo, Copenhagen, Beijing, and Istanbul. They now form international networks—spanning the globe, connected to the Internet, and conferring by electronic mail. Famine, civil strife, affronts to the environment, and deep-rooted practices such as female circumcision are now the business of the global international community, and a rallying cry for the emerging global civil society to take action.

The fall of the Berlin Wall is symbolic of a million more walls that are beginning to fall throughout the world. Impenetrable walls have stood between sectors of society in much of the South and newly independent countries of the former Soviet Union and Central and Eastern Europe. Until recently, it was virtually inconceivable for grassroots organizations in many countries throughout the South and East to interact positively with local business leaders or municipal governments. Seemingly insurmountable social and ideological differences stood in the way. But now old enemies are partners in development, thanks to democracy, the rule of law, citizen participation, and the will to join forces for the common good. The problem today is not how to start a process of global change and transformation, but how to identify and develop the most effective methods and strategies to sustain it.

About The Authors

MIGUEL DARCY DE OLIVEIRA—Cofounder and Executive Secretary of Instituto de Ação Cultural (IDAC) since 1979. He has coordinated educational programs in the areas of human rights, health care, and the environment with women, slumdwellers, and street children. Mr. Darcy de Oliveira began his career as a member of the Brazilian Delegation to the United Nations in both Geneva and New York. Currently, he is a consultant to the International Labor Organization and UNESCO. He is also a postgraduate instructor at the Catholic University, a lecturer and workshop leader, and author of books and essays about education, peoples' empowerment, democracy, and development.

GONZALO DE LA MAZA—Codirector of Foro Privado con Fines Publicos and a Member of the Board of the National Council for Overcoming Poverty. Mr. de la Maza is the former President of ACCION, the Chilean NGO Association, as well as a University professor, consultant, and author of many works on social movements, international cooperation, and evaluation of social programs, including those on youth, gender, and local development.

LESLIE M. FOX—An independent consultant with 25 years of international development experience, primarily in Africa. As a development practitioner, he has managed a number of long-term programs targeting the capacity-building needs of African NGOs and grassroots organizations. Over the past five years, he has undertaken a wide range of assignments for such clients as the World Bank, USAID, CIVICUS, and the African Development Foundation, working primarily in the emerging field of democracy and governance, with special emphasis on enhancing the role of local-level civil society in policymaking in an era of decentralized local government. Mr. Fox has written extensively on this and related subjects.

SUSANA GARCÍA-ROBLES—Special Projects Director at the Global Work-Ethic Fund. Since 1994 Ms. Garcia-Robles has represented the National Institute of Womanhood at several U.N. Conferences. Her previous position was as Program Director for the Executive Council on Diplomacy. A native of Argentina, she has lived in the United States since 1982. She is currently pursuing a Master's degree in International Affairs at Columbia University.

ELAN GARONZIK—A graduate of the Carnegie-Mellon University, the George Washington University, and the American University of Paris, Elan Garonzik has extensive experience working with nonprofit-sector support organizations in the United States and Europe. From 1982 to 1986 and from 1989 to 1991, Mr. Garonzik was employed by the Foundation Center in New York, as Assistant Director of Publications and as Project Director for the implementation of the Center's grants classification system. He joined the European Foundation Centre in 1991 and serves there as Deputy Director and Orpheus Programme Coordinator.

ALFRED GUGLER—Policy Officer in the Debt-for-Development Unit of the Swiss Coalition of Development Organizations since 1991, which he helped to set up. From 1989 to 1991 he served as Coordinator of the national NGO debt campaign carried out in Switzerland that led to the Swiss Debt Reduction Facility. He has also worked for an ILO project in the informal sector in Mali, West Africa.

MALCOLM HAYDAY—Director, Investors in Society, Charities Aid Foundation (CAF) and former President of the International Association of Investors in the Social Economy. Mr. Hayday is a contributor of articles on social investment and new financing resources for charitable organizations.

RICHARD J.V. HOLLOWAY—Senior Associate and representative in Zambia for Private Agencies Collaborating Together (PACT). Previously he was the PACT Representative in Bangladesh, and before that worked for CUSO, and for OXFAM in Asia. Prior to that he worked as Asia Director for CUSO, and Indonesia Country Director for OXFAM. He is the author of "Exit Strategies—Transitioning from International to Local NGO Leadership" and editor of "Doing Development—Government, NGOs, and the Rural Poor in Asia." He has also worked in Ethiopia, Botswana, South Sudan, the West Indies, and the South Pacific.

EVA JESPERSEN—Policy Analyst in the Division of Evaluation, Policy and Planning at UNICEF. From 1995 though July 1, 1997, Ms. Jespersen was responsible for UNICEF's debt swaps for children. She played a key role in conceptualizing and promoting the 20/20 Initiative for mobilizing resources for basic social services, and has contributed to a range of UNICEF publications including "Adjustment with a Human Face," "Africa's Recovery in the 1990s," "Poverty Monitoring, An International Concern," and "20/20: Mobilizing Resources for Children in the 1990s."

DANIEL Q. KELLEY—After receiving degrees in City Planning from MIT and Harvard, Mr. Kelley became the executive director of a community center for Mexican and African American workers and their families in Chicago, directing the organization's successful fundraising campaigns. An expert in corporate real estate finance, Mr. Kelley stayed active in educational and youth projects while a consultant in Chicago and Houston. He now combines his business and nonprofit experiences as President of the Global Work-Ethic Fund, which provides strategic planning services to CSOs in Latin America and Africa, advising them on local and international fundraising. *Dinero para su Causa* (1994), which he wrote in Spanish, was the first book on those subjects created for Latin American nonprofits. An expanded version for Brazil has been published in Portuguese, *Dinheiro para sua Causa* (1995).

WILLIAM LeCLERE—A Senior Associate with the Institute for Development Research, working with grassroots and nongovernmental organizations in the developing world. He was a founding director of McBer and Company, LMA Inc., and the Institute for Planned Change. He lives in Luray, Virginia.

HORACIO R. MORALES, JR.—President of the Philippine Rural Reconstruction Movement (PRRM), a development NGO that since 1952 has been working to uplift and empower the rural poor. Through the programs of PRRM, the Cooperative Foundation of the Philippines, Inc. where he serves as Executive Director, and the political bloc Movement for Popular Democracy that he chairs, Mr. Morales has played key roles in the formation of national and global coalitions that ensure citizen participation in development and democratization. In 1990, he published a book entitled *A Call for People's Development* dealing with Philippine development issues and alternative strategies that emphasized citizen empowerment. He is also recipient of the prestigious 1997 National Community Service Award given by the University of the Philippines Alumni Association.

FADEL N'DIAME—Since 1993, Founding Member and Executive Director of the West Africa Rural Foundation (WARF), an international NGO whose mission it is to help solve the problems of the rural society in West Africa by strengthening rural organizations through the promotion of participatory methods of research and action practices. From 1991 to 1993, Mr. N'Diame was a Program Coordinator for the pilot phase of WARF, and from 1985 to 1991 held positions at the Senegalese Institute of Agricultural Research. He is the author of numerous research articles on the topic of development.

NESsT—the Nonprofit Enterprise and Self-sustainability Team is an international NGO founded to focus on alternative, sustainable financing strategies for CSOs. It has three Directors. **LEE DAVIS** is currently a visiting lecturer in the Social Change and Development Program at the Johns Hopkins University, School for Advanced International Studies (SAIS) in Washington, D.C., and author of "New Directions in NGO Self-Financing," an international study commissioned by SAIS in 1996–97 as a part of the New Directions in Grassroots Development initiative. **NICOLE ETCHART** is the Executive Director of the Association for Women in Development (AWID), where she engineered AWID's transition to a professional international membership organization of more than 1,000 gender and development advocates; she has more than a decade of experience in the field of international development in program development, institutional development, and policy analysis. **KATALIN ZSAMBOKI** is an economist, researcher, and policy analyst specializing in urban policy, housing, local government finance and reform, and NGO financial sustainability.

M. PILAR RAMIREZ—Board Member of Centro de Fomento a Iniciativas Economicas (FIE) in Bolivia as well as Social Analysis and NGO Specialist for the Resident Mission of the World Bank in Bolivia. Frustrated with traditional aid programs for the poor, in 1985 Ms. Ramirez joined with four other Bolivian women and founded FIE, the first microcredit NGO in Bolivia. She has extensive work experience in NGOs in her country as well as in the United States, where she was Program Director of The Synergos Institute in New York. She has been a university professor in Bolivia and lecturer at Stanford University in California.

LAURIE REGELBRUGGE—Vice President of the Hitachi Foundation, a U.S. philanthropic organization established in 1985 by Hitachi, Ltd., of Tokyo, Japan. Ms. Regelbrugge manages a $3-million annual grantmaking program supporting U.S. nonprofit organizations in education, community development, and global citizenship projects. She also oversees partnership programs with U.S.-based Hitachi companies through which local community action strategies are developed and implemented. Prior to joining the Foundation in 1990, Ms. Regelbrugge worked in several nonprofit organizations directing domestic and international programs in education, community development, and management. She is a coauthor or editor of *Global Corporate Citizenship—Rationale and Strategies* (The Hitachi Foundation, 1997) and *Quilt Makers: Community Education Resources and Challenges* (Futures for Children and The Hitachi Foundation, 1996), among other publications.

GHASSAN SAYAH—Chief Executive Officer of the Young Men's Christian Association (YMCA) in Lebanon since 1975. Mr. Sayah is a founding member and Secretary of the Board of the Lebanese NGO Forum, a member of International Voluntary Agencies (VOLAG), and a member and representative for the Refugee Committee of the World Alliance of YMCAs. He is also a member of the Supreme Health Council in Lebanon. He has initiated many social service projects, including a vocational training program for young men and women, a health education program for public schools, and the YMCA Medical Assistance Program for chronically ill patients, which is a collaborative program with the Lebanese Ministry of Public Health. Mr. Sayah has also conducted training programs on the topics of leadership, management and supervision, and planning.

S. BRUCE SCHEARER—A nonprofit leader with an extensive background in both U.S. public affairs and international development, Mr. Schearer serves as chief executive officer of the Synergos Institute, a private nonprofit organization devoted to fostering collaborative action between government, the business sector, and citizens' groups to overcoming poverty. Before joining Synergos in 1987, he developed and operated a national program of policy briefings for the U.S. Congress, foundations, and corporations on the impact of social and demographic changes on U.S. public policy. Mr. Schearer has worked on development projects with governments, development agencies, and private institutions in more than 20 countries in Asia, Africa, and Latin America. He is the author of more than three dozen publications, including public policy analyses, research reviews, and scientific articles.

DR. RAJESH TANDON—Founder and Coordinator of the Society for Participatory Research in Asia, an NGO that works with grassroots development groups in India. He is also President of the Asia-South Pacific Bureau of Adult Education, Asian Vice

President of the International Council for Adult Education, and International Coordinator of the Participatory Research Network and editor of its newsletter. He aids development groups such as farmers, workers' associations, and women's groups in building their capacity for research, training, and organizational change. He has written extensively on participatory research and development strategies in the Third World. His writings and studies include the history and roles of voluntary development organizations.

DAVID VALENZUELA—As Vice President for Programs of the Inter-American Foundation, Mr. Valenzuela is responsible for managing the IAF grant program in Latin America and the Caribbean. In 1990 he reestablished and directed the Peace Corps in Chile following the country's return to democracy. He has also served as Andean regional representative for Church World Service, and was Latin American program officer for the International Secretariat for Volunteer Service, which was incorporated into the United Nations Volunteers. He was born and raised in Chile.

FERNAND VINCENT—Secretary General, Board member, and Founder of the Research and Applications for Alternative Financing for Development (RAFAD) Foundation since 1994. From 1980 to 1994, Mr. Vincent founded and was the Secretary General of Development Innovations and Networks (IRED) and is currently the editor of the organization's quarterly newsletter. From 1963 to 1980 he founded and was the Secretary General of the Panafrican Institute for Development (PAID). He has written more than 50 papers on management, microfinancing, NGO management, education, and networking and is the author of several books, including *Alternative Financing of Third World Development Organisations and NGOs, Vols. I and II*, and *Towards Greater Financial Autonomy*, a manual of financial strategies and techniques for development NGOs and community organizations.

CIVICUS Task Force on Resource Enhancement

S. Bruce Schearer, Chair
Synergos Institute
United States

Gonzalo de la Maza
National Council for Overcoming
Poverty
Chile

Liam Doyle
L.P. Doyle Associates
Belgium

Amita Kapur
CRY-Child Relief and You
India

Ezra Mbogori
MWENGO, Mwelekeo wa NGO
Zimbabwe

Horacio R. (Boy) Morales, Jr.
Philippine Rural Reconstruction
Movement
Philippines

Fadel N'Diame
West Africa Rural Foundation

Thandiwe Nkomo
Organisation of Rural Associations
for Progress (ORAP)
Zimbabwe

Ghassan Sayah
YMCA/Lebanon

CIVICUS Program Committee

Rajesh Tandon, Chair
Society for Participatory Research
in Asia
India

Farida Allaghi
Arab Gulf Programme for the U.N.
Development Organizations
Saudi Arabia

Tim Brodhead
J.W. McConnell Family Foundation
Canada

Miguel Darcy de Oliveira
Instituto de Ação Cultural
Brazil

Ricardo Govela
PHILOS, A.C.
Mexico

Sandra T. Gray
Independent Sector
United States

Thierno Kane
Federation des Associations du Foula
pour le Developpement
Senegal

Sylvie Tsyboula
European Third Sector Training Network
Belgium

Miklós Marschall, *ex officio*
Executive Director, CIVICUS

About CIVICUS

Vision

CIVICUS is dedicated to pursuing a world such that:

- citizen action is a predominant feature of the political, economic and cultural life of all societies;
- private action for the public good is expressed by a rich and diverse array of organizations operating sometimes apart and sometimes in dialogue with government and business; and
- a healthy society is one in which there is an equitable relationship among citizens, their associations and foundations, business and governments.

CIVICUS' special purpose, therefore, is to help nurture the foundation, growth, protection and resourcing of citizen action throughout the world and especially in areas where participatory democracy, freedom of association of citizens and their funds for public benefit are threatened.

Mission

CIVICUS is an international alliance dedicated to strengthening citizen action and civil society throughout the world.

Specifically, CIVICUS seeks to fulfill its mission by serving as:

- A **global alliance** of citizens and their organizations, to help advance regional and national agendas of common initiatives to strengthen the capacity of civil society.

CIVICUS is committed to: 1) strengthening the visibility and understanding of civil society; 2) working to develop a more supportive environment of laws, policies, and regulations; 3) developing permanent, self-sustaining, and creative resource mechanisms.

- An **open forum**, serving to facilitate and establish cross-sectoral dialogue, exchange information, develop a common understanding and shared identity, solidarity, cooperation, and communication within civil society from various regions, and promote a common vision about the role of civil society.

Programs

CIVICUS meets these challenges through a variety of programmatic activity, including:

- regional and global meetings;
- publications, including the bimonthly newsletter *CIVICUS World*;

- special projects on developing the infrastructure of civil society;
- networking and partnering efforts with other civil society organizations and global agencies;
- a growing information clearinghouse.

Membership

CIVICUS is a membership association. Its members include nongovernmental organizations, private charities, corporate philanthropic programs, research institutions, and interested individuals from more than 60 countries around the world.

To find out more about CIVICUS, please contact:

> CIVICUS Secretariat
> 919 18th Street NW, 3rd Floor
> Washington, DC 20006
> Tel: (1-202) 331-8518
> Fax: (1-202) 331-8774
> E-mail: info@civicus.org
> Web site: http://www.civicus.org

CIVICUS Publications

CITIZENS—Strengthening Global Civil Society. Contains overviews of the state of civil society in each region, as well as thought-provoking essays on global civil society. 1994. 385 pp. Price: US$20 for nonmembers / US$15 for members, per copy, plus shipping and handling.

Sustaining Civil Society: Strategies for Resource Mobilization. This book describes in detail innovative methods used by civil society organizations to fund their programs. Includes chapters on revenues from earned income, engaging corporations, venture capital, microcredit programs, and debt conversion, among others, and uses case studies to illustrate each concept. September 1997. 394 pp. Price: US$30 for nonmembers / US$20 for members, per copy, plus shipping and handling.

Legal Principles for Citizen Participation: Toward a Framework for Civil Society Organizations. An international set of principles for civil society organizations (CSOs), designed to be used both for building good national legal environments, and for building stronger, more transparent and accountable organizations. September 1997. Approx. 34 pp. Price: US$15 for nonmembers / US$10 for members, per copy, plus shipping and handling.

Building Civil Society Worldwide: Strategies for Successful Communications. A handbook of case studies describing how civil society organizations have met the challenge of increasing the visibility of their own programs as well as the sector in their countries. September 1997. Approx. 50 pp. Price: US$15 for nonmembers / US$10 for members, per copy, plus shipping and handling.

The New Civic Atlas: Profiles of Civil Society. This book provides an overview of civil society in 60 countries, including information on the breadth and development of the sector and the particular challenges faced in each country. As a resource, each profile includes contact information for organizations and individuals that are able to provide in-depth information on civil society in their particular country. September 1997. Approx. 200 pages. Price: US$15 for nonmembers / US$10 for members, per copy, plus shipping and handling.

CIVICUS World. The bimonthly newsletter of CIVICUS; each issue features commentary on a particular issue facing global civil society, as well as short book reviews, profiles of interesting organizations, member news, and more. *CIVICUS World* is a service to members of CIVICUS.

For more information on these publications and how to become a member, please contact the CIVICUS secretariat at the address listed on the previous page.